Being Rita Hayworth

Being
Rita Hayworth

Labor, Identity,
and Hollywood Stardom

Adrienne L. McLean

RUTGERS UNIVERSITY PRESS
NEW BRUNSWICK, NEW JERSEY, AND LONDON

Second printing, 2005

Library of Congress Cataloging-in-Publication Data
McLean, Adrienne L.
  Being Rita Hayworth : labor, identity, and Hollywood stardom /
Adrienne L. McLean.
     p.   cm.
Includes bibliographical references and index.
    ISBN 0-8135-3388-0 (alk. paper)—ISBN 0-8135-3389-9 (pbk. : alk. paper)
    1. Hayworth, Rita, 1918–1987.   2. Motion picture actors and actresses—
United States—Biography.   I. Title.
PN2287.H38M35 2004
791.43′028′092—dc22
                                                                    2003018837

British Cataloging-in-Publication information
for this book is available from the British Library.

Frontispiece photo by Ned Scott, 1947.
Courtesy Ned Scott Archive.

Publication of this book was supported, in part,
by a grant from the School of Arts and Humanities at the University of Texas at Dallas.

Manufactured in the United States of America

For Larry, and my parents

Contents

Afterword:
Replacing the Love Goddess
198

Acknowledgments

When the subject of your work is a star like Rita Hayworth, you soon find that a lot of people have some fond recollection involving her and are eager to share it with you (I really never came across anyone who actively detested Hayworth or her films). Doing research for this project has thus been far more than a matter of reading books and articles, sifting through archival material, and studying Hayworth's films; it also comprised the joys of more amorphous and informal structures like conversation, fellowship, and the occasional heated debate. I would like to thank everyone who shared his or her Hayworth experiences, memories, and opinions with me in this way over the years; you have been a continual source of inspiration and energy, whether we knew each other's names or not.

I am particularly grateful to Eddie Saeta, Robert Schiffer, Vincent Sherman, and Nita Bieber Wall for talking with me about their work with Hayworth; Fletcher Chan, Dr. Carole Hope Durbin, Fred Hanneman, and the several anonymous respondents to my lengthy questionnaire about Hayworth; Caren Roberts-Frenzel, president of the Rita Hayworth fan club; and most of all Jeanne Kramer and Constance McCormick Van Wyck, for having the foresight to save so much ephemeral and valuable material about stars and for making it available to people like me.

Hayworth's home studio, Columbia, remains an archival blank spot—melancholy rumors continue to circulate about whether its archives even exist, as well as whether they will ever be opened to researchers—so I would like to thank Terrance McCluskey, at one time an archivist for Sony Pictures Entertainment, for providing me with some crucial information about Hayworth's studio contracts and the Beckworth Corporation. I am also very grateful to Norm Scott and the Ned Scott Archive for permission to reprint several photos by Ned Scott, especially the wonderful photo on the front cover; I learned a lot from Norm, not only about his father but about Hollywood studio photography generally. The Ball Brothers Foundation provided me with a visiting fellowship to work in the Orson Welles Collection at the Lilly Library, Indiana University, Bloomington, and I deeply appreciate the patience and consideration of the library's staff. Other libraries, archives, and institutions on whose help and superlative staffs this project has relied include the Cinema-Television Library, University of Southern California, especially the peerless and peerlessly generous Ned Comstock; the Margaret Herrick Library, Academy of Motion Picture Arts and Sciences, Los Angeles; the British Film Institute, London; and the Dance Collection, New York Public Library for the Performing Arts. Nor could I have gotten far without the help of the libraries and staffs of Emory University, Hollins University, and the University of Texas at Dallas, all of which have been extremely helpful at various critical times.

Other individuals and colleagues whom I would like to thank for their intellectual and emotional support through the years include Amy Schrager Lang, my mentor, adviser, sternest and most helpful critic, and dissertation codirector at the Institute of the Liberal Arts at Emory University; Robin Blaetz, a kind and generous teacher, colleague, and friend; Michael Wilson, a limitless font of all sorts of information, as well as a valued colleague and friend; and Dennis Kratz, dean of the School of Arts and Humanities at the University of Texas at Dallas, who makes all things possible. I also thank others involved in the genesis of this book as a dissertation at Emory University: David Cook (dissertation codirector), Matthew Bernstein, Gaylyn Studlar, and Allen Tullos. Here at the University of Texas at Dallas, I have received additional support and encouragement from all of my colleagues, especially Susan Branson, R. David Edmunds, Erin A. Smith, Marilyn Waligore, and Dan Wickberg. I am grateful also to Steven Cohan, Mary Desjardins, Ina Rae Hark, David Lugowski, and Ann Martin for their kindness and conference conviviality over these many years and to my friends and relatives Barbara Cooper, Judy V. Jones and Scott Belville, Charley and Annie Morgan, Cindy Hinton, and Jim and Jo McLean. I also want to thank Larry Thomas again, one of the people to whom this book is dedicated, for locating so many of its illustrations during his travels.

Finally, I offer my deepest and warmest thanks to everyone at Rutgers University Press, especially Joe Abbott, for his expert copyediting; Marilyn Campbell, for all of her logistical help and guidance and her patience with my obsessive tendencies; and Leslie Mitchner, just the best editor in the world, for her wisdom, enthusiasm, energy, and commitment to this project and for making it such a rewarding, satisfying, and purely pleasurable experience.

Portions of this book have been previously published elsewhere. Some sections of chapter 1 appear in different form in " 'I'm a Cansino': Transformation, Ethnicity, and Authenticity in the Construction of Rita Hayworth, American Love Goddess," *Journal of Film and Video* 44 (fall 1992 and winter 1993): 8–26. Small sections of chapters 4 and 5 appear in different form in " 'It's Only That I Do What I Love and Love What I Do': *Film*

Noir and the Musical Woman," *Cinema Journal* 33 (fall 1993): 3–16, copyright 1993 by the University of Texas Press, P.O. Box 7819, Austin, TX 78713-7819. I thank the editors and presses of these journals (and their unheralded anonymous and very helpful readers) for publishing the work and for giving me permission to reproduce it here.

Being Rita Hayworth

Introduction

Why Rita Hayworth?

"**M**en fell in love with 'Gilda,' but they woke up with me."[1] This quotation can be found in virtually any biography, book-length or otherwise, of the movie star Rita Hayworth. The context and the wording may vary, but always the statement is produced as a sort of revelation whose poignancy derives from the combination of bruised self-awareness and utter powerlessness it demonstrates on the part of an ordinary woman who has been engulfed or entrapped by an image (in this case the title role of the 1946 film noir *Gilda*) partly of her own making.[2] Expecting Hayworth to be like Gilda, a fictional femme fatale who was a "roaring, sexy woman,"[3] men were attracted to her. Later, they discovered that she was actually quiet and not at all sirenlike, and were disappointed.

"A man goes to bed with Rita Hayworth and wakes up with me."[4] This version of the quotation, attributed to Hayworth (born Margarita Carmen Cansino) by journalist Leonard Michaels, is apparently a mistaken rendering of the first, and Michaels does not give a source for it. But it is a very interesting mistake, because it implies that men went to bed with one Rita Hayworth and woke up with a *different* Rita Hayworth, someone of Latin antecedents named Margarita Carmen Cansino. Unfortunately, Michaels's essay, which concerns his awakening teenage sexuality and its reaction to seeing *Gilda*, makes no other reference to Hayworth's ethnic origins; so he does not explain the basis on which one would recognize, the morning after as it were, that Hayworth had suddenly become, or reverted to being, Margarita Cansino.

Moreover, the fact that a great many people, male and female, claim personally to have heard Hayworth utter some version of the first quotation over the course of several decades makes it intriguing in other ways, too. It has been so widely published in so many venues that, regardless of how one interprets it, its very ubiquity and frequency of repetition *as* a line suggest that Rita Hayworth was not only aware of but might have employed various fictive aspects of her identity in strategic ways. That is, to read the line quoted now is probably to feel some sympathy for Hayworth as the victim of men unable to distinguish screen image from real woman (with Michaels's confused version interjecting the notion that Hayworth was being mistaken for a yet *more* "real" real woman, Margarita Cansino). But to imagine the line spoken, as part of a conversation with different people at different times, produces a more incongruous and paradoxical sense of who Hayworth might have been. In what manner did she confide the information? What was the next line, for example, or the reaction and response of her interlocutors? What, or who, *was* Gilda—and did Hayworth (or Margarita Cansino) herself act like Gilda (or Margarita Cansino) some of the time and, if so, to what ends and with what distinguishing features? In short, what was the nature of Hayworth's agency in manipulating her public and private images—how might the relationship between being Gilda, a fictional character in a narrative film, and being Rita Hayworth, a Hollywood star who was born with the name Margarita Carmen Cansino, be rearticulated not as the sign of the constructedness and phantasmatic nature of the star image but of a more familiar struggle to understand and control the terms of one's identity and subjectivity?

In her book *Negotiating Hollywood: The Cultural Politics of Actors' Labor,* Danae Clark also considers the kinds of issues raised by thinking about stars as social subjects as well as commodified objects.[5] Rather than focusing, as many scholars already have, on the fetishistic relationship of the spectator to the actor-as-image and the functional role of that image in constituting the spectator's subjectivity, Clark argues persuasively that, from a Marxist-inflected cultural studies perspective, the same unequal relations of power that construct the fragmentary and contingent identities of spectating subjects also constitute the movie star "economically, politically, and discursively." Although their connections to the specific practices of film production and to film texts are not the same, actors and spectators are always already "caught up in a continual process of cultural resistance, pleasure, and negotiation" in relation to their work and their place in the world. Thus, "actors are not that different from spectators" because they too have heterogeneous subjectivities, and Clark's main project is to show that labor power differences—"the fragmented and fought-over position of the actor as a subject of film labor and film representation"—produce a geography on which actors' struggles to define themselves, now and in the past, can be mapped. Primarily because of the lack of specific information about particular labor practices that can be linked to actors' involvement in known historical "events," however, it will always be a "tricky business," Clark notes, to situate "issues of subjectivity within actors' labor history" other than as broadly conceived "modes" or "positionalities" marked by labor power differences.

The most significant of the positionalities Clark names is that of the "actor as worker." Within Hollywood, historically as now, the actor as worker is not the "true" identity of anyone or anything but the site of "intersecting discourses involving the sale of one's labor power to the cinematic institution, the negotiation of that power in terms of work performance and image construction, and the embodiment of one's image (onscreen and offscreen) as it becomes picked up and circulated in filmic and extrafilmic discourse." To write about a historical movie star's subjectivity, then, will mean always, if not only, to seek and to consider the discursive signs that at once indicate and produce struggles between being and doing, between working at making films and working at having a private life, between defining oneself and being defined by others.

This book is about these signs as they circulate in the star image of Rita Hayworth (1918–1987), from her elevation to stardom in the late 1930s and early 1940s through the end of her Columbia studio contract in the late 1950s. I am interested in how her subjectivity, as worker and as woman, and the commercial discourses in which it is produced and located interact with Hollywood's own labor power differences and with the social tensions and concerns of the culture at large. Clark's discussion focuses primarily on the labor of acting in relation to films. But for many women stars, work performance clearly included domestic labor too, the ability to perform successfully as a wife and a mother as well as a film character or glamour figure. Rita Hayworth was a constructed image, a persona, but that construction rested, as all star images do, on something that could be (as it is now with "our" stars) understood to be a "real person." Whatever else was significant and powerful in Hayworth's image, or powerfully deployed by Hollywood's publicity and promotion machinery as well as film texts, for much of her career she seemed to matter most as someone who found it extraordinarily difficult to negotiate the competing demands of family, domesticity, and professional labor.[6]

Indeed, it is the discursive agency of a conventional glamorous woman star like Rita Hayworth that makes her so fascinating as an object of study. Such stars are not only among the most famous of Hollywood's products, but they often can be just as interesting and complex, albeit in different ways, as Mae West, Dorothy Arzner, or any of the more overtly exceptional women who worked in the studio system. In Hayworth's case, particularly, she is a star on the screen during the period under consideration, but she is as big a star off of it, both because her stardom began as a process of publicized commodification and transformation (from Margarita Carmen Cansino to Rita Cansino, ethnic starlet, to the all-American Rita Hayworth) and because she was involved in a sequence of failed but nevertheless "enriching" marriages (most famously to Orson Welles and

Prince Aly Khan) that became part of an ongoing debate about the compatibility of work, marriage, and family in American women's lives.

I do understand, however, that there are still many working in film studies who would hesitate to grant anything resembling subjectivity and agency to a female star image, much less a star so well known for her commodification, objectification, passivity, and one-dimensionality as a performer and as a pinup. Therefore, another concern of this project will be to trace the ways that, from the 1970s on, some scholars working in film studies have helped, if inadvertently, to flatten and collapse the meanings of the very vital Hayworth that emerges from study of her image as it circulated in publicity and promotional materials, as well as in film texts, in the 1940s and 1950s. At this point, at the beginning of the twenty-first century, film studies is well ensconced in the academy, with debates ongoing about how and what Hollywood stars mean on a number of levels and from a number of different critical approaches. In this sense scholars in the field no longer, if they ever did, merely study stars but also participate in the configuration of star images and the marking of their relevance to larger questions of identity politics. Thus, if I am interested in Rita Hayworth as a star in her own historical context, I am no less interested in the ways that this same Rita Hayworth has been positioned and made use of within academic film studies, particularly feminist film studies.

Additionally, Hayworth's most recent biographer, Barbara Leaming, has made childhood victimization at the hands of an abusive father the controlling structure of Hayworth's life (and, as is well known, the star was made yet more pathetic by her death from the Alzheimer's disease she began to suffer in the early 1960s, thus bringing that disease to widespread public attention for the first time).[7] I do not substantially deny that these are all important aspects of Hayworth's star image now. But I will show that, Alzheimer's aside, virtually all of them—even her unhappy childhood—were investigated, negotiated, and contested in the promotional and publicity materials that constructed Hayworth's meanings as a star. Contrary to certain assumptions about Hollywood discourse—that it worked predominantly to contain women's agency, for example, by emphasizing not their labor as stars or even as actors but their faces and bodies or their frustrations at failing to achieve domestic happiness—I demonstrate here that Hayworth's image was actually as interesting and, in many instances, *more* invested with agency and autonomy in the 1940s and 1950s than it is now, after a spate of biographies that purport to show us the real Rita Hayworth.

That I concur with Clark about the potential subjectivity of stars as actors and as workers does not mean, then, that I believe that Rita Hayworth, Margarita Carmen Cansino, and even Gilda are available in the present except as images. But once one allows for the "possibility of actors' labor and resistance," then one can engage and consider the struggles—produced in and by the interaction of film texts, fan-magazine articles, studio publicity, and other available resources from the past—that mark and define them all. I will pay attention not only to Hayworth's construction as "a social subject who struggles within the film industry's sphere of productive practices," in Clark's terms, but also to how the mediated labor of constructing and negotiating the terms of one's own identity at different times and places—the conjunction, even collision, of that star's personal history with the machinery of image making and performing itself—is likely to be a major constituent of the movie star's political power, of her ability to *mean things* to spectators because of what she also means to herself.[8]

Given the abandon with which I have been quoting from Danae Clark's work, it should by now be obvious that I am greatly indebted to it and that I have made many of her insights a subtext for my own investigation into identity, labor, and subjectivity. *Negotiating Hollywood* itself negotiates new strategies for dealing with a central problematic of film spectatorship: that subjectivity is always to be located in the actions of the spectator in relation to the film image, even as it is always absent from the actor who embodies the image—especially when that actor is a woman. As is well known, the feminist historiography of classical Hollywood cinema moved in the 1970s away from attempts to reclaim and to make visible women's creative presence in the past toward an overriding concern with representation and spectatorship. Although certain women, like Arzner and West, who had participated in the man's world of the film industry as directors and writers became subjects of scholarly scrutiny, other women's extreme visibility (those women up there on the movie screen) became the very sign of their *in*visibility as historical women, as agents at work in the world.[9] If what drove early feminist social history was a sense of identification and empathy with women of the past—most tellingly exemplified, perhaps, by the title of Nancy F. Cott's 1977 classic *The Bonds of Womanhood*—film feminism has, at least with respect to film actors, called for critical distance and alienation from a scopic regime in which woman's image has been stolen from her, in Laura Mulvey's terms, precisely in order to reify phallocentric power at the expense of women's agency.[10]

The same criticism of much early work in women's history—that its attempts to recognize and to reclaim from obscurity women's experience in the past also tended to universalize or essentialize the meanings of those experiences without regard for race, ethnicity, nationality, age, class, sexual orientation—has also been leveled at feminist psychoanalytic criticism. My critical stance here can be seen, I hope, as a merging of Danae Clark's interests in the constructed subjectivity of the actor as worker with an explicitly feminist historiography informed by my recognition of and empathy for a subject's struggles to define herself and her own identity and by the knowledge that female stars are positioned within a phallocentrist economy of representation. As in Judith Mayne's study of Marlene Dietrich, it is "both/and" rather than "either/or" that marks my feminist reading of Hayworth; like Dietrich, Hayworth is at once "contained by patriarchal representation and resistant to it."[11] The risks of ignoring this "both/and," the conditions under which historical audiences engaged with, learned from, or interrogated the wide spectrum of information about Hayworth produced by various mass-media outlets, is that we might also be ignoring the implications of a woman's star image as having material effects in the social world, conflicted and ambivalent and *unexpected* effects, that can be participating in the formation of a feminist consciousness rather than only keeping patriarchy in place.[12]

To consider the diachronic shifts and alterations in Hayworth's image is to demonstrate how the discourses produced about her (and ostensibly by her, in some cases, as in the quotations with which I began) represented her as a weak but resisting figure who knew about, and often protested, the appalling power relations that worked to keep her in her place. Her image was continually being reconfigured in her films, in promotional texts circulated about her films, in publicity about her offscreen life (and again, more recently, in film studies itself). I am not attempting to endow a commodity, fabricated according to theories of spectatorship by the patriarchal unconscious of classical Hollywood to signify lack and loss, the not-male, the passive, with some sort of transcendent, true subjectivity and agency. Nor am I writing a biography of some real person "behind" the persona. Rather, I engage the processes of commodification itself—extremely well elucidated in Hayworth's case—and suggest some of the ways in which the mechanisms of commodification, promotion, publicity, and performance also produced conflicted and variable modes of subjectivity.[13]

Of course, analysis of all of these intersecting discourses depends on their existence or availability in the present and, in turn, on my own labor as their interpreter. And it would be impossible for me (or anyone else) completely to disengage the work of cultural analysis from my own subject position as a reader/spectator (nor would I want to). But my study of Hayworth's star image does obviously depend on taking seriously points of attention that are not the same as those considered by other scholars working from different perspectives or on other stars. Danae Clark laments the fact that even to attempt a "single narrative" of something as complex as actor-producer relations is a "rather messy" process, and her own study ends up restricted to analysis of an archival gold mine: a document-loaded eight-month period in 1933 in which the terms of screen actors' labor were contested and defined in discourses, including film texts, relating to Roosevelt's labor policies and the unionization of extras and screen actors.[14] But whatever the difficulties in attempting to apply some of Clark's methods to a broader period and a much less coherent body (in every sense of the term) of evidence, the framework Clark provides for analyzing the material and discursive existence of the movie star as a historical entity can usefully be employed to address a number of questions that have been more or less bracketed out thus far in the canon of feminist film studies.[15]

For example, a number of star images have been examined for their relationship to subcultural or minority audiences, whose members identify with or appropriate stars in unique, often counterhegemonic, ways. Richard Dyer's essay "Judy Garland and Gay Men" falls into this category, as do the "resistant readings" of, say, Marilyn Monroe's and Jane Russell's screen personas in Howard Hawks's 1953 *Gentlemen Prefer Blondes* or Andrew Britton's study of Katharine Hepburn as a feminist star.[16] Although these important and useful studies do attempt, as Ramona Curry puts it in her work on Mae West, to reconstruct the "diversity and variability" of particular female star images, most of the stars so considered have tended to be labeled or understood already as "exceptional historical figures," in Curry's terms.[17] Mae West, as is well known, was what Curry calls a "successful female cinematic author," invoking an analytic framework of writerly and directorial auteurism that would be pointless to apply to Rita Hayworth. None of this is to say that Hayworth's star image has been ignored by scholars, even feminist scholars. But with few exceptions—the most important of which is arguably Richard Dyer's 1978 essay "Resistance through Charisma: Rita Hayworth and *Gilda*"—the results have heretofore been to emphasize those elements presumed to be usual in, or typical of, female stars of the sort who are now known generally for their glamour and physical allure rather than for their acting skills—namely, her erotic specularity, objectification, and, hence, passivity.[18]

The title of this book, in fact, was suggested partly by Amy Lawrence's discussion, in her otherwise extremely valuable and scrupulous 1991 study *Echo and Narcissus: Women's Voices in Classical Hollywood Cinema,* of Hayworth's 1953 film *Miss Sadie Thompson.*[19] Without mentioning any of

Hayworth's other films, or anything else about her star image, Lawrence writes that Hayworth is a "sex goddess." And by "being Rita Hayworth," a "packaged" star whose sexuality is conventionally marked by signifiers of Western femininity, the character of Sadie Thompson is "lock[ed] into spectacle on all sides." Certainly there are some obvious foundational texts of Hayworth's—her World War II pinup photos, for example—that could be used to reduce Hayworth to such a one-dimensional, iconic image. But Lawrence's statements are a bit too simplistic, even for *Miss Sadie Thompson*. When one begins to examine Hayworth's star image in any depth at all, this becomes more noticeable.

I can pinpoint the precise moment at which I began to consider Hayworth's image seriously and to ponder the issue of her subjectivity, as well as my own, so to speak. I was a student in a film studies course, the topic of which was Orson Welles in all of his many permutations—child wonder, writer, political liberal, radio star, actor, director, victim of the venality of others, but most of all genius—and over the course of a few weeks had become completely enthralled with him as a personality and as an artist. As we began to discuss the women in Welles's films, I had no trouble entering easily into a conversation that revolved around which precise variant of the appellation "bimbo" should be applied to Susan Alexander Kane and, by implication, to Marion Davies, the woman on whom all of us by now knew Susan Alexander's character was based. As we talked freely and pejoratively about Davies, lamenting her nails-on-a-blackboard screechiness, her lack of talent, and most of all her stupidity, at one juncture someone said, "After all, not knowing that New York City is in the same time zone as Florida; that's pretty stupid." We easily conflated fictional object with historical subject, in other words, drawing conclusions about a real woman, a historical agent, based wholly on a Hollywood film and the discourse produced about it over the years (never, of course, by Marion Davies). I did hesitantly point out that surely *Davies* knew that Florida was in the same time zone as New York City even if Susan Alexander Kane did not, and since everyone agreed that this was probably true, I let my case rest. I had never even seen a Marion Davies film, so what did I know anyway?

But a few days later we were at it again, this time in a discussion of the 1948 film *The Lady from Shanghai* and Welles's misfortune in having to use Rita Hayworth in the starring role of Elsa Bannister. We covered all the bases: Hayworth was a pinup, an actress of very small abilities, and any deficiencies in *The Lady from Shanghai* were mostly linked to those of Hayworth and the fact that Welles had been forced by Columbia studio boss Harry Cohn to build up her part lest the film do damage to her glamorous and static star image. Everything from cost overruns to schedule problems, the banality of the glossy close-ups and of that terrible song Hayworth sings on the yacht, the poor box-office and critical reception of the film, the fact that it ended Welles's studio career in Hollywood—all this, and more, was laid at Hayworth's feet in her guise of commercial Hollywood star. Indeed, according to the bulk of the reading we were doing for our course, among Welles's many services to history was exposing the hollowness and depthlessness of constructed stars like Hayworth (and it was always Rita Hayworth who was the subject of our discussions, never Elsa Bannister). But these assertions—especially our casual agreement, mirrored in the scholarship we were reading, that this was all somehow Hayworth's *fault*—I found harder to accept, and in fact my inability to do so took on the status of revelation.

For if I did not know much about the films of Marion Davies, I *did* know something about those of Rita Hayworth. I had watched many of her musicals—*You'll Never Get Rich* (1941) and *You Were Never Lovelier* (1942), with Fred Astaire; *Cover Girl* (1944), with Gene Kelly; her own star vehicles *Tonight and Every Night* (1945) and *Down to Earth* (1947)—during the "nostalgia boom" of the 1970s, and I knew that Hayworth was not an emptily glossy and fabricated image but a performer of unusual ability. She was a *dancer,* a really talented dancer, as well as an accomplished musical comedy actress; she was competent and able in ways that relatively few of the Welles scholars we were reading were acknowledging. I decided to look further into the disjunction between what might be called the Wellesian or academic version of Rita Hayworth and what I had seen in other of her films, and that became the subject of my research paper for that course. What I found was enormously productive for my subsequent work in film studies and has led finally to this book.

In some ways, then, I hope to extend the possibilities of Danae Clark's work to allow one to consider not only labor qua labor in relation to subjectivity but the issue of *how* that labor is performed and at whose cost.[20] For example, to say that the musical numbers of Hayworth's films provide textbook examples of "woman-as-spectacle" may be indisputable within the terms of Laura Mulvey's classic paradigm of visual pleasure. But what of issues such as competence and ability—how *well* does Hayworth dance, does she get more accomplished over time, and how might we evaluate her performances as the result of struggles to perfect a craft that, after all, we are willing to take seriously if executed by a Gene Kelly or a Fred Astaire? How *well* does she act or inhabit fictional roles in narrative films? Do the terms of Hayworth's stardom make her, too, no more than a version of what one critic in the 1950s called the "blobs, faceless wonders," "undistinguished girls, not particularly talented," who "seem to come from nowhere"—all characteristics he identified in the era's most popular stars?[21] I have also struggled to find a way to articulate the political importance of two of Hayworth's most remarked-on qualities, as expressed in countless sources, primary as well as secondary: namely, that she was *nice*, that she tried never to hurt anyone, and that she was naturally talented but also an extremely hard worker of extraordinary professionalism who, throughout her studio years, was always prepared and ready to do her job. These terms are familiar to anyone who studies the construction of femininity in American culture, for women are *supposed* to be nice and to work hard to please others. But Hayworth's essential decency, like her professionalism, was not circulating in discourse that tied her to predominant women's issues of romance, marriage, and family. Rather, these were her personality characteristics and behavior in the dog-eat-dog world of Hollywood filmmaking and studio politics.

That Rita Hayworth was not exercising power in institutionalized ways that are clearly articulable *as* agency speaks, I believe, to her strong and underacknowledged appeal to women audience members—to the sense that she was recognizable as someone who was always trying to negotiate between being herself, being a woman, and being an actor-worker who wanted to improve, to learn, to overcome deficiencies in education, experience, and the like. I was surprised to find that, although my interrogation of Hayworth's image can never itself be interlocutory (she never speaks back *to me*), the mediated discourse of the 1940s and 1950s often was; that is, articles and writers (as well as Hayworth herself) frequently responded to and attempted to counter specific points made in other articles by other writers. In her 1994 book, *Star Gazing,* Jackie Stacey researches the meanings of wartime and postwar star images to woman audiences in Britain and argues that it is simplistic to define categorically women's relationship to the female star image as one of narcissistic over-identification, such that what women learned from such stars was how to be appealing to men—and to compete with one another for men—through particular forms of consumerism and commodification (clothes, makeup, hairstyles, as well as mannerisms and behavior).[22] Hayworth's obituaries tended to emphasize her status as the "American love goddess," as she was "officially" named by a *Life* cover story by Winthrop Sargeant in 1947, and inevitably tie her to other tragic love goddesses such as Jean Harlow and Marilyn Monroe.[23] But a major goal of this book is to suggest that Hayworth had a much more interesting value as a star to her contemporaries—and therefore could to *my* contemporaries too—than as the object of the fetishistic and fetishizing or narcissistic gaze or as a perpetual and perpetually passive victim.

Again, to say that subjectivity is constructed does not mean that it is not affectively felt as real and as deployable by others (not only Hollywood but its audiences and scholars) in personally and socially useful ways. In some sense I am arguing that what Michel de Certeau has famously described as *poaching*—one of the many *tactics,* or "ways of operating," employed by the weak or the marginal, those who are in places where they have "no choice but to live" and who therefore must "vigilantly make use of the cracks that particular conjunctions open in the surveillance of the proprietary powers"—is a component of many star images, as well as of readers' or spectators' interaction with those images.[24] The sort of power that fame and a high marquee value give to the female star is not a proper power, in de Certeau's words (that is, it is not power that operates from "within the stronghold of its own 'proper' place or institution"). Hayworth was a powerful *commodity,* but because she was a commodity—because what mattered to her studio was her exchange value—her power was still exercised from outside the stronghold, from the place of the weak, from the same space occupied and recognized by many of her fans.[25] I believe, in short, that even so apparently victimized and powerless a woman as Rita Hayworth, and by this I mean Rita Hayworth as she comes down to us through and as representations produced by Hollywood and other mass media forms, participated in the struggles that helped to produce the very feminist advances that allow me, now, to write about her.

These claims are not outlandish or utopian. I want to underscore the fact that although we can never know very much about Hayworth's own feelings about the terms of her specific agency as an actor (and this applies to any number of other female stars who represent a blank spot in the archival record in this sense), the Rita Hayworth examined here is not my personal fantasy construction. I have indulged in no orgy of interpretation, reading any sort of meaning I want into the discourse constructing Hayworth's image.[26] On the contrary, the claims I make are quite straightforward; in fact, it took very little research to find that Hayworth's abilities and efforts were all foregrounded rather than repressed in her star image from the end of the 1930s through the 1950s—to find, for example, that contra the assertions of Danae Clark and others about the "erasing" of an actor's previous identity, name, and personal history during his or her ascent to stardom, the half-Spanish Margarita Carmen Cansino was always present in Rita Hayworth as a star text.[27] Or that although Hayworth came from a reputedly close-knit family, her father was also strict and abusive and removed her from school to be his dancing partner, lied about her age, and presented her publicly as his wife, thus setting the stage for his daughter's later problems with self-image and her relationships with men. Or that during her glory years in the 1940s and early 1950s Hayworth was the protégée of one of the few women executive producers in Hollywood, Virginia Van Upp, who also wrote, but was not given screen credit for writing, *Gilda*. Or that although Hayworth was both a pinup girl and a film noir femme fatale, she was also a musical comedy star and dancer who not only worked with Astaire and Kelly but collaborated on two of the three films—*Affair in Trinidad* (1952) and *Salome* (1953)—made by one of the very few women choreographers to work in classical Hollywood, Valerie Bettis. Or that although Hayworth was at first defined as a conspicuously consuming clotheshorse, she was later criticized for being a woman "dangerously" unconcerned with her appearance. Or that, although she was sometimes described as being passive, bending easily to men's wills, looking only for someone to take care of her, she never stayed married for long and herself ended each of her five marriages. Or that she was a devoted mother who eventually put both of her daughters through college without material support from their fathers yet in the 1950s also, in spending too much time catering to the wishes of one husband (Dick Haymes), ended up charged briefly with child neglect. Or that although she supposedly yearned only for a simple domestic life, she repeatedly stated that she could not be happy unless she was working; in fact, Rita Hayworth was among the first stars in studio-era Hollywood to form her own production company, the Beckworth Corporation (founded in 1947, its name derived from hers and that of her daughter Rebecca), which gave her script approval and a share in the profits of her films.[28]

All of this information has been presented in recent biographies about Hayworth as a revelation of a hitherto unknown reality, the result of research involving everything from birth certificates to declassified FBI files to interviews with people who claim to have known Hayworth well. But virtually all of it can also be found in fan and mass-market magazines from the late 1930s through the 1950s, produced not by revisionist historians with fresh or freshly uncovered information but by hack writers and gossip columnists. We may have less information, in contrast to the case of Orson Welles or even of Mae West and Katharine Hepburn, that appears to emanate from Hayworth herself, but that does not mean that there is no point in attempting to understand, through the evidence that *is* available, a different sort of commodified image: that of the social subject constructed by her own labor and resistance, as well as by Hollywood's (and some academic scholars') attempts to market her precisely as a fetishized object, a "sex goddess," someone whose only power resides in the negative erotic space of her emptiness and passivity. If my organizing premise is obviously not that Rita Hayworth was a closet feminist, the issues confronting her as a star (and as many of the characters she plays in her films) are nevertheless recognizable as issues that feminism attempts to confront and ameliorate.

I take as a given that we continue to live in a patriarchal society and that any consideration of identity politics must begin with an acknowledgment of the structural oppression of women that patriarchy depends on. I also agree, however, with the many scholars who have worked to characterize the "both/and" mutability of certain conservative mechanisms—a mutability that marks Hollywood's own modes of discourse, from film texts to fan magazines, but also the interactions of its workers with the conditions of their own commodification. Kaja Silverman, drawing on the work of Fredric Jameson, writes, "Although no area of the social formation escapes discourse, that formation is under constant siege from what remains outside discourse—from the biological, from the ecological, and from what [figures] as 'history.' "[29] As a social formation and an individual subject Hayworth's public identity, what she was supposed to mean as a star image, was always running up against events Hollywood's discursive machinery was not engineered to handle, such as the psychic effects of her own dysfunctional childhood, divorce, scandal, illness, even her talent. In order to assimilate these life events—to bring them under what Silverman and Jameson call "linguistic control"—the social formation itself had to change through the reshaping required to cover up the "hole" torn in its ideological fabric.[30]

These sorts of life events have been the primary focus of Hayworth's previous biographers, where they are employed to explain some of Hayworth's specific actions in the world. But they figure in my discussion primarily as they were rendered textually in popular culture—always an "imaginary popular culture," in Lynn Spigel's words, constructed of the assumptions, often erroneous, made by media institutions about their publics—contemporary to the small-scale history I want to write.[31] Conversely, I will also read this discourse symptomatically, for signs that Hayworth's own social reality is actively confusing or blocking the iterative conventions of mass-mediated discourse. Along the way, as my invocation of other women's names has suggested, I hope to introduce further affirmation, however sketchy or limited by the paucity of documentary evidence, of the extensive networks of women's labor power and friendship that also supported stars as commodities and as social subjects.

About Evidence Good and "Bad"

My investigation of the texts that construct Rita Hayworth as at once a resisting social subject and a salable commodity image is the practical result of a consideration of available resources, on the one hand, and an ongoing interest in the 1940s and 1950s in relation to the history of feminism in America on the other (about which I will say more in a moment). Jackie Stacey has remarked that it is "puzzling" that "feminist work on Hollywood cinema has paid little attention to stars."[32] What makes this puzzling is, as Stacey puts it, the amount of "complex and contradictory negotiation" in the "ideals of femininity" that she finds inscribed in classical Hollywood films. Stacey barely mentions ancillary texts such as fan magazines, where I find that the questioning of women's cultural status during this period was much more overt and contentious than in films themselves.[33] If one of the technological developments that has made my study not only simpler but actually possible is that most of Hayworth's Hollywood films survive and have been released in several home-video formats, the point remains that what stars mean is not limited to their films. Indeed, during Hayworth's years of greatest media coverage she was often off the screen entirely, her stardom preserved in and conveyed by what are now yellowed and crumbling pages and clippings from magazines and newspapers. "What to do with Hayworth" was also the subject of studio memos, letters, production schedules, and the like that are preserved in various archives and libraries around the country.

The fact that antique and flea-market dealers refer to this material as *ephemera* suggests more than the difficulty of preserving decomposition-prone paper products for long periods. The term also signifies something of the ideological issues that are often raised by that which is, by definition, not meant to be permanent. Much of the material I consider here was supposed literally to disappear, to be thrown away, to be supplanted by a continual stream of new information. To study a movie star thus means comprehending what Anne Friedberg calls the "imaginary else-when" of film texts—whose "images of a constructed past" are "a confusing blur of 'simulated' and 'real'" and are felt, in their effects, as happening "now"—in addition to more fragmentary, randomly preserved discourse whose very material form more profoundly embodies age (the yellowing pages of ephemera are where the real age of the past often shows itself).[34] Encountering the past through such material can be extraordinarily productive precisely because it is so attached to its own cultural moment (conversely, that someone felt attached enough to the material to *save* it, to *keep* it, is also meaningful) and because even material produced for the commercial or mass market often had a rhetorical or hortatory purpose.

Indeed, many scholars see fan magazines as being merely an auxiliary format of consumerism through which Hollywood supported and promoted the familiar ideological conservatism of its films.[35] According to this line of reasoning, whatever one were to find in a fan magazine would represent a priori the interests of the dominant patriarchal institution that was Hollywood itself. Fan and other mass-market magazines are therefore considered by many historians to be "bad evidence," as Lynn Spigel puts it; they are generated not by "people" but by the "culture industry." [36] Yet as Spigel pointedly remarks, "[T]here is no source that is without its own conditions of power and its own conventions of representation through which it speaks to its imagined publics." Media products like fan magazines and films and even movie stars themselves form an "intertextual network" that, in the case of postwar media, became "an arena of cultural struggles over exactly what and who constitute public and private spheres." What is often overlooked about the relationship of readers and audiences to media products is, as Spigel shows (drawing from Janice Radway's 1984 *Reading the Romance*), the differences demarcating various texts from one another—their specificity rather than the regularity that might be assumed from performing some sort of "scientific" quantifying of data terms, for example.[37] Readers and audiences (still) do *choose* their texts rather than merely consuming them; and although the range of choices is not unlimited, the resources offered are much more nuanced and particular and various than a broad survey would suggest.[38]

Conversely, when historians *have* found evidence in mass-market discourse of a "progressive view of women's changing sexual and economic roles," in Gaylyn Studlar's terms about fan magazines of the 1920s, it is likely to be during periods already recognized as "progressive" with regard to gender roles and expectations.[39] Studlar already knows, in other words, that the 1920s were a time in which "large numbers of American women were perceived as departing from longstanding gender norms in courtship behaviors, in the dynamics of marriage, and in their expression of economic independence." Even the early 1940s, during which there was what Michael Renov calls a "media blitzkrieg" to glamorize work for women outside the home, are dismissed by Renov as a time of "cultural

(as well as economic and political) eccentricity" rather than a real challenge to the status quo.[40] Should one expect, then, to find any "progressive" attitudes about gender in a fan magazine produced during the 1950s,
a period in which large numbers of American women were thought to
have accepted and reinscribed traditional conservative gender stereotypes? If so, would these attitudes be marked by what Studlar refers to as
the "contradictions and ambiguities" of textual and extratextual discourse
of the 1920s, "an era of intensified (and anxious) gender awareness"?[41] In
fact, my research supports other work that has shown that there are as
many if not more "contradictions and ambiguities" marking the commercial discourse about Hollywood stars and their films in the late 1940s
and the 1950s than in either the 1920s or during World War II. I also demonstrate that studies of Hollywood stars in the postwar era—even, if not
especially, stars whose personal lives were as important as their films—can
quite easily be folded into other revisionings of the 1950s as the crucible
for, rather than the barrier to, the emergence of the second wave of feminism in the 1960s.

One of the most useful examples of such revisionist work is the 1994
collection, edited by Joanne Meyerowitz, *Not June Cleaver: Women and
Gender in Postwar America, 1945–1960*.[42] In her own essay, "Beyond the
Feminine Mystique," Meyerowitz examines nonfiction articles in eight
women's mass-market magazines published between 1946 and 1958.[43] She
shows that Betty Friedan's famous formulation of the postwar era as a
time of enforced domesticity for women is flawed by its reliance on a
handful of conservative writings, writings that have since also served as
primary sources for a number of historians. Rather than depicting an era
in which domesticity was glorified, mass-market sources from the 1950s
were seldom unified in their message. Instead, "domestic ideals coexisted
in ongoing tension with an ethos of individual achievement that celebrated nondomestic activity, individual striving, public service, and public success."[44] Friedan's account of the "feminine mystique," then, may
have "hit such a resonant chord among middle-class women" in part
because, Meyerowitz concludes, it was a reworking of already familiar
themes.[45]

The widely accepted view of the 1950s as reactionary and conservative
with regard to women's roles and cold war politics has powerful adher-
ents, and Meyerowitz is quick to point out that a dogmatic domestic ideology *is* a "piece of the postwar cultural puzzle."[46] But it is one piece, not
the entire puzzle. Conservative domestic ideology might be thought of
as the ground against which, or on which, competing discourses stood

out in ever sharper relief. It functioned in the 1950s as what Noël Carroll calls the "cultural commonplace," because its rhetorical strategy was to present itself as a "natural" set of generalized assumptions about behavior and conduct.[47] But however apparently conservative the material I came across—a fan magazine article about Hayworth called, say, "Marry the Boy Next Door," "She's the Marrying Kind," or "Love's Lonely Fugitive"—it, too, was always "varied enough and ambivalent enough," in Meyerowitz's terms, to call into question much of our received wisdom about the prevalence of the feminine mystique.[48]

The social history that Meyerowitz's work elucidates is another important supporting structure for my analysis here, as is the work of other scholars interested in illuminating the historical and discursive contradictions of the postwar era—Lynn Spigel, Elaine Tyler May, Glenna Matthews, Maxine Margolis, Steven Cohan, and others.[49] What May calls an ideology of domestic containment coexisted, as is now well known, not with the departure of women from the public labor force after World War II but rather with a continual and steady increase in women's labor outside the home (albeit back in the white- or pink-collar jobs they had held before the war), particularly married middle-class women's labor.[50] This increase was undoubtedly driven substantially by an ethos of "emulative consumption" and "status striving," as Vance Packard put it in *The Status Seekers* in 1959, such that middle-class women worked in order to contribute to the acquisition of the goods needed to maintain the family's status within the community.[51] Others have suggested that emulative consumption does not convincingly account for statistics that still have the power to astonish—that between 1950 and 1960 more than four million married women took jobs, accounting for 60 percent of all new workers, male and female; and that between 1940 and 1960 the proportion of wives with jobs was double the 1940 figure of 15 percent, and the number of working mothers increased by 400 percent.[52] Even where emulative consumption *is* cited as the motivating reason for a wife's or mother's labor outside the home, it is this labor's ancillary benefits and satisfactions—increased self-esteem, the feeling of being useful beyond one's own limited sphere of influence, the companionship of people with whom one could discuss something other than dinner or diapers—that keep her there over the long run. The popular magazine articles Meyerowitz examines, by "applauding the public possibilities open to women, including married women, may have validated some readers' nondomestic behavior and sharpened some readers' discontent with the constraints they experienced in their domestic lives."[53] As I will show, the discourses constructing

Hayworth as someone whose work continues to matter to her even as husband after husband is left by the wayside support this feature of women's existence in the postwar era as well.

Although I remain extensively indebted to poststructuralist feminist film theory, I am hardly alone in wanting to work through how its theoretical claims sometimes depend on generalizing extensively, but not always carefully, about the past.[54] The illusory simplicity of gender-based models of spectatorship has already been ruptured by scholars working in areas of class, age, race, ethnicity, nationality, and sexual identity politics.[55] This work helps us to remember that we still do not know much about what parts of the past do and do not produce recognizable ideological effects in the present. If stars like Hayworth appear always to lack control over their own images, it is partly because we so often read these stars according to persistent assumptions about the objectification of women by the cinematic apparatus itself rather than taking into account contradictory or more complex historical evidence.

In her study of Mario Lanza, Marcia Landy warns of the "vanity of trying any longer to connect the star to the affective dimensions of identification and belief that belong to a vanished world"; dead stars are commodities who, "uprooted from [their] earlier context," now float in a world of "fantasy" made possible by the new consumer-based technologies of preservation and circulation.[56] I am interested in a different sort of "vanished world," however, and that is the absence of virtually any real "earlier context" for Hayworth's image in film studies' version of the historical record. Patrice Petro has written that even those periods of the past that appear to be most "unified" are always "precarious conglomerates of tendencies, aspirations, and activities."[57] Like Petro, I see the period that I focus on, no less than that in which I live, as a "complex cultural space." Anyone may use the texts and intertexts of the past for his or her own purposes; I am using them not only to suggest that there were affective dimensions in Hayworth's relationship to her audiences in the 1940s and the 1950s but to produce a basis for feeling differently about her image *now,* in the way we think about women stars, industrial and social history, and film feminism.[58]

Before turning to summaries of individual chapters, I want briefly to demarcate what I am *not* going to do here or why I am doing certain things but not others. As mentioned, much of what I study in the chapters that follow can be considered both primary source material and "bad evidence." That is, these discourses are primary not in the sense of their origination in the consciousness and production practices of an individual but as the first-level and originary location of meaning contemporary to, and constitutive of, the several subjectivities in question (Hayworth's as well as her audiences'). This primary material has been gathered from a diversity of sources—libraries and archives, flea markets, online auction houses, and the collections of several individuals.[59] Although I would never claim to have seen everything written about Hayworth over the course of her career, the patterns identified across time do indicate to me that I have examined a demonstrably representative sampling. Equally important, the research for this book was always conducted comparatively, with an eye to understanding how Hayworth was similar to, as well as different from, other star images whose more or less heterogeneous subjectivities were being constructed along with hers.

Generally, most women stars are given core values like integrity and honesty and kindness by fan-magazine writers and publicists in the 1940s and 1950s, and all women stars want domestic happiness and children whether "now" or "eventually." But beyond this basic feature of what John Ellis has named the star paradox—that stars are at once always ordinary as well as always unique and specially talented—the discourse on stars has to distinguish them from one another (Janet Staiger thus defines a star economically as "a monopoly on a personality," his or her "unique qualities" deployed as a "means to differentiate product").[60] In this sense, although I will make only a few passing references to other stars (an exception being my discussion of Kim Novak, Hayworth's "replacement," in the afterword), my work is always operating from an awareness of how other stars were positioned at the same time. For example, I know that Rita Hayworth's ethnicity marks her as different from Betty Grable, Joan Crawford, or Lana Turner but as similar to Dolores del Rio, Marlene Dietrich, Hedy Lamarr, or Ingrid Bergman. Conversely, her Americanness separates her from del Rio, Dietrich, Lamarr, and Bergman and links her to Grable, Crawford, Turner, and Ginger Rogers. Hayworth's domestic problems make her similar to all but a very few stars (Irene Dunne, for example, who stayed married to one man throughout her career, or Eleanor Powell), but her unhappiness with her domestic failures is marked much differently from that of Grable, Crawford, Turner, Rogers, et al. Hayworth never played a mother in any of her studio-produced star vehicles, whereas most of these other stars did. Like Hayworth, Grable and Rogers made musical comedies, but Crawford and Turner did not (and so on). Thus, my analysis takes off from a knowledge of Hayworth's star image as sometimes similar to and at other times different from those of other women stars, as well as from a deep familiarity with the conventional banalities of mass-mediated and film-promotional discourses.

Also missing from my discussions of mass-market magazines and other promotional and publicity material is any sustained analysis of reader response. That is, here there is little reference to such things as Stuart Hall's encoding/decoding model and whether I believe audiences were employing preferred, negotiated, or oppositional strategies in response to the texts in question.[61] Primarily this is because I have become convinced of a certain incompatibility of these and similar models with the reading of fan magazines especially, even those intended for a predominantly female audience. For example, in her 1993 book, *Decoding Women's Magazines,* Ellen McCracken analyzes women's magazines as "pleasurable, value-laden semiotic systems" whose primary purpose is to "conflate desire with consumerism" through the intersection of editorial content with advertising.[62] All of the segments within these magazines, McCracken argues, "foreground a pleasurable, appealing consensus about the feminine" and "exert a cultural leadership to shape consensus in which highly pleasurable codes work to naturalize social relations of power." McCracken believes that a hypothetical reader's first perusal of a magazine will focus on ads and on broadly identifying editorial content, the second on a closer reading of specific articles, and a third on the alternation between levels one and two. Fan magazines certainly contain ads for products aimed at women as consumers (although almost never, at least in the 1940s and 1950s, in the main features sections); however, the star as at once agent and commodity—as her own advertising for her films and for her image but also as her own self with its own social reality—complicates such models of reading and interpretation, as well as any real consensus about femininity or even social relations of power.[63]

For whatever else it might be, the basis of our relationships with stars is primarily felt as a social relationship.[64] The star circulates in multiple and contradictory versions at the same time as well as across time—as many stories in many fan magazines running simultaneously, as brief mentions in gossip columns appearing in many different venues, as movie roles and newsreels, as radio spots, and so forth. McCracken invokes the notion of an Eisensteinian intellectual montage to show how ads interact with text and photos the more firmly to make their consumerist points.[65] But in the case of stars this montage also functions across time, continually refiguring any consensus that may have been briefly achieved in the past. Magazines and films come and go throughout the period I am discussing, but Rita Hayworth remains; and if one is a fan of Rita Hayworth, then what matters about any magazine or film is the information it offers about *her.* And because of the intertwining of discourses of transformation, ethnicity, authenticity, labor, domesticity, scandal, pleasure, unhappiness, and pain it would be extremely difficult to accept the contents of articles about Rita Hayworth without question or even merely to absorb "the dominant ideology which underlies the production of the text," as Jacqueline Bobo puts it in her description of Hall's preferred reading strategy.[66] Even if there were *a* dominant ideology underlying the texts I examine, the texts themselves are rarely less than confusing in their rendering of it. In other words, any reader who might have ardently wished to accept the dominant or preferred meaning of the material I study here would always have had to block out, or to negotiate around, a certain—often quite overwhelming—amount of competing or contradictory discourse.

And finally, although my discussions of film texts involve textual analysis of the visual image, I pay relatively little attention to the appearance—the photographs, the layouts, the colors, the advertisements—of the printed material I examine (I do employ several facsimile reproductions as illustrations). Many readers probably did focus their attention on images and ads as opposed to the text within the articles (cutting out photos for scrapbooks or wall decoration, for example), but most of the material I am employing was saved in its entirety, text and all, by a variety of usually unknown fan-readers (many of whom, unfortunately, did not follow proper scholarly procedure in the labeling of clippings and the like). I do want to note, however, that in my experience of the visual material of commercially produced fan discourse there are few obvious patterns, whether within specific journals or across a variety of them, over time. Sometimes images and text "anchor" each other, to employ Roland Barthes's well-known terminology, and support each other's message—as when an article stressing Hayworth's "new-found happiness" with one or another of her husbands is accompanied by photographs of a smiling, "happy" Hayworth.[67] But equally often the photos and text are more at odds or in bizarre juxtaposition.

A May 1951 issue of *Silver Screen* with Hayworth on its cover, for instance, offers "a tip to teenagers from Rita."[68] The "tip" turns out not to be "from" Rita but from Gladys Hall and can be "reduced . . . to two words: *Be feminine.*" As described by Hall, this means being "considerate of mens' *[sic]* feelings" and "agreeable to any plan or suggestion the current beau might make." Quoting approvingly from Winthrop Sargeant's 1947 *Life* article, Hall claims that Hayworth's success in winning Prince Aly Khan, to whom Hayworth was then still married, could be attributed to her "passivity," her ability to "be" what men want her to be. Yet the "tip" ends finally as follows:

"A Tip to Teenagers from Rita," *Silver Screen,* May 1951. Inside, the cover image is described simply, if redundantly, as a "color portrait in natural color of Rita Hayworth, soon to star in Columbia picture," but *The Lady from Shanghai* is never referred to by name. One of the captions for the article proper, by Gladys Hall, reads "Devastantingly *[sic]* feminine Rita Hayworth reveals secret of adding all-important plus to yourself. Rita had much to overcome in her early days. But she kept improving and improving herself until she became a goddess." Copyright 1951 by J. Fred Henry Publications, Inc.

Whether a movie star, in the uniform of Wac or Wave, a champion tennis player, golfer, channel swimmer, weight-lifter, private secretary, trained nurse, whatever or wherever, be feminine. For if you, like Rita Hayworth, so dress, talk, behave and feel that never for a moment does a man forget you are a *woman*—well, you may not wear a crown . . . but you'll wear a wedding ring, you'll get your man and that's what you want, isn't it?

But as if unconsciously acknowledging the incongruities of this sort of advice, the cover photo is not, as might be expected, a glowing or even a shyly smiling or "feminine" Rita Hayworth. Rather, it is Hayworth as predatory blonde femme fatale Elsa Bannister from the 1948 *Lady from Shanghai,* animal pelt draped over her shoulders, eyes narrowed as she puffs on a cigarette. Against this image the accompanying "tip to teenagers" caption—the only caption on the cover—takes on a more perverse valence, as does the reason, couched as advice, given in the article for Hayworth's "almost boyish bob" in *The Lady from Shanghai:* "To please Orson" ("pleasing Orson" did not make her marriage happy; in fact, it had already ended in divorce). To say that I am not devoting specific or extensive attention to publicity photographs and the like does not mean, then, that I have not been influenced by them or even that the way Hayworth circulates as a still photographic image is entirely ignored. Rather, my project takes off from the assumption that images and text— as with the actions and gestures of the filmed body as opposed to the words it may be asked to speak—are frequently performing different kinds of labor.

Organization

My own labor in discussing these differences is organized as follows. The book is divided into two sections, the first dealing primarily with what might be called Hayworth's labor as a star away from her films (her stardom off the screen)[69] and the second adding extensive analysis of the embodied, performing, filmed Hayworth and the various contexts, including academic film studies, in which she signifies in certain of her best known or most successful star vehicles. That the Hayworth films we know best now are not necessarily the same as those most popular during her heyday is one of the issues in question. (See the filmography for a complete list of Rita Cansino's and Rita Hayworth's commercial films.) My discussion will seem at times an uneasy mixture of history and theory, but that cannot be helped. I want to present the evidence as I find it, but at the same time I cannot remove from my work my interest in the theoretical as well as historical contexts for this material—in placing it into the theoretical frameworks that construct my own subjectivity, as it were, as a scholar. Without these preexisting frameworks—those whose contours I believe this project might also alter—the evidence would not speak at all.

In chapter 1 I consider the processes by which Margarita Cansino became Rita Cansino and then Rita Hayworth and the ways in which this transformation—and its discourses of ethnicity, authenticity, and labor— continued to inflect her meaning as an all-American star. The biographies

and scholarly exhumations of Hayworth vary substantially in their accounts of the role Hayworth's fabrication played in her appeal to her contemporary audiences. Barbara Leaming claims that it struck a particular
nerve in 1940s America—that the notion that someone could be "magi-
cally transformed" into a star "utterly enthralled" audiences of the time.[70]
In his 1992 article about Hayworth William Vincent calls her "the perfect
example of the fabricated Hollywood star" but claims there was "nothing
new" in this (he quotes Carl Laemmle's assertion that fabrication of stars
is "the fundamental thing" in the film industry).[71] What Vincent misses
completely is that, although fabrication of stars was not new, the extent
of the public's awareness of it in Hayworth's case was quite unusual.
Leaming is closer to the mark in acknowledging that the public was "enthralled" by Hayworth's transformation, but, as I show, there was little
that was magical about it. Hayworth was frequently a contentious subject
whose own feelings about her transformation varied over time and whose
professional labor, ending in this chapter with the formation of her own
production company, came to be associated with a gradual independence
from and rejection of that process.

In chapter 2 I examine the ways in which Hayworth's actions in what
is so often called the domestic sphere—her childhood and family life, her
marriages, her relations with her children, the conflicts between domesticity and career—were discussed in the popular press. To borrow Joanne
Meyerowitz's phrase, "the theme of nondomestic success was no hidden
subtext" in the stories about Hayworth, and neither Hayworth's marriages nor the failures of her attempts at domesticity were "prerequisites
for [her] star status."[72] In fact, Hayworth's domestic failures became part
of a very complicated negotiation of the value of stars' labor and, in the
case of Hayworth's relationship with Aly Khan, her meanings as an American woman. Hayworth's divorce from Aly Khan was represented to
American audiences through a racist and nationalist discourse that ended
up valorizing women's social and economic equality to men in contradistinction to the "Moslem world" in which women were figured as "less
valuable than men." From the failure of her very first marriage to a much
older father figure, Ed Judson, in the early 1940s, Hayworth is named one
of "Hollywood's unhappiest stars," an inflection that continues throughout her career and the final marriage I consider in depth, that to Dick
Haymes in the mid-1950s.

As mentioned, in many crucial ways the "real" Hayworth (the one depicted in biographies such as Leaming's) turns out not to be all that different—in her behavior, her problems, her confused and confusing ac-

tions, her responses to culture and its meanings—from the discursive Hayworth produced in and by the "bad evidence" of popular culture. The pressures of Hayworth's own history on the range of representations circulated about her gave her image an agency born of her labor struggles within Hollywood and her very public "private" struggles to accommodate herself to postwar domestic ideology. Over time the contradictions—the wiggling back and forth between alternately valorizing marriage, motherhood, family, work—become too great for even the conventional framework of fan discourse to bear. If only in a modest way, Hayworth's image perhaps helped some women (and, one hopes, men) to begin to articulate overtly feminist feelings of dissatisfaction, frustration, and anger with the impossible double binds of their lives.[73]

The book's second section continues my interest in the discursively produced subjectivity of Rita Hayworth, but its three chapters also focus on textual analysis of several of her major star vehicles—*Gilda* (1946, produced [and substantially written] by Virginia Van Upp), *Down to Earth* (1947), *The Lady from Shanghai* (1948), and *Affair in Trinidad* (1952, also written by Van Upp)—and discuss their production and reception contexts in addition to the scholarly contexts in which they now circulate (or do not) within academic film studies. One of these films is a generic musical, and the others are most often identified as films noirs. In addition to considering the films as texts, however, I consider them as commodities, looking for the ways, in Danae Clark's terms, that the social relations of labor and subjectivity—the traces of hegemonic "labor policies and labor discourses"—have been "embodied in the textual terrain" of the film text itself.[74] I also introduce and explore a different kind of subjectivity, which dance scholar Jane Desmond calls "kinesthetic subjectivity," in Hayworth's image as well—the ways in which her embodiment in and of a variety of dance styles and performance modes generates its own complex forms of agency, signification, and meaning.[75]

Chapter 3 is devoted to the backstage "women's musical" *Down to Earth,* one of Hayworth's most successful but noncanonical musical films, because the dominance of women in its narrative and numbers undermines the prevalent notion that the musical is by definition a conservative genre, particularly in terms of female representation. *Down to Earth* deals with the issue of women's agency and professional labor on several levels: its narrative, in which a goddess is impersonating a human who is impersonating a goddess and trying to exert her will in the face of massive opposition from the show's [male] director and his best buddy; its musical numbers, some of which are meant to be understood as badly performed as against others that are "good"; and, finally, its invisibility *as* a women's musical, because *Down to Earth* is interesting primarily for the performances of the women in the film rather than as a showcase for a male auteur (neither its male star [Larry Parks] nor its director [Alexander Hall] nor its choreographer [Jack Cole] have been granted auteur status by the academy and its canons). By concentrating so extensively on the underlying structure or form of the musical, as scholars such as Rick Altman have, rather than on its many modes of performance, or by defining women's musical performances so frequently as [heterosexual] male-directed erotic spectacle, we have blocked out much of the ideological criticism that the genre and its stars are best suited to make *through* performance (with performance here referring to skill in execution, success in the accomplishment of difficult tasks, demonstrated excellence in ability, and so forth).[76] Many musical numbers in many musical films, particularly those that star talented and competent women, say, in effect, what the conventionally romantic narratives in which they are embedded often cannot. *Down to Earth,* then, foregrounds textually what is implied in all of the mass-market discourse described in the first section of the book, namely the difficulties that women faced in the postwar era in being recognized as themselves, in being "seen and heard."

Musical numbers are also examined in chapter 4 but in a somewhat different sense: namely, their production by and effects on Hayworth as the textual protagonist of the films noirs *Gilda* and *The Lady from Shanghai.* I explore how Orson Welles systematically works in *The Lady from Shanghai* to subvert, taint, or demolish Hayworth's kinesthetic subjectivity and what his success in doing so means for our understanding of female "charisma" (Richard Dyer's term) both theoretically and historically in classical Hollywood cinema.[77] I trace the ways in which film scholars, if unintentionally, have sometimes helped Welles in this task in their accounts of Hayworth's function within the diegesis of *The Lady from Shanghai,* as well as historically, in terms of the making of the film and the context of its reception. My goal, here as elsewhere, is to complicate prevalent assumptions about the "flatness" of Hayworth's star image in the 1940s and 1950s, to restore to her image the volume, effort, and expressiveness put there by dance and her skills as an actor as well as by the discursive contradictions and struggles explored in the first part of the book.

Chapter 5 focuses on the musical numbers in a third Hayworth film noir, *Affair in Trinidad,* usually acknowledged to be a "rehash" of *Gilda,* in order to consider the menace, both narrative and extratextual, that they seemed to represent to several industrial and critical power structures. Although *Affair in Trinidad* is largely unknown within the academy, it is long overdue for scholarly scrutiny because, first, its musical numbers were choreographed and directed by Valerie Bettis (1919–1982), an important modern concert dancer and choreographer, and, second, it caused a stir on its release because of the nature of the female eroticism in those musical numbers, which were taken by film, but not dance, critics to be "grotesque," "vulgar," and "unattractive." Much of my analysis focuses on the film itself, as well as on the response of its contemporary critics. But I also want to delineate as far as possible the logistics of the film's production in order to relate the extraordinary power of the musical numbers in *Affair in Trinidad* to the material circumstances of their collaborative creation by Bettis and Hayworth, including the pair's public battles with studio personnel over the terms of Hayworth's visual representation. In concluding the chapter I also consider similar issues in relation to Hayworth's final three nonmusical films at Columbia: *Miss Sadie Thompson, Salome* (also choreographed by Bettis), and *Fire Down Below* (1957).

Among the major points of the second section, then, is to show how Hayworth's labor as a star performing fictional roles in narrative films intersects with, yet is not the same as, the labor required to be a dancer and musical comedy star and that the passivity and objectification with which Hayworth has been associated in academic film studies is partly a result of a failure to consider this difference. My attempts to elucidate these fundamental concerns engage, sometimes explicitly but more often implicitly, a noticeable split in the definition and theorizing of performance between acting- and dance-based claims that "the body writes" and linguistically derived models of the body as always already "written [upon]." Linguistically based models of the gendered body and performativity tend to equate performativity with enforced mimesis and repetition— such that performativity is understood, as Judith Butler writes, "not as the act by which a subject brings into being what she/he names, but, rather, as that reiterative power of discourse to produce the phenomena that it regulates and constrains."[78] To the dance theorist, on the other hand, the body is capable of performing on many levels that themselves call into existence the discursive frameworks in which the performances "make sense." The relevance of this split for film studies is that it opens up a space in which to consider performance and performativity as process as well as artifact.

And indeed, as Peter Lovell and Peter Krämer point out, much of the work on gender and film has heretofore consisted of "discussions of a fictional character" rather than in analyses of "how that character is embodied (the work of an actor)."[79] Textual analysis often tends to valorize "objective" narrative concerns, such as dialogue, plot points, and narrative closure, over more "subjective" issues of performance style, music, and emotional affect. This emphasis is perfectly reasonable on some levels—it is much easier to prove *that* someone said a particular thing in a film, and when, than to prove *how* they said it. Music and dance, conversely, are often relegated in film studies to the arena of textual noise. Here their expressivity will become the focus, as well as the ways in which different modes of discourse—singing and songs, dancing and choreography, costuming and body type and stance, makeup and facial expression, tone of voice and dialogue—vie for dominance. The usefulness of both these approaches is that together they can help us to understand the filmed, and therefore always historical, body as both agent and object and, most important, to see and to hear how that agency and objectification are accomplished. As Ann Daly writes, the "gaze" as a "metaphor of representation" may not be well suited to dance, whose "apperception is grounded not just in the eye but in the entire body."[80] To rework Danae Clark's formulation, singing and dancing bodies are not that different from spectating bodies in terms of their heterogeneous subjectivities, and clearly there is more at work in spectatorship generally than merely meets the eye.

In summary, I believe that each image of Margarita Cansino, Rita Hayworth, and Gilda (along with Elsa Bannister, Sadie Thompson, and all of their sisters) is an active instigator rather than passive victim of the ambivalence, the paradoxes, the complexity of the discourses they all are represented by.[81] As I consider these women from my embodied present (I was born in 1957), I am alternately bewildered, cheered, offended, saddened, astonished by who they were and were not—indeed, are and are not—able to be. The desire to know them all better is what drives this study forward, into the past.

PART ONE

Stardom Off the Screen

Hayworth at her most conventionally beautiful and glamorous, circa 1946. Collection of the author, photographer not named.

From Cansino
to Hayworth to Beckworth

CONSTRUCTING THE STAR PERSON(A)

In February 1940 Rita Hayworth made her first appearance on the cover of a national mass-market magazine, *Look*. She is dressed as a Spanish dancer: there are red flowers in her black hair, her dress is red, and she brandishes a pair of maracas. The cover's inside spread mentions that Hayworth is "half Spanish," but what makes her worth an additional four-page photographic layout is that she has been named "the screen star with the smartest personal wardrobe."[1] In these photos there is nary a maraca in sight, and Hayworth's black hair turns out to be dark red. The importance of the *Look* cover and the spread to Hayworth's career is that both signal the beginning of her rise to national prominence as a visual image and as a commodity. Her identifying features are an excessive femininity (she is mainly interested in clothes), the fact that she is married (to "oil-man-husband" Ed Judson), and her Spanish background. The article notes also that Hayworth has appeared in several films, among them *Only Angels Have Wings* and a musical with Tony Martin.

What the article does not mention, however, is that by 1940 Rita Hayworth, born Margarita Carmen Cansino, had already appeared in twenty-five movies, close to half of her lifetime output. Ten of them she had made as Rita Cansino, a shortening of her original name. Equally important to this discussion, then, is that the *Look* cover plays up stereotypical visual features of her Spanish heritage, but the article inside does not. Since her name had been anglicized only in 1937, the year she signed a contract with Columbia Studios, this ambivalence could be taken as a sign that her commodification as a star was not yet finished. She had not, in other words, been *completely* transformed from Rita Cansino, who had clearly failed to become a star, into the more marketable and more desirable Rita Hayworth.

Yet contrary to popular belief this ambivalence remains a constant of Hayworth's stardom throughout the rest of her career, and Margarita (or Rita) Cansino is herself virtually always present in Hayworth as a star text. In some sense the process of Hayworth's transformation does conform to

"Rita Hayworth: Best-Dressed Girl in Hollywood," on her first mass-market magazine cover, *Look,* February 22, 1940. Photo by Earl Theisen. Copyright 1940 by Look, Inc.

Danae Clark's assertion that Hollywood studios consolidated their power over their star labor force by "erasing" an actor's real name and personal history in order to create a "coherent, salable persona" whose public circulation the studio controlled.[2] But in other ways the continuing existence of Margarita Cansino belies or complicates this scenario, as do the ways in which Hayworth's own words—whether truly "hers" or not—participate in (changing) the meanings her star image produces over time. Rather than finding that "white" was always the symbolic "apotheosis of female desirability," as Richard Dyer has put it, or that only in the "decomposition stage" of her star image did Hayworth's "original name" begin to crop up in the discourse, as Jane Gaines has claimed, I will show that Hayworth's ethnic background was always a prominent element in her star appeal and that Hayworth herself continually referred to it in public as an important motivating source of her success as a star and even the locus or justification of her identity and behavior as a woman, wife, and mother.[3]

Another equally significant factor in Hayworth's development as a star was the process of fabrication itself, which again seems a familiar component of Hollywood's compulsion to erase a star's previous identity. In Hayworth's case, accomplished according to her biographers at the hands of various male mentor/Svengali figures, this involved diet and body reshaping through exercise, strengthening and homogenizing her voice with diction and singing lessons, changing her hair color from black or dark brown to red, and raising her low forehead through two years of painful electrolysis on her hairline. References to these aspects of Hayworth's transformation are relatively common also in discussions of stardom in classical Hollywood cinema, the details of the whole appalling process offered up as the shocking revelation of what once (surely) had been a hidden, dirty secret.[4] Thus, Hayworth is an obvious and very useful example of how women in American culture are consistently rewarded for undergoing extreme physical and psychic duress in an attempt to attain an impossible, but desirable, physical or moral ideal. As a corollary to this Hayworth also embodies the cultural imperative by which, in Mary Ann Doane's general terms, a woman can be "encouraged to actively participate in her own oppression."[5]

But to leave Hayworth's transformation at this level ignores one of its most profound and seldom acknowledged features: that it was all accomplished in full view of the public and with her own shifting responses to it and her struggles to find her own identity in the course of this transformation made part of the discourse as well. Here the coherent, salable persona is revealed publicly to be what it in fact was: bifurcated along the lines of the actor's collusion with—or conversely resistance to—the terms of persona-making itself. Neither Hayworth's victimization by a series of powerful men nor the strength it took to react against or escape from that victimization was concealed. Hayworth was at first weak, pliable, and excessively tied to her body and its appearance. By the mid-1940s, however, she had become more assertive and much more outspoken about the nature of that oppression and more openly defiant of the conventions of correct behavior.

This chapter chronicles the process by which Margarita Cansino became Rita Hayworth as represented in the popular press and discusses Hayworth's struggles as signs representing the star as "both labour and the thing that labour produces," in Richard Dyer's words.[6] It is this process—as commodification, as a set of discourses about women's cultural value, as a performance strategy revealed to be such by Hayworth herself, as her feelings about her own work—that provides the space in which to interrogate what Clark calls the "fragmented and fought-over position of the actor as a subject of film labor and film representation."[7] (In these years Hayworth also goes through five marriages and five divorces, becomes part of an international scandal, has two children, and becomes a single working mother accused of child neglect. Her public struggles to be successful in the private sphere of domesticity, and the links of these struggles to her own troubled childhood, are explored in the next chapter.) Only when one examines Hayworth's construction in detail, as an advertising strategy with often competing rhetorical purposes and as a series of mutable, evolving representations, can one begin to understand the means by which women stars were confined to the ground of the "cultural commonplace"—those purportedly natural and generalized assumptions about behavior and conduct—yet at the same time helped to alter the terrain of that ground.[8]

Below I focus on a range of texts that delineate the basic terms with which Hayworth's transformation from Cansino to Hayworth was accomplished and with which her labor as a star was defined through the end of the war and the formation of her own production company, the Beckworth Corporation, in 1947. The purpose of the concluding section of this chapter is to underscore the fact that stars like Hayworth were not merely significant as embodied representations of an exotic or domesticated femininity but also as laborers endeavoring within the machinery of Hollywood to develop and improve their skills, to rise through the hierarchy, to be true to their own notions of fairness and equality, to acquire "firm authority over what [they] will and will not do."[9] As will become clear, even mass-mediated discourse was often quite interlocutory in a textual sense, such that the contents of one article can be seen as commenting on or arguing with another (in these contexts, Hayworth herself often was represented as the agent of her own image management).

That's One Reason I Changed My Name

Rita Cansino played primarily bit parts in her first films, beginning with a dancing specialty in *Dante's Inferno* (1935). These films were all low-budget programmers (several of them westerns) made for Fox, Crescent Pictures, Grand National, and Republic before she signed with Columbia (and changed her name) in 1937. In the hierarchy of Hollywood publicity, starlets were usually confined to advertisements or to photo layouts that

Two versions of Rita Cansino, both identifying her simply as a "20th Century Fox Player." Exact date of images not known. Collection of the author.

were extended advertisements for clothing, makeup, and other products. Neither Rita Cansino nor the new Rita Hayworth were exceptions to this (I am particularly fond of an often-reprinted 1940 ad for Autolite spark plugs that features a black-haired Rita Hayworth in a hula skirt). The photo captions of layouts in fan magazines, whose readership was presumed to be female, mainly provide information about the products ("a playsuit of black and white," "an Ensenada slack suit of blue California hopsacking," "hand laced Dundeer Mocc-Sans in soft brown and white"),[10] but even after the name change they also consistently remind us either that Rita Hayworth is half-Spanish or that she used to be Rita Cansino (often both).

Thus for *Motion Picture* in June 1938 Rita Hayworth is "a newcomer who hails from a theatrical family. She is part Spanish and knows her Spanish dances—including the tango and rhumba. But would gladly give up dancing to demonstrate an emotional talent." In a 1938 sheet music ad she is "Daughter of the famous Spanish dancer, Eduardo Cansino," and is "now devoting all of her time to dramatic and light comedy parts, and never intends to dance professionally again." For *Movies* in September 1939, in a brief article called "She Dances but Prefers Acting," Rita Hayworth is someone who, "with her Spanish ancestry and known as a Cansino," has "hurdled the stumbling-block of so many hundreds of actresses—*she's overcome her type.* Hollywood no longer thinks of her as a

Spanish dancer!" As Hayworth herself "explains," "That's one reason I changed my name. . . . I didn't want to be known only as a dancer."

In these and countless other articles like them Hayworth's Spanish heritage is folded into an activity conventionally associated with it: dancing. Despite the number of films she had already appeared in, the *Movies* article continues, she's a "newcomer" because she has only now managed to "overcome her type," which had limited her appeal in the past. And in spite of how much she has (been) changed physically, she has an "utter lack of pose and affectation. She is as natural as the dawn."

After the *Look* cover and article Edward Judson becomes a much bigger player in the publicity, and commodification itself a pronounced structure in Hayworth's appeal. As a 1940 *Screenland* article called "What It Takes to Be a Hollywood Husband! 'Mr. Rita Hayworth' Tells" puts it, "[A]fter marriage [to Judson] this modern Pygmalion took his Galatea in hand and transformed her."[11] It was "not magic, but Judson":

> Eddie Judson is a shrewd businessman. He used the same business principles to sell Rita that he employed to sell automobiles and oil contracts. He mapped out each step of his wife's campaign just as he would map out a sales campaign. . . . To Eddie Judson it was safe and sound business principles to put a commodity across. . . .
>
> "You're lucky you aren't too well known in Hollywood," Ed told her, not unkindly. "Because you're going to start all over again, and this time the right way. Here's the way we ought to plan it: *Step No. 1* will be self-improvement. *Step No. 2* will be self-display. *Step No. 3* will be making a name for yourself. *Step No. 4* will be getting the right rôles and keeping you smack before the public so that you'll be 'hot' at the box office."
>
> Rita listened breathlessly to her husband's ambitious plans.

In quick succession the campaign to make Rita Hayworth "Columbia Studios' 'glamor girl' " put her on the cover of *Life* as well as *Look*, and most of the fan magazines. Because of her cooperative attitude toward the press ("Katharine Hepburn, Ginger Rogers and Margaret Sullavan may appear in dungarees and polo coat and scowl at the camera boys as though they were boogey men, but not Rita. She gives them their money's worth"), she became "the most widely photographed actress in Hollywood."[12]

The fact that a "business campaign" could make someone well known is not that surprising. What is remarkable is that a campaign *about* a campaign, a detailing of the process itself, produced such results. Rita Cansino, according to *Silver Screen* (February 1941), had actually "abandoned all hope" of making it in pictures. Again and again the "family-rocking [name] change" by which she "transformed herself from dancer to potential dramatic ball of fire" is acknowledged. "I didn't want to be typed as a Spanish dancer, so I decided to discard dancing," Hayworth tells *Movie Stars Parade* (1940). She is "hell-bent" on becoming an actress, the *Silver Screen* article continues, and "an intuition which told her to chuck dancing into the ash can *(even though it was responsible for her debut in pictures)*" is "vindicated" by her success in dramatic films such as *Only Angels Have Wings* (1939), *Angels over Broadway* (1940), and, most important, *Blood and Sand* (1941). Hayworth used to be Spanish, but now her name has a "good old American ring, which is completely orthodox, for Rita is a New Yorker, born October 17, 1918" (*Motion Picture*, September 1940).

Through 1941, then, Rita Hayworth is a glamour girl who is working very hard to "become a fine actress."[13] The "weary employment" in B westerns is over. She no longer has to "prove" that she can speak English instead of Spanish. Dancing, because it is tied to the type she is trying to overcome, has been discarded ("I never really cared for dancing"). She's happily married to an older man who is managing her career successfully, helping her to get to all the right places to see and be seen. (In her own reported words, Hayworth has spent "something like $75,000 investing in myself. It was at Ed's insistence.") She has done publicity stunt after publicity stunt, the "one which paid the biggest dividends" being the time in 1940 that she modeled a $250,000 dress made entirely of pearls. We know that, in addition to changing her name, she has dieted, taken voice and acting lessons, dyed her hair, and dresses glamorously "even when she doesn't feel like it." Her duty, as a wife and as a woman, as well as a potential star, is clear: to make the most of her assets and to alter or minimize features that do not fit the dominant (white) paradigm. That the process *itself* has been foregrounded is admittedly "truly unique," at least according to the articles that are doing the foregrounding.

Yet Hayworth's next career move contradicts one of the primary features of the campaign thus far: that dancing is never going to get her anywhere. Only a few weeks separate the last mention of her intention to become a (nondancing) actress in 1941 and her second *Life* magazine cover story (August 11, 1941), which announces, "Rita Hayworth rises from bit parts into a triple-threat song & dance star."[14] Suddenly, Hayworth *is* dancing, with Fred Astaire. It seemed, in fact, as though "she had never stopped dancing, that there never was a four-year gap." Hayworth now "never went out" because she was rehearsing "tirelessly," seven hours a day, for five weeks. Her dancing ability, not her status as a "clotheshorse,"

RITA HAYWORTH RISES FROM BIT PARTS INTO A TRIPLE-THREAT SONG & DANCE STAR

At various stages of her career Rita Hayworth (cover) has appeared in LIFE demonstrating a zipper-front bathing suit, going on a bicycle picnic, or wearing a $250,000 pearl dress. Now Rita poses on her own bed in her own home where she lives near Hollywood with her husband, an oil man. In her black-and-white nightgown Rita needs no excuse for decorating a page, but she has a good one. Playing the seductress in 20th Century-Fox's *Blood and Sand*, Rita stole the show from Linda Darnell and Tyrone Power when she did a Spanish dance in a tight red dress. She was taught to dance as a child by her father, a Spanish dancing teacher. Now as a result of her hit, Rita is becoming a triple-threat singing, dancing glamor star. In her next movie, *You'll Never Get Rich*, she dances with Fred Astaire who says Rita matches any partner he ever had.

Possibly the most famous photo of Rita Hayworth in the 1940s as it appeared for the first time in *Life* magazine, August 11, 1941. Note that the caption and blurb refer to Hayworth as a "Triple-Threat Song & Dance Star," who was earning unqualified praise from Fred Astaire. Photo by Bob Landry. Copyright 1941 by Time, Inc.

is what allows her to "make the leap to stardom." This second *Life* cover story is the one that contains the celebrated Bob Landry photograph that would become a popular wartime pinup. On the one hand is the flat, two-dimensional representation, "stable, an object, an artefact," to use Laura Mulvey's terms.[15] But on the other is Hayworth's "triple-threat" ability as an actress, a performer, a trained professional dancer.

Given the ubiquity of the Cansino references thus far in Hayworth's career, one would expect them to continue in the descriptions of her dancing prowess. Although by and large they do, there are some pointed exceptions. In an October 1941 article, "Born to Dance—Together," in *Movie Stars Parade,* Fred Astaire is "quoted" as saying that Hayworth is

Lobby photo of the now completely all-American(ized) Hayworth with Fred Astaire in *You'll Never Get Rich.* Copyright 1941 by Columbia Pictures Corp.

"a natural" ("She's constantly surprising me. Nothing is too difficult for her. She watches, goes home, practices up, and the next day she's got it perfect"), but she is no longer mentioned as having been a Cansino. *Life* acknowledges that "her father" was a "Spanish dancing teacher," but the construction is ambiguous (Spanish *dancing,* or *Spanish* dancing teacher?). One possibility for representing the "new" dancing Hayworth, then, would be to phase out Rita Cansino entirely.

But this did not happen. Between the end of 1941 and May 1942 the flurry of articles that accompany the box-office success of her two musicals with Astaire, and her less quantifiable success as a pinup girl and wartime entertainer (she performed in troop shows and toured camps), Rita Hayworth's distinguishing and most publicized features become her Latin heritage, her ability as a dancer, and the fact that her good looks are the result of much manipulation.[16] According to one 1941 article Hayworth deserves to be Astaire's partner ("Fred Finds the Right Girl at Last!") because she is "daughter of the once-famed fast-stepping Cansinos, who taught her to dance before she could walk." Although Hollywood once *tried* to capitalize on Margarita Cansino's "Spanish background," dying her hair "jet black," today "she's through being pushed

Publicity still in *Life*, November 9, 1942, of Hayworth and Fred Astaire dancing the "Shorty George" in *You Were Never Lovelier*. This feature, like others on Hayworth at this time, is anointing her the worthy successor to Ginger Rogers on the basis of Hayworth's appeal and dancing talent. Copyright 1942 by Time, Inc.

around. Her name is Rita Hayworth, top-ranking star!" *Time*'s November 1941 cover story, "California Carmen," also names her "the right girl" for Astaire and claims, "Those who saw russet-haired, incandescent Rita Hayworth dance before the movies drafted her knew she was a dancer to partner even the great Astaire. But few of them would have expected her to keep up with his wry, off-beat brand of comedy. She fills both assignments."[17]

I Had to Be Sold to the Public

Another of the signs of Hayworth's ascendancy in the Hollywood hierarchy is a shift in the rhetorical strategies employed in the publicity about her, or the sorts of uses to which her face and body were put. Although even the biggest stars had to appear to endorse products in print ads contracted between corporations and the studios themselves, by 1942 Hayworth has become the subject of many more feature articles that purport to be drawn from personal interviews rather than consisting of recycled versions of studio-produced bios and publicity material. In *Modern Screen*'s "Oomph for Sale" (December 1941) the details of her construction as a "product named Rita Hayworth," which could be "exploited with advertising" just like the automobiles Judson sold, are reiterated but this time in her own voice ("I had to be sold to the public just like a breakfast cereal or a real estate development or something new in ladies' wear," the article begins).[18] The events described are familiar by now (the name change, the physical transformation, her hard work, the publicity stunts), but the fact that Hayworth herself is naming and discussing the process of her own commodification, and some of the pain and confusion that the process engendered *for* her, produces a more nuanced sense of Hayworth's agency as at once laborer and product. In response to a question about her failure to acquire a film role she wanted, Hayworth describes her "depression" until "suddenly it dawned on me that there wasn't a single person in all Hollywood who was going to take either the time or the trouble to feel sorry for little Rita Cansino." Once she changed her name, she "expected wonders to happen. But my roles didn't become any bigger or better. I came home one night, desperate, and asked Eddie to tell me what was wrong. He thought a moment, and said, 'You're trying to sell a product named Rita Hayworth. In business, a man doesn't wait for people to discover what he wants to sell. He advertises.'" In response to a final question about being hounded by the press she claims that she loves it when "photographers gang up on me. . . . And why shouldn't I? It's part of my business, my career, isn't it, now?"

However limited and partial Hayworth's agency in the *Modern Screen* story, the central tenets of Hayworth's commodification in her "own" words are not only that she made herself into a product but that she worked hard to "overcome her type" both as an "eternal Latin cafe dancer" and as a "vapid clothes horse."[19] Even when Rita Hayworth is written about rather than speaking for herself, there is a recognition that what she did on the set—"put away her shyness and let her eyelids grow heavy over sultry eyes; moved her slim body in the inviting fashion of sirens from time immemorial; drew her smiling mouth a little awry" before wiping off the "heavy make-up and remov[ing] her languorous false eyelashes"—differs from who she is as a person. Danae Clark claims that this separation of person from image itself represents the "studios' power of creation and naming [that] assured them economic and ideological, if not legal, ownership over the actor's body." [20] Yet the return of Margarita Cansino as part of the new "product named Rita Hayworth" suggests that the studio's ownership of Hayworth was more limited and partial than we assume it to have been. Again, whether Hayworth had any substantial control over her public image matters less to me than the discursive signs of contestation over the meaning of that image. And Hayworth's home studio, Columbia, was not at that time one of the powerful "star-making" majors, and this fact was itself employed, as discussed below, to (re)inscribe authenticity and agency into her image.

The Sweetheart of the A.E.F.

The 1941 *Time* cover story on Rita Hayworth is the first important national discussion of the "new" now-dancing Hayworth, and it is aimed, of course, at a much broader audience than the presumed predominantly female readership of the fan magazine. [21] But this and subsequent national spreads set the terms that will mark Hayworth as a working star—as someone who is primarily interested in making films rather than concocting "publicity stunts"—for the rest of her studio career. Once again the physical transformation is replayed in much lurid detail, but it is now linked to Hayworth's hard work and ambition and, paradoxically, genuine talent. The insufficiencies of Columbia are produced as evidence to bolster her authenticity as a talent: Columbia was simply not "powerful enough to build a star by publicity alone." Having neither "pretensions nor money to burn," Columbia had to rely on "pure ability to turn the trick. To get to heaven, their stars have to be good. Rita Hayworth is. By all the rules of Hollywood she has won her 'S.' It took six years, and it wasn't easy" (there are also photos of "Margarita Carmen Cansino at 6, 17, and 23—Her hair has turned, but her head hasn't").

Almost exactly a year later (December 1942), Jerome Beatty's "Sweetheart of the A.E.F. [Allied Expeditionary Force]," from *American Magazine* (not a fan magazine either), is even more emphatic and detailed in its discussion of Hayworth's transformation and hard work. [22] "Sweetheart of the A.E.F." begins with a reiteration, with occasional hyperbole in the details, of how Hayworth—now "my gal back home" to "thousands of soldiers, sailors, and marines"—was transformed physically:

> The first thing Rita did was to change her name. Putting a "y" in her mother's name, she became Rita Hayworth.

A characteristic example of the way Rita Cansino remains in Rita Hayworth's anglicized star text, from *Time*'s cover story, "California Carmen," November 10, 1941. Copyright 1941 by Time, Inc.

. . . But changing her name wouldn't be enough. Rita had her long, black hair cut short, then bleached. She looked worse than ever, so she tried auburn, lighter in front than in back. "That's it," she said, when she saw her face in the mirror.

However, her face was too round, she didn't have enough forehead. To lengthen her face, for three years she went every week to have her hairline moved back, at the top and on the sides, a hair at a time by electrolysis, until nearly an inch more of her forehead was exposed.

At first her hair was so tough it could hardly be bent by a hairdresser. Daily, her scalp was rubbed with heavy oil, steamed, shampooed, and brushed dry. Two evenings a week she spends two hours having her hair bleached and colored. . . .

After a year of these beauty treatments, Rita was a different girl.

After recording the extent of the physical transformation Beatty notes that it still was not enough: "Her pictures were in all the papers, she was beautiful, but she couldn't act. That was why she wasn't getting better parts. She was tagged as nothing but a specialist in leg art. Now she found time for a daily lesson from a dramatic coach and two or three singing lessons a week, to improve her speech." The effort that Hayworth exerted to "put herself over," including the physical agony of daily rehearsals with Fred Astaire when she "hadn't danced, except ballroom steps, for three years," is set out in admiring detail (" 'Why didn't you tell me you weren't in shape?' [Astaire] asked. Rita smiled proudly, 'I'm a Cansino.' "). Beatty also repeats as common knowledge the fact that Hayworth's film singing voice was dubbed.

Given the extent of the demystification of all of these articles—and there are many more from which I could cite—what accounts for their admiring tone? What is left to appreciate in a star who does not do her own singing and whose looks are not only manufactured but require such extensive daily upkeep? Quite a bit. According to Beatty, Hayworth has "talent, untiring ambition, and brains. It takes all three to make any top-notcher—a star, the president of a corporation, or a first-rate general." Her "magnificent dancing," in theory a side effect of being a Cansino, is "all her own." Although she had help in getting to all the right places to be "seen and admired," in the end it is "Rita's talent and vitality and ambition that put her over." In the final paragraph is reiterated the fact that "Rita will make it" because "brains and breeding count." The article is illustrated with a large color picture of Rita Hayworth and a smaller, black-and-white photo of "the old Rita" in a Spanish dancing costume.

From now on, through the end of her studio years in the late 1950s, there would be references to Hayworth's ethnic heritage (often incorrectly assumed to be Mexican rather than Spanish) and her transformation in virtually everything written about the "California Carmen." Hayworth was "transformed from a Spanish heavy into a livelier, Americanized Hedy Lamarr" (1941); she's the "former Marguerita Cansino" (1942), the "Spanish-American beauty" (1943), and she "looks more typically American than typically Latin since she turned herself into a redhead [but] she is originally a Cansino—one of the dancing Cansinos from south of the border" (1943); she's "little Margarita Carmen Cansino" (1944), "Senorita Cansino" (1945), the "newest Cansino" who "fully metamorphosed at last into Rita Hayworth of Hollywood and the world" (1946); the "dancing Cansino" (1947), the "dark-haired Spanish-Irish-American baby . . . christened Margarita Carmen Cansino [who] blossomed into a red-haired girl" (1947), the "little Spanish girl" (1948), "Margarita Carmen Cansino, known to millions of her motion picture fans as Rita Hayworth" (1949); "the poor, black-headed little girl whose hairline grew too low on her forehead" (1949); "Marguerite Cansino, a shy, dark-haired little Spanish dancer" (1950), the "plump brunette dancer Margarita Carmen Cansino [who] became a slim red-haired actress named Rita Hayworth" (1951), the "chunky" girl with the "too-low forehead, the thick dark brown hair, the olive skin, the little dancer from across the border" (1952), "little Margarita Cansino" (1953), the "shy" girl whose "thick dark hair grew unusually low on her forehead" (1955), and so on and so on.[23] As in the articles previously described, the amazing corporeal malleability they describe in their text is often underscored by photographs of either Margarita Carmen or Rita Cansino.

Theorizing the Former Margarita Carmen Cansino

But now that we have laid to rest the notion that Hayworth's heritage and transformation and hard work to become a star were excluded from public discourse, the issue becomes what to do with the information. For example, if Rita Hayworth is both manufactured and genuine; talented as well as lucky; "easygoing" and "inert" away from the camera and a "laughing, sparkling, nimble-footed phenomenon" in front of it; a Spanish heavy and an Americanized gal back home, one could still simply invoke the star paradox to explain her appeal. All stars, according to Richard Dyer, John Ellis, and others, embody a tension, a paradox.[24] As Dyer and Ellis describe it, the paradox is that movie stars appeal to us because they are ordinary and just like us and also because they are special and uniquely gifted in some way. Certainly this helps us to understand the presence of incongruous elements in Hayworth's image, as does Dyer's notion of the star as a "reconciler of contradictions." Dyer believes that a star succeeds in reconciling contradictions through "magical synthesis," a synthesis or unity made possible because the star is, in the end, only "one person" with a "real existence" as an individual in the world.[25] But Rita Hayworth is not, in the end, only one person, and the fact that Margarita Cansino appears so frequently alongside Rita Hayworth in promotion and publicity material means that Hayworth's body is unable, or inadequate, to bear and reconcile certain contradictions on its own. Otherwise, why would Margarita Cansino continue to exist? Why not suppress her permanently?

In themselves, references to a star's humble origins are not unusual; they form part of Hollywood's continual invocation of the American Dream as a narrative about moving from obscurity to stardom. In turn, according to Leo Braudy, Hollywood stardom sustains and reifies that dream, which is itself also a paradox: the particularly American "character-wrenching need" for simultaneous conformity and distinction.[26] In a country that says, "If you don't look like it, you must not be it,"[27] adopting the outward signifiers of Americanness can be a "necessary" first step toward "feeling" American. But in the case of Rita Hayworth, unmatched to my knowledge by any other American-born star, Hayworth's heritage, the fact of her ethnicity, serves not only as a set of origins to be transcended but as the guarantor of her authenticity as a star. The shadow presence of Margarita Cansino contradicts the notion that Rita Hayworth has been manufactured, even as it reveals the extent to which her physical appearance has been altered. Hayworth's Spanish-Irish background represents the out-of-date but still valuable stock from which she is refined and is provided as evidence that Hayworth's stardom, her talent, her eroticism are genuine rather than artificial.[28]

As recent work by film scholars on ethnicity and race in Hollywood films has suggested, it would be futile for us to try now to prove whether Rita Hayworth was or was not genuinely ethnic or even whether her ethnic heritage was being more or less truthfully depicted. Most of these scholars conclude, implicitly or explicitly, that understanding ethnicity in Hollywood films is not a matter of determining whether images are positive or negative by reading them against what Werner Sollors calls "an elusive concept of authenticity."[29] Instead, as Ana López argues, Hollywood films are ethnographic in their own right, and they determine and produce their own concepts of ethnicity and national identity.[30] These concepts actually help to define or "invoke" ethnic identity for audiences rather than merely depicting true or false variations of it. Thus, as Lester Friedman puts it in his article "Celluloid Palimpsests," Hollywood can continually make and remake ethnic discourse to serve its own ends.[31]

Certainly Rita Hayworth's heritage, like her hard work to become a star, may have been emphasized during World War II for ideological or political reasons. The energetic reactivation of our Good Neighbor Policy with South America in the 1930s, which continued through the 1940s, resulted in many Hollywood films' featuring South American locales and performers, in which "Latin" elements were emphasized but not specifically differentiated (despite some attempts to acknowledge regional and national identities as distinct, slippage still occurred, as we have seen, between "Mexican" and "Spanish").[32] But without knowing precisely how and when Rita Hayworth's image was promulgated throughout Latin America, to claim that as a Latin star she mainly served the ideological interests of the American State Department is too facile an explanation of her prominence. For one of the most significant paradoxes of Rita Hayworth in any incarnation is that she can be read as ethnic *or* American but also as ethnic and *therefore* American.[33]

According to Friedman Hollywood ethnicity minimizes hereditary privilege, or what Werner Sollors calls ethnicity by *descent* (relations determined for us by blood or nature), in favor of ethnicity by *consent* (relations we choose to accept). Descent language, writes Sollors, "emphasizes our positions as heirs, our hereditary qualities, liabilities, and entitlements," whereas consent language stresses our abilities as "mature free agents and 'architects of our fates' to choose our spouses, our destinies, and our political systems."[34] By valorizing consent rather than descent Hollywood films operate as "handbooks of socialization into the codes of Americaness *[sic]*,"[35] superimposing Americanness as what Fredrik Barth calls a "self-ascripting category" on top of race, ethnicity, religion, or national origin.[36] Many Hollywood films are full of ethnic "types," but in the end these films militantly stress cultural uniformity, with value systems ideologically rather than ethnically defined. Although it depicts images of apparently predetermined descent conditions and characteristics like race, religion, and national origin, Hollywood discourse, according to Friedman, preaches "symbolic interactionism and consent values."[37]

The mixing of ethnic types in Hollywood films (Sollors calls this strategy "multiple-choice ethnicity"), or, read another way, the "all-purpose" function of many ethnicities,[38] seems to reinforce Friedman's assumption that consent matters more than descent in the ideology promulgated by Hollywood. Friedman continues:

> The basic value orientations of a Hispanic, a Jew, a black, or an Asian may have been intrinsically different in another time and in another place. But, in America, unique elements in these ethnically discrete value systems must be discarded if they clash with broad national values. In essence, the movies foster what Herbert Gans calls "symbolic ethnicity": actual ethnic culture values are irrelevant, but ethnic identification retains an emotional aura based on outer symbols. Thus, in Hollywood films, the signifiers remain but the signified has been drastically altered.[39]

Some elements, but not others, of Rita Hayworth's image support this assessment. Because of the name she was born with and her initial adoption of the outward appurtenances of skin and hair color that name connoted, Hollywood typed Rita Cansino as a Latin, and being typed as any nonwhite nationality usually meant being confined to playing all-purpose

All-purpose ethnicity. Lobby photo of Rita Cansino playing an Egyptian girl and Swedish Warner Oland playing Charlie Chan in *Charlie Chan in Egypt*. Copyright 1935 by Fox Productions.

ethnic, often foreign, film roles. Thus, Rita Cansino was alternately Egyptian, Russian, Spanish, Mexican, and South American in her early films. The irony is that, as for many other performers ranging from Myrna Loy to Carmen Miranda, it required nearly as much effort to manufacture Rita Cansino's ethnicity as it did Rita Hayworth's Americanness.[40] To conform to the dominant Latin stereotype seemingly required by her name and background, Rita Cansino's normally brown hair had to be dyed black; makeup was needed to darken her fair skin; and whether as Cansino or as Hayworth, she could only speak Spanish "a little."[41] The outer symbols of Rita Cansino, in other words, were manufactured to fit a descent ethnicity that maximized aspects of her hereditary privilege; but Hollywood, as Friedman notes, valorized symbolic interactionism and consent values. Only by choosing to present herself as Rita Hayworth could Rita Cansino become a star, yet through the presence of her shadow image Hayworth was able to retain a discursive subjectivity linked to her labor to transform herself as well as the outer symbols of the richness of her ethnic background and the "emotional aura" it represented.

Because Rita Cansino did not become a star, not much was written to which we can look for information about how her emotional aura would have differed from that of Rita Hayworth. However, one article from 1935 suggests what might have been the result had Rita Cansino continued to work toward success under her "own name." In this article, "Dancing Feet Lead to Stardom" (apparently written by another "ethnic" performer named Gelal Talata, with whom Rita Cansino had once "shared a dressing room . . . at the Foreign Club in Tia Juana"), it is not eroticism or sexuality that is emphasized as much as breeding and lineage.[42] We learn how many generations in the Cansino family have been performers and which part of Spain the family clan comes from. We learn that Rita's maternal Irish grandparents were Shakespearean actors. We learn that she is a "fiery" dancer but in person shy, gentle, sweet, and "retiring to a fault" (like all "well born latins and celts") and that her father guards her virtue closely. (In appearance Rita Cansino has "a flawless ivory white skin, and the beautifully carved features of the Castilian Spanish. Her hair is midnight black.")

The most interesting passage in the article is when the interviewer asks her subject how she feels about being in the movies. For rather than being asked simply whether she wants to be a star, the precise way the question is posed to Rita Cansino is, "Do you want to be another Dolores Del Rio?" Her response is as follows: "No, I don't want to become another Dolores Del Rio. I want to remain Rita Cansino. If I become a star I want to do so in my own right, and not because I imitated somebody else. I believe that most of my people have made the mistake of trying to be some other picture personality, thereby losing their own identity completely."

The assumption the article makes is that despite being born in America (Brooklyn, to be exact), Rita Cansino as is, however talented, cannot hope to be anything but some variation on Dolores del Rio.[43] And, in a sense, this is true. To be a star and not be a variation on del Rio meant becoming Rita Hayworth and, in the process, altering if not entirely losing Rita Cansino's "own identity." Of course, few seventeen-year-olds fully understand the complexities of identity politics in general and female identity in particular. What does it mean to be oneself, much less in a profession requiring that one be able to become with facility convincingly *other* than oneself? Fabrication intervenes in the creation of any public persona; indeed, the purpose of Talata's article was to establish the terms by which Rita Cansino could be identified.

The tragedy is not that Rita Cansino could not remain herself, for modern identity in America can best be understood, Braudy claims, as an amorphous or paradoxical construct anyway—*"fame without a city,"* as he puts it.[44] But because we now know how insecure Hayworth was as a child and as an adult, we regret her inability to escape the "feeling of inauthenticity" that plagued her about what she was doing.[45] Rita Cansino's "sundered self," to use Andrew J. Weigert's term, is partly the result of what he calls a "structured identity crisis," the "double-bind paradox" that affects all ethnic Americans:

> The metamessage . . . is paradoxical: it asserts that, in order to succeed, the Hispanic American must become an hispanic American, in short, cease being an Hispanic at heart, become an American only, and succeed to the extent that skill, structure, and luck allow. . . . [The] person must disobey the everyday meaning of the command, and in fact cease to be what it affirms, namely, American, successful, *and* Hispanic. Taken as a total social fact in a single imperative, it is contradictory and cannot be fulfilled.[46]

Yet Rita Hayworth was able to keep Rita Cansino as part of her self, if not visually, if not "authentically." One of the most striking revelations of Talata's article, in fact, is how much of Rita Cansino remains in her Americanized double. As would be said countless times of Rita Hayworth, Rita Cansino had a "mind of her own" but used it in a "shy, different *[sic]* way," was sweet and unassuming but fiery on the screen, and was a protected member of a doting but strict family. Again, this sort of discourse is constant throughout Hayworth's career, and as will be explored further in the next chapter, the emphasis on heritage, tradition, and family is particularly marked in articles written to celebrate domestic events such as marriage and, most notably, the births of her two daughters—"Hayworth's Child Has Rich Heritage" (1944), for example, or "A Baby with a Heritage" (1945).[47]

In fact, the consistency of the tone of this material suggests that the difference, rather than the similarity, of Rita Hayworth the star as person from her film roles is *the* characteristic that functionally differentiates Hayworth as a commodity from other stars. Although we do not have access to documentation sufficient to indicate that this was Columbia's actual strategy, Hayworth's star image seems to have been closely aligned to what in some sense she was—a woman whose erotic impact on the screen was belied by her sweet and down-to-earth "real-life" ways, a "tempestuous glamour queen caught by the camera and a nice, quiet girl who lives in a cottage," a "reserved girl" with a "quietness about her that is definitely contradictory to the roles she plays," a woman who was Rita Hayworth "up there" but who never forgot that she had been born Margarita Cansino.[48] (It is telling that Barbara Leaming quotes one of Hayworth's private secretaries, Shifra Haran, in 1989 as "revealing" that "Miss Hayworth herself said she was two people. . . . She was the movie star on the screen, and she was the person. People expected things of her that she wasn't as a person." Yet gossip queen Hedda Hopper, among many others, was producing exactly the same "revelation" in print in the 1940s.)[49] Only after the war and the success of *Gilda* (1946) did there come to be something recognizable as a "Rita Hayworth role"; and as characterized by one fan-magazine writer it was as a "shy siren," an oxymoron that perfectly describes the tensions in her image.[50]

A case can be made, therefore, that the obverse of Lester Friedman's assertion about how ethnicity is signified in Hollywood is also true: even when visual or narrative signifiers of ethnicity are missing from the discourse about the Americanized Hayworth and from her film roles, much of the signified remains. The transformation from looking like Rita Cansino to looking like Rita Hayworth removed the outer ethnic signifiers of pomaded black hair and olive skin but not what they stereotypically signified. Photographs abound of the quintessential *My Gal Sal–* or *Gilda*-style Rita Hayworth (masses of red hair, "peaches-and-cream" complexion) sitting at a table at the Stork Club and identified as the Spanish-American beauty. Is Hayworth therefore a subject whose "legitimacy," to use Lauren Berlant's term, "registers . . . according to the degree to which she can suppress the 'evidence'" of her national identity in her body?[51] In her films Rita Hayworth is a body on which the evidence *is* suppressed, but I would argue that, given the above, she is always also the subject of a discourse that insists on the constant presence of a national, ethnic identity in that same body. Hayworth's film image always draws on the potency, the emotional aura, of stereotypical assumptions about Latin sexuality—even when she plays all-American characters, which she does in all of her most successful star vehicles, the musicals particularly. The exotic locales of many of Hayworth's films of the 1940s and 1950s—*Blood and Sand, You Were Never Lovelier* (1942), *Gilda, The Lady from Shanghai* (1948), *The Loves of Carmen* (1948), *Affair in Trinidad* (1952), *Miss Sadie Thompson* (1953), *Salome* (1953), *Fire Down Below* (1957)—perhaps also intend to indicate an association between milieu and erotic content, although such locations were common in other films.

To some all of this may simply make Hayworth what Homi K. Bhabha has described as a "colonial hybrid," a fetish object that represents the intersection of the mastery of the colonizer with a simultaneous fear of and fascination with the colonized "Other."[52] According to this logic Hayworth's difference is disavowed but also present rather than repressed, as a "mutation," in this case a sexual mutation. But unlike Dolores del Rio,

Lupe Velez, or Carmen Miranda, for example, whom Ana López claims *are* colonial hybrids, Hayworth's sexuality need be "neither too attractive (to dispel the fear-attraction of miscegenation) nor so powerful as to demand its submission to a conquering North American male"[53]—no more so, that is, than would be true for any female star working in classical Hollywood cinema. And Hayworth's hybridity is always produced as a sign of her own agency, her own desire to remain herself, as well as her commodification.

Richard Dyer's analysis, in his essay "White," of how Bette Davis's star image and character function in *Jezebel* can also be applied to Rita Hayworth's image and is more useful, I believe, than fetishism in accounting for women's demonstrated fascination with Hayworth's films. According to Dyer's argument, *Jezebel* presents an "ironic counterpoint" between what is acceptable and not acceptable for white women to express, by showing Davis, a white star, adopting an ethnic mode of expression.[54] The scene in which Davis/Julie "[merges] as nearly as possible and [joins] in" with a group of singing black slaves allows her, Dyer claims, to express "her pent-up feelings of frustration, anger, jealousy and fear, feelings for which there is no white mode of expression, which can only be lived through blacks." The "ambivalence" of *Jezebel* as a film, writes Dyer, lies in its being a vehicle for Davis, who, as Julie, both deserves punishment and "is to be adored" by her huge, primarily female, audience "precisely . . . because she does not conform to notions of white womanhood."

Hayworth was also a star with a huge female following and is, like Davis, "to be adored" and for the same reasons.[55] Hayworth's most successful films also present an ironic counterpoint between what is acceptable and not acceptable for white women to express.[56] But the ambivalence of *Gilda,* for instance, is harder to characterize. Gilda, a North American, is a "roaring, sexy woman" (to use Michael Wood's term again) who, despite her sexual voraciousness, is both decent and even domestic.[57] Unlike the female protagonists of *Double Indemnity* (Billy Wilder, 1944), *The Postman Always Rings Twice* (Tay Garnett, 1946), *Dead Reckoning* (John Cromwell, 1947), *Out of the Past* (Jacques Tourneur, 1947), and particularly Hayworth as Elsa Bannister in *The Lady from Shanghai,* Gilda is punished for her sexual life with marriage rather than death. And unlike Davis, Hayworth is able to express her feelings of frustration, anger, jealousy, and fear (and also *joy*) not by attempting to merge with other ethnic or racial groups but because she is already herself "nonwhite." This all is certainly true of her musicals, as well as *Gilda,*[58] and helps to explain the presence of Hayworth numbers utilizing types of music and dance often characterized as torrid or hot—stereotypically modes of "nonwhite" expression—in virtually every film, generic musical or not, that Hayworth made as a star at Columbia (the notable exception being *The Lady from Shanghai*).[59]

Finally, Rita Hayworth's film roles are, as several scholars have noted, most interesting not for their eroticism alone but for the way they integrate sweetness and innocence with erotic power.[60] This mirrors the doubleness of the discourse, particularly evident in the 1940s and early 1950s, by which she was constructed as exotic and erotic but also as patriotic, modest, hardworking, and eager to marry, settle down, and have a family. Indeed, when Hayworth actually appeared as the heartless Spanish Carmen in *The Loves of Carmen,* reviewers noted that it was her "unquenchable wholesomeness," her all-American girl-next-door image, that prevented her from being fully convincing in the role.[61] Nevertheless, Hayworth's Latin blood, in combination with her Americanization, does remove from her some of the limitations imposed on a "white" star like Davis, allowing Hayworth often to escape the drastic punishments normally inflicted on sexually potent women in classical Hollywood narratives.[62] Hayworth's ethnicity allows her to integrate wholesomeness with eroticism in her films, and this—combined with her hard work to "put herself over"—is one of the things that made the "shy siren" such a popular American star.

The Many Meanings of Star Labor

The invocation of America's Good Neighbor Policy in relation to Hayworth's ethnicity also brings up the issue of how women's labor was strategically engaged during World War II. The wartime rhetoric, by which the "cultural commonplace" limiting women's work outside the home was shifted to accommodate increased demand for industrial labor, looms large in this context. One could argue that the fact that a woman's hard work and ambition (as well as transformation) are stressed so profoundly and in such laudatory terms in the early 1940s is a result of the "eccentricity," as Michael Renov puts it, of the wartime context in which the articles were written.[63] Pressured by government agencies such as the Office of War Information, virtually every kind of channel of popular communication was enlisted to take part in a media campaign to glamorize women's work outside the home.[64] At the same time, women were

The sweetheart of the A.E.F. in a patriotic ad for Royal Crown Cola (and for *Cover Girl*) that circulated in a number of forms in 1943 and 1944. Collection of the author.

still required to use their femininity to keep up the morale of men overseas, something Hayworth, as a pinup and Sweetheart of the A.E.F., was obviously doing. And of course it can also be argued that *any* of the pieces about Hayworth's physical transformation and anglicization simply reinforce dominant stereotypes about women's role in beauty culture. Popular culture and its discourses have always been used to tell American women that one of their primary duties is to make themselves over whenever necessary to fit dominant, and always white, standards of visual beauty.[65]

These are valid points, but they do not go far enough: Rita Hayworth did not *only* anglicize herself, and women not only worked outside of the home during the war but continued to do so afterward, and in ever-increasing numbers—this in spite of another media campaign to get them back into the domestic sphere. And I want again to invoke Joanne Mey-erowitz's study of postwar nonfiction magazines in which "domestic ideals coexisted in ongoing tension with an ethos of individual achieve-ment that celebrated nondomestic activity, individual striving, public service, and public success."[66] Moreover, although Clark claims that stars were "perceived [by other studio personnel] as a privileged class of work-ers that was undeservedly pampered by the front office," this was not al-ways true either.[67] Hayworth's struggles as a social (and economic) sub-ject, her attempts to negotiate the terms of her labor power within the relations that constituted her as an "actor as worker" as well as a star, are implied in the discourses of transformation described above. They are also addressed overtly in much that was written about her from the early 1940s on. I have chosen several texts that can serve as nodal points around which the power relations of Hollywood, locally, and patriarchy, more generally, seem to swirl and in which the arrogant and complacent assumptions of a hegemonic discourse that operates at women's expense suddenly seem ex-posed as cultural rather than natural. These texts are a January 1943 letter to the editor in *American Magazine;* the famous (or infamous) Novem-ber 1947 *Life* cover story, which proclaimed Rita Hayworth the "Ameri-can Love Goddess," and some of Hollywood's reaction to this story; and in publicity surrounding the formation of the Beckworth Corporation in mid-1947. A discussion of these texts also helps to show that Hayworth's stardom was never completely imbricated within Fredric Jameson's "social formation" but was also placing that formation "under siege."

The letter to the editor, from a Columbia wardrobe department repre-sentative, was written in response to *American Magazine*'s "The Sweet-heart of the A.E.F."[68] Although not part of the normative discourse we assume to be engaged in constructing the star commodity, it enumerates and praises precisely the characteristics that have marked all of the public-ity materials about Rita Hayworth that I have examined so far. Even more interesting, in 1943 audiences had described for them, in publicly circu-lated material, a Rita Hayworth that, once again, all of her recent biogra-phers have insisted was not only the "real" Hayworth but one that was substantially unknown to and hidden from her public at the time.

"Having worked with Rita Hayworth on practically every picture she has made," Helene Henley writes, "I read with unusual interest your grand story about her. . . . I was with her on her latest picture at Colum-bia, *You Were Never Lovelier.*" Henley continues:

In one dance number with Fred Astaire, Rita wore slippers with laces that crossed around her ankles. One day, after several hours of

dancing before the cameras, she came to her dressing-room ex-
hausted. Not only that, but the laces had cut into her flesh until she
was bleeding.

I told her that Mr. Astaire wouldn't hear of her continuing if he
knew about it, but she made me promise I would tell no one, because she knew that if she didn't keep on schedule, it would cost the
studio a great deal of money in lost time.

By the time the picture neared completion, the dance routines
had caused her to lose considerable weight. We had to refit her
gowns. You could tell she was terribly tired, although she never said
anything, and her disposition was as even as ever. Right after the picture finished, she went on a month's bond-selling tour through
Texas—in the heat of the summer!

An evenness of temperament under duress and in relation to subordinate
workers; a willingness to work to the point of exhaustion; an awareness of
her own commodity value (and the cost of producing that value) in relation to studio economies—although these attributes hardly fulfill that
"seductive or politically pleasurable" desire, in Clark's words, that a
feminist film historian might have to make actors the "victorious subjects
of a self-determined history," nor are they veritably the signs of Hayworth's construction as a "passive worker" rendered as an equally "passive image."[69]

I am drawn to Henley's letter, in short, for the ways in which it makes
the personal political and vice versa. All of the features she describes so approvingly are the very means by which women stars supported the status
quo of studio politics as well as patriarchy (be feminine, work hard, don't
complain, don't cause trouble no matter how bad things get), and, of
course, in the context of the war, proved their patriotism. Yet in contrast
to the discourse discussed above, in which Hayworth's labor to construct
herself as a star body and a star image is foregrounded, here the labor described is not directly self-aggrandizing but instead is part of the collective but hidden efforts of a number of studio workers whose livelihoods
all depend on the success of the film product. We already know that Rita
Hayworth is a hard worker, but here she is constructed as a worker who
collaborates rather than operates at the expense of those whose own labor
supports hers. This changes in 1943, during Hayworth's courtship by Orson Welles. The complex intersections of the shifting discourses from the
1940s through the 1950s relating to Hayworth's ambivalent positioning as
an "American working girl" (in the words of a 1952 fan magazine) and as
a wife and mother (with a very troubled childhood) feature more promi-

THE CULT OF

THE LOVE GODDESS

IN AMERICA

Rita Hayworth, a movie star and princess of American glamour,
symbolizes a phenomenon of profound sociological significance

by WINTHROP SARGEANT

APHRODITE, Greek love goddess, was the predecessor of girls like Rita.

CONTINUED ON NEXT PAGE 81

The first text page from Winthrop Sargeant's *Life* magazine article "The Cult of the Love Goddess in America," November 10, 1947. The caption under the headless and armless statue of Aphrodite, "Greek love goddess," names her, or rather it, "the predecessor of girls like Rita." Copyright 1947 by Time, Inc.

nently in the next chapter. But I produce Henley's letter here as a background for what follows, as a contrast to the more "official" and widely circulated 1947 *Life* cover story proclaiming Rita Hayworth a "love goddess." What I want to investigate is how easily the terms that make Hayworth a "trouper" (the heading to Henley's letter) in 1943 could be transmuted into a malign discourse that converts her cooperative labor and "even temperament" into a much more conventional representation of feminine passivity and, or as, objectivity.

By the mid-1940s Rita Hayworth was "the fourth most valuable property in the business," according to Columbia studio boss Harry Cohn. This "affectionate" characterization is found in Winthrop Sargeant's *Life* essay "The Cult of the Love Goddess in America."[70] Written when

Down to Earth was reaching theaters, Sargeant's essay asserts that Hayworth—who, in the film, plays Terpsichore, the muse of dance—"symbolizes a phenomenon of profound sociological significance," namely, the "age-old sex goddess." (Sargeant uses "sex goddess" and "love goddess" interchangeably.) For Sargeant, Hayworth is an "overwhelming, industrialized Molochian idol to which millions of otherwise sane Americans pay daily tribute," with the "important historical distinction" between her and Aphrodite, say, being that love goddesses of the past were "regarded with considerable skepticism" (the particular variant of Aphrodite Sargeant chooses as illustration is a nude statue with no head and no arms). In a section entitled "The Feminine Point of View" Sargeant notes the "curious fact" that there are not any equivalent male counterparts for the sex goddess and claims that "American women regard [the goddess] with an abject, slavish worship that suggests the goose-stepping uniformity of the totalitarian state." He continues:

> From 18 to 80 they watch the goddess' slight changes of appearance, character and mood, cutting their clothes and coiffures, shaping their lips and hips in a determined and relentless effort to be as much like her as their physical limitations will permit. . . . [The] theoretical end product of which would be the emergence of an abstract, mechanical, ideal woman, endlessly repeated like the car that issues from the end of the production line, differing from others of its kind only in such minor features as color and optional extras.

Men, on the other hand, are "comparatively humble" in this "religious hierarchy," because they "symbolize action rather than passion, masculine yearning and human fallibility rather than the deified essence of sex."

In a section Sargeant entitles "The Real Rita" he first writes that she is "likable, simple and completely unaffected" but in all other ways "looks and acts very much like her public personality. All the little mannerisms that the faithful have identified with her impersonation of the goddess— the graceful walk, the speculative smile, the way of tossing her head, the helpless shrug and grotesque, little-girlish strut with which she accompanies a humorous sally—are characteristic of the real woman. The only thing conspicuously missing is the dialog." Under "The Power of Passivity" Sargeant defines "the fundamental trait of Rita's character" as "simply the desire to please people." The power that she wields is that of "merely existing"; she "causes or inspires action, but she does not act herself except in response to the desire of others. . . . Rita, like Helen [of Troy], is totally lacking in ambition and is mentally incapable of initiating anything on her own." Rita Hayworth has been manufactured by "masculine effort," and "this fact, added to her rather remarkable physical qualifications, goes a long way toward explaining her success." Her reputation as "being, with the possible exception of Bette Davis, the hardest worker in Hollywood" means only that she works hard at doing what others ask her to do; she has no will of her own. Sargeant does note that she has a "complete indifference to clothes, which causes her to spend practically all her nonprofessional time dressed carelessly in slacks" (which he later refers to as "the inevitable slacks").

The misogynistic terms with which the twin labors of female stardom and female spectatorship are defined here are depressingly familiar. Sargeant's points conform programmatically to the paradigms of Hollywood's visual pleasure described by Laura Mulvey, and the baldness of his presumption in speaking both for "the feminine point of view" and "the real Rita" suggests that what we now read as contempt was viewed then as simple reportage, a statement of the facts rather than a rhetorical strategy designed to undermine women's authority in the world. As part of mainstream postwar discourse, however, it is impossible now not to notice its fissures and contradictions, the ways in which a woman's passivity is made to seem generated by her own lacks rather than being the result of a structural oppression in which women's "point of view" is always already that of men *about* women and their actions. Although he does not specifically champion domesticity over, say, Hayworth's hard work as a star, Sargeant does explicitly characterize the star as being like a "little girl" appearing in a "school play," only happy if she can "[elicit] an approving smile or a pat on her shaggy head" from a "director or the publicity man or some other factotum in charge." What makes Hayworth an "extraordinary relief" in Hollywood is that she is precisely *not* one of those "ambitious, self-propelled, predatory, sugar-cured, artificially glazed and chromium-plated" women with which the city "crawls."

As Joanne Meyerowitz notes of the representation of women in postwar culture, "feminine stereotypes sometimes provided convenient foils that enhanced by contrast a woman's atypical public accomplishment," but they also served as "conservative reminders that all women, even publicly successful women, were to maintain traditional gender distinctions." [71] To leave Sargeant's essay as the last word, as the sign of the failure of the war to produce lasting changes in women's ability to participate in the public sphere except as objects of exchange within it, is to ignore the reaction it provoked from Hayworth herself.

Moreover, to deny the "possibility of actors' agency and resistance," Danae Clark writes, is to "risk leaving the impression that actors were

readily complicit with their employers' desires."[72] As I have already made
clear, however, I am not concerned here with producing the true facts of
Hayworth's life and work as proffered by her biographers to answer
the falseness of the publicity material circulated about her as a star commodity. But in actuality, the agency ascribed publicly to Hayworth after
1947, particularly in relation to the formation of her production company, is substantially *more* impressive than that granted to her in retro-
spect by her biographers, and this is why I believe it deserves more attention than it has heretofore received.

Several articles from 1948 explicitly refer to Rita Hayworth's *anger* at
being named a "love goddess" and a "dope" and about the passivity with
which her image was inscribed by the *Life* article. In "Ask the Boss," by
Louella Parsons (*Photoplay,* March 1948), Hayworth is quoted as follows:

> "The idea all through the story is that I can't make up my own mind
> on anything. That I let other people make all my decisions. . . .
>
> That's the most unfair, most ridiculous thing that was ever writ-
> ten about me. I'm sure my business associates know I am quite ca-
> pable of making up my own mind. My producing unit, the Beck-
> worth Company, has just been formed. I sign all the checks—I've
> got one of the best contracts ever drawn up for an actress in motion
> pictures. Does that sound like I'm doubling for 'Dulcie'?"[73]

In response to the suggestion that "the men in the lovely Hayworth's life
have made her decisions for her," Hayworth responds: "'[What] I've accomplished, I've accomplished by myself. No man has done it for me. Perhaps when I was married to Ed Judson, he did lead me by the nose, but
I've come a long way since then.'" In fact, Parsons writes, the "main thing
wrong with that article is that it was not up-to-date on Rita. It played up
the shy, diffident girl of eight years ago and not the independent woman
she has become in her thirtieth year." Rita Hayworth is "doing a whale
of a job of managing her own affairs and her own life" and has "a new
determination in her voice, a new light in her eye no man has ever been
able to put there. . . . She is a woman who has learned to stand on her
own two feet." When asked if she would change any aspects of her past
life if she were given the chance, Hayworth replies, "without a moment's
hesitation,"

> "No. Not anything. Not anyone. I haven't always been happy, that's
> true. But I feel I have learned much from all my experiences, good
> and bad.

If it is true I have an easy going disposition, I am glad of it. I can feel bitterness when someone has hurt me—but as time goes on, I can forget. I never hold grudges against people."

There is, however, "'one statement in that magazine story,'" Hayworth claims, "'that is very true: I want people to like me!'" Nevertheless, Parsons concludes her story with the statement that "A far better label than The Goddess of Love for Rita as she is today is 'Miss Independence.'"

Hayworth's responsibilities and the challenges and obstacles she faced as a producer are highlighted in many articles over the next several years.[74] In "Goddess with a Grin" (*Screenland,* June 1948), Hayworth is at first "jittery" about being "more or less her own boss" on *The Loves of Carmen;* but now, she says, "I'll save up all the worrying time for after the picture finishes shooting, when my troubles will really begin." This, according to the article, refers to the "editing, musical scoring, and the other heavy chores which give a producer nightmares and king-size headaches." An article by Hayworth's brother, Vernon Cansino, mentions how "burned up" he was to read Hayworth described "as a simple, placid, rather vegetative person. Nothing could be farther from the truth. Just because Rita doesn't talk ALL the time, merely because she has never set herself up in business as a Great Brain, no one should make the mistake of thinking that Miss Hayworth hasn't a smooth, fancily-functioning mind of her own," as evidenced by her new status. *Newsweek*'s cover story "Carmen Hayworth" (August 1948) also mentions Beckworth as "her own production company" and her contract as "the best contract" that anyone has "ever negotiated with a major-league distributor like Columbia." (And here is where Hayworth's "unquenchable wholesomeness," the "hard time" she has being "as dirty and nasty as the part requires," are cited—despite Carmen's being a "natural" role for Hayworth because of her Spanish "antecedents"—as the "principal thing one can complain of" about *The Loves of Carmen.*) Jack Lait wrote in *Photoplay* (November 1948) of Hayworth's previous shyness and her submission to "aggressive men," but "now it is different. Now Rita has her own company, with a share in the profits and firm authority over what she will and will not do." Even in the early 1950s her return to work after her divorce from Aly Khan continues in this vein: writes *Photoplay* in 1952, "After a day as Actress Rita rehearsing and shooting, Producer Rita has to see the rushes, read scripts, puzzle over advertising contracts." In 1953 Aldo Ray—ostensibly writing about the "Rita nobody knows" as her costar in *Miss Sadie Thompson*—also claims that Hayworth "knows every detail of what's happening on the set. As the principal stockholder in her own

Spread of Hayworth as Carmen in *The Loves of Carmen,* as mother to Rebecca (Welles), and as executive of the Beckworth Corporation. From Jack Lait, "Sho' Is All Woman," *Photoplay,* November 1948. The images of Hayworth as Carmen also give a sense of the all-American wholesomeness and general cleanliness that some critics complained marred her conception of the role. Copyright 1948 by Macfadden Publications, Inc.

Beckworth Productions she needs to know about such things as budget, shooting schedules, wardrobe, number of days on location, the Technicolor footage shot today and the day before, and a million and one things which the average actor never bothers his head about."

According to all of Hayworth's biographies and to the few surviving coworkers with whom I was able to speak, Beckworth was a releasing company that protected some of her income from taxation by giving her a share in the profits of her films. Hayworth also won script approval and therefore more control over what films she made at Columbia, which would continue to distribute them. But her Beckworth contract did not otherwise substantially alter her place in the daily routine of filmmaking itself.[75] Despite the sorts of material cited above, then, Rita Hayworth apparently did not make many "heavy decisions" about editing, scoring, and the like. Yet this fact does not mean that the discursive construction of Hayworth as an involved and hands-on executive was not taken as real or inspiring, that her image as an executive had no important ideological effects on her audiences. Rather, this version of Hayworth "complicate[s] our stories of the past," in Joanne Meyerowitz's words—not only Hayworth's past, but ours.[76] There *was* an element of passivity in Hayworth's image, but the question is why, and when, and what sort of passivity it was and how stars like Hayworth might have deployed their own oppression at the hands of men, their victim status, in order to have their own desires met within the confines of their immediate situations. All of the discourse about Hayworth is *also* conservative, but it is not *only* conservative. Her status as a woman who had not merely "overcome her type" as a Latin starlet but also her own shyness, lack of confidence, domination by men, diffidence, and so forth helps to remind us that "[d]espite the conservatism and constraints, the postwar era [was] a time of notable social change and cultural complexity."[77]

Reconciling Contradictions

As this chapter has shown, many of the adjectives used most often to describe stars and star texts in classical Hollywood—*manufactured, created, commodified*—are inadequate to explain the success of specific stars in specific times and places. In the process of trying to reconcile what scholars and biographers have claimed about the construction of Rita Hayworth with discrepant material contemporary to Hayworth and her films, I have concluded that ethnicity, transformation, and labor—far from being denied or even substantially repressed in Hayworth's star image—served, in fact, as guarantors of her authenticity as a dancing talent, as an erotic symbol, and, equally important, as an all-American woman. Her ethnicity, particularly, combined with her transformed all-American looks, allowed Hayworth's image and films to incorporate disparate (to Hollywood) and even "paradoxical" elements, most strikingly eroticism and decency. At the same time, much of the inadequacy of the "star as commodity" model is that what it signifies is widespread and unexceptional. The manufactured star "is us," in some sense, standing in for and representing our drives for fame and recognition as well as our fear of being discovered for what we "are"—inadequate, inauthentic—rather than what we "consent" to perform. That Hollywood differentiated Hayworth by her ethnicity means only, perhaps, that it found it profitable to do so; as an ethnographer in its own right, Hollywood also created the ethnicity it ostensibly merely reproduced.

I have also wanted to show that Hayworth's identity, whether "real" or imagined by the studio, was in constant negotiation over agency and the economic power represented by stardom. Hayworth's struggle was not only to make herself visually attractive, white, or a good wife. Although

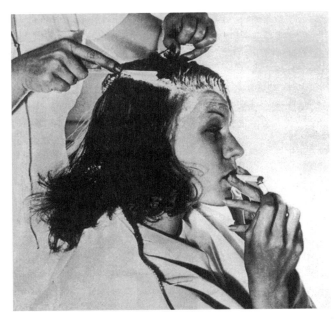

Not all publicity photographs obscured stardom's daily grind. From "Is Rita Hayworth Washed Up in Hollywood?" by Hedda Hopper, *Look* magazine, March 15, 1949. Acme photo. Copyright 1949 by Cowles Magazines, Inc.

her struggles with marriage, domesticity, and motherhood are discussed at length in the next chapter, we can already begin to question the well-known notion that, in Danae Clark's words, "stars did not work."[78] Clark does note the exception of "some stars" who were "distinguished for their acting ability" but otherwise repeats the cliché that stars were "personalities" who "merely displayed the qualities they possessed or the personalities that were packaged for them by others." The horizon against which Hayworth's struggles stand out is, of course, Hollywood's own self-aggrandizement as an institution, and we should not expect to look in mass-market magazines of the 1930s, 1940s, or 1950s for any real critiques of celebrity culture as such. But at the same time, clearly one of the major discursive features of Hayworth's life as a starlet and a star was unrelenting, grinding, but nevertheless rewarding and interesting labor.

Chapter 2 centers on one of the best known tropes of women's stardom, that all woman stars want to have children, are seeking domestic happiness, and would gladly give up their careers if the "right man came along." I consider the waxing and waning of Hayworth's designation, by 1942, as "one of Hollywood's unhappiest stars" and how her promise and potential power as "Miss Independence" gets derailed in the 1950s through a series of domestic scandals that take over her star image. What follows can be read as a series of collisions of life events—among the most important Hayworth's childhood abuse by her father—with the publicity and promotional machinery of popular culture itself. It is also an analysis of how the coding of these life events through euphemism and convention might have been recognized at the time by audience members who themselves had learned (*had* to learn) to couch their lives and problems in more decorous language as well. Much like Hollywood's Production Code constrained the range of representations possible within Hollywood films between the early 1930s and the late 1950s, so did conventions of a hegemonic middle-class gentility work to set the boundaries of acceptable taste within what was written about those films and their stars. The sheer effort required to mask or reconfigure unexpected divorce, extramarital affairs, or out-of-wedlock pregnancies could also help to complicate and subvert the very meaning of what constituted acceptable taste.

Rita Lives for Love

THE FAMILY LIFE OF HOLLYWOOD'S UNHAPPIEST STAR

The revelation at the center of Barbara Leaming's 1989 biography of Rita Hayworth, *If This Was Happiness,* is that Hayworth had been sexually abused and beaten by her father throughout her childhood and adolescence.[1] Leaming acquired this information from Orson Welles, in whom Hayworth had presumably confided during the course of Hayworth's and Welles's marriage in the 1940s. According to the biography's jacket copy Leaming also employs "medical records, government documents, trial transcripts, movie-lot memoranda, and the testimony of hundreds of eyewitnesses" to create "an astonishingly moving portrait of a woman at odds with herself, whose present was continually compromised by her past." Through these documents Hayworth's story is "finally told." Although there had been at least two previous serious biographies about the star, the publicizing of Hayworth's childhood abuse, such copy implies, makes Leaming's the only one with explanatory power, the true one, the one that is able actually to account for why Hayworth had a "tragic compulsion toward men who would victimize her."

To this date the only source for Leaming's revelation remains Orson Welles, yet I have no trouble believing that Rita Hayworth was abused by her father and that the effects were traumatizing and long-lasting. It is ultimately Leaming, curiously, who hedges her bets on the issue, specifically in the chapter in which she chronicles the dynamics of Hayworth's "'incest family.'"

As Leaming notes, part of Rita Hayworth's star image from the beginning was her show-business lineage. Winthrop Sargeant summed up this aspect of Hayworth's past in his 1947 *Life* "Love Goddess" article, writing, "At the age of 4, Margarita Carmen Cansino started her career of pleasing people by pleasing her father. She used to run the bathwater for him in the New York hotel where the Cansino family lived the restless, impermanent life of Broadway show folk."[2] (Leaming produces this anecdote, too, but without acknowledging its pop-culture source.)[3] At the age of fourteen, Sargeant states, Eduardo's daughter was being presented "as her father's partner" while dancing with him "in nightclubs across [the] border in Agua Caliente," where she was "discovered" for pictures. For Leaming, however, it is the *way* that Margarita was presented by her father, and the fact that she and her father were the family breadwinners (she had two younger brothers) from her adolescence on, that was itself abusive in its implications. Leaming writes:

> Love, sex, motherhood: In each of these key areas of Margarita's life the memory of childhood abuse would have a clear and disastrous impact. For all that, even if one were still inclined to doubt Margarita's disclosure to [Welles] about what her father had done to her in private, there can be no doubt whatsoever of the very public exploitation to which Eduardo subjected his daughter. . . . Removed even from the possibility of a normal childhood among others her own age, Margarita passed as Eduardo's wife (he forbade her to call him "Father" in public). . . . Had an incestuous relationship not taught the child, as it so often does, to use sex to get and hold attention, the sexually provocative role that her father encouraged her to play onstage *would have done the same.*[4]

In other words, Leaming asserts that the *public exploitation* of the child by the father, that Margarita Cansino played sexually provocative roles onstage, and the misrepresentation of their relationship (husband and wife rather than father and daughter) in the nefarious contexts in which they performed would themselves have resulted in Rita Hayworth's inability to be successful in "love, sex, motherhood." Although in the previous chapter I quite vociferously problematized the notion that Hayworth's contemporaries saw her only as a sex goddess or as an object of men's manipulation, clearly her father's abuse, and the family dynamics in which the abuse was embedded, does help to account for some of the tragic dimensions of Hayworth's life story. What I *do* question, however, and equally vociferously, are two assumptions whose relationship is a bit paradoxical: first, that all of Hayworth's tragic past, and its continual "compromising of her present," was hidden from the public and, second, that her failures in the domestic realm resonate only as the predictable results of a highly individualized personal trauma.

The sexual abuse of children has only relatively recently become a widely acknowledged social problem; although it has always occurred, only recently have we begun to talk about it openly—to seek ways to prevent it, punish its perpetrators, and ameliorate its effects.[5] Therefore, the language in which childhood sexual trauma was couched in the 1940s and 1950s cannot be expected to reproduce the explicit and overt discussions we are accustomed to now. Nevertheless, there is a clear line in Hayworth's star image—including even the fluffiest of fan-magazine pieces—in which her insecurity, her shyness, her liaisons with a series of victimizing or unsuitable men, her intense desire for a happy home life and her continual failure to achieve one are all tied to what is expressly named the "hurt" Hayworth suffered as a child. Even when her "close-knit" family is being described ostensibly in positive terms (as in Sargeant's "Love Goddess" article), it is frequently disturbingly close to tipping over into Leaming's "incest family." In *Stars* Richard Dyer notes in passing that "surprisingly enough," fan magazines seldom featured relationships involving family life, parents, children (other than as the event of their births).[6] If this is true, then the mere fact that Hayworth's unhappy family life, and its connection to her later problems, is so prominent a part of her star image suggests once more the need for closer examination of the many meanings of the female star.

In this chapter I explore Hayworth's mediated public and private personal life during the 1940s and 1950s, not only because I want to show that many of the claims Barbara Leaming makes in the "first full biography of Rita Hayworth" are significantly similar in some, if not all, of their narrative details to those made by fan magazines and other mass-market instruments at the time. I also want to consider ways in which Hayworth's family and domestic problems may have been useful (although in ways that cannot be precisely tracked) to many working- and middle-class women's lives in the postwar era. Jane Gaines claims that in the 1940s "[o]f course the fan mags never yielded up the real lives of the stars" but instead "were mainly residue of star life."[7] She also notes, however, that these magazines often "raised issues of social adjustment . . . in the absence of other vehicles for dealing with the problems of young women coming to maturity" and that stories about stars could be "adapted to offer solutions to perplexing personal problems."

To get at how Rita Hayworth's perplexing personal problems might have been interpreted and adapted in the way Gaines describes, I have adapted the well-known strategies of what in other contexts would be queer reading—not, in this case, to look for the queer codes of gay and lesbian identity circulating in Hollywood's film and star texts but, instead, to search for the ways in which these texts are "silent on the subject," in Alexander Doty's words,[8] of family and domestic abuse, as well as more prosaic problems in family relationships. "In representation, as in life," Doty claims, "you might never know for certain, as silences and gaps in information can be as telling and meaningful as what is said or shown." And although "representation isn't 'real life' . . . representation can be understood in ways as subtle and complex as those with which we understand real life." The precise dynamics and sordid details of the parental abuse were not explicitly discussed in the public press at the time for reasons, to paraphrase Doty, both psychosocial and/or commercial, but Hayworth's family life and upbringing *are* continually linked to many of her best-known star features: her pathological shyness, her fears of never measuring up, her frustrations about her lack of formal education, her failures as a wife and mother (and therefore as a woman).

It should be clear to any feminist reader, however, that the sorts of "failures" listed above, although certainly "telling and meaningful" in relation to abuse suffered in childhood and adolescence, are also the familiar demons of many average (unabused) women as well. To a large degree insecurity and the fear of being found out as a fraud (even of using sex and femininity to get what one wants) remain, still, the malign and often debilitating undertones of women's professional achievement. Rita Hayworth's image, in short, particularly her offscreen image, at once engaged issues relating to the successful performance of femininity in a patriarchal society (and of professional success in the public sphere) and the traumatic effects of abuse.[9] So, on the one hand, we are dealing with historical problematics of recognition of what in one context was "literally *unthinkable*" because of prevailing social conditions;[10] child abuse, like homosexuality, was similarly unthinkable and therefore unspeakable except by implication and innuendo. But, on the other hand, Hayworth's image as a woman repeatedly victimized by men is not much different from that of the many other female stars who fail to achieve domestic happiness and who are also struggling to be taken seriously for their work.[11]

From 1942 on, when she divorced her first husband, Rita Hayworth was often characterized as a woman who had been hurt, but the hurt could itself be seen as an ordinary feature of women's lives, as well as being the result of childhood trauma (even bracketing out the issues of ethnicity and transformation discussed in the previous chapter and the labor of acting and dancing foregrounded more specifically in the next three chapters). In the end the continual looming presence of Hayworth's father as well as father figures in the discourses about her personal and professional achievements (or failures to reach same) and as compulsively reiterated components of her unhappy image across time lead me to believe that her particular constellation of problems, however unthinkable, might have been useful to fans who were experiencing similarly generated trauma in their own lives.

In exploring the unhappiness in Rita Hayworth's star image I also continue to address the ways in which the personal lives of stars intersected with other elements of the labor of stardom. As it tried to negotiate the real-life dilemmas posed by Hayworth's own history, her own personal experiences, and the direct and indirect increase in her bargaining power because of the growth of her commodity value, Hollywood ended up frequently having to valorize Hayworth's status as a working woman over what Elaine Tyler May refers to as the "pervasive endorsement of female subordination and domesticity" in postwar America.[12] This, too, functioned as an enormously important but underacknowledged facet of female stardom generally and Rita Hayworth's image specifically. Although all Hollywood stars are "really" just looking for love, the other side of the star paradox is that women stars, if not men, are always already failing at domestic life because being a star depends on their performing a labor that is special, unusual, and de facto undomestic.

In this sense all of Rita Hayworth's five marriages—I focus most on the first four, each of which lasted from two to three years—represented a sort of problem to Hollywood's discursive machinery, one whose "vast contradictions," in Lynn Spigel's terms, were "smoothed over" but never completely resolved.[13] I begin my discussion with the dissolution of Hayworth's first marriage to the much older Edward Judson, in 1942, and continue with her second marriage to Orson Welles in 1943 (daughter Rebecca Welles was born in 1944), her third "Cinderella" wedding to Prince Aly Khan in 1949 (daughter Princess Yasmin Khan was born in 1950), and finally her "skid into the rhinestones," in *Life*'s words, with Dick Haymes in 1953.[14] Rather than producing a blow-by-blow accounting of how Hayworth's personal life was written about in the popular press for fifteen-plus years, I again focus on specific representative articles to delineate in some detail the several recurring but mutable themes that mark this discourse over time: that marriage was for Rita Hayworth a continuation of a perverse paternal dominance by other means and that divorce, therefore, could represent a form of escape from malign influence; and that studio work could be seen as a form of oppression and a hindrance to the achievement of personal happiness but also as the most reliable and effective source, aside from her children, of any real joy and satisfaction Hayworth was shown to have experienced once she became a star. If the question posed of all female stars can be reduced to some version of whether they want "career or love"—the "big question" Hollywood was asking about Hayworth, according to a 1952 *Coronet* article—then Hayworth's case shows the extent to which Hollywood's own publicity machinery helped to subvert the domestic ideology on which the meaning of such a question ultimately rests. Her marriage to the abusive Haymes is particularly interesting in this regard because Hayworth's loyalty to and

Spread from Florabel Muir, "She's the Marrying Kind!" *Photoplay,* October 1953, showing Hayworth husbands number 1 through "?" ("Some girls manage to live alone and like it. But not Rita Hayworth. She's a girl who has to have a guy to call her own.") From left to right the husbands are Edward Judson, Orson Welles, Aly Khan, and Dick Haymes. Copyright 1953 by Macfadden Publications, Inc.

domination by "her man" made her seem like a perfect domestic totem figure; but Haymes's marked deficiencies as a husband and a father (Haymes was even more unpopular in Hollywood than Welles was) ended up igniting a print campaign urging Hayworth to leave Haymes, to abandon her search for a husband, and to devote herself to being a single working mother.

Well, Let's Examine the Facts

By the time of Rita Hayworth's first *Look* cover story, in 1940, she had already been married to Edward Judson, a man twice her age, for three years.[15] Therefore, many of the articles surrounding her first big movie successes—*Only Angels Have Wings* (1939), *The Strawberry Blonde* (1941), *Affectionately Yours* (1941), *Blood and Sand* (1941), *You'll Never Get Rich* (1941), *My Gal Sal* (1942)—refer to the fact that she is "happily married to Texas oil man, Ed Judson" (*Movie Life Yearbook,* 1942).[16] Leaming quotes many of Hayworth's friends as having been "puzzled" by Hayworth's

relationship with Judson, but Leaming ties the marriage to escape: "Like
a great many incest victims who seek to escape their fathers by running off
with powerful, older men, Rita saw in Judson a protector capable . . . of
freeing her from Eduardo."[17] Moreover, Leaming notes, the marriage itself not only perpetuated but extended the trauma of the incest: "Never
having developed a proper degree of self-regard, and dependent as she was
on Eddie's approval and affirmation, Rita learned to see and judge herself
through his eyes: a persistent theme in her relations with husbands and
lovers for years to come when—as her longtime friend, the makeup man
Bob Schiffer, explained—'She reflected what the men wanted. Unfortunately, that's the way she thought it should be.'"

As I have already shown, however, these dynamics hardly require the
elucidation of Hayworth's "longtime friends" because the relationship of
this "modern Pygmalion" to his "Galatea" was already a dominant feature
of Hayworth's public image. As *Screenland* put it in 1940, Judson was the
"shrewd businessman" who employed "sound business principles to put a
commodity across," and he was the one who "realizes the importance of
eye-catching gowns for his wife."[18] Judson had to "make his wife a star,"
but he also had to "preserve his own ego and personality in the face of his
wife's accumulating success." In fact, the only thing standing between
Rita Hayworth and stardom was that she had not *yet* learned to "judge
herself through [men's] eyes." Only once Judson entered the picture was
the "obscure, drab bit player" transformed into a "breath-taking girl,"
something that Judson was "shrewd" enough to figure out: "'There's a
potential keg of dynamite if only she'd let up [Judson thought]. That girl
could be the greatest siren in pictures if she only knew what to do with
herself. Why, she could make every other girl look like Miss North Clam
Beach of 1925.'" A *Silver Screen* article (April 1942) called "How I Keep
My Husband from Getting Jealous" also catalogs the "well-known process" by which Judson exploited Hayworth with advertising as though
she were "the automobiles he sold or a bottle of ravishing perfume."[19]
Hayworth *knows* that "her publicity is due to her husband's ability as a
salesman to exploit her," but the writer is careful to note that Hayworth,
"if you stop to think, is perhaps the only glamour queen around whom a
romance, or the slightest breath of scandal, has never evolved. Not a single
news-making item."

But by the time the *Silver Screen* article appeared, Hayworth had sued
Judson for divorce. (The 1942 *Movie Life Yearbook* claims on one page that
Hayworth is "happily married" but on the next page that it "looked like
a happy marriage, but it has now terminated in a divorce court.") Instead

of more about the "years of happiness he and Rita share and expect to share forevermore," then, by mid-1942 (the month after "How I Keep My Husband from Getting Jealous") the fan magazines were scrambling to print articles like *Movie Stars Parade*'s "Don't Blame Hollywood" ("The Hayworth smash-up might just as easily have occurred in Bangor, Ske-dunk. Here's why") (May 1942) and *Photoplay*'s "Love and Rita Hay-worth: The Story of a Daring Fight for Freedom" (July 1942). It is at this point that the real unmasking of Judson, and the exploration of her hor-rid life with him, begins. All previous analyses to the contrary, "The for-mer Marguerita Cansino has often been tagged 'one of Hollywood's un-happiest stars'" (*Screen Guide*, 1943).

In "Love and Rita Hayworth" Judson is referred to as the "graying" husband who had thought of "Rita in terms of a property, to be improved and guarded constantly; but that, in a sense, had been Eduardo Cansino's attitude toward his daughter, too. . . . The important thing," the writer continues,

> is that she has made her escape from what she has always believed was domination, but which has been called by another name, "guid-ance," if you like. She believes she is ready to try it on her own, now after all the years of obeying first one man, then a second; of not be-ing able to choose her own clothes or the location of her evening's entertainment, or decide how she would work, or for whom, or for how much.[20]

Quite explicitly, moreover, this writer links Eduardo Cansino's exploita-tion of his daughter to her marriage to Judson. Since Cansino held Hay-worth in "enforced seclusion," she had "lived always in adult company, and she had never had another beau with whom to compare Eddie." She had been taught that what was "utterly necessary" was "sanctified re-spectability," so if she wanted freedom—"and she wanted it desper-ately"—she was going to have to "marry to get it."

In "Don't Blame Hollywood" the retrospective evaluation of the Judson-Hayworth marriage occurs along much the same lines:

> Well, let's examine the facts. Let's start at the beginning. When Rita and Ed were married, she was just eighteen; he, well along in his thirties. What she didn't know about life and love would have filled the Encyclopedia Britannica. Brought up in the strict con-fines of her family, she'd never even dated until she was through

high school [Hayworth never completed high school]. He'd been married, divorced. He was engaged in a successful business career. She, a struggling nobody. He knew important people, traveled in smart international sets, knew his way around. She was shy, retiring, unsophisticated and terribly young, even for eighteen. He'd formulated his ideas, his way of life, she was groping, unsure.[21]

The publicity campaign, too, is now rendered in much more opprobrious terms. Under a photograph of "Rita and Ed in [a] festive mood at Ciro's" is appended the qualification that "[e]ven these gay evenings were planned with an eye to furthering her glamour build-up."

Jane Gaines notes that during the war years fan magazines "used stars to lend credibility to advertisers' claims and to define 'respectability' for their readers."[22] For publishers "the supreme function of fan magazines was to channel fantasy and envy into practical consumption." Much, if not most, of the scholarship on fan-magazine discourse during the 1940s focuses on woman as consumer who, in the words of Mary Ann Doane, desires to "bring the things of the screen closer, to approximate the bodily image of the star, and to possess the space in which she dwells," experiencing "the intensity of the image as lure and exemplif[ying] the perception proper to the consumer."[23] The relationship of the fan magazine itself to advertising, product tie-ins, and consumerism is clear, but that women experienced fan magazine discourse only or predominantly as consumers is not, as much scholarly attention to the subject has shown (nor, of course, were fan magazines the only sources of public information about stars). If the "miscellaneous detail" of star life, in Gaines's words, was not "real," this does not mean that actual events in the lives of stars did not demarcate the *range* of material that a fan magazine could reasonably present. Thus, because Hayworth sued Judson for divorce, and because that divorce happened, the fan writers could only try to incorporate the event into Hayworth's image as it existed at the time. No matter how ideologically complicit in the oppression of women the fan magazines were, even they could not make the divorce instantly logically compatible with what they had published only weeks, even days, before.

This sudden irruption of history, of life events, into the popular discourse is one of the ways that terms like *respectability, love, happiness* (much less *happy marriage*) themselves become, if momentarily, unstable. Or, rather, the terms become suddenly separated from their history in relation to a particular series of events—such that Hayworth's "happy marriage" was no longer a reference to something authentic but to a fraudulent representation of a truth we had not been allowed to see. In either case the unmooring of terms from what they had purported to represent opens up a space for reflection and questioning, a cognitive dissonance that may have forced readers to make up their own minds, to choose whether to believe what *had* been the truth or, instead, what was now there in its place.[24]

What the fan magazine writers, at least, now put in the place of Hayworth's scandal-free domestic happiness and marital bliss was a life of restrictions and inhibitions related to her strict upbringing and a continual, ultimately demeaning, process of commodification. As above, many fan articles tied the divorce to Hayworth's inexperience and need for freedom and to her oppression at the hands of both her father *and* her husband. In recounting the appearance of the pre-Judson Hayworth ("a dark, Spanish-looking, overdressed girl with black hair growing close over the temples" is typical), and explaining the process of transformation and Judson's role in it, the divorce is now cast as Hayworth's only means of escape from what is expressly paternal domination. As this material begins to suggest, the shadow presence of Margarita Carmen Cansino in Hayworth's image might not have served only as a guarantor of Hayworth's authenticity as a star or even as a love goddess; Margarita may also have been read or recognized as the reminder of the unceasing demands made by patriarchy itself—writ small as well as large—on its daughters. In the end, as "Love and Rita Hayworth" concludes, "the answers lie, of course, with Rita herself. One thing is true; Ed Judson could not have made her the star she is, if she had not had what it takes. She still has that, will always have it." The marriage *and* the divorce "nearly tore her to ribbons," according to a *Movieland* story (August 1943) reporting on Hayworth's "triangle" romance with Victor Mature and Orson Welles, but then "Rita has never been a lucky kid with the men in her life."[25] The only "men" to that point in her life had been her father and Ed Judson.

Feeling "Kinda Sorry" for Rita Hayworth

Once Rita Hayworth was divorced from Judson and back in circulation as an eligible "bachelor girl," the new meanings given to her marriage made its failure acceptable to her transformed all-American image, where she was not only erotic but also a "nice kid," as James M. Flagg called her at the time.[26] Again, what stars mean when they are married is not necessarily what they mean when they are ostensibly alone and lonely. Several scholars have examined the way that fan magazines from the 1920s through the 1940s seem to valorize and, therefore, theoretically to steer

women toward "romance, marriage and consumption," as Diane Waldman puts it, at the same time undercutting this message by representing
stars and their labor as routes to social mobility and financial success.[27] Although "consumption idolatry," in Gaines's words, was discouraged by
the advice columns of fan magazines, especially in the 1940s (with stars,
"incredibly, [recast] as models of practicality, constraint and thrift" during the war), the rotogravure and glamour-portrait sections (as well as the
advertisements themselves) "[suggest] a different message."[28] However
much articles (and film narratives, as well) stressed the militant conformity of stars to desires that were "just like" those of their fans and the
magazines' readers for domestic happiness and a home of their own, the
actual labor of stardom itself created a form of agency at odds with that
conformity.

Clearly, however, Hollywood's version of unhappiness meant domestic
failure. So unhappy was Rita Hayworth on these terms that Louella Parsons found herself "almost knocked off [her] pins" in 1946 by a "little
bobby-soxer, a little girl who might be having dreams of her own about
someday being rich and famous, feeling 'kinda sorry' for Rita Hayworth"
because Hayworth's love life was not working out. ("It is as though the
gods, in a capricious moment, had said, 'We shall make a woman of great
beauty—she shall have everything, talent, fame, youth. But happiness she
will know—only in bits and snatches.'")[29] If it is not a star's labor that
makes her unhappy but her failures in love and romance, then the question arises as to whether a star is more transgressive when she is married
but is still making films and performing other labors of stardom outside
the home than when she is "free" and merely "on the market for romance." A January 1950 *Screen Guide* article foregrounded this problem
when it offered up a "secret for marital success" in Hollywood: "career
sacrifice, particularly on the part of the wife." Men "being the way they
are, very few are capable of playing second fiddle to a more famous wife."
However, "[t]here are many actresses who refuse to give up their careers.
What about these women? you ask. Are they doomed to spinsterhood or
unhappiness?" The question of whether a woman's career might be rewarding in itself is not posed, much less answered, here. But the article is,
after all, about *stars*—stars who would not be stars without their careers.
To be married and a woman, in other words, means to give up being a star
(except in those very few cases where the husband is "equally as prominent" in another field).[30] As the anecdote of the "little bobby-soxer" suggests, stars *are* "rich and famous," as well as unhappy, and they get rich
and famous through the work of making films, posing for glamour shots,
going to Ciro's and the Mocambo and the like rather than being wives

and mothers. Marriage is what makes American adults *normal* (as now), but it is also what makes them the less interesting *norm*, such that stardom is always also performing its own rhetorical difference from that norm (everyone can be married, but not everyone can be a star).

As any number of star scandals over the years have usefully pointed out, what stars were supposed to want and what they actually laid claim to through their actions were frequently and spectacularly at odds.[31] Even without a scandal in a star's life, however, the labor of star work was essentially incompatible with Hollywood's own valorization of domesticity in its films and its mediated representations of star life. Being a star often functionally trumps being a wife, especially when the husband is thought unsuitable by Hollywood's own power structure and its machinery of image making. The effort required to assimilate Rita Hayworth's "unexpected" divorce from Ed Judson was, as we have seen, minimal because of his advanced age, his lack of importance in Hollywood's hierarchy, and the ease with which the discourses of her construction could be recast as signs of his brutality and obsession. With Hayworth's romance with and marriage to Orson Welles in 1943, the hole torn in her image and in Hollywood's was much larger, longer-lasting, and more interesting in its implications.

The Wonder Boy and the Vitamin Girl

Danae Clark maintains that studio publicity departments and fan magazines constructed a positionality for actors "that drew audience attention away from the goals of labor, reinforced studio discourses of entertainment, and thus sought to deny actors' subjectivity by defining them solely in relation to a salable image."[32] The place of Orson Welles in 1943 Hollywood meant, however, that the studios had to draw attention *toward* their "goals of labor" in order to manage a variety of incompatible desires: to reduce the importance of Welles himself in the Hollywood hierarchy, to keep Rita Hayworth fully functioning as a viable star commodity with an ever-increasing marquee value, and to pay lip service to domestic ideology. Thus, when Welles was apparently courting Hayworth in August 1943, a *Movieland* article could point to how Hayworth was on suspension from Columbia—which "some say" was because of her refusal to star in a film but "others say" was a disciplinary measure because "the studio right from the first told all and sundry it did not want her to marry. Whatever was the real cause—the result was that Rita, who would have been far happier working and occupying herself from day to day, was left with four months of idleness on her hands" and made the mistake of falling in love with Orson Welles.[33]

Welles's reputation in Hollywood in 1943 was, in the words of *Movie Stars Parade,* as the man "who came to Hollywood with the announced intention of revolutionizing picture making and committed the unpardonable sin of doing it, successfully, in *Citizen Kane.*"[34] But his reputation had already been significantly tarnished by his "ousting from RKO, his fiasco in South America *[It's All True],* and his relegation to a mere starring role in *Jane Eyre* at 20th." Now, with the war (Welles was "turned down as 4F by the Army"), Welles had "popped [back] up, brash, unpredictable and jaunty as ever," full of "patriotic fervor" and ready to entertain servicemen with the Mercury Wonder Show—a magic and variety act—in Los Angeles and, later, at military camps elsewhere.

That the Mercury Wonder Show was to have starred Rita Hayworth became the topic of press attention because Columbia refused to grant her permission to appear in Welles's show. Columbia's ostensible reason for not allowing Hayworth to perform was its investment in *Cover Girl,* one of her biggest star vehicles to date. Because the Mercury Wonder Show would have been a public-relations boon to Columbia—the show was free for servicemen and had been endorsed by the Hollywood "Victory Committee"—the "David and Goliath set-to" (presumably Welles was David) seems an odd risk for Columbia to have taken. But although, according to the same *Movie Stars Parade* article, "Just why Miss H. is not allowed to appear with the Wonder Show has never been disclosed officially," it was Columbia's own patriotism that ends up being, however feebly, endorsed. Had Hayworth been "at work on a set all day and appearing on a stage all night," she would not have been able to produce an "A-1 performance on either, and since [Columbia] has millions tied up in her picture . . . which will eventually reach and entertain many hundreds more servicemen than Orson's opus ever will, she should devote all her efforts to it." The "Hubbub over Hayworth," then, has been read by Welles's biographers (Leaming is one of them) as a power play between the studios and Welles, such that not Hayworth but Welles was being punished for his refusal of Hollywood's verdict on his films and his failure to bend his unconventional working methods to studio law. The "set-to" became more interesting when, in the midst of it all, "the Wonder Boy and the Vitamin Girl" (otherwise known in Hollywood as "Beauty and the Brain") got married (September 7, 1943), and a bit more than a year later their daughter, Rebecca, was born.

So strongly does Hollywood disapprove of Welles here that it is forced

Sequence of pages from *Look,* February 4, 1947. The first, printed in color, is a typical publicity shot of Hayworth in a bathing suit, here advertising the forthcoming *Down to Earth* (photo by Bob Coburn). The following two pages contain an even larger "exclusive" black-and-white photo of Hayworth, still in Elsa Bannister haircut, in her *"favorite* role" as mother to daughter Rebecca (photo by Earl Theisen). Copyright 1947 by Cowles Magazines, Inc.

to "tell all and sundry" that Hayworth's job is more important than her domestic happiness. Although the wartime context makes this attitude less noteworthy than it would become later, it also works to show the mutability of even one of the most ingrained rhetorical flourishes of fan-magazine writing—that all stars *want* to be married and *should* be married because they are always also ordinary. Hayworth's marriage to Welles, then, becomes a novel sign of her resistance to paternal and paternalistic domination by her studio, which needed to keep her image respectable and marketable at the same time that it was veering close to calling her marriage unpatriotic. Hayworth's subsequent motherhood fit well into Hollywood's discourses of stars as adhering to basic tenets of middle-class respectability, but to shift the tone from disapproving to suddenly laudatory required forgetting virtually everything that had come before.

What is most noticeable in the publicity surrounding the birth of Rebecca Welles is the way that it combines what can only be called a dynastic tone, an almost hysterical invocation of the importance of the baby's show-business antecedents and family tree to its future, within an otherwise familiar framework of the importance of motherhood to female stars. As is well known, very few Hollywood babies have ever *not* been the apple of their mothers' eyes, the center of their households, the thing they rush home to be with after studio work is done (the litany is fairly standard). As is also well known, virtually all Hollywood women with young children are characterized as devoted mothers. But Hayworth's own upbringing had heretofore been described with some ambivalence in the popular press. Now, Hollywood's publicizing of Hayworth's own motherhood seems to invoke a conventional and familiar framework by which Hayworth's childhood becomes linked to that of her daughter. "Unto the fourth generation" begins a photo caption to one of gossip queen Hedda Hopper's syndicated articles, this one called "Hayworth's Child Has Rich Heritage" ("Baby can look toward career as scion of talented Cansino family").[35] Whether as an attempt to mitigate the force of a more obvious source of Rebecca's "talent"—her father Orson Welles—the new emphasis on the Cansino family produces a very strange effect read against much of the previous characterization of the Cansinos, especially her father.

Hopper's article begins, for example, "What a heritage for Rita Hayworth's baby!":

> Everybody knows, of course, that little Rebecca's mother is one of the most successful and most popular of all our feminine stars and that her father, Orson Welles, is a remarkable young man (too remarkable sometimes!) in many fields—writing, acting, producing. But Rebecca's heritage is a matter of generations famous in the theater.
>
> That baby's great-grandfather on the distaff side is the great Antonio Cansino, one of the famous dancers of all time. The story of his life and of the 16 children he begot, and of his grandchildren, is one of the fascinating sagas of the theater. What a book it would make! What a movie!

The dismissal of Orson Welles in favor of the generations behind Hayworth's fame relates well to the ways in which her authenticity as a transformed ethnic all-American star depends on, and is made to stem from, her ancestry and heritage as well as her hard work to commodify herself and so on. "Little Rebecca" is limned as a baby Hayworth here, the story of her mother's assimilation the predictor of the baby's own future success. But if we assume that Hollywood's aversion to Welles is at least partly behind this valorization of Hayworth's (and the baby's) Cansino lineage— a valorization that continues, of course, after Hayworth's separation and divorce from Welles in 1947 and 1948—the result would have been pecu-liar, even disturbing, to those attuned to Hayworth's previous official Hollywood biography and what her childhood had previously been in-voked to represent.

The Time of Eduardo and the Dark-Eyed Girl

Two 1946 *Photoplay* articles, appearing in August and November respec-tively, illustrate this dichotomy well. The first, called "Exciting Woman," is by Charles Vidor, as told to Ruth Waterbury. Vidor directed several of Hayworth's star vehicles at Columbia: *Cover Girl, Gilda* (the film being indirectly publicized by the article), and *The Loves of Carmen*. The second piece, by Dorothy Deere, is called "Feet That Danced" and is once again about Hayworth's past, "the time of Eduardo and the dark-eyed girl who danced beside him, Marguerita—who was destined to become Rita Hayworth."

Vidor's remarks (the article is written in the first person) about Hay-worth are tinged throughout with the by now familiar contradictory tropes of the female star image: she is "one of the most beautiful, one of the most talented, and one of the sweetest of human beings," and she is also "like a trusting child—the most beautiful and obedient child in the world."[36] But she is also "conscious that she is a star and has, as a result, certain prerogatives." She is hardworking, emotional, and "has tempera-ment—but it is wonderfully under control." She knows "exactly what she wants. She will stick indefinitely to an ideal or an ambition—but she doesn't fight for it."

On the second page of the article, after discussing the filming of the second "Put the Blame on Mame" number in *Gilda* ("she did that elab-orate, difficult [number] in two takes. The whole set broke with sponta-neous cheers. . . . But she didn't take advantage of it. She never does"), Vidor suddenly begins a new section midway through the article with the statement that "[s]omewhere along the line of her childhood, Rita was, I fancy, very hurt. As a reaction to it, she is today considerate and thoughtful with everyone." Yet during the shooting of *Gilda,* Vidor re-minds us, Hayworth separated from Welles, and he has no idea why. People have asked him what happened, but he can only "very honestly an-swer I do not know." Although he realizes "from her acting power that she feels everything deeply," to "the world, she very seldom shows it." Hayworth is "no talker at any time"; she has "never talked to [Vidor]" about anything personal; she "keeps her own counsel," and as far as Vidor can tell, she has "never had anyone around," no "chum," no "best friend" in whom she confides. Hayworth is (of course) a "wildly devoted mother," as she was "an intensely devoted daughter to her own mother. In fact," Vidor continues, "I have never seen her be as outwardly devastated as she was when her mother died, not very long ago. . . . And that, I repeat, is amazing for her" because she so seldom showed her true feelings to the outside world.

In his final paragraph Vidor poses an answer to a rhetorical question: "Do I think that Rita will marry again? She says that she won't but I think she will, for within her half-afraid, half-repressed, little-girl soul, she is lonely and insecure. Will she find the right man? of that I'm not so sure—but with my whole heart I hope she does. Rita is a lovely creature who could make a perfect wife, a very great mother. She looks sophisticated—but she isn't at all." He claims that she likes "clothes and her career for identical reasons—they both give her assurance." Nevertheless, Hayworth would of course give up her career "without so much as a backward glance" if the "man wise enough to understand her and great enough to be worthy of her" came along. After a final remark about how any child of this marriage would be "most extraordinary and very possibly be a genius," the article is over.

The version of Hayworth that Vidor produces is familiar: she is unhappy. She has been hurt somehow, damaged so severely that she cannot talk about it; is almost always alone (another section discusses how surprised Vidor and his wife were to discover that Hayworth tended to arrive at social events by herself, something about which they "[o]bviously did not question her"); and, of course, is shy, sweet, and quiet in person despite being tempestuous, emotional, and glamorous in her work. That this Hayworth is also the one "discovered" by Barbara Leaming's personal interviews with large numbers of Hayworth's colleagues and friends years after the fact should not be surprising at this point. Rather, making allowances for a few of the clichés—all female stars are talented and beautiful, all stars are wildly devoted mothers, all directors know how to get stars to do things that the stars "don't understand themselves"—what seems most astonishing now is how closely this discourse resembles Leaming's own assessment of the *effects* of childhood sexual trauma on Hayworth's social life, as well as professional interactions. Of course many of Vidor's statements loom large precisely because we are reading them through the framework provided by the "horrifying secret" Leaming discloses. At the same time, however, Leaming herself gives the secret the power to "make sense" of the "hitherto disparate, puzzling, and seemingly inexplicable details of [Hayworth's] adult life." [37] And I cannot help but believe that others, even in the 1940s, were also wondering about the puzzling or inexplicable nature of Hayworth's problems and coming up with their own reasonable conclusions. Indeed, the attempts made to reorganize the explanatory power of Hayworth's past over her present always ended up recontextualized—and therefore themselves open to speculation—by the recurring tropes of her unhappiness and pain.

If we take to heart the Freudian or Foucauldian perception that we compulsively attend and return to that which we desire most to disavow, then the second *Photoplay* article, "Feet That Danced," adds more than a little credence to Vidor's (and, we have seen, many others') tendency to relate Hayworth's unhappiness to her childhood and adolescent home life. Although the article may have been intended simply as publicity for *Gilda,* too, the film is not so much as mentioned. There is a single reference to Hayworth "soon to be seen" in *Down to Earth,* but, in fact, that film would not be released until the fall of 1947. Instead, the entire article is about Hayworth's past, specifically her relationship to "her dancing partner, Eduardo, her father." Why it appeared at this point in Hayworth's career, and to what purpose, is difficult to discern. Given that her Cansino past had been part of Hayworth's image from the beginning, what made *Photoplay* decide that another piece—much less a full feature article—about Hayworth's relationship with her father was needed at this particular time?

Whether consciously or not, Deere paints the relationship of "Marguerita and Eduardo" as romantic, tipping over into erotic. Rather than employing conventional reportage, this is a fairy tale of the once-upon-a-time variety; no interviews seem to have been conducted, and the narration is omniscient (we move between "being" Eduardo and "being" Marguerita or 'Rita). The opening paragraph reads as follows: "In the spotlight a girl was dancing. An exotic bloom of a girl with blue-black hair and full red lips, swaying from a slim, scarlet stem of a dress. A sensuous gust of music swept her now toward, now away from the man who followed her there on the floor. A man who danced with arms outstretched yet with eyes that showed no expectancy of ever holding her. . . . [ellipsis in original]." [38] The "measure of [Marguerita's] loveliness," the article continues, was not only in the "glances of the customers who watched her" but "in the eyes of Eduardo—dancing with his daughter for the last time, there in the smoke-filled air of a night club in Tiajuana." (By way of comparison, a Louella Parsons *Photoplay* article in May 1946 called "Intermission for *Romance*" [italics mine]—about Hayworth's rumored relationship with Tony Martin—had begun in virtually identical fashion, to wit: "The ballroom spotlight made a halo of burnished gold around the head of the red-headed girl as she stepped onto the floor. . . . The good-looking, dark-haired man who circled her waist with his arm began to sing softly . . .").[39]

Eduardo then watches his daughter from the wings: "'Rita is growing up,' he told himself. 'She is growing into a beauty.'" When he "comes upon" his daughter being criticized by her cousin Jack, whom Eduardo had picked to be her first partner, he finds Rita "saying nothing, taking it the way all her life she had taken scoldings . . . with the hurt hidden inside and only her red lips trembling. 'He is young and excitable—he is mean to her,' decided her father. 'I will be her dancing partner from now on.' And so Eduardo and his talented child became a team."

"'Rita's" mother enters the picture eventually:

> "But it must not all be work. She must have fun," said her mother.
> "Yet, she is too young, too pretty, to be left here in a gambling town to have her fun alone," said Eduardo. Heeding the Latin custom of vigilantly chaperoning daughters until they are married, it was he who played tennis with her, swam and rode horseback with her.
> Night after night, while he was dancing, Eduardo had scanned the ringside at the Agua Caliente for personages who would be important to Marguerita's future.

Once Marguerita is noticed, "by Winfield Sheehan, who was head of Fox Studios," now it is Eduardo who has to force her to leave him, to grow up, to take responsibility for her life, because Marguerita does not want to leave "Daddy": "'I am not going [to the screen test] tomorrow. I am not going anywhere that takes me away from you.'" Eduardo therefore, "[f]rom necessity, [made] his own tones gruff":

> "You have outgrown me," he said shortly, as if it were a fault. . . . "What kind of a dancing partner is that for a man, a girl who is already a full inch taller? It is awkward for me, I tell you—"
> Her lips, the soft and tremulous lips, showed their hurt but he pretended not to notice it. . . .
> Marguerita's eyes were beginning to be rimmed with what was left of the night's faint purple, but the answer was still the same. "You are going with me—somehow—" she said softly.

'Rita's contract with Columbia, her "first" big success in *Only Angels Have Wings,* and her transformation into Rita Hayworth are then renarrativized and recast into a tale of how she was pushed by her father toward a success she was too insecure to desire. She is helped along, finally, by Cary Grant of all people, who tells the young Rita: "'Why don't you lighten the color of your hair and give that unforgettable mouth of yours a chance? It will make you famous.'" And so, with the help of Eduardo and the "handsome Mr. Grant," "Marguerita" Cansino becomes Rita Hayworth, the "Rita whose hair is now a dancing flame around the white oval of her face, and whose long, slim hands have the grace of waving flowers." The end of the article offers the only mention of Hayworth's other domestic situations, her marriages: "during those days when the unhappy ending of Rita's second marriage added a new curve of poignancy to that lovely, vulnerable mouth of hers, they were again very close, these two—Marguerita and Eduardo."

The creepiness of "Feet That Danced" lies not just in the way it sexualizes the relationship of daughter and father even as it justifies it as "Latin custom" (or in the fetishization of trembling lips and flowing hair) but in the dropping out of virtually all of the labor involved in Hayworth's career to that point and any sense of her own agency in accomplishing it, as well as voluminous previous material in which Hayworth's childhood and work with her father had been rendered on much more oppressive terms. The reassigning of the duties, as it were, attributing Hayworth's transformation to her father and Cary Grant—a star whose name had never appeared in previous stories about her personal life—could not have gone unnoticed by fans who had paid even only passing attention to previous publicity material. A textbook example of the way Danae Clark describes the discourse of stardom as opposed to discourses of actors' labor—stars do not work, they merely display "the qualities they possessed or the personalities that were packaged for them by others"—the purpose of this article is hard to fathom.[40] It seems to want to repackage the star, to remake her past and its relationship to her stardom into a family romance. But if one were to psychoanalyze Dorothy Deere, *Photoplay,* and the Hollywood machinery that supported both, one might reasonably conclude that the article is a sort of Freudian slip, an inadvertent but nevertheless powerful statement about Hayworth's relationship to her father. Precisely because of the weight given already to the *effort* and work of transformation previously in Hayworth's star image, this repackaging fails and, instead, highlights the perversity of that family romance. Conversely, the fairy-tale rhetoric might also be taken to indicate Deere's (and Hollywood's)

discomfort with analyzing Hayworth's personal life, because the essay refuses the markers of journalism—even fan-magazine journalism—in favor of those more usually associated with fiction.

Practically speaking, both Vidor's and Deere's articles fall into the
space left by Hayworth's separation from Orson Welles, a separation that
was going to end in divorce. I have suggested that the domestic lives of
women stars presented something of a problem for Hollywood in that a
star's success in the studio hierarchy depended on her willingness to forgo
home and family life in favor of labor to *publicize* her home and family life
in addition, of course, to making and publicizing films. If one brackets
out what was understood to be the biological imperative of all women's
desires to have babies (usually followed in fan-magazine parlance, regardless of star, by "and lots of them"), then the question that begins to loom
large after a star's second or third or fourth marriage is "What are husbands *for?*"

Through the late 1940s the discourse about Hayworth closely resembles that about other working stars whose marriages were continually
failing and underscores Richard Dyer's remark in *Stars* that in Hollywood
fan magazines "love is often not so much celebrated as agonised over."[41]
Hayworth's perpetual unhappiness, as noted, marks her as special or different, but otherwise the use value of her discarded husbands is articulated
over and over again as having helped to correct childhood deficiencies in
her formal education, social experience, self-confidence, and so on. And
because a discarded husband—unless the husband is himself the star—is
a useless commodity, his own agency no longer matters. Given the vitu-
peration already demonstrated against Orson Welles by many studio-
linked journalists and gossip columnists, it is not surprising that his image
would suffer the most in any conflict with a star as dependent on, and
heretofore cooperative with, the goodwill of the press as Rita Hayworth
demonstrably had been.

What makes the Welles-Hayworth break different from her divorce
from Judson, however, is that Welles had never, even after the birth of Rebecca, been portrayed as either an ideal husband or father. Barbara Leaming believes that Orson Welles was the "love of Hayworth's life," the marriage the only one that Hayworth wished had "worked out."[42] Leaming
quotes all sorts of friends and acquaintances who note that, despite how
badly he treated her, Hayworth refused to say a word against Welles in private or in public. Since the way Hayworth responds in the press to criticism of Welles and criticism of her marriage does not vary much, I focus
on representative articles in which Hayworth's marriage to and divorce
from Welles are "explained."

I Must Think for Myself

Like virtually all of the popular material describing Hayworth's marriage to and divorce from Welles, Louella Parsons's "It's Like This, Louella" (*Photoplay*, July 1947) pays backhanded compliments to Welles's genius: "The first time Rita separated from Orson she was very frank in saying she could not live up to his giant intellect. . . . But after this last separation she has little to say, only, 'It's hard to enjoy life with a genius.'"[43] The discourse is, as is usual, bifurcated and contradictory in the sense that a photo caption of Hayworth and Rebecca declaims that Hayworth is "Mother first, then artist," yet Hayworth is about to depart for an extended trip to Europe—"because [she's] never been there"—leaving Rebecca in the care of an aunt. At first glance the article would seem to be useless as real information; we know that Parsons was herself in the pay of Hollywood's power structure and therefore tended to protect it in her work, and she was as bent on her own self-aggrandizement as on publicizing the lives of the stars whom she always "knew personally" from "way back." But once again many of the quotations Parsons seems to extract from Hayworth are reproduced verbatim in biographies such as Leaming's, and a sense of the star's agency is constructed in her discursive resistance—however misguided or wrongheaded in Parsons's view—to the words Parsons wants to put in her mouth, the sorts of opinions Parsons wants her to have.

Parsons, for example, strenuously criticizes Orson Welles for treating Hayworth as "a beautiful statue, something to admire." Unlike other columnists Parsons "cannot feel he is carrying the torch for her as many columnists have said. His pride is hurt because she left him, walked out without a word. . . . Orson was so taken by surprise that he said to all enquiring reporters: 'It's ridiculous. Mrs. Welles and I have not separated. She has merely gone to Palm Springs to rest.' When it could no longer be denied that she *had* left him his silence could have been heard from Hollywood to New York." (This is only a more strongly worded version of Leaming's account, in which Hayworth also turned the tables on the apparently unsuspecting Welles by leaving him: "Rita surprised him, however. No sooner had he left for New York than she decided to divorce him. The sexual betrayals, the long absences, the excessive preoccupation with his work, at the expense of a homelife—Rita couldn't take these anymore.")[44] Yet, as both Parsons's and Leaming's accounts maintain, Hayworth did not denounce Welles in public and continued to argue that she had learned a lot from him. As Parsons "persists" in asking Hayworth,

"Are you glad to be rid of Orson?"

"Let's not underestimate what Orson did for me, Louella," she answered. "He helped me a lot, educationally speaking. But he is pretty difficult to live up to. I think he's best when left alone. And," she said this a little wistfully, "I think it's better for me too. I must think for myself and no one can have a personal thought that Orson doesn't want to intrude upon."

I certainly agreed with her there.

However much Parsons disapproves of Welles's treatment of Hayworth ("It is a great pity he did not appreciate what a fine woman she is"), she notes that the star now has the courage to want to "learn and see things [she's] never had a chance to learn or see before." Welles not only "gave" Hayworth the gift every woman supposedly wants—a child—but he has helped to build another "new Rita," in Parsons's words, who is more sophisticated, poised, and at ease in public. Parsons ends by praising Hayworth's decision to "put her marriage behind her" and to break free from "the Svengali spell of Orson." Now that she has "started to live her own life—something she has not done for too long—she will be a happier and lovelier woman than ever before."

The publicity about Hayworth's personal life after her divorce from Welles would continue to praise her increasing maturity and growth as an actor, her interest in self-improvement, and her overcoming of the "inferiority complex" that (in the words of one "noted psychologist," Gardner Maxwell, who wrote an article for *Screen Guide* in 1948 titled "Psycho-Analyzing Rita") was the result of her strict and limited upbringing and her being removed from school at the age of fourteen by the "the force of economic circumstance" afflicting her family.[45] Indeed, the deficiencies of her upbringing have led Hayworth, in Maxwell's words, to "an incredible position of anomaly, for here she is, a wealthy, glamorous, popular screen queen who knows in her heart that life for her is lonely, incomplete, inadequate; that her intellectual horizon is limited by a cultural background whose development was aborted in her youth." Hayworth has "beauty, kindness, simplicity, unselfishness. She is honest, straightforward, unsophisticated, and sometimes at the mercy of needling newspapermen." She "regrets her lack of formal education," but she "learns quickly and her hunger for knowledge is genuine and avid." Hayworth knows that Welles's intellectual curiosity was "good for her," just as she knows that being married to him, "to live with the man—that's a problem." She is now "free" from the domination of the men in her life who have made her unhappy. With the formation of the Beckworth Corporation she's also "the boss" of her own production company, and although, of course, she'd "like to marry again someday," she's not portrayed as sad or lonely outside of marriage but rather as sad and lonely *within* the wrong ones.

Jane Gaines writes that in their address to young women during the war fan magazines frequently "contradicted themselves in their advice, first recommending wartime marriage, then warning against it; scolding young women for infidelities, while encouraging them to date others if the men they loved were overseas." [46] Obviously there is contradictory advice being circulated about stars after the war too—insisting, on the one hand, that marriage and motherhood constitute the Holy Grail of personal fulfillment but approving, on the other, both of the discarding of husbands who do not treat their wives with the respect they deserve and of labor outside the home and an ethos of fulfillment based on individual achievement. [47] In Hayworth's case, if not those of all female stars, it is the period between her marriages that I find to be the most significant ideologically. Although linked up romantically with several eligible bachelors after her divorce from Welles—David Niven, Tony Martin, Kirk Douglas—there is no sense that Hayworth is merely marking time between men.

In 1947 and 1948 "Miss Independence" may still occasionally have "pain in her eyes" because she was not able to make her second marriage a success, but she is also constructed as enjoying being a mother to her child, forming her own production company, scrapping publicly with Winthrop Sargeant's designation of her as "passive" and a "love goddess," and making a film that had been "her dream" since childhood, *The Loves of Carmen* (directed by Charles Vidor). [48] If "in reality," as Leaming claims, Hayworth was in fact utterly unhappy and depressed, anxious to move out from under Harry Cohn's thumb at Columbia and eager to give up working for a living, still seeking someone to love her "as she was" and to take her away from Hollywood (and so on), her public subjectivity was at the time much more invested with an ethos of self-improvement and independence. [49]

In a winter 1948 *Film Album* cover story called "Hayworth Shocks Hollywood," for example, Hayworth's "previous" problems—"the confusion which surrounds and baffles her"—are again attributed to the "failure" of her "well-intentioned but super-strict" parents. [50] Hayworth was "not permitted even the broadening of an innocent experience or two which normal girlhood demands," but now she has finally emerged from her shell and is a "new, scintillating personality." Sheilah Graham names Hayworth one of "Hollywood's Dangerous Women" in another *Photoplay* cover story (November 1948).[51] Why is she dangerous? Because after coming out of her marriages with that inferiority complex, Rita has decided that it "was her turn. She began concentrating on her career" and was "a very different woman than Marguerite Cansino started out to be." In the same issue of *Photoplay* a "close friend" of Hayworth's, Jack Lait, writes that Hayworth is "no longer a shy siren." She has always been "too shy to assert herself. Orson and the other aggressive men she loved have always dominated her. Now it is different."[52] Lait continues:

> Now Rita has her own company, with a share in the profits and firm authority over what she will and will not do. . . . The first time she landed in Europe, because she had not yet sufficiently mastered her shyness to protect herself in countries where she was unfamiliar with the customs and language, she left herself open to criticism.
> This year it was different.

The Love Goddess Steps Out

What happens next in the public versions of Hayworth's personal life is one of the best-known and well-documented romances of classical Hollywood, her initially scandalous liaison with and marriage to Prince Aly Khan in 1949. *The Loves of Carmen*, then, was Hayworth's last film for three years; she left Hollywood to live with Aly and their children in Europe. I have written extensively elsewhere about how, in contrast to Ingrid Bergman (another married woman who was involved simultaneously in a scandalous affair with Roberto Rossellini), the scandal of the Hayworth–Aly Khan romance (Hayworth's divorce from Welles was not yet finalized, and Aly was not yet divorced from his wife) was displaced by the fortuitous timing of the rest of the relationship—all divorces coming through on time and without acrimony directed at Hayworth by Aly's former wife, the spectacular wedding (May 27, 1949) on the French Riviera, the "premature" birth of princess Yasmin seven months later.[53] After an early but brief bout of shaming by the gossip columnists and a few British clubwomen (who wanted Hayworth to end her affair with her "colored prince"—"this affair is an insult to all decent women"—and threatened a boycott of her films), Hayworth was able to become the "Cinderella Princess."[54] Her departure from Hollywood was described as being at once temporary (she would probably make a film or two again, if she felt like it) and permanent (she had naturally left work behind in favor of blissful romance and motherhood).

Photo of Hayworth and Aly Khan on their wedding day in France, May 27, 1949. From a fan scrap-book devoted to "Rita Hayworth Khan," collection of the author.

Between 1949 and 1952 Rita Hayworth was a movie star circulating out-side the traditional locus of the star's reason for being, namely, the full-length feature film. The fan magazine articles continued, with titles such as "She Married Her Prince," "The Fabulous Life," "The Most Fabulous Love Story Ever Told," "And So They Were Married," "Love Affair," "Title to Happiness," "At Home with Princess Rita," and "Rita's Great-est Challenge." In many of these articles her entire life story is reiterated along the ambiguous lines now familiar from the material cited above. What is different is that her freedom, growth, and independence between the end of her marriage to Welles and her new relationship with Aly Khan now have to be reconfigured in light of her apparent lack of interest in making films.

Elsa Maxwell (who took credit for introducing Hayworth to Aly Khan) refers in a *Photoplay* cover story, "The Fabulous Life" (October 1949), to the Beckworth Corporation now as the source of a "million-dollar in-come," but although that income can do "wonders, most of them pleas-ant," it offers "no surcease for loneliness."[55] Hayworth continued to be "a stimulating, provocative woman of ideas," but she was "desperately lonely," and that is why she "departed for Europe." Maxwell has "never [known] two more devoted" than Rita and Aly, and she rejoices that it was her "good fortune to pull the strings in this great modern love story." In a July 1950 *Photoplay* article, "Title to Happiness," Maxwell writes that the "more success [Hayworth] attained, the more responsibilities she had to assume and the harder she had to work and neither of her previous marriages offered her any escape from this pattern."[56] That is why Maxwell was so moved by Hayworth's "new happiness." And of course although Hayworth was now living a "fairy-tale life," she had "not gone chi-chi" and was still down-to-earth.

Despite the paeans to Hayworth's newfound contentment as a wife and mother, then, the repeated references to her unhappy past might have been serving the paradoxical purpose of accounting for, even setting up, the discursive framework in which the marriage would fail as well. The by now secondhand burblings of a Louella Parsons or an Elsa Maxwell about any star's "new" life were familiar and familiarly hyperbolic and untrustworthy (most of these "new" lives ended in divorce). Nor did other members of even the fan press fail to notice how unlikely a proposition this "most dangerous marriage of the year" was. In 1950 *Hollywood Yearbook* wrote:

> Rita Hayworth is now an Indian Princess, but it remains to be seen if there's enough love—or money in the world to stabilize a marriage subject to so much pressure as this one. . . . You can say, so what? Rita's got nine million diamonds, and more chateaus than any one girl can use, so let her forget about movies. She doesn't need a public life; her private life is dazzling enough. But maybe part of Rita's fascination for Aly was the fact that she *was* a movie star, that men fought to be introduced to her, that her face was famous, that she was a celebrity. Aly saw *Loves of Carmen* four times, and was enthralled by it. If Rita turns into a wife-and-mother, with no outside interests, will she be able to hold her man? Then there's the difference in backgrounds. Rita's known what it was to have very little, materially speaking. When she came to Hollywood, she was Marguerite Cansino, a shy, dark-haired little Spanish dancer. . . . She's probably not a very religious Catholic (Aly is her third husband) but even so, she's not likely to become a disciple of Mohammedanism. . . . There's the discouraging history of previous marital failure on both sides. There's the problem of the children, too. . . . Whether there can be peace and harmony in a household with so many step-mother-father-sister-brother relationships hasn't been proved yet.[57]

This, in a nutshell, is very close to Leaming's version of not only the pressures on but the explanations for the failure of Hayworth's third marriage.[58] Rita Hayworth may have hoped privately that this marriage was the one that would take her away from the pressures of Hollywood, but life with Aly Khan was also lived substantially in public and was therefore equally demanding in terms of what was expected of her—most apparently the continuous evaluation of how well she was "performing" as the scintillating and dazzling star that Aly Khan indeed wanted her to continue to be. (Later, in response to accusations that he did not provide Hayworth with the "home-and-fireside" life she wanted, Aly publicly retorted, "[B]ut she doesn't look like a home-and-fireside girl.")[59] So, as had been the case with her first two marriages, Hayworth's brief turn as a princess was characterized retroactively by, first, how unhappy she had been during its run and, second, how much she had learned from the experience.

Recuperating Hayworth from her "royal marriage" or, more precisely, the dissolution thereof, required some particularly interesting contradictions. For example, overtly racist and orientalist terms are employed to denigrate the "pampered playboy," the "Oriental potentate," the "spoiled, egotistical, Oriental prince," the "fabulously wealthy Moslem prince"—the list of epithets is appalling and extensive. But these terms are embedded in a nationalist framework that also identifies itself as such by an allegiance to the equality of women and men. Rita came out of her "royal marriage" with some "unique advantages"—"Her range of interests widened greatly. She met on an intimate plane the very people who make international affairs. More importantly, she can talk about international affairs today with comprehension and understanding and in French and English!"[60] These advantages, however, are less important than the differences marking "Moslem" and "American" attitudes about women's value and, in turn, the value of women's labor.

Rita Hayworth, American Working Girl

I can only assume that few if any of the journalists writing after Hayworth's return to America in 1951 really knew much about the tenets of Ismaili Islam, yet references to Moslem law are frequent and consistent. Gossip columnist Igor Cassini—who mistook Yasmin in one article for a prince rather than a princess—wrote in *Motion Picture* (August 1951) that Aly had married Hayworth in a "secret Moslem ceremony dictated by the laws of Mohammed" and that the "Oriental mind follows a preconceived

course, and the importance of a wife to a man like Aly is necessarily secondary to such interests as race horses, gambling casinos and the like." [61]
Because "[d]aughters don't mean too much to Orientals, anyway," Rita
Hayworth is paying for Yasmin's upbringing herself. "By Moslem law," repeats *Screen Guide,* "a female child is entitled to half" of whatever
amount is settled upon a male heir in a divorce. [62] Although Rita Hayworth, in the words of *Modern Screen* (November 1951), "feels that
women are just as valuable as men," unfortunately in "the Moslem tradition, this is not so, which is why Aly Khan offered to settle far less on Yasmin than he has on his two sons by a previous marriage." [63] Therefore
"Rita spurned Aly's offer. 'Yasmin is every bit as valuable as a son,' she insists." *Modern Screen* notes that Aly tried to "make Rita happy by treating her as an equal and a beloved wife," but this is against the fact that
"Moslems never treat their wives as equals." Rita had to "study protocol"
in her marriage, too, of course, writes *Movieland* in 1952, "because 'face'
is vital to Eastern peoples." But everything that happened to Hayworth
"happened to an American girl; a girl, in many respects, exactly like you."
And that girl has said "goodbye forever to life in a palace," because from
"now on she is going to be Rita Hayworth, American working girl." [64]

That Hayworth returned home—"Home," continues *Movieland,*
"[t]he biggest word in the world"—from "life in a palace" was not, then,
only because of Aly's publicized dalliances with other women, dalliances
that, according to Louella Parsons, "Rita refuses to discuss." Rather, as
Hayworth tells Parsons in *Modern Screen* (1951), "Perhaps I did not realize how completely American I am until I was brought face to face with
the differences in our ways of life in almost *everything.*" [65] Hayworth reports that one "big difference" was that Aly surrounded himself with
"hangers-on"—people who "come just to drink and eat your food." But
more than that, Hayworth claims, "I know now that I really love my work
and how much I have really missed it." Hayworth comes "home" because
she believes, in *Movieland*'s terms, "that working for one's living was a
normal way of life and that there is a human obligation to be useful." According to another November 1951 *Modern Screen* article, "Rita Hayworth
believes that all able-bodied men should work for a living, and she doesn't
mean working over a roulette table." [66] As Sheilah Graham also wrote in
Modern Screen (February 1953), "Okay, so Moslems don't think a daughter's so hot. Rita's American, and girls in this country rate as much as
boys." [67] Worse, without Rita's money, "I guess the pampered playboy
would have to work. Even as Rita has worked since she was 12 years old to
reach her present pinnacle of success." In fact, Graham continues, "Let us
never forget that in Moslem tradition a woman counts for nothing except

to bear sons for the glory of Allah. You can bet that Rita will rear Yasmin for the glory of the little girl's happiness whatever the religion. She's a good mother in spite of her frenzied and pathetic non-stop search for the perfect romance, which has in the past taken her away from her children very frequently when she'd rather be with them."

The shifts in tone across the relatively brief period of Hayworth's romance, marriage, and divorce are striking. In the service of racism and nationalism the discourse about Hayworth's return to Hollywood and "home" ends up employing a quasi-feminist version of the rights and privileges cherished by American womanhood and, as a corollary, eulogizing the value of women's independence and their labor in the public sphere. If "the victory was abortive and pyrrhic," to recast terms Sheilah Graham used in describing Hayworth's attempt to make Aly Khan "fit the pattern prescribed by American wives for American husbands," it was no less important for having occurred and at such a tension-ridden moment in American social history. Hayworth's first film on her return, *Affair in Trinidad,* was an enormous box-office success and was followed by only two more—*Salome* and *Miss Sadie Thompson*—before she was off the screen again for another three years and once more embroiled in an unhappy and publicly abusive marriage to lounge singer and sometime screen actor Dick Haymes. That Hayworth was in her early thirties throughout most of the 1950s marks her liminality in the postwar ethos of containment and conservatism during which women were continuing to enter the workforce in ever-increasing numbers (again, by 1962 married women made up 60 percent of the female workforce).[68] In some sense the rhetoric employed to reinsert Hayworth properly into the hierarchy of sexual difference after her return to America and to her job resembles that directed at returning women to the home at the end of World War II. But just as that rhetoric could not help but be riddled with ambivalence, so was that circulating around the "not-so-private life of Rita Hayworth," as a *Photoplay* writer characterized it (October 1952).[69]

The *Photoplay* article continues:

> There is love in Rita's life these days. But it's not of a romantic nature. Rita's in love all right. She's in love with her children. That's enough for now. And then there is her career. Once again it has come to count. For three years, she ignored its existence. However, even in temporary retirement, Rita was a star. . . . Now that she has returned to pictures, the spotlight will be even brighter. It will be focused primarily upon her work and her dates. And, of course, the things that mean the most to Rita—her home and family.

Now that she has acquired the "self-confidence she needed," Rita has one more task: she is "learning—to be herself." Once she is working again (and, as recounted above, realizing how much her work "means to her"), the reports from the set are glowing in their praise of her work habits, her professionalism, the fact that she will "never be a jerk like some of the others" because she has none of that "ultra-ultra stuff" (despite having been a princess). Hayworth "gets to the studio at six-thirty in the morning, and sometimes doesn't leave until eight-thirty at night. She's now a producer at Columbia, so things that do not concern other actresses do concern Rita. And for a lazy girl, she's holding up pretty well. She is ambitious for herself as an actress." If there is any mystery about Hayworth, it is "no mystery at all. She is finishing 'Salome,' enjoying renewed friendships in Hollywood and having a wonderful time with her children. If at times she is lonely, she's busy enough hardly to notice it."

This Doesn't Make Sense

The "big question," then, does come down to whether Hayworth wants "career or love." The significant word here is *or* in that it offers at least the illusion of choice, as well as implying that career and love are incompatible *as* choices. Across all of the articles and columns promising to tell us the truth about Rita Hayworth, one can see the confusion over what really was at stake in the struggle to define women's place in the postwar world—between public labor and domesticity, on the one hand, but between being a mother and being a wife on the other.

In Hayworth's case, because of the accretion in her image of discourses of personal unhappiness related specifically to oppressive patriarchal mechanisms in which her "ego was flattened to the ground" first by her father and then by all of her husbands—with the divorce from Aly Khan able to set into play a racist assertion of America's, if not Hayworth's, ideological superiority over her temporary "Moslem prince"—the bifurcation of career and love is more interesting than in most other star images I have examined. Generally, the references to Hayworth's loneliness continue in uneasy symmetry with the valorization of her new life as a working mother, and there emerges a noticeable consternation about her failure to consume and to flaunt the conventional trappings of her femininity. In asking "Should Rita Change?" (December 1951), *Photoplay* suggested that it was okay for her to wear "jeans and moccasins" in her private life and that the American public will be "very pleased with Rita's desire to settle down with her little family." [70] But it also admonishes that

"Rita needn't overdo. No one wants to see pictures of Rita, the glamorous, cooking oatmeal for the children or hanging out the family wash. There's no need for her to be 'the girl next door.'" But although Hayworth continues to be featured in various forms of "leg art" from 1951 on— primarily shots around a swimming pool—these shots begin routinely to appear in the context of others that downplay her glamour. If the Hayworth of jeans and moccasins does not utterly replace the "love goddess," then, she does suggest more mutable meanings to each. ("Wouldn't it be wonderful if someone, some day, just wrote a story about me—my work, my future, the love I have for my children, and not mention once my last marriage!" she exclaimed to *Screenland* in 1952; "Can't I behave as I would like to behave—by *being* myself?").[71] And to anyone who had been following her career from the beginning, it would seem that Hayworth herself had decided on the image change after years and years of adapting to the desires of all of those father figures.

"Is Rita Hayworth Just a Lonesome Gal?" (*Movieland,* May 1953) is another typical example of the contradictions of a discourse that at once questions and endorses the ideal of domestic containment. The article notes on its first page (under a photograph of Hayworth dressed in jeans and reading a book) that "[a] sad and disillusioned Rita returned from Europe to divorce Aly Khan; but that doesn't mean she's nixed romance, marriage."[72] On the same page the article quotes Hayworth as saying, "Look, I want to be a wife, mother and movie star. Without any of those elements, I can't be happy." (On the following page this is reiterated in slightly different terms: "Rita is the first to admit she is happiest when she is a 'wife, mother and actress.'") In fact, Hayworth repeats again, "Remember, I said I want to be a wife, a mother and a movie star. Well, I missed working. It's part of me. I don't think it strange that you eat three meals a day, and for me it's just as natural to act." In describing the marriage the article poses Rita ("the most informal person in the world") against living with Aly in a house that was "like a hotel." Hayworth found herself "bored. She longed to be working." Now she is "back where she belongs, she is with people to whom she can talk about show business." Pain remains a consistent element of Hayworth's personal life—but so is the only way that pain can be dulled, by work ("it's a great consolation to wrap yourself up in your work. If I didn't know it before, I know now," as *Screenland* had also reported in 1952).

But after another two pages about Hayworth's career and the casualness, simplicity, and contentment of her new way of life, the final two paragraphs of the *Movieland* piece kick in with the expected closure: "However, money is not that important to Rita. Love is." Yes, she plays with her children ("they all danced together. It was the gayest scene imaginable"), but in the end it is another "long, lonely evening." "Rita— lonely and out-of-love? This doesn't make sense. Rita wouldn't be Rita if she didn't fall in love again, and marry. And she wouldn't be Hayworth if she thought it all out."

In a May 1944 *Coronet* article by Gretta Palmer titled "Boom in Broken Homes," women who are arranging for divorces—even from men whom they do not love, who are brutes, who drink, or who adopt "the maddening European custom of spending [their evenings] in the local café while [the wife] tends the baby alone"—are setting themselves up for "lonely and poverty-stricken futures for themselves."[73] Such women "ought to be spanked for abandoning passable spouses for a Social Security card and a divorce decree. Many of them will be." Any number of articles in Hollywood fan magazines also follow this sort of logic, which Jane Gaines describes as tautological; all women want to be married, so advice columns focus on how to get a man rather than offering even tentative suggestions for ways to negotiate the world without one.[74] And in her analysis of data measuring the marital satisfaction of white middle-class couples in the mid-1950s, Elaine Tyler May notes that several of the women surveyed describe their independence "as if it were a chronic disease or allergy that flared up now and then to bother [them]."[75] Independence, May continues, "did not fit well with domestic containment," and it was clearly safer for many married women to adapt to domestic containment rather than defy it and risk "loss of economic security, social reputation, or community support." But according to the same data women were twice as likely as men to report that they were dissatisfied with or regretted their marriages, and 20 percent more women than men said that they had considered divorce.[76]

So how would a divorced woman who *was* able to support herself and her family fit into this discursive universe in which women alone are always already "at risk" and lonely? Most of the sorts of contentment and satisfaction middle-class women indicated as resulting from their marriages in May's data derive from the security of having a husband as provider, a home of one's own, consumer goods, children. If these marriages satisfied "at least some of the needs of their participants," it was primarily because, May claims, "there were few alternative routes to a fulfilling life at that time," and "material considerations made it nearly impossible [for women] to abandon their marriages."[77] Many of the themes in the discourse about stars support the notion that women are incomplete without husbands. But, at the same time, the reasons May cites for women's adherence to the institution of marriage in the mid-1950s are not applicable to Hayworth's case.

Therefore, the rhetorical claim that for Rita Hayworth to be "lonely and out-of-love doesn't make sense" can be made to mean something entirely different than that Hayworth doesn't make sense without a man. Women who have children and a secure economic and social foundation for raising them instead don't make sense as figures defined only by their lack of a husband. The support provided to Hayworth by her "close-knit family" of Cansinos is more frequently mentioned as well during this interstice. And although this might have been read ambivalently by certain of her fans, it also works to postulate one sort of "alternative route" to satisfying two out of three of Hayworth's "requirements for happiness," mother and movie star. But this route was cut short by another marriage.

She's the Marrying Kind

After 1950 Hayworth's marriages were being placed into the context of her "frenzied and pathetic non-stop search for the perfect romance." Although, as we have seen, some lip service was paid to the validity of this "pathetic search," the unsuitability of Hayworth's next husband, Dick Haymes, put the final ambivalent cap on the "career or love" controversy. Initially, the 1953 marriage, the final one of her studio years, was characterized according to routine as the end of the "long, lonely evenings." But at least partly because Hollywood was rapidly losing control over the promotional machinery by which it attempted to define the images of its stars, the marriage was almost immediately characterized publicly as a mistake. Among Haymes's faults were that he was still married (to Nora Eddington) during the initial stages of the "romance," that he was tainted with the "stench of draft evasion" in *Motion Picture*'s words (Haymes had claimed Argentinean citizenship to get out of service in World War II), and that he was being sued by wife and government for child support and back taxes.[78] When he left the country to visit Hayworth in Hawaii during the filming of *Miss Sadie Thompson*, he at first was not allowed back into the United States and subsequently, by late 1953, was being threatened with deportation.

Hayworth's marriage to Haymes helped to prevent his deportation, but Hollywood found it more than usually difficult—although its attempts were heroic—to construct the union as even *necessary*, much less ideal. Haymes's private nickname in Hollywood, I have heard, was

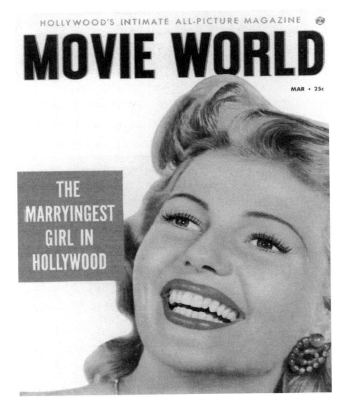

HOLLYWOOD'S INTIMATE ALL-PICTURE MAGAZINE

MOVIE WORLD

MAR · 25¢

THE MARRYINGEST GIRL IN HOLLYWOOD

A cheerful-looking Rita Hayworth is proclaimed "The Marryingest Girl in Hollywood" by *Movie World*, March 1954. The article inside is much less sanguine, and its images are not smiling ones: "Is a happy marriage the most important thing in life for Rita? Friends say it is . . . yet, why does she marry and divorce, only to marry again?" Copyright 1953 by Interstate Publishing Corp.

"Mr. Evil," and certainly there was little enough in his publicly rendered behavior toward Hayworth and her children to challenge that appellation. Before the end of the marriage barely two years after it began, Hayworth was accused of child neglect by the state of New York. The charge was linked to her privileging of her relationship with her husband over that with her children and was made in the midst of a custody battle Hayworth was waging with Aly Khan over visitation rights with and financial support for their daughter, Yasmin. Haymes also pressured Hayworth to dissolve the Beckworth Corporation because he wanted control over her career—and his own stardom within it—and an immediate infusion of cash. Ironically, *Miss Sadie Thompson* was Hayworth's last film for more than three years, at which point the legal wranglings forced the now-thirty-seven-year-old actress to play out the remaining years of her Columbia contract with *Fire Down Below* and *Pal Joey* (both 1957), in the final film costarring against the blonde star Columbia had engineered as Hayworth's replacement, Kim Novak.

Many of the fan magazines writing about Hayworth's romance with Haymes seem to have been written before the marriage but to have appeared in print after it occurred; for example, "She's the Marrying Kind," from *Photoplay* (October 1953), points again to the fact that Haymes is "still married to Nora Eddington," and several others appearing as late as November 1953 refer only to "Rita's alleged romance with Haymes" or "no matter what people say, one day Dick Haymes and Rita Hayworth will be married."[79] Although "She's the Marrying Kind" portrays the "romance" in typically euphemistic terms ("Rita Hayworth is in love again! And when her passionate heart begins turning flipflops nothing else is so important to her as being with the man who's the cause of it all. This time it's Dick Haymes"), the others are much more critical. "Rita's Forgotten Child," from *Modern Screen* (November 1953), is subtitled "A Tragic Sidelight on Hollywood Glamour" and openly, if hypocritically, castigates Hayworth for not spending enough time with her children, particularly Rebecca Welles.[80] "Rita has always professed devotion to Rebecca," but the problem is Hayworth's "turbulent existence—the demands of her career and her need to rest and relax between pictures—has kept her away from Rebecca four to six months of every year of the child's life." Yet "Rita, as everyone knows, has made mistakes of judgment, but not of the heart." This gave Hayworth "a great deal in common with other working mothers who are constantly torn from their children."

At first, then, this article criticizes Hayworth's excessive devotion to her career, a familiar theme of the 1950s, but by the end of its barely three pages, it touts Hayworth's career as crucial to ameliorating the "harm" done to Rebecca and Yasmin because of the "tumultuous life" to which they have been subjected: "It is a pity that Rita, who came from such a warm and loving family, has not succeeded in duplicating such a home life for herself. She has complained loudly of her husbands' lack of interest in 'home life.' Has she ever shown them what a loving home life is like? When she is busy with her torrid romances, doesn't she neglect her family?" The posing of the dilemma as a series of contradictory questions is most interesting here, for even in this short essay the answers appear to be not all that obvious. In the end the writer is forced to point out that Hayworth "finds herself in the same position as thousands of other American mothers who are divorced and unable to collect support for their children from their ex-husbands. Fortunately, she has enough earning years left to be able to compensate for some of the income she has lost. But this film star has much more to recover than her fortune." Rather, the article concludes, Hayworth needs to devote herself to "making her daughter's life happier," and if she does, "she may find more contentment in her own life. Rita will learn that the sparkle in her child's eyes can outshine Aly's diamonds, her own name in lights, and the fleeting glow of romance."

As in many of the previous articles that attempt to explain Hayworth's inappropriate public behavior as a failure to fulfill the requirements of a hegemonic domestic ideology, the advice given is ultimately impossible to follow. Here Hayworth's romances are the problem, not the solution, and she is urged to abandon the search for a husband in favor of spending time with her children. Indeed, her former husbands are also criticized for not contributing to their own children's support. But Hayworth has spent too much time in pursuit of a career, and this has also taken her away from her children. Yet she is "broke" and is raising her children "alone," so it is good that she has "earning years" left. Hayworth thus is urged to stay home and to stop working *at the same time* that her career is named as being all that she has left with which to support herself and her children.

By the time the discourse catches up to the fact of the Hayworth-Haymes marriage, it falls back on previous renderings of the married Hayworth: that although she "may not look like a 'home-and-fireside girl,' [that's] exactly what she is."[81] The contrast between the previous "lavish French wedding to Aly at his villa on the Riviera" and her Las Vegas nuptials is noted here as elsewhere (with *Life* again baldly calling the wedding a "skid into the rhinestones" [October 1953]), but now Hayworth is "wonderfully happy": "After all, I'm getting Dick Haymes and that's all that matters. It's enough that we love each other." But much of the rest of this article—as of most of the others ("Goddess of Love" [*Movieland,* April 1955]; "She Lives for Love" [*Motion Picture,* August 1955]; "Lovely in Love" [*Screen Stars,* n.d.])—is devoted to an enumeration of all of the financial and legal difficulties confronting the pair. And although Haymes "thanks God" that he has Hayworth to "inspire" him to work and "take care of all of [his] troubles," virtually everything that has come before in Hayworth's life, if not in that of every other many-times-divorced Hollywood star, suggests that love is *not,* in fact, enough.

When the neglect charges against Rita Hayworth broke in April 1954—the children had been left in the care of a woman in New York while Hayworth and Haymes took a car trip to Florida incognito—her status as even a working mother was called into question. How could she have left her children in the care of a woman in White Plains, New York, with a junk-strewn porch and yard and who seemed not to notice when reporters were questioning the children? Especially when Hayworth was fighting a battle with Aly Khan over visitation rights and support for Yasmin and the FBI was still investigating some anonymous letters threatening Yasmin with kidnapping? (Yet both Aly and Orson Welles quickly swore out affidavits attesting to Hayworth's excellence as a mother, implying that Haymes was to blame rather than Hayworth.) What Hayworth had done was no more and no less than privilege the wishes of her husband, Haymes, over her relationship with her children. According to Earl Wilson, in *Motion Picture,* Dick Haymes was "distinctly and unqualifiedly her guy. He hardly left her side. He was the lord and master."[82] Wilson's tone is similar to that struck by most of the fan magazines at this time—treading the line between condemning Hayworth outright for uncharacteristic and inappropriate behavior toward her children but maintaining fealty to the idea of "everything for love," in Wilson's terms: "Will the love they've demonstrated for each other crush all opposition? A better question—will their love survive all this pain and grief? My answer is theirs: 'You're --- right it will!'"

By the mid-1950s, then, Rita Hayworth seemed no longer to be making films and, instead, to have become tied to a "one-man-and-no-one-else routine" (*Movieland,* April 1955).[83] In essence Hayworth had taken the cornerstone of domestic ideology—that "women should adapt to men's interests and needs"—to its ultimate logical conclusion: she never left her husband's side, and she began to live her life essentially in the service of that husband.[84] The vertiginous feeling of the discussions about Hayworth's personal life at this time results precisely from their alternately blithe and tortured deployment of buzzwords, cliché, and convention to account for a problem that is rendered ultimately as an inelastic double bind. *Movieland* could piously remark that "Hollywood has never been able to teach Rita that love for one man need not necessarily shut her off from friends and family and work." But as the data Elaine Tyler May cites remind us, many middle-class women in the 1940s and 1950s had internalized a very similar message. Among the most common dilemmas faced by the married women on whose lives May reports is that their husbands came first, as well as demanded the most, and therefore these wives, too, could not properly maintain allegiance to friends, family, and work.[85]

Love's Lonely Fugitive

Although from roughly 1955 on Hayworth is still quoted from time to time in the press, more often she is rendered as a remote object, observed from the outside, described, discussed, spoken of rather than speaking herself. Her cooperativeness with both her studio and the press is called into question, even as it is noted that Haymes is making the decisions about Hayworth's actions. Whether any committed fans believed that Rita Hayworth was "wonderfully happy" during her marriage to Haymes is difficult to assess, but at least one fan magazine (*Movie World,* March 1954) announced the marriage in a feature article and predicted its demise simultaneously in a nearby gossip column: "Even though this is the 'honeymoon year,' gloomy predictions are already made for the dissolution of this marriage contract within the next three years. Such dire prophecies are based on their respective personalities and not on mere cynicism." Given Hayworth's marital history and the continuing shifts in the discourse about her family life, then, it probably was no surprise when Hayworth left Haymes abruptly, "never to return." But the break, instituted by Hayworth and at first denied by Haymes, looms much larger as a defiant gesture in the public press than it did to her close friends and coworkers, for example. (As choreographer Jack Cole noted of Hayworth in an interview in the 1970s, "I like Rita Hayworth, she's a very nice lady, one of the nicest ones in the movies to work with. She wasn't really as dependent on men as one might suspect.")[86]

Leaming, of course, links Hayworth's monstrously self-destructive and self-abnegating behavior during her fourth marriage to the continuing traumatic effects of childhood abuse. But so, albeit in more euphemistic terms, did the popular press at the time. That Rita Hayworth had become the victim—but a resistant and resilient victim—of yet another unscrupulous man comes out most clearly in the new tabloids that emerged from and also represented Hollywood's declining power in the mid-1950s. *Confidential* magazine released a story, "Why Rita Hayworth Walked Out on Dick" (January 1956), that documented the fact that "not just one night but the entire two years of their marriage were a non-stop nightmare for Rita, during which the best-loved pin-up girl of World War II *was subjected to countless cruel beatings!*"[87] Leaming's description of the perpetuation of abusive patterns associated with childhood trauma—Hayworth's fear of not adequately protecting her children turning into neglect charges; Hayworth's abuse at the hands of her father causing her to equate physical violence with love—certainly gives her analysis explanatory power, and I do not question its validity. At the same time, however, it has been my assertion that although Hayworth's behavior patterns might have been recognized as representations of the *unthinkable* to some audience members, they also are discussed in ways that associate her dilemmas more generally with tensions within domestic ideology itself. If we read Hayworth's forays into short-lived and horrid marriages as part

A spread from Alfred Garvey, "Why Rita Hayworth Walked Out on Dick," *Confidential* magazine, January 1956, in which Hayworth is depicted as Haymes's punching bag. The article is very much on Hayworth's side; the caption above the photo of her daughters, below left, reads, "Haymes once publicly announced he wanted to adopt Rita's daughters, Yasmin and Rebecca, but his actions hardly recommend him as a father." Copyright 1955 by Confidential, Inc.

of her "psychology" and her "inferiority complex," as so many writers did, that does not obscure the fact that others would not know how to explain them except as failures within the hegemony of female subordination and domestic ideology, as well as marriage as "togetherness"—that mid-1950s term for the defining and desirable attribute of heterosexual marriage.[88] From this divorce on, Rita Hayworth will be urged to "come home—back to the work she needs and that needs her," to stop "looking so desperately for someone to love her," to take up again with the "many friends who have been heartbroken at some of the foolish things this beautiful young woman has done," to stop making herself and her two daughters "lost and lonely fugitives" (*Movie Secrets,* August 1956).[89] The result of all of this is to problematize togetherness and even the essential value of marriage itself, especially as the inevitable outcome of love and romance. (There would be one more short-lived marriage for Hayworth, from 1958 to 1961, to producer James Hill. In his "memoir" about Hayworth he describes her as wanting at that point in her life to retire to paint, to travel, to read, to enjoy a fulfilling life away from Hollywood; she

Spread from Ruth Seymour, "Love's Lonely Fugitive," *Movie Secrets*, August 1956, urging Hayworth to stop looking for husbands and to concentrate on work and children. "From husband to husband—from place to place—Rita Hayworth has gone seeking happiness—able to escape everything and everyone but herself." Photo captions on the right state that "Edward Judson was almost twice her age, helped make her a star. Then Orson Welles tried to make her a 'brain' and dashing Aly Khan made her a lonely Princess. Then [came] Dick Haymes—who seemed to love her 'just for myself'—til[*sic*] time and creditors proved otherwise." Copyright 1956 by Sterling Group, Inc.

left him to do these things alone because, promises to the contrary, he too saw her as a project—he wanted to mold her into a fine serious actress—and in the end had become another of the "manipulative men in her life.")[90]

The discourse about Rita Hayworth's failed marriages and offscreen family life often employs a rhetoric of victimization to account for her problems. Nevertheless, Hayworth was also equally an "American working girl," as she was called in 1952. Her frequent public struggles to achieve independence from her family and a series of overbearing husbands; her repeated insistence through the middle of the 1950s that she needed a husband, children, *and* career to be happy; the muting of this emphasis as she apparently gave up and granted a husband her complete "loyalty" and control over her private and her public lives and then reasserted her independence and became a female head of household who could conveniently again be castigated for being alone—these can all be

"Out of 'Bondage,'" spread from *Look,* January 21, 1958. The central photo caption reads "Rita and daughters, Rebecca Welles and Princess Yasmin, live together in Beverly Hills. The girls go to public school. Rita says the two 'get along just like any sisters.'" Rita Hayworth had turned forty a few months before and had just married producer James Hill (her final husband). The bonds Hayworth had cut are named as her marriage to Dick Haymes and her alliance with Harry Cohn at Columbia, where she had been "pampered as a doll-child and minimized as a person." In the photo on the lower right Hayworth is shown in the "tousled, outdoor, un-made-up look she has privately favored all her life." Photos by Sam Shaw. Copyright 1958 by Cowles Magazines, Inc.

read as an allegory of the trajectory many women's lives followed throughout this period. Although Hayworth, like these women, tried to make the complexities of her life and experience fit within the contours of conventional respectability, her struggles and her failures were themselves a component in the gradual reshaping of those contours. I still cannot explicitly claim that real or historical audiences either grasped or agreed with the various rhetorical turns of the discourse I have been describing. Some, I believe, probably did link, if only unconsciously, Hayworth's failures in "love, sex, motherhood" to early abuse, and this recognition was important. But Hayworth's ordinariness as a star cannot be discounted either. Her unhappiness was extreme, but it is equally telling that it did not require the overt acknowledgment of childhood trauma to explain it (and by the mid-1950s her extended family of Cansinos was being given the favorable valuation seen to be lacking in her marriages). Nor was this unhappiness constant, and it is crucial to remember that the "hurt" of her life was ameliorated most frequently by her pleasure and satisfaction in her work, her professional achievements in making films, as well as by her children. In short, I believe that the ways in which Hollywood's publicity machinery chose to characterize its female stars' private lives in the 1940s and 1950s is full of surprising juxtapositions and contradictions that make stars like Rita Hayworth a crucial component of, rather than merely an obstacle to, a nascent feminist consciousness that was itself born of frustration, fear, hope, and bewilderment.

To this point I have focused primarily on Rita Hayworth's star image and how the labor of its construction was accomplished and discussed in the popular press. What Hayworth meant to her audiences was not confined to her film performances; in fact, the significance of Hayworth's star image was substantially tied to her offscreen authenticity, in Richard Dyer's sense—her "private and natural" meanings as a woman struggling to be herself, to learn and grow, to adapt to the competing demands of domesticity as well as the Hollywood marketplace.[91] In the second section of this volume I turn to concentrated discussion of several of Rita Hayworth's film performances (as Danae Clark notes, film studies "seems incomplete without the study of films")[92] to explore how these aspects of her star image interacted with the fictional characters she portrayed on the screen and how other elements of her star labor, especially dance, were characterized in the popular-press accounts contemporary with the films. Because this labor has not received sufficient attention in the body of scholarship that currently makes up academic film studies, I also spend more time discussing that scholarship, as well as the popular and archival material by which I mean to reorganize some of its assumptions.

PART TWO

Film Stars, Film Texts, Film Studies

Lobby photo taken on the set of *Affair in Trinidad* of Glenn Ford possessing the gaze but deriving no apparent pleasure from it. The photograph he is glaring at is of Rita Hayworth in "Trinidad Lady" and was itself a photo used to publicize the film proper. Photo by Lippman. Copyright 1952 by Columbia Pictures Corp.

3

*I'm the Goddess
of Song and Dance*

PERFORMING COMPETENCE
IN *DOWN TO EARTH*

In its review of the Rita Hayworth musical *Tonight and Every Night* (1945) *Weekly Variety* remarked that "In Rita Hayworth, Columbia has a protagonist of musicals second to none in the industry."[1] Her skills in dancing, acting, and "simulated singing" (everyone knew her voice was dubbed by others) had become "expert" and "top-ranked" across the two musicals she had made with Fred Astaire, *You'll Never Get Rich* (1941) and *You Were Never Lovelier* (1942). In fact, Hayworth was regularly touted as a suitable replacement for Ginger Rogers. Hayworth's performance in *Cover Girl* (1944), with Gene Kelly, was even likely to make audiences "forget that there ever was such a perfect combination as Ginger and Fred," in the words of Kate Cameron of the *New York Daily News*.[2] As the box-office success of *Tonight and Every Night* was demonstrating, however, even without an Astaire or a Kelly to support her—and even without doing her own singing—Hayworth was able to carry a major motion picture musical as the primary star attraction. Both *Tonight and Every Night* and her subsequent musical, *Down to Earth* (1947), were testaments to Hayworth's competence and skill as a musical performer, as well as to her ability to be "eye-filling" in Technicolor. ("Rita Hayworth's dancing is more alive than all the rest of the film rolled up," wrote Eileen Creelman of the *New York Sun* about *Tonight and Every Night*.)[3]

Tonight and Every Night has no major male stars (Lee Bowman was the love interest and Marc Platt a supporting player). Nor does *Down to Earth,* although costar Larry Parks had had notable success impersonating Al Jolson in *The Jolson Story* (also Columbia) the year before. Both of these Hayworth musicals, like the three with Astaire and Kelly, made substantial profits for Columbia, and critically they were no less lauded (or conversely lambasted, primarily for the predictability of their plots).[4] So if *Tonight and Every Night* and *Down to Earth* remain virtually unknown in the canon of film musicals, it cannot be because they were not popular at the time (they were as successful as two other well-known canonical

Ad for Hayworth's 1945 star vehicle *Tonight and Every Night* attesting both visually (the original is in color) and verbally to Hayworth's dominance in the film. The image on the right is of Hayworth performing "You Excite Me," choreographed by Jack Cole. Copyright 1945 by Columbia Pictures Corp.

musicals, Vincente Minnelli's *Yolanda and the Thief* [1945] and *The Pirate* [1948], for example) or because they received bad reviews.[5] Rather their obscurity seems related to the fact that neither *Tonight and Every Night* (directed by Victor Saville) nor *Down to Earth* (directed by Alexander Hall) offer scholars "the security of a major author," in the words of Bruce Babington and Peter William Evans.[6] More specifically, they do not offer the security of a major *male* author.

Both *Tonight and Every Night* and *Down to Earth* are, like many other musicals carried primarily by female star performers, what I call "women's musicals." It has always been striking to me that despite their ubiquity as performers (and as underacknowledged choreographer-performers),[7] and however often we give the nod to the collaborative basis of all musicals, relatively few women's names appear in the most prominent discussions of the genre. In his 1981 book *Dance in the Hollywood Musical,* for example, Jerome Delamater describes the "considerable overlapping" of creative personnel involved in making musicals, particularly in the golden age of the Freed unit at MGM in the 1940s and 1950s.[8] But in his listing of this personnel he names seventeen men and two women—Judy Garland, a singer, and Betty Comden, a writer. Neither of the women, in other words, are related to *dance,* the subject of his book.

Women's omission from discussions of creative personnel and the film musical involves more than textual oversight, for the creativity of male musical performers is seldom at issue—on the contrary, it is admired and widely praised. Whereas in his book on the American film musical Rick Altman will refer to a female dancer as graceful or beautiful, he eulogizes Gene Kelly as "a self-confident and energetic individual whose talent and style turn the entire world into a realm of gaiety and dance. Watching him dance makes us want to dance, seeing him express his joy makes us joyous in turn. In short, Kelly does what every performer does, just more so and better, and in a particularly American way."[9] Further, Altman claims that Kelly embodies the "secret of eternal youth. . . . Be happy, dance, and clown—and somehow the impossible can be achieved. . . . Gene Kelly shows us the way."

Equally disheartening to me is the contrast between the terms with which Michael Renov describes Rita Hayworth and partner Fred Astaire in *You'll Never Get Rich:*

> Hayworth's glamour potential is exploited in *You'll Never Get Rich,* but not without contradiction. The eye is mechanically drawn to her during an early rehearsal sequence (the camera individuates her through a tracking movement), because Hayworth's dancing prowess will not suffice to do so (or at least such a display is suppressed). . . .
>
> Conversely, Astaire's appropriation of the look is based upon an irrepressible kinaesthetic potency achieved through the coupling of meticulous precision and "effortless" grace.[10]

Even when Astaire is framed by a group of "marching beauties," Renov continues, "the eye is drawn to Astaire's famous feet . . . perhaps to catch the subtlest syncopation of step, the sign of a joyful expressiveness undaunted by repression. . . . In effect, the struggle for control of the gaze is settled by a marriage of the twin currents of fascination—those attached to the glamorized female form and to the energized male body."

I am myself a big admirer of Gene Kelly and Fred Astaire. But what I am concerned about here is why female performers, for whom repression really *is* an issue, are hardly ever described this lushly, with this much reference to their energy, their "kinaesthetic" potency, their precision, their ability to achieve the impossible. That women are not described in these terms can of course be linked precisely to their status within film studies as "glamorized female forms," as objects rather than performing subjects. But if women's skills *were* routinely discussed along with those of male performers and choreographers, then it would paradoxically become much more difficult to justify relegating women to the status of object. Compare Altman's and Renov's comments to those of William Vincent in a 1992 essay about Rita Hayworth, for example. The primary remarks Vincent can make about Hayworth in *You Were Never Lovelier* focus on her clothes: "Especially beautiful is [her] costume for the 'I'm Old Fashioned' sequence; the gown shows off Hayworth's shoulders and back and thrusts her breasts forward in a manner that is anything but old-fashioned."[11] Vincent claims that one of Hayworth's most technically exacting and explosively performed numbers, "You Excite Me" from *Tonight and Every Night,* is "heavy-footed," makes "few demands of her," and requires her only to "rotate her pelvis and look sexy." The number he describes, choreographed and directed by Jack Cole,[12] is actually a difficult and intricate three-minute routine shot in four long takes, and surely Vincent could not fail to notice (given his prurient interest in the surface allure of her body) that Hayworth's very visible working legs bulge with the sorts of sinewy muscles seldom found in pinup photographs or that the male chorus dancers are as fetishistically dressed as any of the women in the number in ruffles, tight pants, and midriff-revealing shirts (they also engage in considerable pelvis rotating).

Even when the lack of attention historically paid to female film performers is precisely the issue under consideration, somehow women's authority as performers still gets bypassed—to wit, in Virginia Wright Wexman's discussion in the chapter called "The Love Goddess: Contradictions in the Myth of Glamour" in her 1993 book *Creating the Couple,* Wexman writes that "although women actors are more likely than men to sing and dance onscreen, their roles are less likely to 'spill over' in a way that could endow their offscreen personas with the status of musical professionals. Thus, Fred Astaire is known primarily as a dancer-star of the movies, Ginger Rogers as a movie star who danced with Astaire. Further, female performers are often positioned as images whose skill in these areas must be manufactured by technological sleights of hand: for example, there is no male equivalent for Marni Nixon."[13]

Rita Hayworth being given an award in 1942 by the Associated Dancing Teachers of Southern California for "advancing the cause of both North and South American dancing," notably in *You Were Never Lovelier,* then in release. Photo by Don English. Collection of the author.

Wexman's last remark is not exactly true, for there were several male singers whose voices were dubbed in whole or in part during the musical's heyday (Gene Kelly in *Cover Girl* was one of them; Larry Parks in *Down to Earth,* as discussed further below, was another). But this issue is not what I want to address here. Rather, my point is that women performers in Hollywood films could *also* do all the things we so routinely ascribe to an Astaire or a Kelly (Eleanor Powell is another major underacknowledged figure). And not considering these women and their productive labor does a serious disservice to them, to us, and to their contemporary audiences ("productive labor" is Wexman's term; she claims that for women "except in rare instances like the backstage musicals of the 1930s, [singing and dancing] do not appear to involve any activity that the audience could construe as work").[14]

Nor do I want to deny the importance of the work of those scholars who are now engaged in the important task of interrogating the presence of exhibitionist males in the musical as a film genre.[15] But the fact remains that surprisingly little attention has been paid to how dancing women, in particular, contributed to a destabilization of the presumed gender divisions of classical Hollywood cinema, how their representation interacted with other ideologies of gender and sexuality in the postwar era, and how their abilities and performances are both constrained by and struggling against what Judith Mayne calls the "dominant visual and narrative momentum of the classical cinema."[16] Steven Cohan suggests that the film musicals of Astaire and Kelly "imagined an alternative style of masculinity, one grounded in spectacle and spectatorship," yet only in a footnote does he mark the potential for certain female stars, such as Judy Garland and swimmer Esther Williams, to "transform the showgirl basis" of the musical into "something quite different."[17] That difference is in fact quite widespread throughout musicals as a genre (and some nonmusicals as well). Once one begins to recognize this, the whole "showgirl basis" of the musical and musical performance, as an academic construct, can be called into question.

The continual defining of Hollywood's performing women in academic film scholarship as passive and fetishized showgirls can be traced to the "device of the showgirl" described in Laura Mulvey's classic "Visual Pleasure and Narrative Cinema" (1975).[18] Mulvey's psychoanalytic and deterministic model of spectatorship has been criticized over the years on a number of grounds—mostly relating to the model's neglect of other components of identity politics such as race and ethnicity, class, and sexual orientation, and the passivity it assigns to the female spectator—and I am not going to tread what is now well-worn ground. Rather, my engagement with Mulvey's work centers on breaking apart and questioning the definition of the showgirl herself, or rather itself. Whatever else has fallen away from Mulvey's model, the device of the showgirl has been left standing as a unitary cinematic strategy that de facto objectifies women— whether strippers or ballet dancers—and renders them passive, beautiful, and reassuring objects of the male gaze.[19] Indeed, I have found very few studies that so much as question what a showgirl might be, what it is that showgirls do, or why one showgirl should always be like another.

Rita Hayworth is, on the surface, very easily assimilable into both the heterosexist narratives of her films and binary models of film spectatorship in which spectacle—the locus of all showgirls—is aligned with passivity and objectivity. But as I will show, Hayworth also was engaged in transforming the showgirl basis of the musical into something quite different: in her musicals and musical numbers Hayworth's performances *also* can be described perfectly using the sorts of laudatory, transcendental, inspirational language with which Astaire and Kelly are so frequently characterized. Hayworth's physical competence as a dancer—the demonstrated ability to employ her talented, trained, and disciplined body in the performance and, equally important, enjoyment of difficult and expressive physical feats—complicates almost all of our assumptions about classical Hollywood cinema's routine ordering of the visual world along the lines of sexual difference. What Judith Mayne finds fascinating about Marlene Dietrich is, then, no less true of Rita Hayworth and other of her performing sisters: they are both "contained by patriarchal representation and resistant to it," producing again a "both/and" that constitutes the "very possibility of a feminist reading of performance." [20]

Because I am interested in how we have come to accept male performers' subjectivity in the musical and the musical number while denying this potential for women performers, I first lay out several influential examples of the ways that film scholars have analyzed women's music and dance performance in Hollywood cinema. Then I suggest some of the ways that dance scholars would theorize such performances differently and employ this theorizing in my own analysis of the multiple discourses of women's labor and performance in Hayworth's 1947 star vehicle *Down to Earth*. These discourses are both part of the film's narrative and strategies of its own self-reflexivity as a backstage musical featuring several shows-within-the-film. Again, I want to argue both for the importance of the disordering potentials of the women's musical as a subgenre that deserves serious attention and for the usefulness of an interdisciplinary approach to theorizing performance for feminist film scholarship more broadly.

Rethinking the Showgirl

One of the most frequently reprinted and cited of the few feminist studies of women in musicals is Maureen Turim's 1979 article (revised 1991) about *Gentlemen Prefer Blondes* (Howard Hawks, 1953).[21] Turim mentions that *Gentlemen Prefer Blondes* is a musical and that its stars, Marilyn Monroe and Jane Russell, perform in musical numbers, but she never discusses music and dance except as the type of "generic" spectacle defined by Mulvey—that represented by showgirls who, through their fetishization as erotic spectacle, play to and signify male desire.[22] Lucie Arbuthnot and Gail Seneca's 1982 piece about *Gentlemen Prefer Blondes,* on the other hand, suggests the possibility that the erotic spectacle might have been addressed to, or found responses in, female spectators as well as male.[23] Yet Arbuthnot and Seneca also seem scarcely to notice that the film's spectacle is *musical* spectacle. Neither Turim nor Arbuthnot and Seneca refer to performance style or mode of address, music, or choreography, in other words—all of the things that set the musical number off from other types of spectacle, as well as from the film's narrative. And without an acknowledgment that there *is dancing* taking place in *Gentlemen Prefer Blondes,* then, of course, there can be no discussion of how the dance functions.

Nevertheless, what all three of these writers admire about *Gentlemen Prefer Blondes* seems to derive largely from what Turim calls, in a later addendum to her piece, the "appeal of the two women performing movements in rhythmic coordination," an appeal that seems to puzzle Turim, given that she finds the film ideologically abhorrent otherwise.[24] "How do we understand," Turim asks, "the fascination of . . . this dancing team?" One obstacle to such an understanding is the way the female body is defined as an object in feminist film theory itself. As Turim writes, "The female body is not only a sex object, but also an object of exchange; its value can be sold (prostitution) or it can be incorporated into another commodity which then can be sold (the film)." Put another way, the female body, even the dancing female body, is only a sex object *or* an object of exchange in classical Hollywood cinema (this is one of the best-known axioms of feminist film theory). Woman as spectacle represents and reinscribes sexual difference, functioning as a component part in one of the mechanisms of defense (fetishization) generated by the cinematic apparatus to defuse the threat of sexual difference (castration) that women represent to men in patriarchy.[25]

I am hardly the first to argue with this theoretical paradigm or to point out that it makes women interchangeable such that Rita Hayworth would fill the same psychic function as any other female performer, from Marilyn Monroe to Lena Horne to Joan Crawford, in any film's diegesis. More significant to my project is the inattention paid in this paradigm to the material basis of the Hollywood musical, the fact that, as Richard Dyer put it in 1977, the musical's performing "work force" is in a "better position to determine the form of its product than are, say, secretaries or car workers."[26] There is already, and arguably always has been, an "implicit struggle" within professional entertainment itself because of the important roles it grants to "structurally subordinate groups in society—women, blacks, gays." Despite this, many film scholars remain, even today, less than comfortable studying female performers in classical Hollywood cinema as *professional* performers, as talented women, particularly if they are dancers.

This is not to say that some scholars have not made tentative moves toward studying women in the musical on levels other than the structural, but their work has not been as influential as it might have been. Robin Wood, in his 1975 article on the MGM musical *Silk Stockings* (Rouben Mamoulian, 1957), notes how musical numbers can transcend their "local ideological function" in the diegesis.[27] The solo dances of Cyd Charisse are motivated narratively and even ideologically to produce an "image of woman-as-object," for example, but although the "invention" of Charisse's solo is all "almost entirely 'within the ideology'" (it depicts a woman changing from the drab gray body coverings of Soviet communism into the silk and satin of Hollywood-Parisian consumer culture), ideology cannot account for its effects. Wood concludes that there may be "certain fundamental drives and needs that are not ideological but universal—drives which certain ideologies can suppress but which no ideology creates—and that such things as freedom of expression, delight in bodily movement, instinctual spontaneity, are among them." Ideology may help to determine "the forms in which the drives find embodiment, but it can't account for the drives themselves."

In a later introduction to Wood's piece Rick Altman also speaks of the "supplementary nature of dance," how dance and its "very components (rhythm, movement, grace, rapport) carry a message of their own which often seems to rise above the narrative aspects of a film," and suggests that Wood's argument is "one which deserves to be employed more widely in analysis of the musical."[28] Yet fifteen years after the appearance of Wood's and Altman's (much less Dyer's) remarks, Angela McRobbie noted that scholars continued to be "negligent" of dance in cultural studies, and this despite the "extremely strong, almost symbiotic relationship" that dance is known to have with its audiences, particularly girls and young women.[29] Because dance carries within it a "mysterious transformative power," McRobbie states, it can create fantasies of change, escape, and achievement for girls and women. Although McRobbie notes that this power depends on "holding at bay" other issues of family relationships and sexual success, she nevertheless concludes that dance allows the female body to speak "at least . . . in a register of its own choice."

Jeanine Basinger arrived at similar conclusions in her 1993 book *A Woman's View: How Hollywood Spoke to Women, 1930–1960*, in her discussion of the "contradictory" situation of Rita Hayworth in *Cover Girl*.[30] Through glamour and her dancing talent the character Hayworth plays, Rusty,

Ad for Hayworth and Gene Kelly in *Cover Girl* that ran in numerous magazines in color in 1944. Copyright 1943 by Columbia Pictures Corp.

becomes a star, but Rusty then is told that she can never be happy without the love of a poor man (played by Gene Kelly). Basinger also compares the "passive," static posing models of the film's final number ("The Girl on the Magazine Cover") with Hayworth's participation in it, which is "the total opposite. She is a dancing, whirling, twirling, active, and alive force . . . running down from above in a dancing attack, smiling, laughing, with young men dancing out to meet her. Hayworth, in other words, is no stationary cover girl. She is a living, breathing talent. She is also free and unleashed, in control of her dance, the center of the universe." This contradiction, Basinger believes, is the *real* message of *Cover Girl,* and thus it is more "open" as a text than its story line alone suggests.[31]

That *Cover Girl* (which was written by Virginia Van Upp) is a canonical musical in film studies derives not from these contradictions, however, but because it is a Gene Kelly musical, significant for the way his "alter ego" number (in which he dances out an internal conflict with a superimposed mirror image of himself) presages Kelly's innovations in the integrated musicals he would make later at the Freed unit at MGM (*The Pirate, An American in Paris* [Vincente Minnelli, 1951], *Singin' in the Rain* [Stanley Donen/Gene Kelly, 1952]).[32] *Cover Girl* is also canonical because it has an easily decipherable male-female dual-focus structure, which Rick Altman suggests characterizes the musical genre as a whole.[33] *Cover Girl* is both generically typical, in other words, *and* exceptional because of Kelly's extraordinary implementation of the genre's requirements. Basinger's analysis is unusual, therefore, not only because it focuses on Hayworth rather than Kelly, or even on the contradictory nature of the film's message, but because she makes a distinction between "posing" and "dancing," between being passive and being active, in the same structural situation, the musical number.

I, too, believe in Basinger's contradictions and in what McRobbie and Wood call the "transcendent" and "transformative" potential of dance (and, I will argue, of the music that so often drives it, of the singing that so often precedes it), even when that dance takes place in a Hollywood film. I, too, believe that dance may allow the female body to speak in a register of its own choice and that we need to examine more closely both how and what (as well as when) even the preserved or recorded body is speaking. But I am less inclined to grant dance transcendent or transformative power, as such, out of the historical contexts of its production or to make agency a condition or attribute of all dance; I do not believe that all dancing everywhere in film means the same thing. Rather than make dance into another blanket structure like the device of the showgirl that affects the meaning of the female image in film in some occult or automatic or automatically transgressive way, I am interested more in how music and dance performance in particular films at particular times affects that image in particular ways.

In order to construct a methodology with which to investigate women's difference from each other rather than their functional equivalence in postwar Hollywood films (and the power of dance and, by extension, music to instantiate these differences), I have turned to dance scholarship itself. This scholarship suggests useful and compelling ways for understanding the "encounter between bodies and some of the discursive and institutional frameworks," in Susan Leigh Foster's words, "that touched them, operated on and through them, in different ways."[34] Yet much of the power of the cinematic musical number (which is where most meaningful dancing occurs in Hollywood films) depends on particular features, devices, and techniques that are conventional only to film as a medium and are not components of live theatrical performance, so these have to be explored briefly as well in order to provide a new and experimental "discursive and institutional" framework for the final analysis of *Down to Earth*.

Disrupting Meanings, Reversing Hierarchies

None of the claims made by Wood, McRobbie, Altman, Basinger, et al. about the mediating or transformative potentials of dance would be news to dancers and dance theorists because they have long known and argued that, in Ann Cooper Albright's words, dance performances are always sites of "complex negotiations between somatic experience and cultural representation—between the body and identity." [35] Even when initial "recognition" of a dancer occurs according to normative visual categories based on gender, race, age, and the like, these visual categories, Albright states, can be "disrupted by the kinesthetic meanings embedded in the dancing itself." Sondra Horton Fraleigh writes of the dancing body using several of the same terms that Maureen Turim employs in her discussion of *Gentlemen Prefer Blondes* but arrives at entirely different conclusions: "The body is not the instrument of dance; it is the subject of dance. The body cannot be an instrument, because it is not an object as other instruments are. Even when it is objectified in dance, it retains its subjectivity." [36] Historically, according to Judith Lynne Hanna, women use and have used dance in this way because it enables and allows them to be "agent rather than object." [37] Philosopher Francis Sparshott notes that dance always embodies the possibility of transformation: "in whatever mode of dance, . . . however quotidian or even vestigial, to stand forth as a dancer or to enter the dance is to undertake what amounts to a marked change in one's way of being." [38] Joseph Margolis claims, finally, that dancers use their "personally and culturally idiosyncratic selves as the very medium of their art—*not* steps, movements, positions, or styles primarily focused on denotative and symbolic import." [39]

Moreover, for the self to be expressive in dance does not require that the self be an essential or unified self; dance theorists too know that the self is always fractured or partial or divided. Indeed, the potential power of dance as an art form is that it draws on multiple aspects of the self, transforming them through performance into a comment on the nature(s) of one's own felt identity. Ramsey Burt writes of the "visceral response" he often feels while watching dance, an "imaginative sympathy [that] comes from a recognition of commonality—of what I as an embodied spectator have in common with the dancing body—and it not only draws on my experience but adds to it." [40] Just as we cannot necessarily see the organs inside our bodies but accept that they exist because of the evidence that they work, so can dance and its ability to produce a "recognition of commonality" function as evidence of the existence of a potentially unified self that helps to make up the "historically contingent" meaning of a particular dance.[41]

The Rita Hayworth I recognize in films is so often a dancing, sweating, and moving body, whose training as a dancer was obviously extensive. She was adept at many Latin dancing styles, of course, but from my observations she seems especially to enjoy performing difficult and complex rhythm tap and jitterbug-style routines and is as competent at ballet-based lyrical styles as many other stars (like Eleanor Powell) whose dancing skills are even more significant elements of their star images. Hayworth's dancing line is fluid and graceful, especially from the "legs up," as one of her dancing colleagues at Columbia described it to me.[42] She has extraordinary range of motion in her neck and head, spine, shoulders, and arms—she easily accomplishes the hip and shoulder isolations required by Latin dance styles—and her long hands and fingers are fully integrated into the gestures of her upper torso. Because her hips are relatively narrow and her legs naturally parallel rather than turned out from the hips (she is somewhat pigeon-toed and her feet long but with a relatively flat arch), her movement range in balletic styles that require the free and open extension of fully stretched legs and feet is more limited but only in comparison to the extremes of turnout and extension expected of theatrical dancers, even musical-comedy dancers, today.[43] As is the case with virtually all film dancers, some performances are shot with more care than others, in some numbers she seems more confident than in others, sometimes she is costumed in ways that inhibit her ability to move (dancing in high heels and very tight skirts is especially difficult). I pay more attention to these issues as they relate to specific numbers below and especially in the next two chapters, but as a rule Rita Hayworth's performances, alone and as part of a couple or a group, are always interesting, often dazzlingly so, their appeal deriving from the way she embodies and performs her talent, hard work, skill, energy, and pleasure.[44] Tracking Hayworth's "kinesthetic history," as Jane Desmond calls it, leads in "two directions simultaneously": toward the ways in which Hayworth expresses her own felt subjectivity and how she is repressed by the material and ideological conditions under which her performing takes place.[45]

In short, clearly any number of women were always more, even in Hollywood films, than "glamorized female forms" who only play to and signify male desire.[46] The female body can also be an energized body; a dancer like Rita Hayworth (or Ginger Rogers, Josephine Baker, Eleanor Powell, Cyd Charisse) can also make us want to dance, and expressing her joy she, too, can make us joyous in turn. The theoretical "mushiness," to use Sparshott's term, of dance (and music) is daunting (because neither dance nor music can be deconstructed usefully into any formative substance or raw material).[47] But this mushiness should not obviate attempts to elucidate the ways that dance and music complicate the assumed clear meanings of women in classical Hollywood cinema. If we widen our field of inquiry to include music and dance as complex forms of communication, expression, and transformation, we can also address associated issues—not only the absence of women from the film musical canon but how to augment the dominant structuralist models of the Hollywood musical with a historicized understanding of variables such as technical competence in performance, costuming and its effect on female deportment (and when and by what standards female deportment could be considered threatening or transgressive), and the interrelation between filmic techniques and mise-en-scène and how we are given access to music and dance.

Sound Identifications

Paradoxically, a primary issue of relevance to a feminist valuation of the Hollywood musical is a characteristic generic feature, one that Rick Altman claims is exclusive to the musical as a film genre: the reversal of Hollywood's "normal" image-over-sound hierarchy.[48] In the musical number, if nowhere else in Hollywood films, image actually becomes subordinate to sound. This reversal is accomplished by an audio dissolve from the diegetic dialogue track to the music track, across an intermediary sound bridge usually of diegetic music. Diegetic music is made "supradiegetic"; it is brought forward through close miking and becomes, as Alan Williams puts it, suddenly "thoroughly noticed and felt."[49] Now the "active force in the production of meaning," the sound track invites people "to move in time to prerecorded music."[50] The invitation is often direct: total frontal address to the camera is also a common mode of the musical number.[51]

Altman considers the reversal of the image-over-sound hierarchy to be one of the identifying features of the film musical, for "only in the musical does the sound actually generate the movement within the image."[52] Its significance to my argument should be obvious: when the sound track drives the image track, rather than vice versa, our relation to the image is likely to undergo significant changes. Not only do the performer's movements, the shot lengths, the editing respond to musical phrasing, but so does the audience as well.[53]

Unfortunately, the mushiness of music scholarship is as great as that of dance. As Susan McClary writes, "By far the most difficult aspect of music to explain is its uncanny ability to make us experience our bodies in accordance with its gestures and rhythms. Yet this aspect is also what makes music so compelling. If music were not able thus to move us, the human race would not have bothered creating any of it for formalists to dissect, for musicologists to catalogue, or for sociologists to classify."[54] On the other hand, McClary states, even if it is "difficult to account definitively for how music precipitates such transformations, its political potency must be acknowledged. And any human discourse with this much influence not only warrants, but demands serious scrutiny."

One of the most important of music's "uncanny" properties is its ability to foster not only a sense of unity in the listener but of community between listener and performer. What is important about music's audience/performer communality is that it is not only amorphously emotional or ideological but constructed somatically, through rhythm and synchronization. The audience is synchronized, according to David Burrows, with the music and, metaphorically, with its source's activity.[55] This synchronization is not gendered in a way that precisely corresponds to the visual image, recalling Ann Cooper Albright's statements about the ongoing tension in dance performances between recognizable and normative visual categories and the often contradictory meanings produced by the dancing itself. Visually, we may sort out the world and fix it into discrete entities according to patriarchal psychic economies predicated on sexual difference. Sound and, even more powerfully, singing, on the other hand, can provide what Burrows calls "the great alternative" to this fixity.[56] Even Stephen Handel, a physicist, concludes his 1989 examination of the psychophysics of music with the following statement: "My sense is that I am part of my auditory world but that I am looking into my visual world. It is perhaps for this reason that music is so closely tied to religious experience. The rhythm and melody of music bonds the experience in ways that I am at a loss to explain."[57]

In opposition to speaking, singing, as music, can transform speech into a force that dissolves the separations among singer, audience, and object of discourse. As Mark Booth puts it in *The Experience of Songs*, identification with a singing voice, any singing voice that signifies as human (whether heard live or not), is "a remarkably strong force, sweeping us past the stage of aesthetic contemplation and even past the fantasy that the words are directed to us."[58] Writing about European and American songs of the nineteenth and twentieth centuries, Booth notes that "the more vigorously such songs declare lonely alienation, the better they function as rituals of solidarity." Of particular consequence to identity politics is the fact that audience identification with the singing voice (as "teller") can be "so compelling as not necessarily to respect even a difference of sex: a man who hears a woman sing a declaration of love generally identifies himself, I think, with declarer and not with beloved," Booth continues. In fact, we do not, Burrows claims, really sing *to* each other; rather, we sing *for* and are sung *by* each other.[59]

When a woman begins to sing, as well as dance, she can become a point of identification and community in addition to, or possibly instead of, a figure or object representing only sexual difference. In fact, Altman and Williams posit that dance in film may by definition involve the primacy of sound over image, for dance as I am considering it—that is, as a theatrical performing tradition—is usually a response to music and musical rhythms. Dance completes the process begun by music of enlivening the passive, still, inactive female image, through what Randy Martin calls the "dimensionalizing force" of the body in motion.[60] The musical number can be thought of in this sense as what Mulvey calls the "no-man's-land," a discursive regime that offers a clear challenge not only to the supremacy, the triumph, of narrative but to "pure" spectacle as well.[61]

Moreover, even if one leaves out the specific functions of music and dance in the Hollywood musical as *product,* as *process* the musical represents a form of discourse in which different modes of expression compete for attention. All Hollywood films are collaborative, but the musical is collaboration's limit-text.[62] The interaction of choreographer and performer, choreographer and director, performer and director, and all of these with music has always allowed for both the interplay of disparate voices and the possibility that normally marginalized voices might suddenly become dominant. Musical spectacle may represent not simply a different mode of performance from narrative but a competing form of discourse,[63] coming from those whom the narrative works otherwise to minimize or suppress.[64] Turning away for the moment from the salient issue of the musical's relationship to gay men and male camp discourse, obvious examples of this competition would include any classical musical that features nonwhite performers as specialties (Josephine Baker, the Nicholas Brothers, Lena Horne, and countless others) or a strong female performer of outstanding or idiosyncratic ability as a lead (Eleanor Powell, Ann Miller, Vera-Ellen, as well as Sonja Henie and Esther Williams). In the first case the romantic courtship model of the musical's narrative does not allow for the inclusion of nonwhite performers in what Rick Altman calls the "primary" male-female couple that "is the plot" of the classical Hollywood musical.[65] Thus, these performers are relegated to a sec-ondary pairing with another nonwhite performer and/or set off from the narrative by the special brackets of the musical number itself. As with the Nicholas Brothers in *Orchestra Wives* (Archie Mayo, 1942) or Gypsy Fla-menco dancer Carmen Amaya in *Follow the Boys* (Edward Sutherland, 1944),[66] the musical number happens to be the only place in the film in which the named performers appear, *and* it is a privileged location in which the performers exert some control over their self-presentation, as well as how we are given access to them through camera angles and shot lengths. In the second case, as in almost any of the films of virtuoso tap dancer Eleanor Powell, the musical numbers stick out so severely from the plot in both style and content, and have so little to do themselves with the formation of Altman's heterosexual couple, that they are obviously of an-other order of existence—the product of other wills, other creative vi-sions—than the conventional narratives in which they are embedded.[67]

Patricia Mellencamp suggested this long ago when she noted in 1977 that the musical as a genre is always marked by tension between the "mo-mentarily subversive fantasy" of the musical numbers and the narrative superstructure that brackets them. Mellencamp characterizes musical numbers as subversive because of their effects on the spectator, who is "awakened to the 'here and now' of performance and to the awareness that the events of the 'once upon a time' of the fictive narrative are not 'real.'" In the specific numbers Mellencamp describes, from *Singin' in the Rain*, Gene Kelly and Donald O'Connor "are *really* dancing, but Lock-wood and Brown [their characters] are only acting." Although in the end Mellencamp concludes that these effects are temporary because they are "ultimately contained by the process of narrativisation," I would argue that "really dancing" can never be fully recuperated by narrative closure because dance in film is subversive in a practical sense as well. Although a sort of dancelike movement can be insinuated into any film through edit-ing, camerawork, music, and so on, even the briefest shot of a dancer who is actually dancing can betray the essential duality, the distance between, narrative and spectacle. Dance cannot be a fictional treatment of itself in performance. To dance, one has to be able to do it, not merely to suggest it (as Albert Johnstone puts it, "The soaring leap is not *indicative* of a soaring leap, it *is* a soaring leap").[68] In film, then, dancing can make plain, in a way that no other performance style can so easily, the distance be-tween the real-life authority and complexity of a film's performers and the narratively defined and bounded fictional characters they play.

Annette Kuhn claims that performance "proposes a subject which is at

once both fixed in, and called into question by, this very distinction between assumed persona and authentic self. Performance, in other words,
poses the possibility of a mutable self, of a fluid subjectivity."[69] But when
combined with a performance mode that involves the body (which con-
notes fixity), Kuhn notes that a "distinctly contradictory quality" can be
conferred on the activity. Thus, even without an extended discussion of
the meanings of particular dances or dance styles, the conjunction of the
body and performance can at its simplest produce a "contradictory quality" that might highlight dance's capacity to bring forward features of
deportment or personality or attitude other than those simply classed as
feminine (or, indeed, masculine, white, upper-class, and so forth).[70] It is
not that we watch the real Hayworth or the real Eleanor Powell in dance
but that we watch a persona over which they have some creative control,
and it is this that gives women dancing in film their potential to enact a
fantasy of achievement with particularly potent effects on female viewers.[71]

Another factor in dance's marginality is its association with gay men,
both in its theatrical and its filmed forms.[72] There is persuasive evidence
that the association of dance with gay male choreographers, designers,
and performers led homophobic Hollywood directors consciously to dis-
sociate themselves from musicals generally or at least from the musical
numbers in their films.[73] Conversely, the recognition that men assume the
"to-be-looked-at-ness" of women in musical numbers—whether they are
Gene Kelly in khaki pants and black loafers, Fred Astaire in top hat and
tails, or the near-naked and oiled athletes whom Jane Russell ogles in
Gentlemen Prefer Blondes—has recently become the subject of considerable scholarly attention paid to the industrial, as well as spectatorial, camp
dimensions of the Hollywood musical.[74] The blurring in visual terms of
the representation of sexual difference, as well as the varieties of authorship implied by industrial considerations and production contexts, also
helps to make the musical number an arena in which gender politics are
negotiated in a less hierarchical fashion.[75]

For both women and men, then, dance represents the power to create
and lay claim to time and space through movement.[76] When filmed, the
dancing body often becomes not only a theatrically expressive body but a
working, sweating body—despite all the attempts by Hollywood to abol-
ish, through makeup, costuming, lighting, and editing, what James Naremore calls the "biological" or physically symptomatic basis of cinema re-
alism.[77] Gene Kelly exploits his muscularity and the effort it supports; the
"effortless grace" of Fred Astaire, on the other hand, owes much to his
slight physique and the loose and unrestrictive clothing he favors. Even

the fetishizing impulse represented by the scantily clad dancing girl can be subverted by the activity of dancing itself. Indeed, dance critics, if not film scholars, have frequently complained that one of the problems with transferring dance to the screen is that film destroys the illusion of ease in dance. In language that is strikingly apposite to that characteristically applied to the female image in film, Edwin Denby wrote in 1943 of the "discomfort" that films of female dancers "close-by" produced in film viewers: "We are embarrassed to see her work so hard."[78] Even though Denby does not explain *why* this is embarrassing, one might begin by thinking about the contradictory desires that underpin film labor. If films of men dancing "close-by" are not embarrassing, it is because we are accustomed to watching men work and to granting men the agency implied by that work. Women, on the other hand, although they work equally as hard in this area, commonly are supposed to disguise the terms of their labor precisely in order to render them more comfortably into spectacular but unthreatening objects. (On these terms alone it is possible that the spectacle of women performing the labor of dance—and conversely of men engaged in narcissistic displays in which their labor is hidden by costuming, for example—helps to explain the anecdotal displeasure generated in so many male spectators by film musicals over the years.)

In short, music and dance are complex forms of expression and systems of performance *even if* they are located in a Hollywood film. When women are dancers, their bodies are "not disciplined to the enunciation of a singular discourse," in Elizabeth Dempster's words, but instead are a "multi-vocal and potentially disruptive force which undermines the unity of phallocratic [language]."[79] As dancers, Hayworth and others like her can problematize through performance their films' basic narrative assertions—and those of Hollywood cinema generally—about what women can and cannot, should and should not, do.[80] For full demonstration of this I turn to *Down to Earth,* a fantasy film whose historical specificity (it began production in 1945 and was released in 1947) and plot make it valuable on a number of levels: it is overtly, as well as covertly, concerned with women's and men's roles, public and private, in postwar America; and its particular oddities of form and performance help us to understand why rigid valorization of structural models of the film musical, like the dual-focus model (described further below) that Rick Altman proposes in *The American Film Musical,* actually has blocked out many of the most interesting and useful (as well as popular) examples of Hollywood's own inabilities to reconcile the competing discourses of domesticity, labor, and identity.

A Women's Musical in a Man's World

Down to Earth is, again, what I have termed a women's musical: a musical that features women as the predominant performers in both the narrative and the musical numbers.[81] It also has an extremely elaborate fantasy plot in which Hayworth plays the muse Terpsichore, "the goddess of song and dance," an actual diegetic character who lives on Mount Parnassus, as well as "Kitty Pendleton," the character Terpsichore becomes on Earth in order to play Terpsichore (that is, "herself") in a Broadway show-within-the-film.

Terpsichore's plight in *Down to Earth* thus foregrounds textually what I have in previous chapters described in extratextual terms, namely, the way women are constrained by patriarchy to misrepresent themselves even when they are "authentically" competent, authentically talented, and authentically able to speak "in their own register." *Down to Earth* uses Rita Hayworth's dancing and performing abilities to validate itself as a musical, but in so doing it produces an irreconcilable split between saying that women are not capable or competent and showing that they are, in fact, both.

Down to Earth was an attempt by Columbia to capitalize on the success of the 1941 comic [nonmusical] fantasy *Here Comes Mr. Jordan* (also directed by Alexander Hall). Several characters, among them theatrical agent Max Corkle (James Gleason), "Messenger 7013" (Edward Everett Horton), and Mr. Jordan himself (Claude Rains in *Jordan,* replaced by Roland Culver), are carried over into *Down to Earth.* The first several minutes of *Down to Earth* review the earlier film through dialogue that takes place in Max Corkle's office. Max is being questioned by the police about a murder, and it is Max who provides the context for the film's complicated and very peculiar action.

From Max's office we dissolve into a dress rehearsal of a Broadway show, "Swinging the Muses," being produced by Danny Miller (Larry Parks). We see a musical number spoofing the nine muses, especially Terpsichore, which angers the "real" Terpsichore (Hayworth) up among the clouds on Mount Parnassus. Upset by the "cheap and vulgar" misrepresentation of herself and her eight sisters, Terpsichore enlists the aid of Mr. Jordan to get down to Earth so that she can correct Miller's misapprehensions and mistakes by appearing in the musical herself. Mr. Jordan has his own reasons for allowing Terpsichore to go down to Earth (she is to save Danny Miller's life, we find out later). Once on Earth and in the show, Terpsichore (as Kitty Pendleton) first simply explains to Danny why he should make the necessary changes, which has no effect. She then se-

Publicity "action" still taken on the set of *Down to Earth,* when Terpsichore "steps in the line to show them how a real goddess dances," according to the tag on the back. Although other photos from this number were published unaltered and the dress was not changed for the film itself, note that here the neckline of Hayworth's dress has been retouched to cover up more skin. The taped mark on the floor, however, which would *not* be visible on the screen, comically remains. (Carol Haney, a Jack Cole dancer and protégée, is visible on the right.) Photo by Ned Scott. Courtesy Ned Scott Archive.

duces Danny into changing his mind. But her "high-brow" version of the show flops in its out-of-town tryouts, so although Danny has fallen in love with Terpsichore, he tells her she must do the show his way ("hot") or she's fired. Furious, she walks out and demands of Mr. Jordan that he take her back to Mount Parnassus.

Mr. Jordan instead takes Terpsichore back in time to a scene in which Danny Miller signs over a suicide note to a gambler (George Macready, straight from Hayworth's previous film noir *Gilda,* cane and all) in exchange for financial backing for Danny's show. If the show is a flop, the backer can kill Danny, with Danny's suicide note absolving him of legal guilt. If the show is a success, the backer splits the profits. When Terpsichore sees how much the show "means" to Danny, she agrees to appear in it as a "hot goddess." She convinces Danny to take her back, and the show opens in New York and is a smash. (The backer not only does not get to murder Danny, but he is himself gunned down by his own gambling partner.) After the opening Mr. Jordan appears to take Terpsichore back to Mount Parnassus (her mission having been accomplished), but she now wants to stay on Earth and marry Danny. Mr. Jordan tells her this is not possible; she must return whence she came. Once there, however, Mr. Jordan takes the despondent Terpsichore into the future to show her that she and Danny will be reunited forever on Danny's death after a lifetime of producing Broadway hits. The film ends with Terpsichore dancing alone in the clouds.

Thirty of *Down to Earth*'s quite bizarre 101 minutes are devoted to musical numbers; this is a high ratio. The numbers, choreographed and directed by Jack Cole, are all carefully and completely integrated into the film's meaning but are bracketed separately as performance through the device of the show-within-a-show. The show-within-the-show is supposed to be *about* the goddess who is also performing *in* the show; this gives *Down to Earth* a doubled narrative that is more than merely self-reflexive.[82] Taken together, the numbers do not further the story but tell a different one—one in which women rather than men are in charge, figuratively and literally.

In the aforementioned first number nine brazen and powerfully muscled muses surround a lone male (Eddie, played by Marc Platt) dressed in military uniform and sing to him about all the creative geniuses—ranging from Socrates and Sigmund Freud to Benny Goodman and, oddly, Madame Tetrazzini—that their kisses have inspired. Hayworth first appears in the second number, a rehearsal for the show Terpsichore wants to "correct." To get into the show, she simply starts dancing with the other chorus girls, then sings one of the show's songs;[83] her abilities cause Danny and Eddie to cast her in the lead. In the third number Danny sings another song from the show to Terpsichore, but she joins in at the end and has "the last word"—"Oh what a flatterer you are!" One of the strangest song-and-dance numbers, "This Can't Be Legal," follows; it features Terpsichore with Danny and Eddie (again in unexplained military uniforms) as two men whom she wants to marry, both at the same time ("Why not?" she asks; that way she "would have a man for lovin' and a man to fix the oven, too").[84]

Then comes the centerpiece of the film, the Greek Ballet that Terpsich-

Rita Hayworth, in costume for "This Can't Be Legal," with Jack Cole on the set of *Down to Earth.* Courtesy Museum of Modern Art Stills Archive.

ore has created. It is one of the longest numbers in the film, and it is at once pretentious, overdecorated (as well as overpopulated), and stunning in its performance values. The female dancers all have washboard stomachs and the legs of athletes, and the male dancers are shaved, oiled, curled, and even more skimpily dressed than their female counterparts. Terpsichore is seen first in a seashell, letting golden sand ripple through her fingers to harp arpeggios. The ballet is meant to be a takeoff on the elaborate "exotic" ballets of Ted Shawn and Ruth St. Denis, with whom Jack Cole had studied and performed. It also satirizes the mythological themes then current in the works of modern concert choreographer Martha Graham.

The length and spectacular production values of the Greek Ballet give it the air of a finale, the culmination of the film's show-making as well as romance. But there has to be another finale that corrects Terpsichore's

A publicity still from the "swing" version of the Greek Ballet in *Down to Earth*. Although the tag reads "BEAUTY AND THE BALLET—Rita Hayworth, assisted by a corps de ballet, performs a classic Greek routine in Columbia's Technicolor musical, 'Down to Earth,'" this is obviously a more candid photo than the tag declares. It does, however, give a good idea of the Graham and Denishawn influence on the décor and costuming and a fine glimpse of the physical pulchritude of Jack Cole's dancers. Photo by Ned Scott. Courtesy Ned Scott Archive.

[corrected] version of the show. First there are glimpses of the "swing" version of the Greek Ballet, and then a new finale, called "People Have More Fun Than Anyone," takes place on a playground. This ends with a tableau featuring Terpsichore as the apex of a triangle formed with Eddie and Danny and her sister muses.

According to Altman's definition of the "musical corpus," the film musical's narrative work is to set up a dual focus and then reduce it to one—to the "lowest common denominator," marriage, "whereby two become one, adopt a single name, and are given the right to procreate." [85] The dual-focus narrative is Altman's model for virtually all musicals of the 1930s through the early 1950s, although he does admit that there may be certain kinds of musicals that do not privilege the romantic couple to such an extreme degree (he posits a separate "childhood initiation" subgenre for the numerous musicals starring children, for example). We might ex-

pect of *Down to Earth,* then, that it contain a primary male-female duality overlaying a secondary dichotomy; that it should have parallel and
repetitive scenes involving each member of a couple or couples engaged
in similar kinds of activities (singing, dancing); and that success in "plot
ventures" (as well as singing and dancing as performance) be tied to success in romance. The film's basic structure should be easy to see, for "the
whole point," Altman claims, "in overdetermining the musical's dualistic
structure is precisely to make sure that the spectator will sense the film's
overall patterns without analysis."

Certainly *Down to Earth* seems to contain a primary female/male duality (Terpsichore/Danny), and it would appear that the secondary dichotomy is high/low, manifest in two forms (heaven/earth, art/enter-
tainment). Yet *Down to Earth* consistently, almost compulsively, raises
issues that it cannot, indeed will not, resolve. If *Down to Earth* is a dual-
focus narrative, in other words, it is one whose parallel scenes, repetitions,
and redundancies often serve not to anchor meaning but to dislocate it.[86]

First, it is not clear that *Down to Earth* has a heterosexual plot as much
as a homosexual, or at least homosocial, one. That there can be any question is a result of the competence and agency of Terpsichore and the
passivity of Danny on the one hand, and the closeness (physical as well
as emotional) of Danny and Eddie on the other (Eddie used to "carry
Danny's books to school" and is continually being slapped on the ass
by Danny). The "erotic triangle," to use Eve Sedgwick's term, linking
Danny, Eddie, and Terpsichore is marked both in the musical numbers
and in the narrative. For example, since Terpsichore's attempts to *speak*
the truth about herself are repeatedly rejected, she uses Danny's attraction
to her to seduce him into doing things her way. The seduction of Danny
takes place under the disapproving eye of Eddie ("That guy never looked
at a dame before in his life," Eddie says bitterly), who actively tries (unsuccessfully) to intervene and stop it.

In fact, Danny spends much of the film functioning as an object of exchange between Eddie and Terpsichore; Danny is passive physically (the
one time he does dance, he dances with Eddie rather than Terpsichore) as
well as narratively. *Down to Earth*'s "erotic triangle," then, does not seem
to represent the homosocial bond that Sedgwick describes, which holds
men together by making women objects of exchange and desire between
them. Instead, in *Down to Earth* Eddie and Danny seem to be navigating,
none too successfully, the "invisible, carefully blurred, always-already-
crossed line" that separates the homosocial from the homosexual.[87]

The "erotic triangle" in *Singin' in the Rain,* by way of comparison,
more closely resembles that described by Sedgwick. Although Don (Gene

Lobby photo of director Alexander Hall (left) and the duo of Marc Platt and Larry Parks hovering above Hayworth on the finale set of *Down to Earth*. Platt has changed out of the military uniform with which he begins the number (paired with Parks). Hayworth appears to have begun taking off her probably painful shoes. Copyright 1947 by Columbia Pictures Corp.

Kelly) and Cosmo (Donald O'Connor) do not compete for Kathy (Debbie Reynolds), Cosmo is the one who delivers Kathy to Don and thus sanctions their heterosexual courtship and marriage. Cosmo dances as an equal with Don; they are more like each other than not. *Singin' in the Rain,* therefore, suggests (in contrast to the situation in *Down to Earth*) that Cosmo will end up *like* Don, with a suitable mate, as well as *with* Don, through homosocial bonding. Nevertheless, the case could be made that *Cover Girl, Singin' in the Rain, On the Town* (Stanley Donen/Gene Kelly, 1949), *It's Always Fair Weather* (Stanley Donen/Gene Kelly, 1955), and many other musicals are also problematized as heterosexual narratives by the prominence given to the male couple (or trio, in the case of *On the Town* and *It's Always Fair Weather*).

Altman's definition of the musical as a dual-focus heterosexual courtship narrative can be made to fit *Down to Earth,* then, but only if we ignore the complexity of its triangular relationship. If it is too much to say that Terpsichore is masculinized (she does wear fedoras and pin-striped suits) while Danny and Eddie are feminized (Eddie wears fewer clothes in the Greek Ballet than Terpsichore does), the "normal" conqueror-conquered/male-female relationship is, if not absent, at least obscured. Thus, although *Down to Earth* may possess the requisite semantic and syntactic elements of a typical fairy-tale musical, its strangeness is what makes it fascinating, not its structural similarity to other examples of the genre.

A second challenge to Altman's dual-focus model is the fact that repetitions and parallel scenes in *Down to Earth* seem intended specifically to confuse, not clarify. In the subgenre of the fairy-tale musical, Altman claims, sexual desire is often displaced onto a battle, which can take the form of anything from physical violence to bickering or simple competitiveness. But the battle between Terpsichore and Danny is between truth and falsehood, authenticity and misrepresentation. In one early scene, for example, Terpsichore tries to convince Danny that she is "the goddess of song and dance," who lives on Mount Parnassus. Danny tells her he "didn't land on his head when he was a kid" and demands to know who she is *really.* When she begins to answer, Danny interrupts her to tell her to "hit" a word a little more strongly; we then realize that they are rehearsing the musical within the musical. The slippage between the shows (the film proper and the show-within-the-show) becomes stronger when Terpsichore tries to tell Danny that her father was not Zeus, as Danny has written in his play, but Dionysus. She also tells Danny that he has got her "drinking ambrosia. Ambrosia's *food;* nectar is the drink." Here the slippage becomes close to vertiginous, for she is correct; she *has* to be correct (she *is* Terpsichore, she knows who her own father is, and ambrosia *is* food). But *Danny* has to be correct in the film.

Danny's angry response to the questioning of his authority ("I take you out of the chorus, give you the lead, and now you're trying to run the whole show") causes Max, on his way out of the theater with Eddie, to mutter "She musta went to college; you know how that'll ruin anybody." There are four such confrontations between Danny and Terpsichore, and Terpsichore's frustration and Max's comment provide the paradox on which both the male/female relationship and the musical-within-the-musical turn. If Terpsichore tells the truth, Danny must be lying. But Max's comment makes Terpsichore's insistence on telling the truth seem only the highbrow intellectual quibbling of a college girl (and her version of her story will flop). Danny's ignorance becomes the *real* truth—his version of the show is a success, and success is always "right" in the musical ("That wasn't too painful was it?" he will ask Terpsichore after she performs "his way").

This is where *Down to Earth* founders, as well as where it becomes most fascinating, depending on one's point of view (the teleological reasoning of William Vincent in dismissing *Tonight and Every Night,* for example, as "more interesting than good" is that it *"deliberately violates several canons of the genre"* [italics mine]).[88] For the show-within-the-show to succeed, Terpsichore must *agree* to misrepresent herself, something we have no reason to believe, given the film's focus on her and her abilities (and the fact that Rita Hayworth is the star), that she will do. Moreover, when Terpsichore's version of the show is unsuccessful—again, unsuccessful, the film says, not *as* art but *because* it is art—she first tries to return to Mount Parnassus rather than submit to Danny's authority to misrepresent her. In other backstage musicals countering art and entertainment—like *The Barkleys of Broadway* (Charles Walters, 1949) and *The Band Wagon* (Vincente Minnelli, 1953)—conflicts are resolved through what Altman calls the mystic marriage of performer and performance, in which the vitality of entertainment is blended with the beauty and prestige of high art.[89] But in *Down to Earth* there is no arena in which such mystic marriage can take place. For Terpsichore to return to the show and to Danny requires the divine intervention of Mr. Jordan, who only now reveals to her that Danny will be murdered if the show is not successful.

Faced with having Danny's death on her hands, Terpsichore agrees to save his show. It is scarcely unusual for a female protagonist in a Hollywood movie to conform to a masculine view of her. But here, because of the film's focus on Terpsichore, her apparent lack of romantic interest in Danny (even reviewers noted the "ambiguous continuity of the romance"), and the fact that such an extreme life-or-death situation is required to get her to change her mind, the fact that she does "give in" is made excessively obvious. When Terpsichore dances, sings, and acts "Danny's way," the show is a hit, and only then—*after* the final number—does a real romantic clinch occur, the only time in the film in which, to paraphrase Altman, success in plot ventures parallels success in romance.

One might reasonably conclude at this point in the film, or through its final number, that *Down to Earth* has labored to integrate Terpsichore from what Jane Feuer calls the "elitist world of high art" into the "populist world of musical theater."[90] But the romantic clinch lasts for all of thirty seconds—and there are another ten minutes of film left (but no more numbers), during which everything falls apart. For Terpsichore is not going to be allowed to remain part of that world, that "community." She has to become a goddess again.

That there is no mystic marriage between art and entertainment in *Down to Earth* (and no real marriage of any kind *on* Earth) simultaneously supports and undercuts Altman's claim that the musical aligns success in love with success in plot ventures. For in *Down to Earth* the very notion of success operates on several levels. The two finales provide the best examples. The Greek Ballet, which Terpsichore controls, is a flop diegetically ("Brother, if those longhairs go for it, you're *dead*," a stagehand tells Danny—and we know this is literally true). There are even two cuts to members of the audience falling asleep. But we also are shown the musical number itself—and it is the best number in the film.

No Hollywood musical—indeed no Hollywood film—devotes more than five minutes of screen time to boring its audience intentionally (and of course the Greek Ballet does not; there would be no announcement, as there is, in the film's opening credits of "Greek Ballet [with] special music by Mario Castelnuovo-Tedesco" if said ballet were meant to put the audience to sleep). Although the Greek Ballet is pretentious and overdone, as it is narratively supposed to be, it also was one of the most enthusiastically admired sequences in *Down to Earth* as a film—by reviewers, some of whom *also* thought that it fulfilled its diegetic purpose (to be *bad*) admirably.[91]

The Greek Ballet is the centerpiece of *Down to Earth* yet a flop (Danny calls it "*phony* art"). "People Have More Fun," the second finale, is a success, but it resolves nothing. Indeed, it actually returns the show to where it began—to what Danny wanted in the first place, before he got "sidetracked" by falling in love with Terpsichore. There is no reason why Terpsichore should succeed in the second show when she could not in the first. That is, there is no reason *other* than to endorse Danny's view of her as the correct one ("That wasn't too painful was it?"). The final number ends with "Terpsichore" (the character) waving good-bye to a wagonful of her sisters who have also come down to Earth and are now returning to Mount Parnassus with servicemen of their own. "Terpsichore" is going to stay on Earth with Danny, and Eddie.

In most musicals the finale is the culmination of both romantic and theatrical success, and the film ends. The finale of *Down to Earth*, however, is what Altman calls false cloture (although he actually claims false cloture does not occur in the film musical until *The Red Shoes* in 1948). That is, the film continues for another ten minutes, during which time Terpsichore learns that despite her desire to be a human being rather than a goddess, Danny can "no longer see her, no longer hear her." She will

live on Mount Parnassus until Danny dies. Then and only then will they
be united—and, presumably, be given "the right to procreate."

Jack Cole later called *Down to Earth* "a sort of *Gilda* in color," and
there are many parallels between *Gilda*'s film noir structure and that of
Down to Earth, one of which is the unconvincing tacked-on manner of
their resolution.[92] *Down to Earth* displays the same apparently unironic
assumption that it can have it both ways—that a romantic clinch and
narrative closure *are* all it takes to restore the proper gender hierar-
chies, even as the film has attested, for an hour and a half, to the fact of
an independent female subjectivity and competence. Turning a musical-
within-a-musical into a life-or-death proposition, one that requires Terpsichore's participation and her acquiescence in subscribing to Danny's
view of her, foregrounds the very myths and codes of romance and success in the musical genre. This is also easily illustrated by a comparison
of *Down to Earth*'s Greek Ballet, Terpsichore's show, the one that flops,
with Jane Feuer's analysis of the "show that lays an egg" in *The Band
Wagon.*

In her classic and influential essay "The Self-Reflexive Musical and the
Myth of Entertainment," Feuer states that the Myth of Entertainment
means, at its simplest, "that entertainment is shown as having greater
value than it actually does."[93] I believe that although *Down to Earth* is
marked by the myth's characteristic "oscillation between remythification
and demystification," it cannot manage all the component myths, particularly of spontaneity and integration, successfully. For example, in all of
its musical numbers the women are the protagonists, the primary performers. The women compete with men in many of the numbers, and
win. They prove, in short, that women can do anything a Hollywood musical requires of them. They can be spontaneous, breaking into perfect
song and dance at any opportunity. They can also labor and create art.
Their performance abilities integrate them into show business and into
the community that show business often stands in for in movie musicals.
The women solicit the attention of both diegetic audience and the film's
audience as well, through direct address to the camera. And all of the female performers, if not the males, are "blessed with the capacity to exude
presence even on film" which, as Altman puts it, they must if they are to
dissipate "the scandal of their celluloid existence."[94]

In Feuer's discussion of "the myth of spontaneity" she claims that Jef-
frey Cordova's early productions in *The Band Wagon* are unsuccessful because in them labor eclipses performance; we are never shown a completed number from the first Cordova show, only the calculation and
contrivance that goes into them.[95] *The Band Wagon,* Feuer writes, "sug-

gests that Cordova fails because he has been unable to render invisible the technology of production in order to achieve the effect of effortlessness by which all entertainment succeeds in winning its audience." But in *Down to Earth*, unlike *The Band Wagon*, we see no preparations for the unsuccessful show; instead, because of the way the numbers are placed in the narrative, we see the *successful* numbers, the ones that will eventually appear in the final, successful, show, along the way.

So, despite Terpsichore's dissatisfaction with the manner in which Danny presents her, she shows us, in performance, that she can do whatever Danny and Eddie give her to do. We are shown, in short, that she can do what musicals themselves valorize—namely, *entertain*. But unlike Danny or Eddie, Terpsichore can also create *art*, without excessive effort or labor. Thus, what Feuer claims about effort, art, and demystification in *The Band Wagon* does not hold up in *Down to Earth*. Feuer writes, "Although Cordova's *Oedipus* is said to be successful with audiences in the film, the extent to which it is demystified for us undercuts its status as a successful show." In *Down to Earth*, on the other hand, art is easy; thus, we might say of it, "Although the Greek Ballet is said to be *unsuccessful* with audiences in the film, the extent to which it is *mystified* for us undercuts its status as an *unsuccessful* show."

In *Down to Earth*, then, entertainment is something you do, not only something that is; entertainment is not only found or naturalized, but it is also created by calculation. Just as the visual representation of Hayworth's Americanness was successful despite its basis in fabrication, spontaneity is shown as successful when it is successfully *performed*, for example in Terpsichore's audition dance. It does not matter whether it is natural or, conversely, contrived. Most important, these points are made as a consequence of the power the film grants to its female star and her abilities: her sheer competence to do *anything* the film requires her to do—except marry Danny. Thus, in *Down to Earth*, whose plot has been said to resemble that of *The Band Wagon* because of the show-within-a-show in which art battles entertainment, the Myth of Entertainment is, at least partly, foregrounded as a myth.[96]

To adapt Bruce Babington and Peter Evans's characterization of *It's Always Fair Weather*, *Down to Earth* is a musical of "real prognostic interest," a "symptomatic work" that registers important historical changes in the genre.[97] For if my description and discussion of *Down to Earth* have proved anything incontrovertibly, it is how carefully the Myth of Entertainment needs to be managed for it to work and how strongly it relies not only on component myths of spontaneity, integration, and the audience but of gender. There is no reconciling of difference in *Down to Earth*;

Terpsichore gives up, not because that is how the romance will be resolved, not to put on a good show, but to save a man from being murdered. Mr. Jordan, showing Terpsichore herself in the future with the now-dead Danny, says that "in all these years he's never had a failure; there's a legend about him on Broadway; they say he was kissed by the muse." Either Danny has spent the past fifty years in celibacy, or he and Eddie finally consummated *their* relationship.[98]

If *Down to Earth* is not a typical musical as Altman and Feuer describe them, the points it makes through Hayworth's extreme competence in performance are typical of the women's musical. Extreme competence is itself a form of authorship, particularly if it occurs in the raison d'être of a genre, as in the musical numbers of a generic musical.

Steven Shaviro has written that the best thing about musicals—and, as I will suggest in the following chapters, significantly in some nonmusical films as well—is the "surplus enjoyment" they provide through their musical numbers. Musical numbers continually exceed "those functions of fantasy and ideological resolution that are highlighted in the most important recent discussions of the genre."[99] The musical number is not always used as the exterior manifestation of interior feelings; in *Down to Earth* and many other women's musicals featuring women playing "showgirls," the "feelings" performed are professional pride and ability. Although there may still be some kind of heterosexual romantic narrative closure, in other cases the narrative takes so obvious a backseat to the numbers that closure seems to serve mainly as a sign that the film is over. Unfortunately, a lack of unity between number and narrative is often used to criticize musicals, and it is true, as Arlene Croce writes, that many great film dance numbers, featuring what she calls "great performers in great routines," occur in films that you "wouldn't want to see again."[100] But it is in the musical numbers of *any* film that the greatest explicit critique of established assumptions—about gender, racial, and ethnic roles, for example—is likely to take place.

Down to Earth foregrounds the ways in which women can be made to subdue themselves and their talents, as well as some of the ways women can "speak," as singers and dancers, their competence and autonomy. If we can never determine exactly what aspect of herself Hayworth or any other musical woman presents through dance, we can know that we see not only an "image" but an act of will, of talent, of ability, of *choice:* one cannot be made to dance *well* and with pleasure.

Perhaps the clearest indication of the subversive pleasures and ideological contradictions provided by *Down to Earth* is how hard other texts about Hayworth worked to contain the "surplus enjoyment" the film provided. This, I believe, is why Winthrop Sargeant's 1947 *Life* article labored so intently to turn Hayworth from the "goddess of song and dance" into the "love goddess," whose primary features as he names them are physical beauty and passivity and whose defining power is the ability to inspire men to act for her.[101] So, too, does Orson Welles labor to reduce Hayworth to the flattened, evil, and passive image of Elsa Bannister in *The Lady from Shanghai,* as is explored in the next chapter. To deconstruct these myths is one of the most compelling reasons for examining musical women more closely, to find the terms with which to discuss their coupling of meticulous precision and "effortless" grace, their energy, and their "joyful expressiveness undaunted by repression."

4

I Told You
Not to Move—I Mean It!

CROSS-EXAMINING *GILDA*
AND *THE LADY FROM SHANGHAI*

The film noir *The Lady from Shanghai* (1948) is undoubtedly the Rita Hayworth film most frequently studied in the academy. As an Orson Welles film its authorship is the primary reason for its scholarly appeal. Few of Hayworth's other films were directed by men whom we would now consider auteurs (the exceptions being two early films in Hayworth's star career, Howard Hawks's *Only Angels Have Wings* [1939] and, perhaps, Rouben Mamoulian's *Blood and Sand* [1941]). Nevertheless, running closely behind *The Lady from Shanghai* in academic popularity is an auteurless Hayworth film noir, *Gilda* (Charles Vidor, 1946), which also has attracted no small amount of scholarly, especially feminist, attention.[1] These two films—or, more precisely, recent critical assessments of them— have probably done more to define Rita Hayworth's star image than any other of her some sixty movie vehicles. Although I am primarily interested in complicating rather than redefining Hayworth's image per se, in restoring to her image some of the variety of meaning and the inconsistency that always characterized it in its contemporary popular discourse, revisionary conclusions are more conspicuous in this chapter than in others because of the prominence of Orson Welles and his films in the cinema pantheon. My goals in this chapter are twofold: to sort through the ways that scholars have discussed *Gilda* in relationship to *The Lady from Shanghai* and to interrogate the assumption that, through the genius of Orson Welles and *The Lady from Shanghai*, we can see through and reveal Rita Hayworth (and by implication other women stars in Hollywood films) for what they "really" were.

As is well known, feminist theorizing about spectatorship and classical Hollywood cinema that began in the 1970s was not interested in the historical contexts of production and reception, and these exclusions helped to create what B. Ruby Rich calls a "monumental absence" of women on-screen as well as in the audience.[2] But it is not that structuralist or post-structuralist theorizing completely blocked out historical evidence; rather,

Putting the blame on Mame. Digital frame enlargements from the two versions of the song as performed by Hayworth in *Gilda* (above to Steven Geray). Copyright 1946 by Columbia Pictures Industries, Inc.

the evidence is virtually always unexamined or presented relatively un-problematically as fact. Laura Mulvey, to use an ur-example, employs an-ecdotal statements (the source for which she does not document) by di-rectors Budd Boetticher and Josef von Sternberg as evidence that women were consciously, as well as unconsciously, relegated to the role of narra-tive object rather than subject in classical Hollywood cinema.[3] Thus, if some feminist film scholars *have* subordinated historical analysis to theo-retical interpretation, as Patrice Petro claims,[4] the fact remains that there are many references to biography, to publicity stories, and to fan-magazine gossip permeating analyses even of the unconscious psychic processes undergirding spectatorship. If an anecdote uttered by or about a star or a director can be used to buttress the argument at hand, in other words, then history, of whatever kind and from whatever source, matters.

This presents a two-pronged challenge: feminist historical analysis, as opposed to theoretical interpretation, has until recently been relatively rare. But much theoretical interpretation is based on a quite small core of information composed of little more than reiteration of the legend and lore that Hollywood produces about itself. Certainly in the 1970s, and even the 1980s, the evidence employed to support much theorizing about the function of women in classical Hollywood cinema was inordinately sketchy and often represented the point of view of those higher up in the hierarchy of Hollywood as an institution. To say, then, that Orson Welles and *The Lady from Shanghai* have substantially (re)defined Rita Hayworth's image in the academy does not mean only that we know less about her than we might otherwise. It also means that her "monumental absence," like that of many other female performers, is partly configured by what scholars have left unspoken—for example, the subjectifying properties of her star labor, or of the music and dance discussed in the last chapter, or of problems in granting someone like Orson Welles the last word in any number of biographies and interviews. The danger, again, is that, in Adrienne Rich's well-known terms, what is unspoken can literally become unspeakable.[5]

Moreover, the ramifications of leaving so much unspoken exceed the reputation of a single film star. Much of the scholarly discourse produced about *Gilda* and *The Lady from Shanghai* seems to set out to illuminate how classical Hollywood cinema *characteristically* represents women, or woman, such that Rita Hayworth stands in for all female Hollywood stars. *The Lady from Shanghai* has received much more critical attention than *Gilda* and is now well established in the cinema firmament, but in the end neither it nor *Gilda* is recognized as *unusual* in terms of how the role of the female protagonist is written, directed, and performed. One goal of this discussion, then, is to participate in the ongoing adjustment of axiomatic assumptions about women's work in classical Hollywood cinema, through textual, contextual, and countertextual analysis—the production of evidence to the contrary of what continues to be promulgated as "truth."

Making Trouble

Although *The Lady from Shanghai* is an undeniably compelling film on many levels, I have derived more pleasure and satisfaction over the years from watching *Gilda* (and I have met many other women and men who have the same preference). The reason (for all of us) is that although *Gilda,* which costars Glenn Ford and George Macready, is eminently conventional in its use of filmic techniques, its vision of femininity and what women "are" is far more interesting than that of *The Lady from Shanghai.* Gilda is decent, funny, sexy, and gets away with almost everything; and although it is true that she seems about to marry the sullen and brutish Johnny (Ford) at the end, she at least gets to keep her robust good health, and we are not even made to watch a final clinch. Elsa Bannister, however, in *The Lady from Shanghai,* looks bad, acts bad, is bad, and as a consequence must be killed off in front of us. Indeed, Elsa is so conspicuously evil as to be boring, at least to practiced and cynical female spectators: she is a conventional element in an otherwise unconventional film. Given the cinematic values of *The Lady from Shanghai* (its deep-focus photography and unconventional framing and compositions in depth, its hard-edged lighting, its use of overlapping dialogue and multilayered sound), the conventionality of the female lead would not be worth scholarly attention except for the fact that so much has been made of the truth of its vision of Hayworth as a synthetic "Hollywood sex goddess," to use J. P. Telotte's term.[6] In my personal experience many film scholars (and, one may infer, the students they educate) know Hayworth primarily through *The Lady from Shanghai* and are unaware that she was also a dancer and musical performer. Even when they are also familiar with *Gilda* they do not necessarily know this in any profound way (never are they aware of the career of *Gilda*'s producer and unacknowledged screenwriter, Virginia Van Upp, or its uncredited choreographer Jack Cole).[7] The questions I am concerned to address further, therefore, are how, over time, the voluminous scholarship about *The Lady from Shanghai* has interacted with the much smaller body of work on *Gilda* and by what means the former has often seemed to succeed in blocking out the latter.

Richard Dyer's 1978 essay "Resistance through Charisma: Rita Hayworth and *Gilda*" is the most significant and insightful essay about Hayworth's performance in *Gilda* and its relationship to her persona as a musical star. But its conclusions, I have found, are seldom really discussed even in subsequent feminist essays either about *Gilda* or *The Lady from Shanghai,* and it is impossible not to wonder whether this absence serves a strategic purpose in some way.[8] Although Dyer deals with *The Lady from Shanghai* almost not at all, his concern with female charisma in *Gilda* begins to reveal how Welles was able to obviate or obscure the same charisma in *The Lady from Shanghai,* and Hayworth's lack of charisma in the second film in turn reifies the presumed passivity and emptiness of the female Hollywood star.

Hayworth, Glenn Ford, and Virginia Van Upp, apparently in the Columbia commissary, during the filming of *Gilda*. Collection of the author. Copyright 1946 by Columbia Pictures Corp.

Briefly, according to Dyer *Gilda* makes "trouble for itself" by, in essence, starring Rita Hayworth in the title role. After noting the salient characteristics of women generally in film noir—that noir women are "above all else unknowable," and thus their presence divides the world into the "unknown and unknowable (female)" and that which "is known (male)"—he concludes that *Gilda*'s "trouble" is the result of privileging our knowledge of the female over the male and of the casting of Rita Hayworth as a generic femme fatale. Although some elements of Rita Hayworth's image fit this generic profile, Dyer writes that others do not, and "this 'misfit' is sufficient to foreground the functions of the *femme fatale* in relation to the problematic adequacy of the hero." The elements that do not belong to the femme fatale are of most interest to Dyer. He ascribes particular importance to Hayworth's biography and her "known image" as a star of musicals, arguing that her association through extra-textual discourse with the "life concerns" of women (domesticity, motherhood), and her energy and "self-expression" through dance, give her a fundamental charisma before the film begins. Because Hayworth is already "constructed and experienced" as almost a "magic presence," this charisma helps to break apart *Gilda*'s noir structure.

A concomitant question that Dyer's conclusions should immediately have raised is why Hayworth's presence was not sufficient to make similar trouble for *The Lady from Shanghai*. How could Hayworth foreground, even transcend, the femme fatale in *Gilda* and fail to do the same barely twelve months later in *The Lady from Shanghai*? Was she not still the same "Rita Hayworth"? The answer is arguably no, she was not. The Hayworth of *Gilda* is actively eliminated from *The Lady from Shanghai* through a process that involves far more than the change in Hayworth's physical appearance (which Dyer calls an "implacable destruction") that her then-husband Welles orchestrated and carried out:[9] in the presence of some sixteen photographers, her famous red hair was cropped short and bleached to a platinum blonde (a stunt that Maurice Bessy would dub both "the execution of Rita Hayworth" and "the birth of the new Rita").[10]

The mutability of Hayworth's physical appearance was, as I have already indicated, a prominent element of her star image from the beginning. The interest attending this particular alteration seems to derive from the fact that there was no obvious reason for it. That is, Hayworth's box-office popularity was on the rise in 1946, and the association of her good looks with her ethnic background and the dancing talent it represented had become one of her most successful trademarks, a means of differentiating her from other performers. Thus, the switch to platinum blonde, to the status of "blonde bombshell" à la Jean Harlow or Lana Turner, immediately raises issues of what "the execution of Rita Hayworth" might denote in ethnic terms. We cannot do more, perhaps, than surmise about why Orson Welles felt he had to make Rita Hayworth completely "white." (In Sherwood King's *If I Die Before I Wake* [1938], the literary source of *The Lady from Shanghai*, Elsa Bannister in fact has "dark red hair" that hangs "loose and wild.")[11] But we can go further in our understanding of what the process denoted and why it worked so well in abolishing Hayworth's charisma onscreen. Welles was himself mistreated and misunderstood in Hollywood, but he will not drop out of the cinematic firmament if we begin to examine more precisely the ideological basis of Welles's reputation—to address the famous Welles misogyny in light of whom it was most likely to affect.

Perhaps because of Welles's marginal status within the classical Hollywood system, feminist scholars have scarcely addressed this issue. E. Ann Kaplan, Lucy Fischer, and others have written about *The Lady from Shanghai* as a male-centered discourse that explores the menacing nature of female sexuality and desire (in terms of the Oedipal journey, or the myth of the Sphinx),[12] but none questions or even mentions the historical or political basis on which the film's reputation rests or its quite explicit relationship to *Gilda*.

Smoking Guns

That Columbia intended us to associate *Gilda* and *The Lady from Shanghai* is made clear by the pressbook the studio released with *The Lady from Shanghai,* in which *Gilda*'s success is invoked over and over again,[13] despite the fact that the later film's release was postponed for some fifteen months because Harry Cohn (the anecdote runs) hated what Welles did to Hayworth in it. The two films also share much of their production and postproduction personnel (assistant director, editor, makeup men, hairdressers, musical director, songwriters, among others). Within *The Lady from Shanghai*'s formal structures and diegesis *Gilda* as a referent is also quite apparent. *The Lady from Shanghai* uses the male protagonist's voiceover to narrate the action in flashback, positions a lone female between two men,[14] utilizes South American locales, and features one of the songs from *Gilda* as background music. Yet even as these sorts of easy similarities become apparent—and there are other, slyer ones—*The Lady from Shanghai* turns them on their heads. That is, it brings *Gilda* to mind in order to taint the audience's memory of it, to demolish its appeal. Since the sort of "trouble" *Gilda* makes for itself renders its heroine enormously appealing and strong, in part by drawing on the audience's presumed awareness of Hayworth's musical/intertextual and extratextual star image, this empathy with and understanding of both the female protagonist and the star who plays her is what *The Lady from Shanghai* must work to subvert.[15]

Although *Gilda* and *The Lady from Shanghai* both begin as flashbacks from the point of view of their male narrators, the omniscience of *Gilda*'s narrator, Johnny (Ford), is undercut by a number of what Dyer calls "moments of privileged access." During these moments we learn more about a character than the narrator has told us and usually more than the narrator can know. There are several sequences in which Gilda appears alone with a character named Uncle Pio (Steven Geray), whose function is that of a seer, a wise man of the people who, as Dyer notes, conventionally has to speak "the truth." Uncle Pio constantly calls Johnny a peasant but addresses Gilda as "little one" and is always solicitous toward her; and through Uncle Pio we learn that although Gilda is unhappy and frustrated in her love for Johnny (he had once walked out on her), she is not bad but instead fundamentally decent. When Gilda sings "Put the Blame on Mame" to Uncle Pio in the deserted casino at five o'clock in the morning, we are alone with her and her pain at being merely what she is, a woman, one of a sex always blamed when the world goes wrong.

Most important, Johnny's narrative about Gilda is often actively contradicted by the content of the scenes he describes. Thus, we know before Johnny does that Ballin (George Macready), Gilda's husband and Johnny's friend and boss, is evil and deviant and "thrives on hate" and that Gilda is afraid of him. As the film progresses, the disjunction between narration and diegetic content, or between what Johnny tells us and what we learn for ourselves, builds. Eventually Johnny's voice-over simply disappears, never to return.

In contrast to *Gilda* we learn very few things about Elsa Bannister in *The Lady from Shanghai* that Michael O'Hara (Welles) does not also know. His point of view drives the film from beginning to end. Indeed, we know as the film opens, in Central Park, at night, that the story is already over and done with, that O'Hara did lose his mind for a bit and is going to tell us about it, but the film comes almost full circle (or to San Francisco, at least) and ends with his narration returning us to daylight and sanity. Because the film allies Elsa with darkness, however, and reveals her first as a hard white beauty emerging from its depths, we are not likely to come to think of her as anything other than a stereotypical femme fatale of the sort made famous already by Barbara Stanwyck in *Double Indemnity* (Billy Wilder, 1944), Claire Trevor in *Murder, My Sweet* (Edward Dmytryk, 1944), and Lana Turner in *The Postman Always Rings Twice* (Tay Garnett, 1946).

Elsa confirms this by engaging O'Hara in what was by then standard terse B-movie double entendre. There is double entendre in *Gilda* too, but it usually seems to be played for laughs. Gilda at least is able to see the humor in the bizarre situations she gets herself into, and there is as well a wry acknowledgment on her part that she is often her own worst enemy. Gilda makes wisecracks, but Elsa obfuscates, speaking always epigrammatically, in tautologies or "Chinese" riddles. Elsa does utter an apparently anguished "Why would anybody want to live around us" at the South American picnic, sans O'Hara, but within seconds O'Hara appears and launches into the famous shark parable—about sharks who go mad at the sight of their own blood and devour each other. Since it is O'Hara who thus provides us with a motive for Elsa's anguish, it can hardly be said to be a privileged moment. O'Hara continually undermines or counters Elsa's statements with knowing, ironic ones of his own, revealing himself always to be fully aware of the situation he is in but choosing to go along with it anyway. By presenting himself as made foolish by love (in the same way, in fact, that Gilda is made foolish by her love for Johnny), O'Hara's self-deprecating narration comes across as artless. In contrast to *Gilda* the narration disguises the actual power that O'Hara holds in defining Elsa for us.

In previous chapters I have tended to downplay the significance of the power of the gaze as such, especially in relation to dance in film; but who looks at whom and when, as well as who talks about whom and when, can obviously fulfill important narrative functions because of the very conventionality of such structures, their relationship to our expectations about what these moments mean in any film. This is especially marked in the cinematic device of the full-face close-up and its attendant reverse shot(s) (when we see through the character's own eyes, more or less). Through this connection to the eyes, facial expression, and point of view, glamour-lit close-ups can also formally signal, as in the scene with Uncle Pio described above, Dyer's moments of privileged access. (Dyer notes that the close-ups in *Gilda* are, to an unusual extent, of people of both genders actively looking, even directly at the camera in the case of Gilda, *while* they are also being looked at.) The close-up can function as an integrating device in this sense, granting us access to what we think is a character's interior life and fostering our identification with his or her desires and motives. It should come as no surprise that the close-ups in *The Lady from Shanghai* seem meant to fulfill another function entirely.

Welles uses close-ups in many of his films as self-reflexive elements that draw attention to the process underlying their creation, through exaggeration or distortion of the normal conventions. Certainly the choker close-ups of a sweating and leering Grisby (Glenn Anders) show us more than we want to know. They are not only about Grisby but about how artificially other close-ups are constructed (this is *really* what people look like up close, Welles seems to be saying). On the other hand, the flat lighting and almost metallic surface sheen that Welles gives to Hayworth's skin and platinum hair in her close-ups may indeed comment on the artificiality of the physical construction of the genus Movie Star, but they also make Hayworth's face a mirror of Elsa Bannister's coldly asexual soul.[16]

Perhaps it was Harry Cohn who (according to Hollywood legend) insisted, apparently against Welles's wishes, that Welles interpolate close-ups of Hayworth and the other stars into *The Lady from Shanghai*. But choker close-ups are not unusual in Welles films, from *Citizen Kane* (1941) through *Touch of Evil* (1958), and certainly *The Lady from Shanghai* would not function so well without them. Welles may have had what Charles Higham thinks is an "ironical last laugh by making the close-ups of Rita Hayworth the most banal and emptily glossy things in the film,"[17] but even Welles could not eat his cake and have it too. That is, the very glossiness and flatness of what James Naremore also calls the "bad closeups of Rita Hayworth" function to make Hayworth's/Bannister's face, from the very first, a mask of the death we already know she represents.[18] The

Digital frame enlargements of the final fade-out on the polished platinum Elsa Bannister as she finishes singing "Please Don't Kiss Me" in *The Lady from Shanghai*. In the final few frames, as shown, her face goes completely slack and still. Copyright 1948 by Columbia Pictures Industries, Inc.

femme fatale is not revealed for what she is at the end, by the discovery that she can speak Chinese and has the "smoking gun" in her handbag; we know what she is from the very beginning *because* of how she looks and how inexorably she works to bend others to her wishes (obscurity of motivation notwithstanding).

The script of *The Lady from Shanghai* continually refers obliquely to "the fake passion," in Charles Higham's words, of Elsa Bannister, who appeals to Michael O'Hara "by making him feel she is sexually neglected (whereas in fact she is . . . sexually lifeless . . .)."[19] A "Glosso-Lusto" hair-oil commercial emanating from the ship's radio also insinuates that Elsa is a lifelessly cosmetic construction, and this is followed by a verbal seduction scene that is another reference to *Gilda*. Gilda is always asking for help getting undressed because she's "not very good with zippers," whereas Elsa Bannister constantly asks Michael O'Hara to help her put something *on*. Neither Gilda nor Elsa really needs such help; but whereas for Gilda such demands are a game, for Elsa they are tests of power. Elsa, in fact, seldom initiates action on her own; *physically* passive, she induces others to act for her.

This physical passivity leads us to the most important element in Welles's manipulation of Rita Hayworth's star image: namely, movement as a form of self-expression—an important element of Dyer's characterization of Gilda's charisma ("No other *femme fatale* dances")[20]—or, more precisely, the suppression of this type of movement. In contrast to the dynamic shot that introduces us to Gilda—Hayworth tossing back her hair—as well as her general physical exuberance and vitality, the lady from Shanghai seldom moves on her own. Elsa is moved or transported—by carriage, by thugs in the park, by car, by boat. She can shiver involuntarily, as when lighting a cigarette before luring O'Hara into a kiss, or strike calendar-girl poses wearing silly costumes and a blank face under rakish hats or doing swimsuit cheesecake. At least one of the two times we do see Elsa in active motion—running away in Acapulco, at night, first along the bay, and then along a colonnade in a border-town street—was apparently inserted by Harry Cohn and shot by a second unit at the Twentieth Century Fox ranch by arrangement with Darryl Zanuck.[21] Even Elsa's dives off of the rocks into the sea as Grisby leers through his telescope are also essentially static, the dives themselves poses in motion, movement with no real impulse other than a reaction to the forces of gravity. Gilda generates movement on her own or in response to music; Elsa, on the other hand, is actually lying flat on her back when she sings her single song.

In fact, the way Welles handles the notorious interpolated commercial song—also apparently included at Harry Cohn's insistence and written by the same pair who wrote the songs for *Gilda*—is a master stroke on many levels: Rita Hayworth is pinned down by the camera's lens like a paralyzed insect, her face in gigantic close-up, slowly mouthing the words of the song to no one in particular. She is a fantastically beautiful object, but this is constriction on a grand scale. As well, since Hayworth was seldom allowed to sing onscreen[22]—and Welles knew how uncomfortable she was about Cohn's insistence that her voice be dubbed—the whole scene seems to be a comment not on commercialism per se but on talent. Whether the intention was to damage Hayworth's reputation or merely to foreground the spurious basis of star worship itself, Welles here makes it seem as if Rita Hayworth herself is incapable of being anything but a surface to admire or desire.

In *Gilda* singing and songs work to make the female protagonist a communicating subject, but in *The Lady from Shanghai* the same activity serves mainly to emphasize her status as an object. Many scholars ignore the former possibility and write about musical interludes in nonmusical films as moments of spectacle, fetishization, and therefore stasis. (As already discussed, Laura Mulvey arrived at her formulation of what spectacle means in terms of sexual difference in Hollywood films partly through looking at the device of the showgirl in musical moments in nonmusical films.)[23] Several scholars writing about music's function in nonmusical films also have adopted this assumption.

Claudia Gorbman, for example, uses Hayworth in *Gilda* as an example of how "significant action" is deferred by the musical number because the narrative "freezes for the duration of the song."[24] A musical number of this sort may provide what Gorbman refers to as "pleasure," but when numbers performed by women are interjected into nonmusical films, she and others tend to dismiss them as moments during which nothing important happens or else as more or less purely fetishizing moments that thus "play to and signify male desire." But, in fact, significant action takes place in many musical numbers, *particularly* when the numbers are in nonmusical films, away from the expectation, set up by the musical's conventional structure, that they will regularly occur; the narrative rupture that musical numbers represent occurs more clearly as such in a nonmusical than in a musical film.

As the discussion of identification and singing in the previous chapter suggests, a woman singing even in a "genre of alienation" like film noir might also counter, if only temporarily, the narrative's drive to make her unknown and unknowable. Depending on whether the song is actually a musical number (in which the image-over-sound hierarchy is reversed and the sound is close-miked and brought forward to drive the image rather than vice versa), she might not at that moment represent only sexual difference that the narrative drives relentlessly to investigate, to control, to punish. Nor must she be only a spectacularized one-dimensional fetish, fascinating us across an irreducible distance. Instead, because she is singing, she can become an active communicating subject, the intervening "sounding air," as David Burrows calls it, "galvanized by the source of the sound into acting as a vibrant connective tissue."[25]

Yet as *The Lady from Shanghai* makes clear, the performer/audience unity and identification fostered by song can be nullified by the determined director. Welles flattens the singer with whom we would identify

into an almost motionless platinum surface. He also keeps cutting back
to narrative action and dialogue during the singing, which fades in and
out as a consequence (this is not, in other words, a musical number in
which music is given actual image-driving prominence). We may well
identify more with Elsa Bannister while she sings "Please Don't Kiss Me"
than at any other time in the film, but the narrative's intervention in the
song, as well as the extreme objectification and fetishization of its singer,
reinforces rather than overcomes her narratively inscribed inscrutability.
Illustrating both the potential power of song and the ease with which it
could be effectively obviated, *The Lady from Shanghai* is a more or less
standard example of how musical performance functions in film noir.[26]
There is one song only; it may draw us into temporary closer identification with the female protagonist, but we probably would not miss it if
it were gone.

Indeed, Elsa Bannister's humorlessness, stasis, and hard physical sheen
are barely affected by her participation in music; she remains an object,
physically and spiritually constituted by the platinum represented by the
color of her hair. Compared to Gilda, Elsa's demeanor and carriage are
strikingly contained. Elsa never hurries and seems to have no natural re-
flexes. She is completely still when O'Hara tells his shark story, completely
still when she finds a butler shot in her kitchen, barely responsive when
she is unexpectedly called to the witness stand to testify against her lover.
She is frozen even during the climactic shoot-out in the fun-house hall
of mirrors. Her face a blank mask, eyes unblinking, and ankles neatly together, Elsa shoots her husband to death and is shot in turn. Then and
only then does the pinup come physically to life, stumbling after O'Hara
to scream that she doesn't want to die. But, as André Bazin puts it, Welles
"let her die like a bitch on the floor . . . while he walked out indifferently,
eager to have things over and done with."[27]

No Other Femme Fatale Dances

Richard Dyer, with reference to Mulvey and her discussion of fetishism,
notes the importance of movement, especially dancing, to the charisma of
movie stars, particularly female stars. In marked contrast to *The Lady from
Shanghai* we *would* miss the musical numbers in *Gilda* because unlike the
song in *The Lady from Shanghai,* or in the majority of other films noirs,
the numbers in *Gilda* are real *musical numbers,* as Rick Altman, Alan
Williams, and other musical scholars have defined them.[28] And there are

more of them. Last, but far from least, two out of three of them are also danced.

This is where Hayworth becomes different from any other musical woman in film noir, and it points up the need for new conceptions of the role of singing and dancing in musical numbers in many nonmusical films.[29] Despite the persuasiveness of Dyer's analysis of the significance of Hayworth's musical persona to female charisma in *Gilda,* his insights have not been built on by other film scholars; indeed, they are rarely mentioned.[30] Kaja Silverman, for example, applying Mulvey's paradigm to the danced reprise to "Put the Blame on Mame," gets caught in the bind of trying to explain Gilda's resistance to masculine authority without reference to music or dance, since neither of course figures in that paradigm.

Silverman begins her discussion by describing Gilda's striptease as "ritual self-humiliation" and notes that it "relies on the equation of female subjectivity with spectacle, and male subjectivity with the look."[31] Yet she has to acknowledge that something is wrong with the theoretical model that this moment should fit. Silverman calls the number

> a classic example of what Mulvey calls the "fetishist" solution to the problem of female lack. However, it deviates from Mulvey's model in that the erotic overvaluation of Gilda's body (her arms, her face, her hair, the black sheath she wears, the necklace and gloves she tosses to the crowd) does not serve to conceal her castration, but to flaunt it. It also involves a rather noisy demonstration of female guilt, in that it is intended by Gilda to provide the final, irrefutable evidence of her promiscuity. Finally, that demonstration is not orchestrated by the male subject, but is "voluntarily" supplied by the female subject; Gilda not only engages in a self-incriminating striptease, but sings a song about the age-old evil of woman ("Put the Blame on Mame"). . . .
>
> The film thus superimposes the two rather contradictory strategies isolated by Mulvey as calculated to neutralize the male subject's castration anxieties.

As the "insufficient figure" of Gilda "loudly" and "voluntarily" admits her guilt, she implicates the male spectator—diegetic and film-audience—in her guilt as well and makes "transparent," Silverman says, the mechanisms patriarchy has built to keep her in her place. The number therefore represents "a point of female resistance within the very system which defines women as powerless and lacking."

But we are left with *how* to account for Gilda's power to do all that Silverman says she does: consign the spectator and the diegetic male subjects to masochism and passivity, while flaunting her own castration and powerlessness. After all, erotic overvaluation and self-incrimination run rampant in classical Hollywood cinema; presumably female resistance does not. Silverman claims that Gilda "exercises fascination precisely by virtue of those things she lacks—money, legal authority, power, the omnipotent and coercive gaze." Yet most women in classical Hollywood cinema suffer from the same lacks. If, as Silverman says elsewhere, film's female subject can be defined as "the mirror reflection not only of the male subject's castration, but of his specularity, exhibitionism, and narcissism," and "manifests so little resistance to [his] gaze that she often seems no more than an extension of it,"[32] how would one explain female resistance in *Gilda?*

I bring up Silverman's analysis not because the power of the "omnipotent and coercive gaze" retains supremacy as a theoretical tool but because of how difficult it *always* should have been for Silverman to account for Gilda's fascination in terms of what she lacks. Dyer's analysis makes sense because it acknowledges that what Gilda possesses, partly because of her incarnation by Rita Hayworth (the ability to sing and dance, to perform professionally, and, as a result, to lead another life than the one Johnny wants her to lead), makes her fascinating too. Because of her abilities Gilda is able to go off to Montevideo and get a job, to humiliate Johnny by performing a pseudostriptease in his nightclub. And as Gilda can from time to time escape Johnny's control, so do the musical numbers escape the "sadistic" course of narrative. Here we have a woman whose singing—dubbed or not—functions as a "ritual of solidarity"[33] and whose actions, for a space of time, are not directed by the narrative but by the music and her obvious pleasure, despite physical hindrances, in responding kinetically to it. (The same is true of *Gilda*'s other song-and-dance number, "Amado Mio.")[34]

"The fetish is stable, an object, an artefact," Mulvey writes.[35] But Hayworth in *Gilda* was never only a leg, a gown, a face, or hair; she was always a dancing human being whose three-dimensionality is presented to us kinetically as part of her star charisma and whose labor as a performer in the public sphere is foregrounded and meaningful and powerful as such. This does not mean that Rita Hayworth was not fetishizable (witness *The Lady from Shanghai* and its platinum pinup girl). One might note and object to Hayworth's physical constriction even in *Gilda*, the painfully tight clothes and excessively high heels that make it impossible

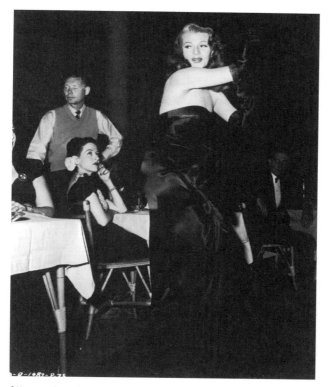

Lobby photo of Hayworth performing the song-and-dance version of "Put the Blame on Mame." Although this photo was part of *Gilda*'s official publicity campaign, I am struck both by the intent gaze of the seated woman on the left and the complete disinterest and closed eyes of the (obviously nondiegetic) man standing behind her. Copyright 1946 by Columbia Pictures Corp.

for her to move as freely and as openly as her comportment elsewhere shows us she can. But even in the face of material and narrative repression, the point remains that the fetishization of Hayworth had to work against a concomitant and continual reinvesting of her image, through music and dance, with the suggestion of the "other life" possible for the professional performer.

Equally important, as Marjorie Rosen points out, Gilda's sexuality "was a very physical one—without mystery or pretense . . . [and] for the first time a heroine seemed to say, 'This is my body. It's lovely and gives *me* pleasure. I rejoice in it just as you do.'"[36] *Gilda* as a film is often identified solely by the dance to "Put the Blame on Mame," and the image of Hayworth as Gilda almost always seems to be the image of Hayworth dancing. Although Mary Ann Doane, like Kaja Silverman, tortuously attempts to reinsert Gilda into the patriarchal system that is classical Hollywood cinema by asserting that Gilda's movements are "the 'moving' representation of stasis"[37]—the stasis generated by her objectification as spectacle, as well as by the sadism of narrative—the fact remains that this film fascinates because, rather than in spite, of its use of woman as spectacle. We would not give the auteurless *Gilda* the attention we do were it not for *both* performances of "Put the Blame on Mame"; but it is primarily through dance itself that Gilda makes transparent the mechanisms patriarchy has built to keep her in her place.

In a brief unpublished essay called "A Femme Fatale Communicates through Dance," dance scholar Svea Becker states that by her dancing "Gilda (and Rita Hayworth) escapes the confines of the noir formula which is defined by masculine rules, including physical mastery of the environment."[38] As an "act of freedom" dancing allows Gilda physically to assert herself and thus to overcome the "passive feminine stereotype." Because Jack Cole's "Mame" is a dance "relying on feelings and emotions" rather than recognizable dance steps, Becker believes that it draws more heavily on modern dance than on "show dancing" (she compares it to dances created by Isadora Duncan, Doris Humphrey, or Martha Graham) and is directly tied to personal expression. Becker also tries to demonstrate through Laban movement analysis that Gilda's movement patterns of scattering and gathering and the energy "radiating outward from her center" actually indicate that she cannot be a "Spider Woman." Despite the obvious constrictions imposed on her by costume and space, Gilda's approach to the movement of the dance indicates that she has "access to physical desire," that she is dynamic and independent, and that she is an "open, warm, generous, loving person desperate to communicate" rather than a manipulative femme fatale. When Gilda dances, Becker writes, "we realize that Gilda is not a sexual object, but a real person." Thus, "Put the Blame on Mame" is not so much a striptease as a revelation of "inner emotion."

Although the precise enumeration and qualification of movement types, shapes, and impulses may or may not indicate that Gilda is by definition not a Spider Woman (Becker is not clear about whether she is discussing Hayworth's dancing or Gilda's or how the two interact, nor does she refer to how costume or camerawork and editing control our access to the dance and its movements), Becker's basic conclusions make more sense in the end than Silverman's. Rather than a loud and voluntary admission of guilt, or a superimposing of two contradictory strategies by which the castration anxieties of male subjects are neutralized, or a flaunting of castration rather than a concealing of it, the choreographed move-

Well-known lobby photo of Orson Welles and Hayworth from *The Lady from Shanghai*. Copyright 1948 by Columbia Pictures, Inc.

ments and performance style of "Put the Blame on Mame" actually contain within them the source of Gilda's unusual nature as a noir heroine. Indeed, it is *out* of the dance situation, as Becker notes, that Gilda is "not free to defend her point of view." The contrast between the powerful, open, and communicating spectacular Gilda and the worked-upon and managed narrative Gilda serves in the end to foreground the impossible bind in which Gilda, Hayworth, and any number of other postwar women all too often found themselves.

I am sure that Rita Hayworth was always ambivalent about her life as a dancer because of its relation to her childhood and her abusive father, but she was also always fiercely proud of her ability and her training.[39] What Welles took away from Rita Hayworth in *The Lady from Shanghai* was not so much an illusion but an important kind of reality, her *work* as well as her innate talent: an extraordinary ability to move, to add an extra dimension to the flat surface of the screen. The "new Rita" that is born from Bessy's "execution of Rita Hayworth" is in effect an image emptied of content, of background, of tension. Rather than making "trouble for itself," *The Lady from Shanghai* banishes the most significant source of the trouble—the resonance, contradictions, and ambiguity of Hayworth's star image. When Michael O'Hara turns a gun on Elsa Bannister in the Chinese theater and says, "I told you not to move—I mean it!" the line signifies beyond its function in the film's narrative. Some scholars have written that women could not identify with Hayworth as Elsa Bannister because Elsa was a "cold-blooded murderess,"[40] but surely this is beside the point. We do not identify with Elsa because there is so little there to identify with.

Thus, if Welles was in fact making an effort to give Hayworth a new image in the eyes of her studio and the world (as he often claimed later he was trying to do), he did it by altering her physical appearance and by suppressing the kinetic source of her unusual charisma. Welles did not uncover hitherto hidden depths but instead masked the ones that were there, and in this way he defined Rita Hayworth according to the standards of the Hollywood and the society whose interest in the superficial he from all accounts deplored. And then he was off and "eager to have things over and done with." Although *The Lady from Shanghai* is surrealistic, imaginative, and brilliant on many levels, it is also, in its mythic view of the evil of woman, extremely conventional. James Naremore writes that "at its deepest level . . . *The Lady from Shanghai* concerns O'Hara's own potential for evil" and that Welles himself was "essentially a humane and liberal man,"[41] but the evil in *The Lady from Shanghai* is a projection onto women and their appearance. We know Elsa Bannister is a bad woman because she looks like a bad woman.[42]

Asking Questions

One obvious question that arises at this point is whether I have too closely associated the historical Welles and the historical Hayworth with their fictional counterparts. And, if there is no such thing as an essential or real Hayworth, what is the point of worrying about whether one construction (star text) is different from another (fictional character)? These concerns are, in fact, the crux of the arguments I have with the minor industry formed over the years around interpretation and analysis of the Welles oeuvre. At best, the actual relationships between Orson Welles and Rita Hayworth and the characters of Michael O'Hara and Elsa Bannister in *The Lady from Shanghai* are only barely amenable to analysis. One barrier to understanding is Welles's penchant for never telling the same story twice (indeed, the ideological basis on which scholars seem to assume that Welles is telling the truth about Hayworth while simultaneously acceding that he rarely tells the truth about anything else needs some examination). Another impediment might seem to be the fact that, as I have discussed in previous chapters, we know very little about Hayworth beyond publicity stories and coworker reminiscences (in fact, about Hayworth in *Lady from Shanghai* we know primarily what Welles has told us).[43] Nevertheless, even the contemporary evidence of fan magazines and other ancillary outlets, as well as that produced by archival research, suggests that, in fact, *The Lady from Shanghai* does *not* reproduce the relationship between the historical figures Orson Welles and Rita Hayworth.

Yet, aided and abetted by Welles himself—especially toward the end of his life, when he was actively engaged in rehabilitating his own persona—several critics and scholars over the years have conflated the relationship of Michael O'Hara and Elsa Bannister with the relationship of Welles and Hayworth and used *The Lady from Shanghai* as an example of how *Welles* was victimized by Hayworth in her guise as exemplar of Hollywood's preoccupation with appearance over reality.[44] Quotations from the literature will best support this contention, and I lay them out more or less chronologically below because they provide a fascinating record of the solidification of what in the end is a prevalent but ultimately wrongheaded assumption.

Maurice Bessy wrote in 1971 that "Welles had taken the 'ideal woman' . . . Hollywood had created—and denounced her as a man-eater, as a praying mantis. For the first time, woman, who had always served as man's saving angel, is as criminal as man, if not more so."[45] Despite the fact that Bessy's assertion makes no historical sense, given the "man-eaters" of *Double Indemnity, Murder, My Sweet, Dead Reckoning,* et al., in 1990 Lucy Fischer repeated the statement in her piece on *The Lady from Shanghai* with no qualification. Peter Cowie in 1973 noted the "remarkable ease and subtlety" with which Welles destroyed "the glamour surrounding" his "second wife" and also mentioned how at "every possible moment he shows her, sardonically, in the conventional, romantic light, and then, at the end, 'he smashes the ideal woman and the *femme fatale* is revealed.'"[46]

Joseph McBride wrote in 1972 that it was "significant that Welles should give to a beautiful woman, his former wife, the most precise formulation of his ultimate sin," noting that the "temptation offered by women in Welles's world is that of passivity, of sentimental and distracting reassurance, of a sheltering from reality which can become crippling."[47] In 1977 McBride also speculated that O'Hara's "foolishness" may have "stemmed from Welles's judgment at the time he was married to Hayworth,"[48] but he leaves uninterrogated the question of why a woman who had been

working professionally since the age of twelve should represent "the ultimate sin" of passivity and distracting reassurance.[49] And in both editions
of his book *The Magic World of Orson Welles* (1978/1989), James Naremore
wrote that Welles turned Rita Hayworth into "a series of insubstantial images which symbolize the gaudy unreality and fascination of movie stars,"
that *The Lady from Shanghai* "can almost be read as an allegory about
Welles's adventures in Hollywood, showing his simultaneous fascination
with and nausea over the movie industry," and that in the film Welles
"gives a rather bitter farewell to his wife and portrays her as a woman
'kept' by rich businessmen."[50]

Jon Tuska claimed in 1984 that in interviews with Welles he got "the
distinct impression" that the "inspiration for *The Lady from Shanghai*
came from his curiosity about having been attracted to a Hollywood sex
goddess and glamour queen in the first place and what it was that the experience was supposed to teach him. The significance of blonde-haired
heroines, in *Citizen Kane,* in this film, or in the later *Touch of Evil* . . . had
its origin in his own personal experience."[51] In 1989 J. P. Telotte called
"Elsa's image" a "paradigm of the Hollywood sex goddess, a vision of the
collective desires that the movies themselves project," and noted how the
"uncharacteristic—for Welles—soft focus close-ups of Elsa and Grisby's
leering views through his telescope further develop her symbolic status
here, that of the movie siren and pinup girl Rita Hayworth was in *real life*
[italics mine]."[52]

Most of this literature, then (whatever its excellence on other levels,
which is not in question here), repeats a similar story, makes the same
connection between the personal experience of Welles—his attraction
and marriage to Rita Hayworth—and the way Hayworth is represented
in *The Lady from Shanghai.* Although there is a recognition on the part
of feminist scholars that the enigma of the female that Elsa Bannister
represents "resists decoding because it is a male fabrication,"[53] their analyses also do tend to accept the literally as well as figuratively conventional
wisdom about the film, including its quasi-biographical nature. Lucy Fischer, for example, repeats McBride's statement that "Columbia was so
horrified at what Welles had done to [Hayworth's] image that it held up
the film's release for two years and rushed her into several more conventional roles."[54] But the only Hayworth film released between *Gilda* and
The Lady from Shanghai was the musical *Down to Earth,* which had been
in production before *Gilda* was released. Repetition of minor incon-
sistencies or mistakes is not cause for concern. But if we are going to
theorize so broadly on the basis of these repetitions, then we risk continu-

ally reifying not only the mistakes of the past but the mind-set that produces them.

E. Ann Kaplan's essay about *The Lady from Shanghai,* an essay otherwise interesting for the distinction it makes between male and female subject positioning, is a case in point. Kaplan first notes that in *The Lady from Shanghai* (as in most films noirs), "the woman's unknowability provides the very impetus for the narrative: the hero's task is to discover the truth about the woman, a truth that constantly evades him, as it does therefore also the spectator, positioned as we are within his perspective." [55] But she maintains that we, the viewers, also "constantly strive to know her from her image, and from what she says in the brief interactions with the protagonist, apart from what he says about her." Kaplan therefore acknowledges that the female spectator may not be "caught up" in the "same mechanism of desire [for refusion with the Mother]," so that Elsa Bannister may appear to the female spectator "ambiguous from the start." But although Kaplan allows for a difference in male/female spectator positioning, it is a difference that involves "moral degradation": "The narrative . . . follows a pattern that first is a reflection of (unconscious) male fears and fantasies about women and second, offers a *warning* to men about the danger of the beautiful, sexual woman, should they give in to their desire for her."

Kaplan seems to be writing, then, about *The Lady from Shanghai* as a narrative built on male anxiety about female desire and sexuality generally rather than on the relationship of Rita Hayworth and Orson Welles, and she never refers to the film's historical or industrial context in any way. But throughout her essay Kaplan undermines the authority of her own approach by continually eliding, with no apparent awareness that she is doing so, the character "Elsa Bannister" with the actress "Rita Hayworth." [56]

Orson Welles, for example, is mentioned by name three times, either as actor, writer, or director; when he is discussed in narrative terms, he becomes, correctly (in terms of Kaplan's argument), "Michael O'Hara" or "O'Hara." Rita Hayworth, on the other hand, is used interchangeably with Elsa or Elsa Bannister, which produces a number of bizarre statements—for example, "The crazy world of the fairground where Hayworth has, literally, transported O'Hara" or "Significantly, Hayworth does not have a point of view here." [57] Of course, *Hayworth* did not, literally or otherwise, transport O'Hara to a fairground; and *Hayworth* did have a point of view "here," whether the character she was playing was given one or not. Although "Rita Hayworth," as a star text, is a discursive construction, this does not mean that her construction takes the *same* form as that of a fictional character in a Hollywood narrative.[58] Kaplan does not conflate "Orson Welles," for example, whose public image is also a construction, with the fictional character Michael O'Hara. To be a professional performer, in other words, is not of the same order of existence as representing a fictional character *through* performing.

It is never that there is some singular or authentic reality we can know from an unmediated or benign perspective. But in the case of the Wellesian representation of Rita Hayworth, to agree to define her solely as a "Hollywood sex goddess and glamour queen" means not looking for, or making use of, material that might confute what has at this point become a canonical stereotype. When *Gilda* was released in 1946, it was publicized as Hayworth's first dramatic role and also as a continuation of her musical career. Virginia Van Upp's authorship as executive producer was regularly mentioned.[59] And, as has been pointed out in all previous chapters, Rita Hayworth was not simply a "movie siren and pinup girl" in "real life" but a complex figure of eroticism and decency, ethnicity and all-Americanness, a devoted mother and a "roaring, sexy woman," a dancer and comedian as well as a pinup girl. Hayworth even once said that she thought of herself mainly as a "comedian who could dance."[60]

Misogyny cannot be left to define the object of its scorn, because accepting the notion that women are always already passive objects in Hollywood cinema creates an endless circle: Hayworth and others like her are punished for not being outspoken, their passivity assumed partly because it was not forcefully contradicted either by themselves or by those who wrote about them. They are punished, in effect, for *being* stars, for taking that role seriously. Emptying a star image of its ambiguities, and of the alternate forms of active communication (singing and dancing, for example) it may have contained, *enables* it to be flattened and, subsequently, defined as insubstantial and its owner passive. Moreover, in the case of Hayworth and *The Lady from Shanghai* archival evidence has been available to scholars since the early 1980s that could have been used to complicate assumptions about Hayworth's star image and her historical reputation—to *differentiate* her star image from the historical agent who "performs" that image. Instead, scholars using this archival material (most of it in the Orson Welles Collection of the Lilly Library in Bloomington, Indiana, as well as in FBI files available since the 1980s) and writing about Welles or Hayworth seem to miss such evidence, or ignore it, thus acquiescing, consciously or unconsciously, in the perpetuation of Hayworth's "monumental absence" from academic film history.

I'd Forgotten That

Briefly, the archival documents in the Orson Welles Collection concerning *The Lady from Shanghai* seem at first glance to rehabilitate Welles's reputation for profligacy in the production, and subsequent lack of interest in the release and reception, of *The Lady from Shanghai*. Certain documents appear to support the notion that Rita Hayworth hindered Welles's efforts to economize on the film by acting "like a star"—for example, she was overly concerned about her appearance, made excessive personal demands, and could not do a full day's work without becoming "fatigued." In fact, according to two memos from Richard Wilson (Welles's Mercury Theatre associate), one to Welles and one to Arnold Grant (Welles's New York lawyer), *The Lady from Shanghai* was over budget and behind schedule because of delays caused by Hayworth's demands and her extended periods of illness.[61] James Naremore, Frank Brady, Peter Bogdanovich, and others reproduce this material to prove that it was actually Hayworth rather than Welles who was responsible for the fiscal problems that beset *The Lady from Shanghai*.

The evidence for Hayworth's illnesses, however, can really be pinned to one source, an undated fifteen-page typed memo by Wilson to Welles. As Wilson writes, the "general purpose" of the memo is to "refute charges of wastefulness or extravagance" made by Harry Cohn against Welles and his associates. The memo, which is a series of entries about "everything" Wilson notes or remembers, "is *designed* [italics mine] to be part of both an answer and an inquiry into the amount we are over the budget." It is only in this memo, written several months after *The Lady from Shanghai* had finished production, and in a brief letter from Wilson to Arnold Grant that "Rita's general condition of fatigue" and her "collapse on the set [from illness]" are ever mentioned.

Wilson's memo states that Rita Hayworth "collapsed" on the set on December 27, 1946, and was at her Los Angeles home (the conclusion drawn by Barbara Leaming in her Hayworth biography) recuperating from her illness for two weeks. In the letter to Grant, dated January 6, 1947, Wilson also writes that "Rita has not been well. . . . We expect her back next week." But in the same folder as both memo and letter is a brief note from Richard Wilson to Rita Hayworth herself dated December 30, 1946 (three days after the "collapse"), addressed to her at the Arrowhead Springs Hotel. The note requests her signature on "two papers." Hayworth was not, then, at home recuperating from her illness; rather, she was in a hotel at Lake Arrowhead, as Welles and Wilson knew.

According to some of the few surviving production personnel of *The Lady from Shanghai* (Bob Schiffer, Hayworth's and Welles's makeup man; and Eddie Saeta, assistant director, responsible for signing off on each day's call sheet),[62] Hayworth was not even ill. Indeed, she was rarely ill or absent during the production, but she *had* walked off the set that day in December. What specific action caused this was not made clear to the two men, but both stated that it likely had to do with her being "fed up" with Welles's actions as director, his public indiscretions with other women, and his erratic production methods. It is interesting that, from Wilson's and Welles's points of view, illness was a better cover than the truth, that Hayworth had walked off the set. Why? Why not tell Arnold Grant that Hayworth had shut down production *willfully* rather than write that she was ill and "resting for a few days"? Was there something incriminating or embarrassing to Welles and/or Wilson about her actions?

Although exactly what happened is unknown, and likely to remain so, the point I want to stress is that Schiffer's and Saeta's recollections tally with the contradictory documents in the Welles Collection itself. Other, equally interesting, issues were raised by Saeta and Schiffer on their own. For example, Wilson writes that "practically from Mexico on" (where principal shooting began) Hayworth's "fatigue" made possible "only about a half day's results no matter whether she worked a full day or not." Schiffer remembers it as the opposite situation, that often Hayworth was scheduled for shooting but never called to the set because of Welles's demands and delays, his decisions to rebuild sets, recostume or remakeup minor characters, rewrite scenes, and so forth—all possibly admirable artistically but none the result of Hayworth's intransigence or temperament.

On the first night of Hollywood shooting involving the scenes in Central Park, although listed on the call sheets, Schiffer says Hayworth was in her dressing room the whole time; "they never used her." In another scene, shot on location in San Francisco, the Wilson memo claims that the production had to close up because of the cold "for Rita's sake before getting the shot." Schiffer recalls that the production closed down that night because *Welles* never showed up. And where in the Wilson memo, both Schiffer and Saeta asked, is the time Welles was found sitting at a bar in Sausalito, while the entire company waited for him? Where is the time that Welles wasted setting up a shot on a pier that he knew in advance had been condemned and would not support the weight of the camera crane? "I don't see that on here," Schiffer said referring to the Wilson memo, "and we lost a whole day because of that." In terms of general cost overruns, when Wilson writes that "a lot of the expense in Mexico is really

Rita's," both Saeta and Schiffer countered that the expense was really Orson's.

Saeta's and Schiffer's stories of Welles-induced delays are numerous, and a few of them are probably exaggerated or mistaken (although neither man had seen the other in years, and their recollections are quite close). The issue is whose discourse prevails; and here, obviously, despite the availability of evidence that might have painted a different picture of one working woman's life in Hollywood, Welles's and Wilson's version has attained the status of not just fact but *revisionary* fact. Barbara Leaming also employed FBI files in her explicitly revisionary biographies of both Welles and Hayworth, but although Leaming describes the way in which the Welles household was spied on by an anonymous FBI informant during and after World War II, she neglects to mention that the informant also passed on the information to the FBI that whereas Welles was "reckless with his money" and had "nothing in the bank," Rita Hayworth by contrast was a "smart woman" who "ran a separate account."[63] Quite recently, in fact, the Wilson memo has even been presented as *new* evidence that reforms Welles and his reputation: in Peter Bogdanovich's 1992 interview-based biography of Welles, Bogdanovich states, "Going through the records [that is, the Wilson memo in the Orson Welles Collection, which is the only such 'record'], I found that the delays in shooting hadn't anything to do with you. Most of them were caused by Rita Hayworth's illnesses." To which Orson Welles responds, "I'd forgotten that. Yes, that's what got the home office into such a tizzy about Mexico."[64]

In short, this brief exposition is meant to demonstrate that one question that arises about *The Lady from Shanghai* and its reputation vis-à-vis Rita Hayworth ("the mysterious, beautiful, and manipulative woman")[65] and Orson Welles (one of the "simple and decent ones of the world")[66] is who really has been shanghaied by whom? Orson Welles has become a towering figure, a cinema monument of a stature so forbidding that even John Kobal, Hayworth's partisan biographer, seems to have had second thoughts about criticizing him. In the 1972 article that brought Kobal the commission for his 1977 full-length biography of Hayworth he wrote that Welles used Hayworth

as he might have used any other box-office name willing to risk herself to Welles's genius, e.g. Barbara Stanwyck, or Lana Turner, or . . . Lizabeth Scott. Hayworth was more than adequate but Welles ignored the things that *Gilda* had shown she could do better than any of her contemporaries, suggesting, to me at least, that he was unable or unwilling to deal with a force on screen as strong as his own and in whose creation he had had no part.[67]

Despite its obvious validity, this sentiment is missing from Kobal's subsequent book.

The biographers of Welles and Hayworth do at times seem puzzled or uncertain about the motivation of Welles's treatment of Hayworth, on or off the screen. She was, after all, the mother of one of his children, and he from most accounts "adored" her, although he could not be faithful to her. Welles knew, no less than anyone who read about her in fan magazines, that Hayworth was shy (sometimes pathologically so), an enormously hard worker, and tried her best to please everyone. And as mentioned, Welles was also the sole outside party to know, according to Barbara Leaming, that Hayworth had endured the trauma of sexual abuse at the hands of her father. Given this, Welles's demolition of Hayworth's professional image, not to mention the way he accomplished it, seems all the more perverse.

But Welles may in the end simply have been, in Molly Haskell's words, only "indifferent" to the lives of women in general, perceiving their "siren songs" to be of "gold, or compromise."[68] ("What a bore—this domesticity!" Welles once "thundered," in the presence of Hayworth and their child, to columnist Hedda Hopper.)[69] This makes Welles less some sort of pathological or vicious brute than a more or less "typical" postwar American male who occupied at least temporarily a position of prominence within a hierarchical and patriarchal system (although Welles was also quoted as saying that women are "things" you have to "use" and that women are "stupid; I've known some who are less stupid than others, but they're all stupid").[70] In this sense Welles's reputation rests as much on his ability to represent what Dana Polan calls "the impositions and prescriptions of a culture"[71] as on his solitary genius, and it would also explain why film noir seems to be Welles's preferred fantasy milieu. But André Bazin, writing in 1958, makes Orson Welles also partly *responsible* for the "misogyny of American cinema" or, at least, its auteurist masterpieces; Bazin calls Rita Hayworth "undoubtedly one of its first victims," as well as, "through Welles's genius, its most glorious martyr."[72]

The "implacable destruction" of Hayworth's star charisma has become one of the most important effects, if not purposes, of *The Lady from Shanghai* and the scholarship devoted to it. This is why I have striven so hard to emphasize available countertexts whenever possible. For as Dana Polan notes, "the very ways that we write history are of consequence for the ways we understand dominance and change." [73] James Naremore equates the scholarly attempt to define the work of Orson Welles as "rather like Thompson's search for Rosebud," which leaves us feeling that the puzzle might be complete yet knowing that a single piece "cannot sum up the story." [74] Naremore also refers to the "feeling of absence" that "hovers" over the material Welles left behind. This feeling of absence is even more pronounced in the case of Hayworth and other female Hollywood stars. Indeed, absence has come to define them as well as their film work.

It is not that the real Rita Hayworth is Gilda and not Elsa, but the real Rita Hayworth was as complex as Gilda, as frustrated, as bound by circumstance, and as talented. As David Thomson puts it in his recent measured biography of Welles, Hayworth, as Gilda, had "never looked more beautiful or played so overtly erotic and intelligent a woman. In *Gilda,* something seems to have educated Hayworth about the emotional dishonesty of men." [75] Rather than reifying or restating, then, what Welles took away from Hayworth and her reputation, I would argue that she was well aware of the constriction imposed on her as such, that she, too, wanted *The Lady from Shanghai* to be read as a deconstruction of image worship in general and of star worship in particular. It would make sense to grant that Hayworth contributed to and participated in the film, that she actually *acted* rather than was always acted upon. [76]

Does it tarnish the brilliance of *The Lady from Shanghai* to refuse to accept what Polan calls a classic film's "aura of accomplishment?" [77] If certain Hollywood stars have not left their own records and reminiscences—if they are, in this limited sense, silent—that does not mean that there was never anybody there. The title of Dyer's essay is, after all, "Resistance through Charisma," with *charisma* referring not only to star power but also to the ability to inspire and control others. And as the following chapter illustrates, it was not only a lone 1940s film that chose to make "trouble for itself" by privileging the discourse, particularly the musical and kinetic or dance components, of its female protagonist (with another film actively engaged in suppressing that discourse in order to avoid such trouble). Consideration of *Affair in Trinidad* also shows that classical Hollywood cinema is not, nor ever has been, as trouble-free ideologically as it was once posited to be—even in the 1950s. In fact, even then there were many more women working in Hollywood's resistance movement, as it were, than we have heretofore been led to believe.

This Is Hayworth as Hayworth Really Is

Some of the most significant action in Hayworth's star vehicle *Gilda* takes place in the musical numbers rather than, or as well as, in the narrative. On the other hand, musical performance is peripheral to *The Lady from Shanghai,* whose protagonist is mainly confirmed as a literal, as well as figurative, siren by her singing. *Gilda* would be a vastly different film, and a much less compelling one, without its musical numbers; *The Lady from Shanghai,* however, would be only minimally affected were its single statically performed and framed musical number excised. *The Lady from Shanghai* establishes, in fact, the extent to which the charisma that Richard Dyer ascribes to Hayworth's star image in *Gilda* depends and draws on Hayworth's skills and abilities as a musical performer, particularly her dancing.[1]

If singing and dancing are critical to a feminist reading of *Gilda* and Hayworth's star image, they are even more so to the primary subject of this chapter, *Affair in Trinidad* (1952). An obvious attempt to capitalize on the success of *Gilda* in terms of casting (through the presence of Glenn Ford), as well as narrative elements and plot (it was even written, as *Gilda* had been, by Virginia Van Upp), *Affair in Trinidad* was one of Hayworth's most financially successful star vehicles. Partly because of the dominance of directorial auteurism in the formation of the film canon, however, *Affair in Trinidad* is still largely unknown within the academy (it was directed by Vincent Sherman, an auteur in no canon with which I am familiar). But like *The Lady from Shanghai*—if for different reasons—*Affair in Trinidad* deserves its own "aura of accomplishment," an aura that this chapter is devoted to discussing. In large part, I will show, *Affair in Trinidad* is noteworthy because it was choreographed by one of the very few female choreographers ever to work in classical Hollywood, the modern dancer and concert choreographer

Valerie Bettis. Even more intriguing is the way that film critics reacted
to Bettis's and Hayworth's musical numbers in *Affair in Trinidad*. In
fact, the film caused a palpable stir on its release that was directly tied to
the nature of the female eroticism in its two musical numbers, especially
the opening "Trinidad Lady" number: in contrast to the oft-cited assumptions of scholars like Laura Mulvey or Kaja Silverman, the spectacle of a glamorized female singing and dancing hardly appeared to
these critics to be "reassuring rather than dangerous," in Mulvey's terms.[2]
Rather, the hostile reactions suggest that the numbers, if not the entire film, evoked in several critics something akin to a fight-or-flight
response.[3]

Although the intervening years have mitigated some of the shock of the
new obviously felt by these contemporary reviewers, the musical numbers
in *Affair in Trinidad*, as in Hayworth's star musicals and *Gilda*, reveal the
extent to which musical performance can exceed or actively contradict
narrative cues and logic. Its musical numbers remain products of Hollywood industrial practice on some levels—lighting, mise-en-scène, camerawork, editing. On other levels, however, they function as a competing
mode of discourse that the industry may produce and exhibit but that it
cannot always control and that allows women to be, if not "themselves,"
something other than signifiers of a hegemonic ideal of spectacular femininity. Here I continue my interest in breaking "star studies' fetishistic at-
tachment to the actor as object," in Danae Clark's words.[4] In fact, one of
the most useful features of the public discussions about *Affair in Trinidad*
is that they specifically and repeatedly invoke the question of who Hayworth "really" is, in which part of the film (and her star image) she is "really" to be found.

I discuss below the nature of Hayworth's and Bettis's collaboration
as it was depicted in publicity and promotional material about the production of the film, and I also make use of several subsequent interviews
with Bettis in which her work with Hayworth always became a focus of
attention. Then I turn to how the nature of the two numbers in *Affair in
Trinidad* and the polarized critical responses to them also help to complicate our understanding of Hollywood discourse of the 1950s, as well as
theories of its representation of sexual difference. As always, I am concerned to show that labor and identity discourses were a prominent feature of Hayworth's star image in the past and that her struggles to define
herself were recognizable and compelling as such rather than merely being anomalous precursors to or symptoms of a feminism that could not
yet know its name.

Publicity photo of Hayworth on the set of *Affair in Trinidad* "ganged up on" by Glenn Ford and, the tag continues, "members of the crew who have worked with them in all their pictures. Left to right are Bob Schiffer, Rita's make-up man; Dorothy Hays, body make-up; Ford; Dave Grayson, Ford's make-up man; Flora Jaynes, hairdresser; Roselle Novello, wardrobe; Hal Clifton, dialogue director." Photo by Lippman. Copyright 1952 by Columbia Pictures Corp.

Facing Monsters

Affair in Trinidad was the first film Hayworth made after an absence from the screen of more than three years, during which time her romance with and marriage to Aly Khan had been continually in the headlines. Following the breakup of her marriage, with two young daughters to support and her money running out, she returned to Hollywood and work. The musical numbers in *Affair in Trinidad* were shot first. Bettis and Hayworth worked alone together for weeks, spending "many hours talking things over and trying out different types of dances" and also in class and rehearsal.[5]

If Hayworth's every action was news at this time, reporters and journalists were pointedly curious about the nature of her collaboration with another woman. Because of Bettis's prestige as a concert dancer, and perhaps because of the ingrained assumption that two beautiful women could not possibly work together in Hollywood without becoming bitter rivals, she was interviewed many times about working with Rita Hayworth. The sorts of questions Bettis was asked—about whether Rita was "difficult to handle" or temperamental, for example—suggest that reporters were most eager to hear gossip about tension on the set. But there appears not to have been much tension to report. On the contrary, Bettis and Hayworth quickly formed a close working relationship and often functioned as a team, battling Harry Cohn and the Columbia management together over costuming, camera setups, musical tempos, and script problems.[6] In a 1952 article headed "Hayworth and Bettis vs. Movie Executives" Bettis described how "[e]very day there was a major crisis, but [Rita] and I won all our battles and of course that gave us great satisfaction, no matter how the studio officials felt." Bettis went on to call Hayworth "the most cooperative artist with whom I have ever been closely associated."[7] In fact, then and for the rest of her life Bettis reported that she loved working with Rita Hayworth. Equally important, their relationship was clearly a partnership, a real collaboration, rather than simply a master/student interaction. Asked by a *New York Times* interviewer in 1952 whether Hayworth was "a truly good dancer by a reputable choreographer's standards," Bettis gave the following "militant reply": "She fed me. . . . She was an Open Sesame. There she was, under a double-edged sword, so to speak, facing the 'monster'—the camera—for the first time in more than three years. I wanted her to loathe it. I wanted her to be so familiarized with the routines she would be contemptuous of it. And she was—like an angel."[8]

Given these remarks, it is all the more satisfying that the amount of discussion that the musical numbers in *Affair in Trinidad* would excite remains, in my experience, unusual for a nonmusical film (as we will see, most of the articles and reviews devote more attention to the numbers than to any other aspect of the film). Also of interest is the attention paid to the meaning of the dances in relation to Rita Hayworth's star image and dance ability and how differently the numbers appeared to dance critics (who regularly reviewed movie musicals and their dance content in dance and stage journals, as well as mass-market newspapers and magazines) as opposed to film critics. Indeed, to compare the accounts of film critics and dance critics is to wonder whether they have seen the same film. Where film critics complain about and scorn Bettis's and Hayworth's combined efforts, dance critics praise the numbers and the radical departure they represented from what usually "passed for dance" in many musical, much less nonmusical, Hollywood films. We are fortunate that Bettis herself was very vocal and articulate not only about her own film work but about the relationship of dance, the body, film, and eroticism. Asked to create a "sexy dance" for Rita Hayworth, Bettis instead worked with Hayworth to show up how limited and limiting were Hollywood's

Publicity photo of Vincent Sherman, Valerie Bettis, and screenwriter Oscar Saul on the set of *Affair in Trinidad,* a Beckworth Production. Bettis is in costume for the role of Veronica. Photo by Lippman. Copyright 1952 by Columbia Pictures Corp.

conventional and stereotyped renderings of what women's bodies could, or should, do on the screen.

You Want What You Can't Have

A distinguished dancer and choreographer of the second wave of modern dance pioneers who came to prominence in the 1940s and 1950s, Bettis received most of her training from Hanya Holm and made her solo concert debut in 1941. Among Bettis's best-known compositions are *The Desperate Heart* (1943), *Yerma* (1946),[9] *As I Lay Dying* (1948), and *A Streetcar Named Desire* (1952). She also danced and acted on Broadway, and the success of her performance in the musical *Inside U.S.A.* (1948), in particular (choreographed by first-wave pioneer Helen Tamiris), brought her to the attention of Hollywood. In general, Bettis is known for the emphasis in her concert dance works on the representation of a character's emotional states through movement. Unlike the mythic or archetypal figures populating the major narrative dance works of Martha Graham, for example, or the precisely technical embodiments of abstraction employed in the ballets of George Balanchine, Bettis created overtly individualized characters whose meaning is tied to their interactions with a recognizable and usually quite ordinary situation or dilemma. For Bettis, dance technique is only what enables the emotion to be represented legibly—the means by which dance could concretely embody a character and his or her feelings. As she put it in a 1979 interview, "if the movement is correct, it will give you [dancer and audience] back the emotion that produced it; it's inside out or outside in. That is, if the whole dynamic of it is fulfilled, you can't help but get an emotion back from it." [10] Whether or not Bettis's dances were specifically feminist on terms we might recognize today, thematically they investigated many principles of perpetual interest to feminism—autonomy, the discovery and disclosure of the inner self, the desire both to "acknowledge" one's status as a female and to "desexualize" one's movement and gestures. [11]

Much feminist writing works to reclaim the body theoretically or metaphorically, yet, as many dance scholars suggest, we also need to consider what Marianne Goldberg calls the "material, experienced body." [12] And as Jane Desmond reminds us, dance is "one of the most important areas of public physical enactment. With its linkage to sex, sexiness, and sexuality, dance provides a dense and fecund field for investigating how sexuality is literally inhabited, embodied, and experienced." [13] In *Affair in Trinidad* two women worked together to create a dance that would not merely connote eroticism through largely external costume conventions, such as high heels or black stockings, or even gestural conventions, such as a hip-swinging walk. Instead, the dance would *be* erotic, in Bettis's terms, because the movement itself was generated as a felt response—of the choreographer to the nature of the dancer with whom she worked and the character that dancer was playing, and of the dancer to her own and her character's sensuality rather than that provided by a stereotyped image repository of coded steps and gestures.

There are two musical numbers in *Affair in Trinidad*, and, like the dual renditions of "Put the Blame on Mame" in *Gilda*, they work to radically different effect. The first number, "Trinidad Lady," is interesting on three counts: its placement within the narrative, its structure and the movement quality it allows, and its use of different modes of address. *Affair in Trinidad* begins in what today is a recognizably noir fashion: it is the middle of the night and a body is being pulled from the ocean, the body of an American man who has apparently committed suicide. Two officials, one

Publicity still from the opening of "Trinidad Lady." The tag reads, "Rita's professed joy at being back on the job seems to be expressed in these terpsichorean gyrations, done for a Trinidad night club scene." Photo by Lippman. Copyright 1952 by Columbia Pictures Corp.

British, one American, go to notify the man's American wife, at the "Caribbee Club." When the American expresses surprise that she would be at such a place so late, the other replies, "She works there." Cut to the nightclub where, after some patter between the two men and the club's owner, "Trinidad Lady" begins. In some two minutes we have been presented with what seems to be a plot (did the man really kill himself and why, and what did his wife have to do with it?), but something important is missing: a strong male figure through whom our first look at the woman will be mediated.

On Laura Mulvey's terms, of course, this lack of "mediation through the eyes of the main protagonist" suggests that the camera's eye is a surrogate for those of the director.[14] But even if this were true, the director here is choreographer Bettis, under whose supervision the number was

Digital frame enlargements from the first close-up of Hayworth in "Trinidad Lady." Copyright 1952 by Columbia Pictures Industries, Inc.

shot, and the very first glimpse we get of the woman's face happens to be her direct look at *us*. This direct address occurs after the audio dissolve and reversal of the image-over-sound hierarchy, and it lasts for several seconds and recurs throughout the singing of the song and even, at significant points, during the dance itself. The words of the song underscore the ironic sense and self-awareness that the direct address implies ("It's only that I do what I love, and love what I do, can't help the mad desire that's deep inside of you. You realize the fault isn't mine, I'm not to blame, you want what you can't have, and you're all the same"). In contradistinction to the apparent fetishization of costume and surface beauty—bare legs and feet, long flowing hair, a single earring—and the theoretical passivity implied by the structure of the woman-as-spectacle, the song's lyrics help negotiate our identification with the woman as singer: we look, but we also feel what it is to be looked at. Ramsey Burt claims that this sort of recognition, when it occurs in relation to theatrical performance, "develops through a form of interactive production. It is based not on lack or loss but on recognition and acknowledgement of sameness, which manifests itself through making connections on the level of knowledge of the common experience of embodiment."[15] This recognition also complicates Hayworth's spectacular status as a "showgirl" who dances.

In some ways, however, my pleasure in Hayworth's dancing in "Trinidad Lady" comes from the fact that it seems to take place in spite of my attention to it. That is, Hayworth's pleasure specifically does not require my identification with her—much less her objectified position—but derives instead from the physical actions of her body and the obvious pleasure she takes in its trained and innate abilities to respond kinetically to music.[16] Autoeroticism is palpably signified by the way she manipulates her skirt; her bare feet, legs, and arms; the way she touches her body; and the correlation of musical climax with the moments of greatest physical exuberance. Then the song is reprised, but with a twist: Hayworth again confronts the spectator directly during its final words and continues to look back until the end of the number a few measures later. She exits, comes back, takes bows; she goes to her dressing room—alone—and pulls a towel around her neck. There are no cuts away from the number once it begins; after it there is a cut to the two officials, and the American utters the uncompleted thought, "Why would a man kill himself when he had—" Such self-aggrandizement is common enough in Hollywood films, but in this case to complete the thought is impossible. For it is all too clear, given what we have seen, why a man might feel himself superfluous to this woman (and in fact we never do find out exactly what went wrong between her and her husband). At the same time, this woman's virtue, unlike Gilda's, is never in doubt. She does not play around with *anybody*. (She does not have to—she *dances*.)

That performance and promiscuity are not the same thing becomes virtually a subtext, whether intentionally so or not, of *Affair in Trinidad*. Although the film was publicized as being another *Gilda*, its Hayworth character, Chris (a more ambiguously gendered name), is very quickly revealed to be trustworthy as well as virtuous. This time, the "Uncle Pio" character is her live-in housekeeper and companion, Dominique, played by Juanita Moore. Through acting and body language, as well as lines of dialogue, it is clear that Dominique takes care of Chris, and vice versa. The

Lobby photo of Hayworth performing "I've Been Kissed Before" in *Affair in Trinidad,* a Beckworth Production. Copyright 1952 by Columbia Pictures Corp.

closeness of the two women, one of the conventionally racist signposts of Chris's virtue and innocence, is demonstrated early in the film. In addition to this narrative signifier of Chris's probity, she is deemed trustworthy enough by the American government to be recruited as a spy for a secret mission. The only problem is that she is not allowed to tell anyone what she is doing, or why, or in whose [patriotic] service. Thus, Glenn Ford (as Steve, the brother-in-law who does not believe his brother committed suicide, and with whom Chris falls in love), in the dark about her motives and mission, misunderstands her relationship to the villain, Max Fabian (Alexander Scourby), whom she is spying on. Jealous and suspicious, Steve confronts Chris at Max's birthday party, but she cannot tell him the truth because Max is watching and she still has her spy job to do. So she begins to sing and dance instead.

Much like Devlin, the Cary Grant character in Alfred Hitchcock's *Notorious* (1946), Steve is unable to think of women except in terms of whom they are sleeping with.[17] Chris knows this but loves him anyway. It is only because he will not listen to her *speaking* that she has to resort to singing and dancing. To protect him (and America, for whom she is working), to get him to leave the villain's house, she offers a gestural performance that she knows he will read as promiscuity. It is not a striptease, as in *Gilda*, but a dance to a song about a fictional checkered past ("I've Been Kissed Before"). If *Affair in Trinidad*, despite its style and form, does not feel like a film noir, partly it is because it acknowledges that female sexuality is not inherently dangerous.[18] Unlike *The Lady from Shanghai*, for example, in which female sexuality lures several men to destruction, *Affair in Trinidad* indicates that, although it is often read as destructive, the reading can be mistaken. And this is expressed primarily through song and dance.

In regard to the presumed function of the device of the showgirl, then, *Affair in Trinidad*, like *Gilda*, proposes that there can be, indeed are, a variety of responses to the same musical performance. For the villain, as well as the guests at the party, "I've Been Kissed Before" is a pleasurable present from Chris. But for Steve it is equivalent to a slap in the face. Not surprisingly, given the film's reliance on obvious tropes from *Gilda*, Steve slaps Chris (as Johnny slaps Gilda after "Put the Blame on Mame") before stalking out.[19]

Thus, the schizophrenia caused in *Down to Earth* and other women's musicals, as well as in *Gilda*, by the tension between numbers and narrative and between women's authority in the musical numbers and lack of agency in the plot is even more apparent in *Affair in Trinidad*. Rather than the musical number signifying spontaneity, or the unforced expression of joy, romantic longing, or utopian affect, in *Affair in Trinidad*—more obviously even than in *Gilda* or *Down to Earth*—dance is not only emotionally significant but able to be deployed as a means to a narrative end. Dance gives women a narratively acceptable outlet through which to express themselves and their own sexuality, but it is also a professional skill. One can be both a sultry dancer and a virtuous woman; one can be genuinely erotic as well as decent. More to the point, these attributes co-exist in Chris and Gilda; neither one is an act, false, a deception. The paradox in *Affair in Trinidad*, especially, lies not in the duality of how Chris is characterized (erotic, decent) but in the way dance and physical expression are allowed to signify both as real, as sincere, and as modes of performance that can be employed to many specific purposes (they can even be directed, with near surgical precision, at specific targets). Despite its derivative and routine plot, *Affair in Trinidad* remains compelling for the way in which it essentially argues for the multivalent nature of sexuality, its performance, and its representation.

Look Closely

There were a variety of responses to *Affair in Trinidad* when it opened in 1952; audiences lined up for blocks to see it (it made more money even than *Gilda*), whereas most film reviewers contented themselves with snide quips about the patchwork and derivative story. As mentioned, however, the musical numbers provoked commentary of their own. The venerable Bosley Crowther of the *New York Times,* for example, fond of musicals generally, was close to vituperative, calling the numbers "both vulgar and grotesque."[20] Another film critic, Otis Guernsey of the *Herald Tribune,* complained about them as well:

> In the old days, movie dances in night club scenes were graceful, swaying routines dedicated to Eros rather than Terpsichore. Nowadays, in most pictures, they seem more elaborate, and this is certainly true of the Valerie Bettis choreography for Miss Hayworth in "Affair in Trinidad." They are the kinds of dances which the extremely able Miss Bettis has done so effectively in Broadway shows—angular and correct rather than flowing—and to this observer Miss Hayworth looks more harassed than seductive in going through these paces. She looks better while simply floating along a garden path in the moonlight, trailing a chiffon handkerchief.[21]

In other words, Hayworth looks better to these reviewers when she is not really dancing. (Also intriguing is the fact that several reviewers, among them Guernsey, refer to the emphasis on "correct" rather than "seductive" dancing in Hollywood movies in terms of an industry trend, one of which they obviously disapproved.) To be sure, many reviews are taken from the pressbook of *Affair in Trinidad* and only refer to Hayworth's performance as "sizzling," "torchy," "sexy," "provocative." But because these terms were used so frequently to refer to virtually any film moment in which a woman performs in a nightclub setting or for the apparent enjoyment of a diegetic audience, as well as the film audience proper, these terms function (much like the "device of the showgirl" in film theory) as a sort of shorthand that does little to elucidate the particulars of the moment at hand. I am therefore most interested in the inordinate attention paid to a couple of three-minute dances contained in an otherwise high-gloss but ordinary spy thriller—the ways in which the inconsistent responses and the level of discomfort that several of the reviews manifest seem to signal that what was pleasurable to some reviewers was felt as a figurative slap in the face by others.

Of course, the tension between reassurance and fear that marks response to the fetishized or spectacular woman is not in itself unusual. Many studies exist of the ways patriarchy has constructed the double bind that both rewards and chastises the woman who assumes "to-be-looked-at-ness." As Patricia Parker notes, there is a "double impulse" within the whole tradition of displaying the female body to public view in which a woman must be presented as "both inviting and under control," praised for virtue and chastity as well as beauty.[22] The relationship between the potentially uncontrollable female sexuality represented by a woman speaking in public and the frequently misogynistic responses to her doing so is the very echo of film narrative's "sadistic" response to the extradiegetic tendencies of woman as spectacle.[23]

But, as in the case of the often ambiguous outcome of the battle between musical spectacle and film narrative, the issue is not merely whether a misogynistic double impulse is deployed but in what context and how successfully. Might not Guernsey's and Crowther's objections to Hayworth's performing—Crowther also thought the numbers in *Gilda* were vulgar—rest on the fact that her pleasure is not contingent on theirs? Since Hayworth displays herself as a professional dancer, her performance here can also be read as a measure of her competence and autonomy rather than of her dependence or objectification. Dance critics like the *New York Herald Tribune*'s Walter Terry and, of course, Bettis herself describe "Trinidad Lady" in terms that underscore the sense of freedom and lack of constraint it produces, not its "vulgarity" or "angularity."

The contrast of the dance reviews to the film reviews cited above is powerful. Terry, for example, first notes that Hayworth is a "dazzling [cinematic] creature" and then that in *Affair in Trinidad* she also is called on to "dazzle in dance"—which, despite this not being "as simple as it sounds," Hayworth succeeds in doing. Terry then turns to a lengthy, detailed discussion of the success and originality of Bettis's and Hayworth's collaboration:

> Here, there is no sense that a dance seems sensual simply because Miss Hayworth is decorating its measures with her sensual presence. Rather do these dances exploit and disclose new aspects of a very vibrant personality. They hardly go so far as, say, Martha Graham's danced revelation of the inner being but they do go beyond mere surface dazzle. . . .
>
> For "Affair in Trinidad," Miss Bettis has choreographed one number ["Trinidad Lady"] which is almost pure modern dance. It is danced in bare feet, thus making possible a sort of primitive earth-

contact impossible to achieve with shoes, and if you look closely you will see that the legs are but infrequently used to make steps for carrying the body from one geographical location to the other but that the legs move because violent actions of the torso propel them forward and backward and sideways. This too makes for earthiness, for a walk or a step is fairly closely associated with practical problems of locomotion, but a torso or a hip is not customarily contracted or lifted or swung without good emotional cause.[24]

Terry then describes how, despite the lack of "emotional nuances or complexities to communicate," the modern dance approach enables Hayworth to give "force and fire and certain depth to movement outlines" that, because of the type of mundane thriller *Affair in Trinidad* is, might otherwise have seemed "like the usual routine."

However much the dances appeal to Terry, he mentions the reproval that "Trinidad Lady" was sparking in the press (if not in audiences, who seemed "delighted" with it) as well: "Could it be that some disapprove of Miss Hayworth dancing in bare feet? But no, we have long since passed that period. . . . The few dissidents, I would guess, feel that modern dance movements look better on Miss Bettis than on Miss Hayworth. Strictly speaking, they do but the choreographer has adjusted this technique of dance so expertly . . . that, in my opinion, a new and more exciting Miss Hayworth has emerged." Yet the second dance ("I've Been Kissed Before"), "performed in high heels, is not nearly as arresting. The star looks handsome and moves easily but not with that fine abandon nor with that movement range manifested in the earlier number."

Richard Dyer claims that the kinetic potency and charisma of Hayworth's danced performance of "Put the Blame on Mame" in *Gilda* is sufficient to upset that film's noir ethos.[25] Svea Becker arrives at a similar conclusion in her movement analysis of "Put the Blame on Mame" when she notes how the "scattering and gathering" motions that Gilda uses in her dance contradict Johnny's characterization of her as a Spider Woman or a femme fatale.[26] But to compare "Trinidad Lady" to "Put the Blame on Mame" (or "Amado Mio") is to be aware of how material the constriction of women can be in classical Hollywood cinema. In "Put the Blame on Mame" Hayworth can display little of "that fine abandon" because her tight clothes and high heels will not let her. Nor will they in "I've Been Kissed Before," which nevertheless exceeds "Mame" in animation and kinetic energy. It does not require the tools of Laban movement analysis to understand that Hayworth is literally free to move, to dance, in "Trinidad Lady" but not in the dances of *Gilda*—or anywhere in *The Lady from*

Shanghai. In contrast to Elsa Bannister, Gilda *is* characterized by motion, by a certain physical ease in spite of her constriction, but Gilda remains earthbound rather than earthy. In "Trinidad Lady" Hayworth as Chris Emery is allowed to feel the ground, to take off from it, to experience the space she moves in as a partner (one of Martha Graham's images) rather than as an inhibiting force by which she is contained.

The Wrong Concept of Sex

Walter Terry's designation of "Trinidad Lady" as no mere "display of surface dazzle" forms part of an interlocking discourse about dance, sexuality, and Hollywood's representation of women that occurred on the release of *Affair in Trinidad.* Terry refers to the fact that Hayworth's bare feet in "Trinidad Lady" were singled out for dismayed attention by several film critics. Why would this particular aspect of her performance generate so much alarm? Valerie Bettis mentioned in a 1952 interview that one of the "main fights" she and Hayworth had with Columbia boss Harry Cohn was over "whether Miss Hayworth could be barefoot or not," which struck her as a "rather silly thing." It was not that he was "afraid people would look at her feet." Instead, Bettis says, "Mr. Cohn seemed to feel that it didn't make [Hayworth] look attractive."[27]

This sort of controversy may seem quaint to us now, but the issue it circles is meaningful, namely, the relationship between a conventional, nearly generic, surface display of sexuality against the actual embodied and deployed performance of what might be called a felt eroticism or sensuality. Elizabeth Dempster points out that in dealing with dance, particularly, we need to learn to look critically at the body and to resist the "seductions of the glittering surface."[28] In the case of "Trinidad Lady" the "glittering surface" of Hayworth's satin costume, jewelry, and flowing hair were not enough to draw attention away from her bare feet and legs and the dangerous "seduction" that they represented. But according to Mulvey, Kaja Silverman, and others, the fetishized woman is not meant to alarm or to threaten but to reassure. If Hayworth is fetishized, in other words, it does not seem to have worked very well in "Trinidad Lady," given the critical comments her performance elicited. When physicality and effort are emphasized rather than obscured, then, the filmic spectacle of a woman deriving pleasure, as well as livelihood, from her own abilities may not be pleasurable but instead can feel threatening to social mores that depend on subjectivity's being defined by or as a masculinized action and effort. Bettis and Hayworth were challenging a long tradition in which eroticism in Hollywood films *was* equated with fetishization and *did* depend on "shop-worn tricks" of costuming, stance, bodily fragmentation, and conventional gesture rather than the active and "honest" (Bettis's term) depiction onscreen of a woman's pleasurable relationship to her own body and its capabilities.

In fact, in almost all of the articles about Bettis's involvement with *Affair in Trinidad* she articulates both the extent to which fetishization had become the rule in Hollywood and her awareness of how little fetishization has to do with actual eroticism: "Hollywood has had the wrong concept of sex for years—you know, black net stockings and high heels. Hollywood thinks that the way you suggest sex is to put on a costume. But that's not my way of doing it. . . . I used the personal qualities of Hayworth in dance terms. This dance isn't Hayworth running through some fancy steps. This is Hayworth as Hayworth really is."[29] Leaving aside for the moment the intractable issue of what a real Hayworth might be, this approach caused a "furor" at Columbia, Bettis said, because "up to now my kind of choreography had not been part of the Hollywood scene." The movies, as Bettis put it in another interview, "don't use dance numbers . . . to communicate something anymore."[30]

In a 1952 interview in New York with Walter Terry broadcast on radio, Bettis also articulated her feelings about film, dance, and eroticism, with particular regard to conventions and the relation of conventional costumes to behavior. The important thing to Bettis is that one feel "comfortable" in one's body, no matter how unconventional the costume (for example, Bettis was wearing pants during the interview, and although at the time *that* was "unconventional," Bettis herself felt "comfortable" that way). When asked by Terry about what movements Bettis might use to depict a "specific sex quality," Bettis elaborated further about how high heels and black stockings were so often used as "signposts" for the audience:

We've taken an awful lot of conventions to say that for us in the theatre, I think, such as costuming and—*exaggerations,* really, of what is taken to be a very sexy person. . . .
    Sensuality is a state of being. . . . You sensualize any movement by *being* sensual.

Indeed, because "I've Been Kissed Before" has a "dramatic point" in *Affair in Trinidad* that requires that it *not* be a real expression of Chris Emery's sexuality, here Bettis and Hayworth do employ the "signpost" approach. There are "many more obvious approaches to a 'sexy dance'" in this number: Hayworth is not only in a tight sequined black dress and high heels, but the bump-and-grind movements and gestures she uses, including placing a flower between her breasts and subsequently removing it and tossing it to a "patron," have been codified by countless repetition in other films to signify exactly what they signify in *Affair in Trinidad*—that Chris Emery is "morally misbehaving"—albeit in *Affair in Trinidad* for a good reason, "for a worthy cause" (at which point in the interview both Terry and Bettis, and their studio audience, all hoot with laughter).[31]

"Trinidad Lady" and "I've Been Kissed Before" are not only described in different terms, then; they represent distinct forms of expression. So do the two versions of "Put the Blame on Mame" in *Gilda;* but in *Gilda* one number is a private performance, a privileged moment, whereas the other is a public, "professional" performance. In *Affair in Trinidad,* on the other hand, neither number is a privileged moment; the film audience is granted no special access to Hayworth's character in the musical numbers, and we have no point of view that is not shared by her diegetic audience—for example, Steve and Max, who each interpret the performance of "I've Been Kissed Before" differently. Yet we have seen that the terms with which "Trinidad Lady" and "I've Been Kissed Before" were publicly discussed are unusual, that the numbers are differentiated from one another in interesting ways. Bettis claims that in "Trinidad Lady" we see Hayworth "as Hayworth really is," and Walter Terry finds evidence of a "new and more exciting" Hayworth. Conversely, the "real" and "new" Hayworths are missing from "I've Been Kissed Before."

Yet according to Maurice Bessy and others, Rita Hayworth had also been reborn, uncovered, revealed for who she really was by Orson Welles in *The Lady from Shanghai.* How do we approach, then, all of these real or new Hayworths? Given my assertions, following Danae Clark and others, that any actor's subjectivity is discursively constructed, the issue is not that there is such a thing as an essential, foundational Hayworth (or indeed an essential, foundational anybody), much less one who is accessible through filmic representation. Rather, the struggle over the definition of the real Hayworth is itself interesting here because such struggle over the terms of one's identity is where subjectivity can potentially be located in whatever fractured or limited sense. Richard deCordova claims that the star system as such actually "leads us toward that which is behind or beyond the image, hidden from sight," and that the star "cannot be reduced" to an enactment of the spectator's vision.[32] In this way the spectator's relation to the star image is not much different from his or her relation to any persona—we see or hear that which is presented to or performed for us, but we desire always to know what is "really" there, hidden or protected by the public image. Thus, it is easy to understand why we might more easily accept the apparently deconstructionist assertions of Bessy and the other scholars writing about Hayworth and *The Lady from Shanghai*, in which the public image is shown to be empty, flat, one-dimensional. The statements of Bettis and Terry, on the other hand, do *not* fit a deconstructionist paradigm, and they also seem to imply that something real and authentic can be found in a moment of film spectacle, the same sort of spectacle that feminist film theory defines as the quintessence of mere "surface display."

Once again, as in the discussions of *Down to Earth*, *Gilda*, and *The Lady from Shanghai*, I raise the fact that to define the singer/dancer only in terms of her fetishization and objectification is to disregard the very elements that make the musical number potentially so valuable—the transformative or communicative properties of music and dance performance, the way in which a woman singing and dancing can contradict or constrain a film's attempts to control and define her narratively. The historical, as well as theoretical, question raised literally by the discourse about Hayworth in *Affair in Trinidad* is whether it is actually possible to locate a particular woman's self in a particular (Hollywood) musical number and how that self might be characterized. Even if we begin by assuming from our (post-)poststructuralist vantage point that there is no such entity as a single, unified Hayworth because there can be no such entity as a single, unified self, we still have to account for what Bettis and Terry were trying to articulate about the different Hayworths in "Trinidad Lady" and "I've Been Kissed Before"—especially in the context of the early 1950s.

Affair in Trinidad is interesting not only because it, like *Gilda*, "makes trouble for itself" but because the trouble it makes more clearly defines the paradox of modern, particularly female, identity. When Judith Butler, for example, writes so famously about "gender trouble," she notes that it "sometimes euphemize[s] some fundamentally mysterious problem usually related to the alleged mystery of all things feminine."[33] More important, "trouble [becomes] a scandal with the sudden intrusion, the unanticipated agency, of a female 'object' who inexplicably returns the glance, reverses the gaze, and contests the place and authority of the masculine position. The radical dependency of the masculine subject on the female 'Other' suddenly exposes his autonomy as illusory." Although Butler does not spend much time discussing this "particular dialectical reversal of power," her analysis clearly fits the performance of "Trinidad Lady" and also elucidates some of the alarm it generated.

Even if, to us, the contestation of patriarchal authority in *Affair in*

Trinidad seems limited, the fact that it had any effect at all reinforces Butler's assertions that agency is not the result of subjectivity per se but is, instead, located within the working of variations by subjects on a *"regulated process of repetition"* that also defines them as subjects. Thus, the high heels and black stockings of "I've Been Kissed Before" might represent a regulated process of repetition, whereas the autoeroticism, gaze reversal, and "modern dance approach" of "Trinidad Lady" are a "reconsideration and redeployment" of that regulated process. The "vulgar and grotesque" Hayworth reconfigures and redeploys the "graceful, swaying" Hayworth, and the multiplicity of responses her performance generated are a signal, however small, that even Hollywood's rigid rules of representation can be bent. The "real" Hayworth that Bettis describes cannot be *the* real Hayworth, the essential Hayworth, the foundation that, or who, precedes or underlies all other performative Hayworths. But the "Trinidad Lady" Hayworth is *a* real Hayworth, one of many constructed, as Butler writes, "in and through the deed," in this case dance as performance. The self, Butler reminds us, is *always* constructed, by tools that are taken up "where they lie, where the very 'taking up' is enabled by the tool lying there." Construction, then, is not "opposed to agency; it is the necessary scene of agency," of the possibility of "subversive repetition." The dance that Bettis and Hayworth produce together "denaturalizes" the natural, producing a bodily surface that begins, at least, to become "the site of a dissonant and denaturalized performance that reveals the performative status of the natural itself." The "real" Hayworth that Bettis describes is a sensual Hayworth who "is" sensual in the world, as a material being, rather than a sensual Hayworth who is signified as such by the conventions of gesture and attire.

Ten pounds heavier than in *Gilda* but superbly fit, muscular, and sleek, Hayworth here is a thirty-four-year-old woman at ease with her body, moving in ways that have less to do with "playing to" patriarchal desire than with "playing out" her own. When an eighty-five-year-old Vincent Sherman was asked to remember Rita Hayworth, Valerie Bettis, and *Affair in Trinidad,* he quickly recalled the shock of seeing Hayworth—till then pleasant and warm but "so quiet"—begin to perform "Trinidad Lady" for the first time: "It was like you'd plugged her in; she hadn't been alive before, now she was electric. She felt comfortable, confident, when she was dancing."[34] (Sherman also maintains that Hayworth "was terribly underrated as an actress, and it was so sad; not because she was tragic, but because of her belief that she needed more than she had"—a belief fostered by her insecurity about her lack of education, not because she was "stupid.")[35]

Rewriting the Discourse of Spectacle

Neither dance in *Affair in Trinidad* contains unusually difficult steps or astonishing technical feats—multiple turns, beats, jumps, balances, and so forth. But one can imagine that, for a middle-class woman sitting in the film audience in 1952 in an underwire bra (padded, of course), a Playtex full-length girdle with garter belt and stockings, spike-heeled shoes with painfully pointed toes and a dress with no elastic in it anywhere, a number like "Trinidad Lady" might have had the same force of revelation that Jane Gaines, for example, claims for *Flashdance* in the 1980s.[36] As Francis Sparshott points out, "to be aware of others dancing, in however refined a way, is to be aware of them as entering upon a transformation such as one might oneself undertake."[37] For this and other reasons, I believe that, more than any other of Hayworth's filmed dances, "Trinidad Lady" at once transcends and reorders the narrative in which it is embedded. Although Bettis hoped that the Hayworth routines in *Affair in Trinidad* would start "a new trend for exciting dances integrated into [the] story line, with the dancers having something to say instead of merely acting as rhythmic puppets," she made only two more films in Hollywood.[38] But the sort of discourse produced by and about Bettis and the dances she and Hayworth created can productively augment ongoing discussions about performing women in classical Hollywood cinema (as well as the function of musical numbers in nonmusical films). As in the case of Hayworth and *Gilda* and *The Lady from Shanghai,* we can continue to explore the ways in which women worked to manage their own images through choreography, costuming, and performance. And, again, it helps if we can understand how some of the most influential feminist scholarship has handled these issues in the past.

Lucy Fischer, for example, employs two Hollywood films—the Busby Berkeley/Ray Enright musical *Dames* (1934) and Dorothy Arzner's *Dance, Girl, Dance* (1940)—in one of the best-known works of feminist criticism, *Shot/Countershot: Film Tradition and Women's Cinema* (1989), to show how the heroine of *Dance, Girl, Dance,* Judy/Maureen O'Hara, "transgresses the male discourse" of Hollywood film both by her famous oppositional speech to the diegetic audience and through "her formulation of a new kind of dance." This new dance is not in the film itself, however, so it is not clear from *Dance, Girl, Dance* how Judy "rewrites" the discourse of spectacle as well.[39] Fischer convincingly argues that in his films Busby Berkeley makes numbers that produce "ironic reverberations" about the status of woman as fetishized image. But Fischer also notes "the curious fact that Berkeley girls did not (and often *could* not) dance—a

phenomenon that accentuates our perception of their role as visual em-
bellishments," and of course there are many Hollywood films in which
girls *do* dance. Fischer compares *Dames* and *Dance, Girl, Dance* with two
1983 feminist experimental films by Kathy Rose. Although in her *Primi-
tive Movers* Rose performs almost nude, Rose, as opposed to the Berkeley
showgirl, is "clearly in control of the strategy, using it for her own (not
patriarchal) purposes." Rose also fragments her body in *Strange Ditties*
into hands, legs, and arms, but Fischer contends that these parts are "not
fetishized," although formally they appear to be. I have no problem
granting that Rose's intention was not to fetishize her body and that this
intention matters, given how frequently we grant explanatory credence to
the intentions of a Welles or a Hitchcock. Fischer concludes her discussion by claiming that the work of Arzner, Rose, and also Chantal Aker-
man "rewrites" the equation of woman as spectacle: "The 'dames' we celebrate in their work are not showgirls, but film directors who rescore and
restore the cinematic musical form." Thus, the showgirl as performer is
de facto excluded from the "rewriting" itself.

My cautious ambivalence about Lucy Fischer's analysis here—or more
generally about the terms of much 1980s and 1990s feminist film theory—
stems not from any weakness in the analysis itself but from how the evidence used to support it depends on our denying that there can be a creative female presence in classical Hollywood cinema that is not a designated
directorial presence. It is fine to look for ironic reverberations in the work
of Busby Berkeley, as long as we also look for them in a song called "Put
the Blame on Mame," which is, after all, sung twice in the same film by
the same woman but with two different voices—a very dangerous thing,
presumably, for a Hollywood film to do[40]—as well as staged by a gay
man (Jack Cole). Yet "Mame," we have seen, is termed by Kaja Silverman
"self-incriminating" and its performance "erotically self-lacerating." And
the "grotesque and vulgar" dances that Valerie Bettis choreographed for
Rita Hayworth were a natural place, one of the first places to which we
might have turned, to seek real "ironic reverberations" about the status of
woman-as-spectacle.

To paraphrase Janey Place, it is not the noir woman's eventual recup-
eration into narrative and patriarchy but her resistance that we tend to
remember,[41] and in the Hayworth films I have described I connect her
"both/and" status to musical performance.[42] But once one acknowledges
musical performance in film noir as important, other films present themselves about which a similar argument can be made. Hayworth's nonmusical films as a whole feature music and dance to an extraordinary degree,
and not surprisingly several of these films—particularly *Miss Sadie Thomp-*

son (1953) and *Fire Down Below* (1957)—also seem to be "in trouble" because of it.

Yet the tendency to conflate musical performance and erotic spectacle persists in much of the scholarly criticism of these films as well. As in work cited in the previous chapter about *The Lady from Shanghai,* the conflation seems to result from an inattention to or ignorance about the *complexity* of Hayworth's star image in the 1940s and 1950s and of music and dance themselves as systems of expression. There is nowhere near the amount of material on Hayworth's 1950s films in comparison to either *Gilda* or *The Lady from Shanghai,* but when the films are considered, the analysis tends to be somewhat predictable in relation to assumptions about Hayworth's star image and the films' industrial and critical contexts.

Amy Lawrence, for example, begins her extended analysis of the female voice in *Miss Sadie Thompson* (in a very interesting essay comparing the film versions of Somerset Maugham's "Sadie Thompson" and/as the dramatization *Rain*) by stating that "the visual and aural representation of 'woman' is central to the narrative, yet the woman's relation to each always (already) exceeds her control. In the third [film] adaptation of Maugham's story, the repressive ideology of the 1950s is reaffirmed, woman and her voice back in their old familiar places as the favored objects of spectacle."[43] Lawrence's reading of the film does not, however, consider the possibility that Hayworth's performance might be *meant* to be "dissonant and denaturalized," in Butler's terms, rather than old and familiar. Lawrence writes, "When she sings, Sadie's voice enters the realm of the spectacular," such that (reiterating the conclusions of Mary Ann Doane and Kaja Silverman) the female voice in *Miss Sadie Thompson* always (already) "signifies" Hayworth's body. Hayworth's voice (which Lawrence does not mention is dubbed here by Jo Ann Greer) *is* her body: both body and voice are put on display—"simultaneously, but separately—as spectacle." According to this "classical text," Lawrence concludes, "the woman's submission to spectacle status in both image and voice is, finally, the only possible course."

However valid Lawrence's claims may be in other contexts—perhaps in *The Lady from Shanghai*—her conclusions are problematic, for historical as well as theoretical reasons, in relation to *Miss Sadie Thompson* itself. First, although Lawrence attributes to Sadie a "highly codified, constantly changing set of characteristics" of femininity, consisting of "her clothes, her smile, her suggestive dancing, cascading hair, and sensuous voice," the fact remains that Sadie is presented narratively *and* visually as being one step away from destitution and is rowdy and noisy rather than sensuous. Lawrence also refers to the " 'packaged' sexuality of Hayworth in her tight-fitting designer clothes and 3-D musical numbers," yet from her first introduction in the film this Sadie is dressed conservatively in all but one scene, spending much of her screen time in a light-red skirt and a plain white blouse with a ruffled Peter Pan collar. Second, and more significant, these features of the film were noticed and remarked on at the time. Reviewers of all stripes mention that Sadie's clothes (of which she owns very few) were designed to look cheap, tawdry, and common rather than the result of any designer's intervention. Instead of "packaging" Hayworth's sexuality, then, her clothes underscore how precarious Sadie's "Western femininity" actually is.

Indeed, as played by Hayworth, Sadie speaks loudly, is boisterous and jovial, even tomboyish—"one of the guys." Her voice is deeper than in her previous films, her hair is shorter, her body beefy and often plain sweaty rather than voluptuous or languorous. Her deportment also suggests ease and purpose; when she walks she covers a lot of ground, and the marines have to rush to keep up with her. And again, all of these attributes were recognized and commented on at the time: the *New Yorker*'s John McCarten, for example, in comparing Hayworth's Sadie to previous film incarnations, reported that Hayworth's "new-day Sadie . . . switches about with the healthy muscularity of a drum majorette in a Legion parade and lines out songs . . . as if she were the song leader on an old-fashioned hay ride." [44] *Variety* also referred to Hayworth's "braving a completely deglamourizing makeup, costuming and photography," and *Cue* magazine's reviewer wrote that he "never thought [he'd] live to see the day when Rita Hayworth would steal acting honors from José Ferrer. But that's exactly what she does." [45] Given both Hayworth's performance and the way that *Miss Sadie Thompson* was discussed in its original reception contexts, then, clearly it would be difficult to argue that "Being Rita Hayworth," in Lawrence's terms, must be the same thing as "being reduced to spectacle for the male gaze," which causes Sadie's voice, as well, to become "a matter of pure surface." [46]

Again, I am not suggesting that it is wrong to claim that women frequently occupy spectacle status in classical Hollywood cinema, only that this is inadequate to define women as signifying—always and by definition—submission, repressiveness, or, as Mary Ann Doane puts it, "a surface which refers only to itself and does not simultaneously conceal and reveal an interior." [47] The single dance number that *Miss Sadie Thompson* contains—"The Heat Is On," choreographed by Sammy Lee—resembles "Trinidad Lady" more than any other of Hayworth's musical numbers in terms of movement quality. Again she is confined by space yet continually pushes against it. Even though she is surrounded by perspiring marines, she again seems to use her body for her own purposes rather than theirs. Sadie's profuse sweatiness and the obvious pleasure she takes in singing and dancing accentuate not her femininity but her resemblance both to the marines and to the "native" Pacific Islanders they live among. Rather than seeming "out of place," as Lawrence suggests, Sadie appears to adapt easily to her physical surroundings while retaining her own "tomboy" identity. When Sadie is raped by a missionary who has converted her, it shocks not so much because the rapist is a "man of God" but because Sadie, like Chris, is so obviously *not* licentious in either her figure or her personality.[48]

In *Fire Down Below,* Hayworth's next film but made after the three-year interstice of her unhappy marriage to Dick Haymes, her impassioned barefoot dance in a Mardi Gras–style street carnival ends with her flopping sweaty into a chair and saying, "That was *won*-derful!" to bemused observer Robert Mitchum. But when Mitchum's character later forces her to kiss him, she is completely unresponsive. Mitchum leaves her with the line "I don't make love to the dead," but we know she is not "dead." We have *seen* that she is not dead; it may be that she does not like kissing *him*—or that she has already had her excitement for the evening.

Interesting Situations

In a 1977 interview for *Dance Magazine* Valerie Bettis was once again asked her opinion of Rita Hayworth. Bettis responded, "Oh, I loved her. Very unpretentious. Worked every day, you know; she really did class with me and worked very, very hard. It was an interesting situation."[49] I have in turn worked hard myself to do justice to Bettis's and Hayworth's interesting situation. Taken together, all of the chapters of this book are ultimately arguing that in too many cases the most consequential effect of emptying a star image of its ambiguities and contradictions is the *production* of insubstantiality and passivity, not merely the location of it in a preexisting form. The fact that dance, in particular, must be performed in order to exist must be taken into account in any discussion of the function and effect of spectacle in Hollywood films. Dance requires dancers, and dancers are, as we have seen, possessed by and possessors of selves and identities that form much of the raw material of dance itself.

Dancers communicate with their bodies, and the female body can be, and has often been, objectified and commodified in Western culture. But objectification and commodification are complicated issues in dance, a form of "interactive production," in Ramsey Burt's words, precisely because watching a dancing body threatens to "break down or blur" the presumed or normative "distinction between subject and object." [50] We have hardly begun, in short, to understand the role of music and dance in the representation of women (and of spectacularized men) in classical Hollywood cinema. The dancing body is not the essential ground of identity nor is it free from the cultural markers of race, class, gender, and sexuality. Yet the convergence of the personal, the idiosyncratic, and the culturally inscribed can produce meaning that, to repeat Robin Wood's expression, transcends the "local ideological function" of the image. [51]

In the end I must caution that there is no global or perpetual or even transcendent power in all, or for all, of Hollywood's musical women (or men, for that matter). Music and dance are not magic tools, devices that make all spectacle a "no-man's-land" or a site of female resistance. Dance has no universal power to dimensionalize the female image in film. My privileging of the transcendence of Hayworth's and Bettis's "Trinidad Lady" in *Affair in Trinidad* occurs in relation to the context of the number's place in the narrative, its reversal of Hollywood's normal hierarchy of image over sound, its movement quality and style, the function of mise-en-scène, and, in particular, our relatively unrestricted access to the dance through the specifics of camerawork and editing. I also used extratextual resources such as reviews and interviews to grant Bettis and Hayworth an intentional purpose in the number, a purpose that my analysis of the resources and the number itself gave me reason to believe they achieved.

But even for the remarkable team of Bettis and Hayworth things did not always work out so well, and another sign of the significance of *Affair in Trinidad* is how quickly the hatches were battened down, so to speak, for their next film, *Salome* (1953), directed by William Dieterle. Here Bettis and Hayworth would not be left to stage and film the musical numbers without intervention from the film's director. There would be no direct address during the number, no reversal of the image-over-sound hierarchy, no pausing of the narrative. Although there is considerable extratextual evidence that the pair meant Salome's "dance of the seven veils," which they rehearsed for many weeks before filming began, to be a "serious" dance, they apparently had no control over how the dance was shot and edited. There are glimpses of a virtuosic and unusual movement quality, but Hayworth's body here is fragmented into legs, arms, hands, head, breasts, and bare torso by camerawork and cutting, so the dancer cannot express much at all through movement but only as a series of culturally inscribed and gendered surfaces. The sound never drives the image; instead, as in *The Lady from Shanghai,* dialogue—here between King Herod

(Charles Laughton) and Queen Herodias (Judith Anderson)—separates us from the music and the movements that are taking place to it. Equally important, the dance is presented primarily from the point of view of the lascivious and leering Herod—multiple close-ups of his loose-lipped and sweating face are edited into the dance—who thus filters our access to Hayworth/Salome narratively and as spectacle.

Much of the discussion in these final three chapters has focused specifically on forms of "non-verbal semiosis," as Horst Ruthrof puts it, that differ substantially in their meanings from those afforded by linguistic, verbal, or narrative systems of representation.[52] Moreover, my examination of the scholarship by which Hayworth has partly been positioned in academic film studies is also meant to suggest that we need continually to revisit our own analyses and to subject them to rewriting and revision as we learn more about the diverse texts of the past. If neither Valerie Bettis nor I can present Rita Hayworth as "Hayworth really is," this is not because there is no real woman behind the image but because Hayworth's agency and subjectivity are constructed in and by the very processes of negotiating the meanings of her image over time.

And as should be obvious by now, I believe that narrative closure is overrated, as well as overvenerated theoretically. Virtually all classical Hollywood narratives end with problems and plotlines resolved and with any strong, erotically active, or recalcitrant female protagonists safely contained and tamed by Production Code–mandated heterosexual marriage or death. Although disruptions or perturbations to the status quo are recuperated by narrative closure in this sense, the fact remains that moments of rupture, of narrative interference, often remain lodged in our memories in a way that the always already conventional Hollywood endings do not. But in books it is always satisfying to point the way to what happened next, to construct a bounded whole out of complicated, unwieldy, and contradictory material. This I attempt to do, however sketchily and transitorily, with the narrative of my own project in the following afterword.

Afterword

Replacing the Love Goddess

Great parts make great pictures! Great pictures make great parts! This girl [Kim Novak] has had five hit pictures. If you wanna bring me your wife or your aunt, we'll do the same for them.

—*Harry Cohn, 1956*

Ironically, Novak was originally nourished to movie life by Harry Cohn and his associates as a threat to Rita Hayworth, Columbia's then number-one star, who was squabbling with the studio. The idea was to build up a girl in order to intimidate the intractable Hayworth and possibly even to step into some of her pictures in case Hayworth should get completely out of hand. Novak, indeed, did inherit Hayworth's regal status at the studio. And now she was doing a Hayworth herself and tangling with the bosses. In due course there would undoubtedly be another girl to take Novak's place.

—*Ezra Goodman, 1961*

Rita Hayworth was a very lovely woman to work with. She was very nice and we got along great.

—*Kim Novak, 1986*

As I have mentioned, closure is never the last word (so to speak), not with Hollywood films and especially not with scholarly studies of them or of their component parts. My study has centered on a single Hollywood star, but the questions I have been concerned to address in relation to Rita Hayworth's film performances and offscreen image only point in the end toward other Hollywood stars and films, as well as to broader and enduring issues of modern identity politics generally.

Although I have referred to other stars and film workers tangentially throughout this book, I need now to confess that one of the most significant things I learned in the course of my research is just how little I myself knew, really, about the ways in which Hollywood stars and their films were represented by their contemporary publicity and promotional discourses and, therefore, how different their meanings might have been then from what they are, now, *assumed* to have been for any number of reasons.

Many times I came across information that simply did not jibe with what I thought I knew about stars—and I had zipped through a lot of star biographies and autobiographies during that nostalgia boom of the 1970s—and certainly not with much of what I had been taught in the course of my academic education. Among the several weighty and humbling questions I am left with are two that perhaps loom largest, and these are supporting some of the most interesting work being done now by others in film studies.

First, although I have focused primarily on song and dance as competing forms of discourse to and in Hollywood's film narratives, there are many variables of performance, ranging from gesture to voice quality and inflection to delivery to bodily stance and posture, that clearly also compete with narrative concerns in similar intriguing ways. (All kinds of specialty acts feature women in unusual performance modes—as jugglers, toe dancers, acrobats, and the like—that yet require vocabularies for elucidating and exploring.) There are no "clean" theoretical paradigms that fit the diversity of women's labor, on or off the screen, in classical Hollywood cinema nor even in the promotional and publicity discourses by which and in which that diversity was constructed.

Second, although some stars, such as Mae West, Katharine Hepburn, and Marilyn Monroe, have been carefully examined through promotion and publicity materials as well as through film texts, many others—for perfectly sound reasons to which I have also alluded throughout this book—continue to function in film studies as barely characterized at all or as adjuncts to a series of male auteurs.[1] Everyone could probably come up with his or her own list, but three such examples from my own experience include Rosalind Russell, whose place in film studies is primarily as Hildy in Howard Hawks's *His Girl Friday* (1940) or as Sylvia Fowler in George Cukor's *The Women* (1939) (the camp dimensions of *Auntie Mame* [Morton DaCosta, 1958] or *Gypsy* [Mervyn LeRoy, 1962], in addition to *The Women,* might also shimmer into consciousness from time to time). Ginger Rogers is significant as the partner of the brilliant Fred Astaire, of course, and occasionally as the star Hawks did not want to use in *Monkey Business* (1952). Olivia de Havilland is Melanie in *Gone with the Wind* (Victor Fleming, 1939), or Errol Flynn's love interest, or that dual role in the evil-twin melodrama *The Dark Mirror* (Robert Siodmak, 1946). In this last case, at least, I *had* learned from my reading in the 1970s that de Havilland was also the intrepid star who, in 1944, took Warner Bros. all the way to the Supreme Court to put an end to the "indentured servitude" created by the suspension clause in the studios' standard seven-year contract. We are now matching our careful textual and industrial studies of films and their directors with similar, perforce intertextual, analyses of stars (as well as other behind-the-scenes production personnel) and the many meanings of their labor, and I hope my work can be seen as participating in this ongoing effort.[2]

I had planned to end this book, quite neatly and logically, by discussing Hayworth's final Columbia film, *Pal Joey* (1957). *Pal Joey* is not only the film Hayworth had to make to finish out her contract with Harry Cohn, but it was also an important testing ground for "the next Hayworth" at Columbia, Kim Novak. I was sure that by summarizing and musing on why and how Novak was engineered into the potential replacement "love goddess" for the "unpredictable" Hayworth, in Cohn's words, as well as the ways in which that engineering ultimately failed, I could close Hayworth's story differently. I would simply employ Novak's insufficiencies as an actress, her passivity and fetishized blonde beauty, as a convenient foil to Hayworth's comparable complexity and depth and would thereby authenticate Hayworth's subjectivity, as it were. The only problem with this plan was that the sum total of my knowledge about Novak's image, as far as I had ever pondered it at all, came from what I had read and been taught about Hitchcock's *Vertigo* (1958). And of that, the only thing that had remained with me forcefully through the years (besides the surpassing immanence of *Vertigo* itself) was the fact that Hitchcock thought Novak was "bovine."

Given what I had already learned about Rita Hayworth's star image, I could hardly claim to be surprised to find—again with relatively little effort—that even Kim Novak (b. 1933), whose career in the studio system was much shorter than Hayworth's, also had a broad and complex range of meanings in the 1950s, as well as later, when she left Columbia behind (she had even been written about a couple of times by film scholars).[3] Indeed, the fluidity and variability of Novak's image in the 1950s and since, especially her explicit refusal of Hayworth's fate as a star, does help to rewrite the discourse not only of Novak's stardom but of Hayworth's as well, although not necessarily in the ways I expected. So I can, after all, follow through on some version of my plan but precisely because of how different Novak proved to be from what I assumed she was.

Filling the Vacant Throne

From the time Rita Hayworth left Hollywood to marry Aly Khan there were any number of attempts, official (by Columbia) and unofficial (by journalists and fans), to fill the "throne vacant in Hollywood: the throne of the Love Goddess," in *Life* magazine's words in 1949.[4] *Life's* purpose in writing about Hayworth's vacant throne was to suggest that it be filled by Corinne Calvet, "a lively, freckled young lady" who did "not make any claim to being a great actress" and who was being "put forward" by producer Hal Wallis at Paramount. *Life,* of course, was where the Love Goddess had been deified two years before, and it should not be forgotten that she had then been characterized as passive, placid, dim-witted, eager to please—she "drove men to madness and women to envy in all countries, classes, creeds and conditions." In essence, this abortive deification of Calvet is a sign of the continued naturalization of the Love Goddess, the rendering of her status as inevitable, immutable: the tautological question for *Life* is no longer whether Rita Hayworth (or any other Hollywood actress) should be designated as such in the first place but who was going to replace her.

Kim Novak is undoubtedly the best known of the official replacements for Hayworth. She was, by some accounts contemporary with her rise to stardom in the early 1950s, manufactured from "nothing"—a Chicago girl whose only performing experience was as a commercial model and who arrived in Hollywood as a consequence of being Miss Deep Freeze for Thor refrigerators.[5] Harry Cohn liked to boast that he had chosen Novak because she was there: after one of his fights with Hayworth in 1953, he proclaimed to a journalist, he vowed to replace Hayworth with the "next girl to walk in my door," and in Novak (then Marilyn Novak) had walked. Of course this is not the way it really happened, but, more important, it was not even the only way it was represented in promotional material either. Once she had proven to be popular with audiences, fan magazines spent as much time on Novak's drive and ambition to improve and to learn as on her "discovery" or her physical appearance.[6] But because Novak had progressed from her first bit part in *The French Line* (Lloyd Bacon, 1954), with Jane Russell, to a billed role in *Pushover* (Richard Quine, 1954), to four more lead roles in little more than a year and the starring role in Josh Logan's prestige production *Picnic* in 1956 and, ultimately, in *Vertigo* in 1958, it also could be argued by any who wanted to that all it took to become a Hollywood star in the 1950s—Novak was named the top box-office draw in the country by exhibitors after her first six films— was a young and beautiful face and body and a willingness to give oneself over totally to the ministrations of more or less benevolent studio heads, beauticians and wardrobe masters, press agents, and directors.

With *Pal Joey* in 1957 Cohn had the chance to pair the original with the copy. Although *Pal Joey* had been owned by Cohn since the 1940s (it was meant to star Hayworth as the ingénue Novak would play and to costar

Gene Kelly, who originated the title role on Broadway), by the time it was finally filmed Rita Hayworth was relegated to the "older woman" role, the society stripper Vera who attempts unsuccessfully to turn Frank Sinatra's Joey into a gigolo (Hayworth was, of course, two years younger than Sinatra), and Kim Novak had been given the role of the professional innocent Linda. At this point some press reports made Novak into the rude bad girl in the face of, or in contrast to, Hayworth's "real" star status; Hayworth was punctual, prepared, and professional (as well as talented), whereas Novak was hysterical, held up production, and demonstrated what Tyrone Power, Novak's costar in *Jeanne Eagels* (George Sidney, 1957), had called Novak's "unfortunate" confusion between "temperament and bad manners."[7] (In fact, Hayworth, like some fan-magazine writers, sympathized with Novak's plight and her status as Harry Cohn's newest "property"; Novak in turn admired Hayworth, and the two women were friendly.)[8] In director George Sidney's own scrapbook of 1957–1958 there is a British article in which Sidney himself claims that Hayworth "wipes the floor" with Kim Novak, Hayworth now being the real thing whereas Novak is the unqualified pretender.[9]

A male psychoanalyst consulted about Novak for a *Time* cover story about her in 1956 was even more contemptuous:

> Girls like Kim Novak, Marilyn Monroe and Jayne Mansfield—the most popular actresses in Hollywood—all reflect the times we are living in. They are blobs, faceless wonders, poor lost souls that go well with an era that suffers from a loss of identity. . . . During the depression, in the Thirties, the movie heroines, like Katharine Hepburn and Rosalind Russell, were much stronger. And in the Fifties, with their pronounced loss of identity, the most popular movie stars are pudding-faced, undistinguished girls, not particularly talented—like Monroe, Mansfield and Novak. Their undistinguished background appeals to most people. These girls have no father or mother, figuratively speaking, and sometimes literally. They seem to come from nowhere.[10]

Whether the male stars of the era—for example, Rock Hudson, Tony Curtis, Aldo Ray—also were pudding-faced and undistinguished goes unaddressed. Paradoxically, however, all of the stars named *do* "reflect" the 1950s but because of their embodiment of so much of the era's ambivalence and tension rather than because they were "not particularly talented." Nevertheless, Ezra Goodman, who wrote the *Time* story, remarks in his 1961 book *The Fifty-Year Decline and Fall of Hollywood* that "Kim

Novak filled this psychiatric bill as well as she filled a sheath gown at a Hollywood premiere. Novak, to be sure, had a face. . . . But the face was blank—except for the eyes, which were deep and haunted. One could call her faceless." Novak was temperamental and driven, then, but however "haunted" she was by the ambitions planted in her by Cohn to succeed ("she was [by 1956] irrevocably committed to screen stardom," said her press agent, "[a]nd she'll never chuck it—no more than a narcotic addict"), she was always going to be a pretend Hayworth, a secondhand Monroe, the thinking man's Mansfield.

So on these terms Kim Novak does participate in constructing Rita Hayworth's subjectivity as a star in the mid-1950s, both because of Novak's publicized failures to match up to Hayworth's standards of professionalism and talent and because the terms of Novak's own stardom also serve to dispel many of the myths surrounding fabricated stars (as, for that matter, did Monroe and Mansfield). Harry Cohn could not (and did not) make Novak into a star "from nothing"; there are many others with whom he had tried and failed. Novak (like Hayworth) did have something more than a face and body, and it is probably not mere nostalgia that leads headline writers to refer now to Novak with epithets reminding us of her "enduring magnificence"; indeed, James Harvey, in *Movie Love in the Fifties* (2001), provides a laudatory chapter about Novak (about *Picnic* he writes she "seems the only *serious* human presence in the film").[11] A 1986 book-length biography of Novak is entitled *Reluctant Goddess,* and, in fact, Novak did manage to chuck that purported addiction to fame and left Hollywood and the film business—Harry Cohn died in 1958 and "old Hollywood" itself not long after—in the 1960s to raise animals on her two ranches in the Northwest.[12] She did not marry until she was in her thirties, has been married to a veterinarian since 1976, and has never had children.

In short, Kim Novak did not replace Rita Hayworth in either the public's or Hollywood's eyes, and she rejected the binding stereotype that the Love Goddess represented. Although, as a consequence, Novak endured slurs and slights more vituperative even than those leveled at Hayworth during her frequent battles with the studio system, Novak was eventually able to control and to manage her own stardom and its aftermath in a way that had been denied Hayworth. After *Pal Joey* Hayworth made several films in which her performances remain among the most critically respected of her career—*Separate Tables* (Delbert Mann, 1958), *They Came to Cordura* (Robert Rossen, 1959), *The Story on Page One* (Clifford Odets, 1960). Ironically, Hayworth is praised for having left the "love goddess" role behind, a role that had been imposed on her but that she had never

Digital frame enlargement of Rita Hayworth and Kim Novak in *Pal Joey.* Copyright 1957, renewed 1985, by Columbia Pictures Industries, Inc.

embraced. But the Alzheimer's disease that struck Hayworth in the early 1960s, and her inadvertent yet crucial role in making the devastations of the disease widely known in America for the first time, meant that her story would never have the happy ending thus far possible for Novak.

What Kim Novak's career and image also mean in the context of my argument, then, is that they remind us that many of the tragic dimensions of Hayworth's stardom stem not from her objectification as the Love Goddess but from the collision of Hayworth's extreme personal torment and history with Hollywood's star-making machinery. Hayworth is not unusual because she was a fabricated star or because she was often objectified onscreen and off. If, in fact, she is unusual, it is because the process of her fabrication and construction made her what she "was"—an all-American girl who was half Spanish, a shy introvert who loved to dance and perform, a working professional woman torn apart by the cultural imperative to desire domesticity and motherhood as well as a personal need to repair, through public acceptance, the psychic wounds left in her by her childhood. In other words, to say that a star is constructed should open up rather than close down discussion—constructed from what and into what? What factors participate in and result from the processes of construction itself? How does a star's labor to construct and to understand herself interact with our own attempts to manufacture and to manage the images we present to others?

As I stated in my introduction, I agree with Danae Clark's argument that star studies needs to be "rearticulated to include a space for the actor as social subject and to intervene in the historical formation of this subjectivity."[13] I have attempted to do this in the five views of Rita Hayworth presented here, by elucidating the ways in which the various subjectivities of a particular star were constructed by a complex series of negotiations among her own history, her own struggles, her own labor, her own understanding of her own identity at various times and places but especially in postwar America, and, finally, the terms of academic film studies itself. The dilemma that Hayworth had to manage did not rest only on the difficulty of differentiating between her public roles and her private self but was the perpetual occupational hazard of being a professional woman whose image circulates in the public sphere, who is unable always to manage or present her various selves according to her own devices and desires. I would like to *replace* the Love Goddess with this "unpredictable" woman who was working so hard at being Rita Hayworth, and to *re-place* this woman, and other stars as yet unstudied, as subject rather than object into the field from and in which I write. If Hayworth's story does not have a happy ending, it is all the more critical that we grant it the resonance and power it did possess, and in such measure, for so long and at such a critical time in American women's history.

Notes

ABBREVIATIONS

AMPAS Margaret Herrick Library, Academy of Motion Picture Arts and Sciences
BFI   British Film Institute
RHS   Rita Hayworth scrapbooks, 7 vols., Constance McCormick Collection, Cinema-Television Library, University of Southern California
VBS   Valerie Bettis scrapbooks, Dance Collection, New York Public Library for the Performing Arts

Introduction

1. Neil Grant, ed., *Rita Hayworth in Her Own Words* (London: Hamlyn, 1992), 31. This collection culls Hayworth's "own words" from a wide variety of extant mass-market articles and biographies about her, and the fact that Grant assumes Hayworth's discursive subjectivity to be a "real" subjectivity—it does not matter whether Rita Hayworth actually wrote or uttered these words—supports the primary notion on which *Being Rita Hayworth* rests. For the same reasons, there are only a few instances here where it is of profound importance whether Hayworth actually said the words she is being quoted as having said.

2. The first part of this book details much of the awfulness of Hayworth's personal life, but throughout I will be suggesting that some of the awfulness derives (still) from the fact that her considerable professional abilities are not taken seriously. As is common with stars, Hayworth's work has heretofore been read mainly for what it can tell us about her private life. A director's life, on the other hand, we read usually for what it can tell us about "his" work. Book-length biographies of Hayworth include John Kobal, *Rita Hayworth: The Time, the Place, and the Woman* (New York: Norton, 1977); Joe Morella and Edward Z. Epstein, *Rita: The Life of Rita Hayworth* (New York: Delacorte Press, 1983); and Barbara Leaming, *If This Was Happiness* (New York: Viking, 1989). See also Caren Roberts-Frenzel, *Rita Hayworth: A Photographic Retrospective* (New York: Abrams, 2001), whose lushly produced and "rare" photographs are meant to allow us to "view the public and private" Rita Hayworth as "she's never been seen before. She is no longer just the 'Love Goddess' but a flesh-and-blood woman with whom we can identify" (8). My argument, of course, is that Hayworth was *always* a "flesh-and-blood woman" with whom her fans identified and that she was accessible as such through widely available promotional and publicity materials. It is important to remember, too, that the sorts of images available to fans were often imperfectly printed, garishly colored, flimsy; there were no coffee-table books about stars in the 1940s and 1950s.

3. Michael Wood, *America in the Movies* (New York: Basic Books, 1975), 56.

4. Leonard Michaels, *To Feel These Things: Essays* (San Francisco, Calif.: Mercury House, 1993), 1. Michaels "signs" the quotation "Rita Hayworth (b. Margarita Carmen Cansino, 1918)."

5. Danae Clark, *Negotiating Hollywood: The Cultural Politics of Actors' Labor* (Minneapolis: University of Minnesota Press, 1995). All quotations in this and the following paragraph are from xi, 3, 11–12, 16. Like Clark I use *subjectivity* as the critical concept relating to construction of the person-as-individual through practices that are at once unconscious and sociocultural but that result in what is felt by that individual as his or her personal identity. My deployment of the term *agency* throughout this book refers to the ability of that subject to exert power and energy that produce desired effects, to operate in the pursuit of goals that are perceived to be his or her own.

    I also want to note that, like Clark, I would not be able to do this work had it not been for the ground laid by Richard Dyer's two seminal studies *Stars* (London: BFI, 1979/1998) and *Heavenly Bodies: Film Stars and Society* (New York: St. Martin's, 1986), as well as Richard deCordova's *Picture Personalities: The Emergence of the Star System in America* (Urbana: University of Illinois Press, 1990). Another useful early study is Cathy Klaprat's "The Star as Market Strategy: Bette Davis in Another Light" (1976), in *The American Film Industry,* ed. Tino Balio, rev. ed. (Madison: University of Wisconsin Press, 1976/1985), 351–376 (page citations here and throughout are to the 1985 edition).

6. In *Stars* Richard Dyer defines promotion as "material concerned directly with the star in question—studio announcements, press hand-outs (including potted biographies), fan club publications (which were largely controlled by the studios), pin-ups, fashion pictures, ads in which stars endorse a given merchandise, public appearances (e.g. at premieres, as recorded on film or in the press)," as well as "material promoting the star in a particular film." Publicity, on the other hand, "is not, or does not appear to be, *deliberate* image-making. . . . In practice, much of this too was controlled by the studios or the star's agent, but it did not appear to be, and in certain cases . . . it clearly was not. The only cases where one can be fairly certain of genuine publicity are the scandals" (60–61 [page citations here and throughout are to the 1998 edition]).

7. Leaming, *If This Was Happiness.*

8. Clark, *Negotiating Hollywood,* xi.

9. As of this writing there is a renewed interest in uncovering, preserving, and restoring the work of women film "pioneers" (implicitly defined as women writers, producers, directors, and production personnel other than actors), for example through Duke University's Women's Film Pioneers Project (for which I hope eventually to write about Virginia Van Upp [1902–1970], the executive producer and writer of *Gilda* [see chap. 4]). See also Ally Acker, *Reel Women: Pioneers of the Cinema, 1896 to the Present* (New York: Continuum, 1991). I also want to note that Viola Lawrence (1895–1973), one of the first and best-known woman editors in the classical studio system, edited ten of Hayworth's films, including the majority of Hayworth's star vehicles.

10. Nancy F. Cott, *The Bonds of Womanhood: "Woman's Sphere" in New England, 1780–1835* (New Haven, Conn.: Yale University Press, 1977); Laura Mulvey, "Visual Pleasure and Narrative Cinema" (1975), in *Issues in Feminist Film Criticism,* ed. Patricia Erens (Bloomington: Indiana University Press, 1990), 28–39.

11. Judith Mayne, *Framed: Lesbians, Feminists, and Media Culture* (Minneapolis: University of Minnesota Press, 2000), 3–22.

12. It should become clear that I am not claiming that I can profoundly understand what Hayworth meant to a large, undifferentiated historical audience. But other scholars, like Jackie Stacey (*Star Gazing: Hollywood Cinema and Female Spectatorship* [London: Routledge, 1994]), have attempted to elucidate female spectatorial responses to stars of the past with results that suggest that I am not making particularly aberrant assumptions here (see the references to Hayworth on 143, 153, 202, 206, 209, and 210 of Stacey). Nor am I positing that a star like Hayworth was any kind of *radical* political influence on her audiences. But I concur with Matthew Tinkcom's reasoned argument that although we cannot "wish up" some demonstrably radical historical fan, neither must we assume that if fans were not radical, then they must have been "complicit." Tinkcom also notes that always to employ the term *spectatorship* in discussing audiences of the past ignores the "other activities that are implied by fandom (reading fan magazines, collecting star images, fantasizing, and daydreaming)." Just because "fans do not transform the culture industries at the level of altering them as capitalist enterprises does not, at least to [him, or to me], disallow the potential of fans to shape their own readings and the subcultural networks that value those readings. Equally, fan labors redirect and refashion the value potential of star publicity beyond corporate profit itself" (Matthew Tinkcom, *Working like a Homosexual: Camp, Capital, Cinema* [Durham, N.C.: Duke University Press, 2002], 142–144). It is in their potential to interact with and affect other "structures of feeling," in Raymond Williams's words, that the trials, tribulations, and triumphs of stars like Hayworth had political value.

I circulated a questionnaire among several individuals who responded to an ad I placed in 1996 in the newsletter of the Rita Hayworth fan club (president Caren Roberts-Frenzel) requesting information from anyone who remembered Hayworth and her films in their original context. The resulting sample, although small (six responses), supports Stacey's conclusion that "the cultural consumption of Hollywood stars does not necessarily fix identities, destroy differences and confirm sameness" (172). For example, one woman (an R.N. and Ph.D. in psychology) who describes herself as "a fan of Rita Hayworth from childhood" identified with her because she was "impressed by her dancing—I became a dancer and sometimes a redhead"—and wrote that "the women—my mother and I and our friends—all loved her. Men seemed to like dumb blondes at the time." One of the male respondents (working class, eighth-grade education) remembers "her beauty, poise, and dancing ability." He does not remember anything about her personal life, and anything he has heard since "would not cause me to change my mind about Rita." Another woman (working class, tenth-grade education) remembers that she "was beautiful and talented" and that "she had pretty soft eyes." She was always familiar with the vicissitudes of Hayworth's private life and frequently "talked to her sister about Rita." She "didn't care for her going with [Orson Welles]" and assumed that she "had to marry [Aly Khan] because she was p.g. She's not the 1st nor the last." One "remembers feeling relieved when she left [Aly Khan]," another that she "didn't care much for her going with [Orson Welles] because she was engaged to Victor Mature. It hurt him." Anecdotally, at least, clearly Rita Hayworth's attributes and actions were judged and measured in the context of these fans' own lives.

13. Following Ramona Curry, *Too Much of a Good Thing: Mae West as Cultural Icon* (Minneapolis: University of Minnesota Press, 1996), 154 n. 14, I will not adhere to a "strict typographical designation" in which "Rita Hayworth" (the "cultural sign") is differentiated from Rita Hayworth (the historical person) by quotation marks. Indeed, I am claiming that, even to her biographers, there is no way for her to be anything but a cultural sign now, so to use quotation marks would be redundant.

14. Clark, *Negotiating Hollywood*, 119–120.

15. For a review of the formation and constitution of the canon of film feminism see Judith Mayne's introduction to *Framed* (xi–xxiii); and Patrice Petro, *Aftershocks of the New: Feminism and Film History* (New Brunswick, N.J.: Rutgers University Press, 2002), esp. chaps. 2 and 9.

16. Lucie Arbuthnot and Gail Seneca, "Pre-Text and Text in *Gentlemen Prefer Blondes*" (1982), in Erens, *Issues in Feminist Film Criticism*, 112–125; Richard Dyer, "Judy Garland and Gay Men," in his *Heavenly Bodies*, 141–194; Andrew Britton, *Katharine Hepburn: Star as Feminist* (New York: Continuum, 1995).

17. All quotations from Curry, *Too Much of a Good Thing*, 135.

18. Richard Dyer, "Resistance through Charisma: Rita Hayworth and *Gilda*," in *Women and Film Noir*, ed. E. Ann Kaplan (London: BFI, 1978), 91–99. By way of contrast to his essay see Mary Ann Doane, "*Gilda*: Epistemology as Strip-tease," *Camera Obscura* 11 (fall 1982): 6–27; Linda Dittmar, "From Fascism to the Cold War: *Gilda*'s 'Fantastic' Politics," *Wide Angle* 10 (1988): 4–18; Kimberly Lenz, "Put the Blame on *Gilda*: Dyke Noir vs. Film Noir," *Theatre Studies* 40 (1995): 17–26. For further discussion see also chap. 4.

19. Amy Lawrence, *Echo and Narcissus: Women's Voices in Classical Hollywood Cinema* (Berkeley: University of California Press, 1991). All quotations here from 147–154.

20. I see in Hayworth's image what Richard Dyer calls "an element of protest about labour under capitalism which you do not find in [certain star images like] [June] Allyson, [Clark] Gable, [Fred] Astaire" (*Heavenly Bodies*, 7).

21. A psychiatrist commenting on 1950s stars in Ezra Goodman, *The Fifty-Year Decline and Fall of Hollywood* (New York: Simon and Schuster, 1961), 272–273.

22. Stacey, *Star Gazing*.

23. See, e.g., *Time*'s obituary, "The All-American Love Goddess," May 25, 1987, 76. The designation came from Winthrop Sargeant, "The Cult of the Love Goddess in America," *Life*, November 10, 1947, 80–96. For fuller discussion see chaps. 1 and 2.

24. All quotations here from Michel de Certeau, *The Practice of Everyday Life*, trans. Steven F. Rendell (Berkeley: University of California Press, 1984), xix–xx.

25. In this sense Hayworth's power was limited to her "earned autonomy," as sociologists call it, in that her popularity was related to her skill as well as to her innate physical attributes: "[But] in any group where the occupational task is performed primarily in concert with others, autonomy is limited regardless of the degree of skill and knowledge required. This may explain why the model of a professional occupation has so little relevance to team players, musicians in orches-

tras, and others who perform tasks as part of a group effort" [including, clearly, Hollywood filmmaking] (Phyllis L. Stewart and Muriel G. Cantor, "Analysis: Occupational Control," in *Varieties of Work Experience: The Social Control of Occupational Groups and Roles,* ed. Phyllis L. Stewart and Muriel G. Cantor [New York: John Wiley, 1974], 319). See also Anne K. Peters and Muriel G. Cantor, "Screen Acting as Work," in *Individuals in Mass Media Organizations: Creativity and Constraint,* ed. James S. Ettema and D. Charles Whitney (London: Sage, 1982), 53–68. Barry King also writes about "low and high autonomy stars" in relation to the control they had over scripts, salary, and choice of vehicles. Hayworth was at first a low autonomy star, but with the formation of Beckworth she became a high autonomy star in King's terms. See Barry King, "Stardom as an Occupation," in *The Hollywood Film Industry,* ed. Paul Kerr (London: Routledge and Kegan Paul, 1986), 172–174.

26. Richard Dyer coined the phrase "structured polysemy" to refer to the ways stars signify many different things that are nevertheless contained by boundaries of gender, ethnicity, race, age, context, and cultural contingency. A star cannot be made to mean *anything,* infinitely, in other words. But stars signify both in complicated ways as individual identities and through the synergistic combination of their identities with those of other stars in particular times and historical situations. See Dyer, *Stars,* 63.

27. Clark, *Negotiating Hollywood,* 22–23.

28. No one has ever been able to tell me, given the date of Beckworth's founding and its terms, why James Stewart is continually cited as the first star to receive a percentage of the profits from his films; Stewart's deal was made in 1950. See, e.g., Connie Bruck, "The Monopolist: How Lew Wasserman Took Over Hollywood," *New Yorker,* April 21 and 28, 2003, 139. Beckworth is discussed further in chap. 1.

29. Kaja Silverman, "Historical Trauma and Male Subjectivity," in *Psychoanalysis and Cinema,* ed. E. Ann Kaplan (New York: Routledge, 1990), 116. See also the chapter of the same name in Silverman's *Male Subjectivity at the Margins* (New York: Routledge, 1992).

30. Silverman, "Historical Trauma," 116–117.

31. Lynn Spigel, *Make Room for TV: Television and the Family Ideal in Postwar America* (Chicago, Ill.: University of Chicago Press, 1992), 8.

32. Quotations here and in subsequent sentence from Stacey, *Star Gazing,* 9, 224. See also Curry, *Too Much of a Good Thing;* and Diane Negra, *Off-White Hollywood: American Culture and Ethnic Female Stardom* (New York: Routledge, 2001). For feminist work on acting see also Patricia Adams, "Dorothy Tutin and J. C. Trewin: An Essay on the Possibilities of Feminist Biography," *Theatre Studies* (1984–85/1985–86): 67–102; and Britton, *Katharine Hepburn.*

33. Mary Ann Doane writes in "The Economy of Desire: The Commodity Form in/of the Cinema," *Quarterly Review of Film and Video* 11 (1989): 23–33, that the "much sought-after address to the female spectator often seems more readily accessible in the discursive apparatus surrounding the film than in the text itself" (26).

34. Anne Friedberg, *Window Shopping: Cinema and the Postmodern* (Berkeley: University of California Press, 1993), 2–7.

35. See, e.g., Diane Waldman, "From Midnight Shows to Marriage Vows: Women,

Exploitation, and Exhibition," *Wide Angle* 6 (1984): 40–48; Jane Gaines, "War, Women, and Lipstick: Fan Mags in the Forties," *Heresies* 5 (1985): 42–47; and Doane, "Economy of Desire."

36. Quotations in this and subsequent sentences from Lynn Spigel, *Welcome to the Dreamhouse: Popular Media and Postwar Suburbs* (Durham, N.C.: Duke University Press, 2001), 14.

37. Ibid. See also Janice Radway, *Reading the Romance: Women, Patriarchy, and Popular Literature* (Chapel Hill: University of North Carolina Press, 1984).

38. Much work has been done recently on analyzing and decoding women's magazines other than fan magazines, as well as romance novels aimed at a female audience. Most of these studies conclude that the pleasure produced for the reader, however significant in the context of her own life, is secured usually at the expense of political change or confrontation with the structural oppressiveness under which she spends that life. See Tania Modleski, *Loving with a Vengeance: Mass-Produced Fantasies for Women* (Hamden, Conn.: Archon Books, 1982); Radway, *Reading the Romance;* Ellen McCracken, *Decoding Women's Magazines: From Mademoiselle to Ms.* (New York: St. Martin's, 1993); and Jennifer Scanlon, *Inarticulate Longings: The Ladies' Home Journal, Gender, and the Promises of Consumer Culture* (New York: Routledge, 1995).

39. Quotations here from Gaylyn Studlar, "The Perils of Pleasure? Fan Magazine Discourse as Women's Commodified Culture in the 1920s," *Wide Angle* 13 (January 1991): 9–10. In the case of the 1920s, then, the "surprises" are not produced by the discourse but by its unusual context and, most important, by the differing theoretical assumptions the context appears to call for.

40. Michael Renov, *Hollywood's Wartime Woman: Representation and Ideology* (Ann Arbor, Mich.: UMI Research Press, 1988), 3, 36–38. See also his "Advertising/ Photojournalism/Cinema: The Shifting Rhetoric of Forties Female Representation," *Quarterly Review of Film and Video* 11 (1989): 1–21.

41. Studlar, "Perils of Pleasure?" 9, 10.

42. Joanne Meyerowitz, ed., *Not June Cleaver: Women and Gender in Postwar America, 1945–1960* (Philadelphia, Pa.: Temple University Press, 1994).

43. Joanne Meyerowitz, "Beyond the Feminine Mystique: A Reassessment of Postwar Mass Culture, 1946–1958," in ibid., 229–262. See also the essays in Joel Foreman, ed., *The Other Fifties: Interrogating Midcentury American Icons* (Urbana: University of Illinois Press, 1997), which aim to locate "struggle, resistance, instability, and transformation in what is for many the least likely place: mass media popular culture" (6).

44. Meyerowitz, "Beyond the Feminine Mystique," 231.

45. Ibid., 252.

46. Ibid., 231.

47. Noël Carroll, *Theorizing the Moving Image* (Cambridge, U.K.: Cambridge University Press, 1996), 281.

48. Meyerowitz, "Beyond the Feminine Mystique," 246.

49. Meyerowitz, *Not June Cleaver;* Maxine L. Margolis, *Mothers and Such: Views of American Women and Why They Changed* (Berkeley: University of California Press, 1984); Glenna Matthews, *"Just a Housewife": The Rise and Fall of Domesticity in America* (New York: Oxford University Press, 1987); Elaine Tyler May, *Homeward Bound: American Families in the Cold War Era* (New York: Basic

Books, 1988); Spigel, *Make Room for TV* and *Welcome to the Dreamhouse;* Foreman, *The Other Fifties;* and Steven Cohan, *Masked Men: Masculinity and Movies in the Fifties* (Bloomington: Indiana University Press, 1997).

50. May, *Homeward Bound.*

51. Vance Packard, *The Status Seekers* (New York: David McKay, 1959).

52. Margolis, *Mothers and Such,* 212, 218.

53. Meyerowitz, "Beyond the Feminine Mystique," 237.

54. Robert Ray has written that the "generalizing power" of poststructuralism's "enormously powerful theoretical machine" arguably has been to make feminist consciousness itself into a poststructuralist development. See Robert B. Ray, *The Avant-Garde Finds Andy Hardy* (Cambridge, Mass.: Harvard University Press, 1995), 7. See also Mayne, *Framed,* xi–xxiii.

55. For one very recent example, among many, see the work contained in Matthew Tinkcom and Amy Villarejo, eds., *Keyframes: Popular Cinema and Cultural Studies* (New York: Routledge, 2001).

56. All quotations here from Marcia Landy, "Mario Lanza and the 'Fourth World,'" in Tinkcom and Villarejo, *Keyframes,* 257–258.

57. Petro, *Aftershocks of the New,* 161.

58. For more on emotion and/as identification see Berys Gaut, "Identification and Emotion in Narrative Film," in *Passionate Views: Film, Cognition, and Emotion,* ed. Carl Plantinga and Greg M. Smith (Baltimore, Md.: Johns Hopkins University Press, 1999), 200–216.

59. As will be detailed further in the notes to individual chapters, the resource of which I have made the most extensive use is the Constance McCormick Collection of star scrapbooks at the Cinema-Television Library, University of Southern California, which contains seven scrapbooks of fan-magazine material (not always documented as to source or date, unfortunately) covering Rita Hayworth's career (cited here as RHS). In addition I have drawn on clipping files (at the Cinema-Television Library, USC; the Margaret Herrick Library, Academy of Motion Picture Arts and Sciences, Los Angeles [cited here as AMPAS]; and the British Film Institute, London [cited here as BFI]); the Hedda Hopper Collection at the Margaret Herrick Library; the Louella Parsons Collection at the Cinema-Television Library, USC; the Valerie Bettis scrapbooks and folders and the Rita Hayworth folders at the Dance Collection, New York Public Library for the Performing Arts; and the standard sources referenced by the *Reader's Guide to Periodical Literature.* I also had access to about fifty additional popular articles about Hayworth, mostly photocopied from movie fan magazines, provided by Caren Roberts-Frenzel. Jeanne Kramer, whom I met through the online auction house Ebay, generously donated an additional extensive collection of original material from fan magazines and tabloids for use in this project, and I am especially grateful to her for her help.

60. See John Ellis, *Visible Fictions: Cinema, Television, Video* (London: Routledge, 1982), 91–108; and David Bordwell, Kristin Thompson, and Janet Staiger, *Classical Hollywood Cinema: Film Style and Mode of Production to 1960* (New York: Columbia University Press, 1985), 101.

61. See McCracken, *Decoding Women's Magazines,* 30, 73–74.

62. All quotations here ibid., 1–2, 7–8.

63. See Virginia Wright Wexman, *Creating the Couple: Love, Marriage, and Holly-*

wood Performance (Princeton, N.J.: Princeton University Press, 1993): "One need not adopt a posture of naive credulity regarding all the 'facts' that Hollywood purveys about its stars in order to argue that the film audience has traditionally percieved *[sic]* this information as being endowed with a kind of authenticity that it does not grant to the fictional forms of the films themselves" (33). See also Samantha Barbas, *Movie Crazy: Fans, Stars, and the Cult of Celebrity* (New York: Palgrave, 2001), 85–108, which discusses the ways that fans negotiated their own methods for distinguishing "the true from the false" in the 1930s—with Louella Parsons, *Modern Screen,* and *Photoplay* being among the most "trusted magazines and reporters" relied on by fans (103).

64. According to John L. Caughey, *Imaginary Social Worlds* (Lincoln: University of Nebraska Press, 1984), "The basis of most fan relationships is not an esthetic appreciation but a social relationship" (40); fans "characterize unmet media figures as if they were intimately involved with them, and in a sense they are" (33). Most of these relationships with media figures are simply an "important but perfectly manageable part of everyday life," as S. Elizabeth Bird puts it. See S. Elizabeth Bird, *For Enquiring Minds: A Cultural Study of Supermarket Tabloids* (Knoxville: University of Tennessee Press, 1992), 3, 155. See also note 12 above.

65. McCracken, *Decoding Women's Magazines,* 24–25.

66. See Jacqueline Bobo, "*The Color Purple:* Black Women as Cultural Readers," in *Female Spectators: Looking at Film and Television,* ed. E. Deidre Pribham (London: Verso, 1988), 90–109.

67. See Roland Barthes, *Image/Music/Text,* trans. Stephen Heath (New York: Hill and Wang, 1977), 39–41.

68. All quotations here from Gladys Hall, "A Tip to Teenagers from Rita," *Silver Screen,* May 1951, 22–23, 51, 53, 55.

69. I do not want to make too much of the play on words, but clearly I am also using "off the screen" in another sense: that which has disappeared from view or is not noticed.

70. Leaming, *If This Was Happiness,* 53–54.

71. William Vincent, "Rita Hayworth at Columbia, 1941–1945: The Fabrication of a Star," in *Columbia Pictures: Portrait of a Studio,* ed. Bernard F. Dick (Lexington: University Press of Kentucky, 1992), 118. This would also raise the question of what to make of the concomitant success of Ingrid Bergman, a star proclaimed by Hollywood discourse to be entirely natural. For a comparison of Bergman's and Hayworth's images in these terms see Adrienne L. McLean, "The Cinderella Princess and the Instrument of Evil: Revisiting Two Postwar Hollywood Star Scandals," in *Headline Hollywood: A Century of Film Scandal,* ed. Adrienne L. McLean and David A. Cook (New Brunswick, N.J.: Rutgers University Press, 2001), 163–189.

72. Meyerowitz, "Beyond the Feminine Mystique," 234.

73. For more on the double bind as a theoretical concept see Michael Renov, "*Leave Her to Heaven:* The Double Bind of the Post-War Woman" (1983), in *Imitations of Life: A Reader on Film and Television Melodrama,* ed. Marcia Landy (Detroit, Mich.: Wayne State University Press, 1991), 227–235.

74. Clark, *Negotiating Hollywood,* 83.

75. Jane C. Desmond, ed., *Meaning in Motion: New Cultural Studies of Dance* (Durham, N.C.: Duke University Press, 1997), 2.

76. My use of the term *performance* also draws on Valeria Ottolenghi's discussion of the professional performer as always mediating between "the presentation of one's social or professional role (the dancer or the boxer)" and the "complete representation of someone or something other than oneself (a disguise, a character)" (Valeria Ottolenghi, quoted in Marco De Marinis, *The Semiotics of Performance*, trans. Aine O'Healy [Bloomington: Indiana University Press, 1993], 49). See also Mayne, *Framed*, 3–22.

77. Dyer, "Resistance through Charisma."

78. Judith Butler, *Bodies That Matter: On the Discursive Limits of "Sex"* (New York: Routledge, 1993), 2. See also Jane C. Desmond, "Introduction: Making the Invisible Visible: Staging Sexualities through Dance," in *Dancing Desires: Choreographing Sexualities on and off the Stage*, ed. Jane C. Desmond (Madison: University of Wisconsin Press, 2001), 3–32.

79. Alan Lovell and Peter Krämer, eds., *Screen Acting* (New York: Routledge, 1999), 5.

80. Ann Daly, "Dance History and Feminist Theory: Reconsidering Isadora Duncan and the Male Gaze," in *Gender in Performance: The Presentation of Difference in the Performing Arts*, ed. Laurence Senelick (Hanover, N.H.: University Press of New England, 1992), 243.

81. In a sense all of the work explored in and embodied by this book involves revision and revisioning. The majority of Hayworth's films in the 1950s are remakes of other films or adaptations of preexisting works (sometimes both). Analysis of these films, augmented by study of the extratextual and intertextual sources on which they draw, helps us to understand the 1950s as a period in which the process of revision—of the past, of one's personal image, of the images of others—itself possessed an unusual ideological relevance.

Chapter 1. From Cansino to Hayworth to Beckworth

1. All references here from "Rita Hayworth, Hollywood's Best-Dressed Girl," *Look,* February 27, 1940, 28–32.

2. Danae Clark, *Negotiating Hollywood: The Cultural Politics of Actors' Labor* (Minneapolis: University of Minnesota Press, 1995), 22–23.

3. Richard Dyer, "White," *Screen* 29 (autumn 1988): 64. The Gaines quotation is in Jib Fowles, *Starstruck: Celebrity Performers and the American Public* (Washington, D.C.: Smithsonian Institution Press, 1992), 234. Despite the prevalence of Hayworth's ethnicity in her image, George Hadley-Garcia's relatively recent *Hispanic Hollywood: Latins in Motion Pictures* (New York: Citadel Press, 1990) was the first study of the Latin image in Hollywood, or indeed of ethnicity in Hollywood generally, in which Hayworth's name is so much as mentioned. Works that do not mention Hayworth include Allen L. Woll, *The Latin Image in American Film* (Los Angeles, Calif.: UCLA Latin American Center Publications, 1977); Randall M. Miller, ed., *The Kaleidoscopic Lens: How Hollywood Views Ethnic Groups* (New York: Jerome S. Ozer, 1980); and Lester D. Friedman, ed., *Unspeakable Images: Ethnicity and the American Cinema* (Urbana: University of Illinois Press, 1991).

4. See, e.g., Patrick Agan, *The Decline and Fall of the Love Goddesses* (Los Angeles,

Calif.: Pinnacle Books, 1979), 69; William Vincent, "Rita Hayworth at Columbia, 1941–1945: The Fabrication of a Star," in *Columbia Pictures: Portrait of a Studio,* ed. Bernard F. Dick (Lexington: University Press of Kentucky, 1992), 119; and Virginia Wright Wexman, *Creating the Couple: Love, Marriage, and Hollywood Performance* (Princeton, N.J.: Princeton University Press, 1993), 136.

5. Mary Ann Doane, "The Economy of Desire: The Commodity Form in/of the Cinema," *Quarterly Review of Film and Video* 11 (1989): 24. See also her *The Desire to Desire: The Woman's Film of the 1940s* (Bloomington: Indiana University Press, 1987), 23.

6. Richard Dyer, *Heavenly Bodies: Film Stars and Society* (New York: St. Martin's, 1986), 5.

7. Clark, *Negotiating Hollywood,* 3.

8. See Noël Carroll, *Theorizing the Moving Image* (Cambridge, U.K.: Cambridge University Press, 1996), 281.

9. The "firm authority" is from Jack Lait, "Sho' Is All Woman (Rita Hayworth)," *Photoplay,* November 1948, 46. Again, because fan and other mass-market articles are not listed individually in the bibliography, I will cite all such articles in their entirety in the notes and give complete pagination whenever possible (if a journal name, date, author, and/or page numbers are not cited in the text or in notes, it is because the information was not available to me at the time this was written). Brief excerpts (two or three words), especially if they are representative of often repeated or characteristic locutions or phrases, are more often cited only in the text.

10. All references here from articles, c. 1939–1941, collected in Rita Hayworth scrapbooks (RHS) of the Constance McCormick Collection, vols. 1 and 2 (see note 9 above).

11. All mentions here from Helen Hover, "What It Takes to Be a Hollywood Husband! 'Mr. Rita Hayworth' Tells," *Screenland,* c. 1940, 26, 90–92.

12. Ibid. According to John Kobal, by 1940 there had been more than thirty-eight hundred stories filed on Rita Cansino/Hayworth, and her photograph had been reproduced more than twelve thousand times. See John Kobal, *Rita Hayworth: The Time, the Place, and the Woman* (New York: Norton, 1977), 81.

13. All references in this paragraph from Dorothy Spensley, "Design for Loving," *Motion Picture,* September 1940, 34, 56, 72; John R. Franchey, "Sultry Siren," *Silver Screen,* February 1941, 36–37, 79–80; Mary Jane Manners, "How I Keep My Husband from Getting Jealous," *Silver Screen,* April 1942, 26–27, 60–62.

14. Hayworth's first *Life* cover (July 15, 1940) accompanied a one-page photo spread about a "bicycle picnic" (58). The second cover (August 11, 1941), of Hayworth eating a hamburger on the Santa Monica beach, accompanies the one-page pinup photo and its brief blurb, from which all references in this paragraph are taken (33).

15. Laura Mulvey, *Visual and Other Pleasures* (Bloomington: Indiana University Press, 1989), xi.

16. All references from RHS, vol. 2.

17. "California Carmen," *Time,* November 10, 1941, 90–95.

18. All references here from James Reid, "Oomph for Sale," *Modern Screen,* December 1941, 36, 95–96.

19. Quotations in this and subsequent sentence from Franchey, "Sultry Siren"; and

Susanah Parker, "Love and Rita Hayworth: The Story of a Daring Fight for Freedom," *Photoplay*, July 1942, 27–28, 76.

20. Clark, *Negotiating Hollywood*, 23.

21. Citations in this paragraph from *Time*'s "California Carmen."

22. All references in this and subsequent two paragraphs from Jerome Beatty, "Sweetheart of the A.E.F.," *American Magazine*, December 1942, 42–43, 72–74.

23. All mentions from RHS, vols. 2–5. In my research it became something of a challenge to find an article, short or long, about Hayworth that did *not* mention the fact that she used to be Margarita Cansino (variations in the spelling of "Margarita" and, more infrequently, "Cansino" are common and will not be acknowledged—e.g., with *sic*—as incorrect).

24. Richard Dyer, *Stars* (London: BFI, 1998); and John Ellis, *Visible Fictions: Cinema, Television, Video* (London: Routledge, 1982), 91–108.

25. Dyer, *Stars*, 26, 82.

26. Leo Braudy, *The Frenzy of Renown: Fame and Its History* (New York: Oxford University Press, 1986), 10, 11.

27. Ibid., 570.

28. Obviously class might also be a factor in the formation of Hayworth's star image, but this is harder to articulate. That is, stardom supplants class or puts one into a "new" class, one in which it is perfectly acceptable to have inferior roots. Paul Fussell groups actors and "celebrities," as well as "*the talented*," in an "X" class of the "self-cultivated" (Paul Fussell, *Class: A Guide through the American Status System* [New York: Simon and Schuster, 1983], 179–187).

29. Werner Sollors, *Beyond Ethnicity: Consent and Descent in American Culture* (New York: Oxford University Press, 1986), 11. On positive and negative images see, e.g., Ana López, "Are All Latins from Manhattan? Hollywood, Ethnography, and Cultural Colonialism," in Friedman, *Unspeakable Images*, 404–421; Lester D. Friedman, "Celluloid Palimpsests: An Overview of Ethnicity and the American Film," in ibid., 11–35; Sumiko Higashi, "Ethnicity, Class, and Gender in Film: DeMille's *The Cheat*," in ibid., 112–139; Gaylyn Studlar, "Discourses of Gender and Ethnicity: The Construction and De(con)struction of Rudolph Valentino as Other," *Film Criticism* 13 (winter 1989): 18–35; Shari Roberts, "'The Lady in the Tutti-Frutti Hat': Carmen Miranda, a Spectacle of Ethnicity," *Cinema Journal* 32 (spring 1993): 3–23; Daniel Bernardi, ed., *Classic Hollywood, Classic Whiteness* (Minneapolis: University of Minnesota Press, 2001); and Diane Negra, *Off-White Hollywood: American Culture and Ethnic Female Stardom* (New York: Routledge, 2001). "Image of" studies include Woll's *Latin Image in American Film* and Miller's *Kaleidoscopic Lens*.

30. López, "Are All Latins from Manhattan?"

31. Friedman, "Celluloid Palimpsests."

32. For information on the Good Neighbor Policy I consulted Bryce Wood, *The Making of the Good Neighbor Policy* (New York: Columbia University Press, 1961); John T. Reid, *Spanish American Images of the United States, 1790–1960* (Gainesville: University Press of Florida, 1977), 150–151, 212–215; Guy Poitras, *The Ordeal of Hegemony: The United States and Latin America* (Boulder, Colo.: Westview Press, 1990). See also López, "Are All Latins from Manhattan?"; and Roberts, "'Lady in the Tutti-Frutti Hat.'"

33. As James M. Flagg writes of Hayworth in 1942, "She's half-Spanish, half-English,

which makes her look just as American as your sister" ("Rita Hayworth Is Sketched by Flagg," *Los Angeles Herald Express,* RHS, vol. 1). I cannot know how audiences read the "old Rita" and the "new Rita" as texts, but fragmentary evidence in archives in the form of fan letters indicates that she inspired "deep liking" in some audience members specifically because of her "Spanish heritage," as expressed in a 1947 letter from American GI José Manuel Torres to Hedda Hopper (Hedda Hopper Collection, AMPAS). Unfortunately, Torres's letter is the only such fan letter in Hopper's file.

34. Sollors, *Beyond Ethnicity,* 6; see also Friedman, "Celluloid Palimpsests," 18–19.
35. Sollors, *Beyond Ethnicity,* 29.
36. Friedman, "Celluloid Palimpsests," 15, 22.
37. Ibid., 22.
38. Sollors, *Beyond Ethnicity,* 33.
39. Friedman, "Celluloid Palimpsests," 27.
40. Loy, e.g. (born Myrna Williams in Montana in 1905), did not become a star as an "Oriental vamp," an identity with which she was typed visually early in her career, but as Nora Charles, the perfect American wife, in the *Thin Man* series. See also Roberts, "'Lady in the Tutti-Frutti Hat.'"
41. Robert J. Schiffer (Hayworth's longtime friend and makeup man), personal communication.
42. All citations from Gelal Talata, "Dancing Feet Lead to Stardom," *Milwaukee Journal,* c. 1935, Rita Hayworth clipping file, AMPAS.
43. See also Joanne Hershfield, *The Invention of Dolores del Rio* (Minneapolis: University of Minnesota Press, 2000).
44. Braudy, *Frenzy of Renown,* 554.
45. Ibid., 576.
46. Andrew J. Weigert, *Mixed Emotions: Certain Steps Toward Understanding Ambivalence* (Albany: State University of New York Press, 1991), 71.
47. Quotations from Hedda Hopper, "Hayworth's Child Has Rich Heritage: Baby Can Look Toward Career as Scion of Talented Cansino Family," *Los Angeles Times* (1944), RHS, vol. 2; Hedda Hopper, "Rebecca of the Welles" (June 3, 1945), Hedda Hopper Collection, AMPAS. See also Dorothy Deere, "Feet That Danced," *Photoplay,* November 1946, 47, 110–114; Louella Parsons, "Cinderella Princess: Colorful Career of Cinderella Girl Told by Film Writer," chaps. 1–6, *Los Angeles Examiner,* May-June 1949, RHS, vol. 4.
48. The "glamour queen" quotation is from "Rita Hayworth Found to Be Two Individuals," *Los Angeles Times,* c. 1948, Hayworth clipping file, AMPAS. See also Hedda Hopper, "Rita's Sweeter Than Ever" ("There are two Rita Hayworths . . ."), July 18, 1948, Hedda Hopper Collection, AMPAS.
49. Hopper, "Rita Hayworth Found to Be Two Individuals" and "Rita's Sweeter Than Ever"; and Barbara Leaming, *If This Was Happiness,* 122.
50. From Lait, "Sho' Is All Woman."
51. Lauren Berlant, "National Brands/National Body: *Imitation of Life,*" in *Comparative American Identities: Race, Sex, and Nationality in the Modern Text,* ed. Hortense J. Spillers (New York: Routledge, 1991), 132.
52. In López, "Are All Latins from Manhattan?" 412. In his "The Other Question—the Stereotype and Colonial Discourse," *Screen* 24 (November-December 1983): 18–36, Bhabha uses the psychoanalytic concept of fetishism to discuss the stereo-

type and its use, but I am reluctant to rely entirely on fetishism because it returns us to making assumptions about all viewers split along binary gender lines. Fetishism does provide a convincing analogical structure for the way colonial power is exercised; it even, as Bhabha suggests, explains the stereotype's inherent failure completely to define the "Other" as other because disavowal always threatens to become knowledge of the "fantasy (as desire, defense) of [the] position of mastery" (34). But it does not aid much in illuminating the nature of the response of either the colonized or of colonized audiences to their own representation *as* such, as stereotypes. Indeed, Bhabha himself wants to complicate the "historical and theoretical simplification" that colonial power and discourse is "possessed entirely by the coloniser" (25). He also raises the one-sidedness of psychoanalytic discourse as a problem and notes that applying the notion of fetishism to the simultaneous fascination with and disavowal of the difference (imposed, as well as "inherent") of the stereotype leaves little room for any other than a masculinized explanation of the prevalence and power of the stereotype. To me the issue is not only what stereotyping represents or means psychoanalytically (as a process, as an activity, as an impulse) but what it means historically or culturally in specific times and places and then to what ideological uses the stereotype is put by those producing it and those consuming it.

53. López, "Are All Latins from Manhattan?" 414.

54. All quotations in this paragraph taken from Dyer, "White," 44–64.

55. According to Gallup's audience research Hayworth's marquee value during the war was only marginally (one or two percentage points) higher with men than with women, and after the war she was, in fact, more popular with women than with men. I was surprised to find that Betty Grable, contrary to what I had always been taught, was more often much more popular with men than with women (*Gallup Looks at the Movies: Audience Research Reports, 1940–1950* [Wilmington, Del.: American Institute of Public Opinion and Scholarly Resources, 1979]; on microfilm).

56. See the section on Marilyn Monroe in Dyer, *Heavenly Bodies,* 19–66. One question that Hayworth's stardom raises is, in fact, whether it is enough to claim "white" as what Dyer calls the symbolic "apotheosis of female desirability." Betty Grable, Hayworth's contemporary, of course fits Dyer's definition of the white star as the "impossible dream" (Dyer, "White," 44–64), but alongside Grable was Hayworth, whose whiteness clearly is not the most important element of her image. Although obviously I believe that Rita Hayworth is a far more unusual star than film scholars have heretofore acknowledged, it may also be true that we need somehow to think about stars as working and signifying much more in synergism with other stars than as single entities. If Betty Grable is, as several have claimed, virtually an advertisement for eugenics, the potential mother of a master white race, what does it mean that Hayworth, "darker" and more exotic, essentially matched her in appeal? Could there have been a Betty Grable without a Rita Hayworth (or a Dietrich, a Bergman, a Miranda, etc.)—or vice versa? See also Richard Dyer, *White* (London: Routledge, 1997).

57. Michael Wood, *America in the Movies* (New York: Basic Books, 1975), 56. References to Hayworth's recent motherhood are frequent in the publicity about *Gilda* (see *Gilda* pressbook, Cinema-Television Library, USC). For more about Hayworth's relationship to domesticity see chap. 2.

58. That Columbia was not all that sure about how to characterize Hayworth's role in *Gilda* (her "first" dramatic film) can be judged by one of its primary advertising tag lines: "Great as is her powerful dramatic portrayal—great, too, is this dancing Hayworth—singing 'Put the Blame on Mame'!"

59. In *The Lady from Shanghai,* which followed *Gilda* and was Hayworth's only real 1940s failure, Elsa Bannister is "sexually lifeless" (to use Charles Higham's term) and dies at the film's end (Charles Higham, *The Films of Orson Welles* [Berkeley: University of California Press, 1970], 116). Significantly, Elsa Bannister is the only role that Hayworth plays as the whitest of women, a platinum blonde. Audiences vehemently protested the conversion. See chap. 4 for discussion of *Gilda* and *The Lady from Shanghai.*

60. See, e.g., Richard Dyer, "Resistance through Charisma: Rita Hayworth and *Gilda,*" in *Women in Film Noir,* ed. E. Ann Kaplan (London: BFI, 1978), 91–99.

61. See, e.g., "Carmen Hayworth," review of *The Loves of Carmen,* dir. Charles Vidor, *Newsweek,* November 23, 1948, 78–80.

62. I have found no evidence that Hayworth's ethnicity was ever used as blame or excuse for transgressive or excessive sexual behavior in her private life, even during the scandal that surrounded her initially adulterous liaison with Aly Khan (see chap. 2).

63. Michael Renov, *Hollywood's Wartime Woman: Representation and Ideology* (Ann Arbor, Mich.: UMI Research Press, 1988), 3.

64. Ibid., 36–38. See also Renov's "Advertising/Photojournalism/Cinema: The Shifting Rhetoric of Forties Female Representation," *Quarterly Review of Film and Video* 11 (1989): 1–21.

65. See, e.g., Lois Banner, *American Beauty* (New York: Knopf, 1983); and Peg Zeglin Brand, ed., *Beauty Matters* (Bloomington: Indiana University Press, 2000).

66. Joanne Meyerowitz, "Beyond the Feminine Mystique: A Reassessment of Postwar Mass Culture, 1946–1958," in *Not June Cleaver: Women and Gender in Postwar America, 1945–1960,* ed. Joanne Meyerowitz (Philadelphia, Pa.: Temple University Press, 1994), 231.

67. Clark, *Negotiating Hollywood,* 26.

68. All citations from Helene Henley in "Letters to the Editor," *American Magazine,* January 1943, 5.

69. Clark, *Negotiating Hollywood,* 20, 57.

70. All citations in this and the following two paragraphs are from Winthrop Sargeant, "The Cult of the Love Goddess in America," *Life,* November 10, 1947, 80–96.

71. Meyerowitz, "Beyond the Feminine Mystique," 233.

72. Clark, *Negotiating Hollywood,* 5.

73. Quotations from Louella O. Parsons, "Ask the Boss," *Photoplay,* March 1948, 50–51, 90–92.

74. Citations in this paragraph are from Lynn Bowers, "Goddess with a Grin," *Screenland,* June 1948, 20–21, 56–59; Vernon Cansino, "The Rita You've Never Met," *Movie Show,* August 1948, 23–24, 63–66; "Carmen Hayworth," *Newsweek,* August 23, 1948, 78–80; Jack Lait, "Sho' Is All Woman," 46–47, 114–115; Jane Corwin, "The Not-So-Private Life of Rita Hayworth," *Photoplay,* October 1952, 50–51, 105–107; Aldo Ray, "Oh, Oh, What a Gal," *Movie Stars Parade,* August 1953, 34–35, 75–76.

75. According to Terrance McCluskey of Sony Pictures Entertainment, the contract, dated June 1, 1947, between Columbia Pictures and the Beckworth Corporation was a production-distribution agreement. Beckworth was to "produce and Columbia to distribute all motion pictures produced by Beckworth," and all would star Hayworth. She would receive 25 percent of the profits of her films. The contract was for five terms of one year each (McCluskey to the author, December 4, 1991). This is all the information I was able to acquire from Sony about anything to do with Columbia and its archives, and subsequent letters to McCluskey were returned "addressee unknown." As I mentioned in the introduction, I do not know why James Stewart's 1950 profit-sharing deal, engineered by Lew Wasserman, is always cited as the first contract that granted a star a percentage of a film's profits.

76. Meyerowitz, introduction to *Not June Cleaver*, 2.

77. Ibid., 5.

78. All quotations from Clark, *Negotiating Hollywood*, 25.

Chapter 2. Rita Lives for Love

1. All quotations here from Barbara Leaming, *If This Was Happiness* (New York: Viking, 1989).

2. Winthrop Sargeant, "The Cult of the Love Goddess in America," *Life*, November 10, 1947, 80–96.

3. Leaming, *If This Was Happiness*, 9.

4. Ibid., 18 (italics mine).

5. See, e.g., Colin Heywood, *A History of Childhood: Children and Childhood in the West from Medieval to Modern Times* (London: Blackwell, 2001), 116–117: "We are bound to agree with Lloyd deMause that by the early twentieth century children in the West were less likely to be killed, abandoned or beaten than in the past (reserving judgment for lack of evidence on sexual abuse)."

6. Richard Dyer, *Stars* (London: BFI, 1998), 45. I should note that in his essay "Four Films of Lana Turner," in *Star Texts: Image and Performance in Film and Television*, ed. Jeremy G. Butler (Detroit, Mich.: Wayne State University Press, 1991), Dyer makes reference to the fact that in the 1940s and 1950s the "true story" of Turner's father—"a gambler and bootlegger [who] was murdered by one of his cronies when Turner was ten"—surfaced in fan magazines and biographies as a "useful" story (approved by Turner's studio, MGM) for explaining Turner's "inexorable link with badness, and its pitiability" (230). In fact, this "true story" did not appear until December 1951, in a long *Woman's Home Companion* magazine piece by Turner, as told to Cameron Shipp, entitled "My Private Life" (see the Lana Turner scrapbooks [LTS], vol. 3, Constance McCormick Collection, Cinema-Television Library, University of Southern California), and it was never "approved" by MGM. More to the point, Turner "adored" her father and claims she had a very happy childhood until his death regardless of what she discovered later about his past (according to a June 1954 *Modern Screen* article about Turner, she wished she "hadn't done the story" [LTS, vol. 4]). Although Dyer writes that "Turner and her father were a powerful image-complex" at this time, it was clearly a different image-complex than that of Hayworth and her father, and it

was rarely referred to again in fan magazines until 1958 (in coverage of the stabbing of Johnny Stompanato in Turner's bedroom). In a sampling of some ten fan magazines from 1948 to 1958 that all feature articles about both Turner and Hayworth, for example, only one even mentions Turner's father (and then simply to refer to his death). In contrast, all of the articles about Hayworth from the same magazines mention or discuss Hayworth's father and family and their influence on her career and home life.

7. All quotations here from Jane Gaines, "War, Women, and Lipstick: Fan Mags in the Forties," *Heresies* 5 (1985): 45.

8. All quotations here from Alexander Doty, *Flaming Classics: Queering the Film Canon* (New York: Routledge, 2000), 3.

9. See Gloria Steinem, "Women in the Dark: Of Sex Goddesses, Abuse, and Dreams," *Ms.*, January/February 1991, 35–37, for a discussion of how many "sex goddesses" (Hayworth, Harlow, Monroe, Kim Novak, and others) were the victims of physical, sexual, and/or emotional abuse as children. For interesting insights into how self-aware Hayworth was as to her objectified status and its link to her *performances* rather than her private identity see Evan S. Connell Jr., "A Brief Essay on the Subject of Celebrity with Numerous Digressions and Particular Attention to the Actress, Rita Hayworth," *Esquire*, March 1965, 115–116; John Hallowell, "Rita Hayworth: Don't Put the Blame on Me, Boys," *New York Times*, October 25, 1970, 15, 38; and James Hill [Hayworth's fifth husband], *Rita Hayworth: A Memoir* (New York: Simon and Schuster, 1983).

10. Here I recast Robin Wood's description of his strong but *"unconscious"* identification as a teenaged and closeted spectator in 1948 with the gay male characters in Alfred Hitchcock's *Rope*. Robin Wood, *Hitchcock's Films Revisited* (New York: Columbia University Press, 1989), 352.

11. Virtually any biography of a female Hollywood star whose major appeal is linked to her beauty and who was married several times—the ur-star here being Marilyn Monroe—will likely feature many references to that star's search for love, search for happiness, victimization by men, and so on. See, e.g., the jacket to Ronald L. Davis, *Hollywood Beauty: Linda Darnell and the American Dream* (Norman: University of Oklahoma Press, 1991): "Driven by a stage mother to become rich and famous, but unable to cope with the career she had longed for as a child, Darnell soon was caught in a downward spiral of drinking, failed marriages, and exploitive relationships." See also Steinem, "Women in the Dark." In its May 2, 2003, issue, *Entertainment Weekly* put the cap on this rendering: "you've seen [it] 10,000 times: A struggling performer triumphs over a tough childhood to become rich, adored, and needy for love" (65). In this case the star in question is Lucille Ball.

12. Elaine Tyler May, *Homeward Bound: American Families in the Cold War Era* (New York: Basic Books, 1988), 89.

13. Lynn Spigel, *Make Room for TV: Television and the Family Ideal in Postwar America* (Chicago, Ill.: University of Chicago Press, 1992), 34.

14. Judson was born in 1896, but I can find no reference to the date of his death; Welles was born in 1915 and died in 1985; Aly Khan was born in 1911 and died in 1960; Dick Haymes was born in 1916 and died in 1980.

15. "Rita Hayworth, Hollywood's Best-Dressed Girl," *Look*, February 27, 1940, 28–32.

16. As in chap. 1, very brief quotations are cited only in the text. Other fan and mass-market articles are cited with full pagination, when possible, in the notes, because they are not listed individually in the bibliography.

17. This and subsequent quotation from Leaming, *If This Was Happiness,* 34, 39.

18. All quotations here from Helen Hover, "What It Takes to Be a Hollywood Husband! 'Mr. Rita Hayworth' Tells," *Screenland,* c. 1940, 26, 90–92.

19. All quotations here from Mary Jane Manners, "How I Keep My Husband from Getting Jealous," *Silver Screen,* April 1942, 26–27, 60–62.

20. All quotations here from Susanah Parker, "Love and Rita Hayworth: The Story of a Daring Fight for Freedom," *Photoplay,* July 1942, 27–28, 76.

21. "Don't Blame Hollywood," *Movie Stars Parade,* May 1942, 14–15.

22. All quotations here from Gaines, "War, Women, and Lipstick," 42, 43.

23. Mary Ann Doane, *The Desire to Desire: The Woman's Film of the 1940s* (Bloomington: Indiana University Press, 1987), 32–33.

24. Taken to its limit, the cumulative result of a number of such moments might easily be cynicism, distrust of the media, a refusal to believe that representation equals reality. For more on the changes in public acceptance of and attitudes toward Hollywood stars and their behaviors over time, see the essays in Adrienne L. McLean and David A. Cook, eds., *Headline Hollywood: A Century of Film Scandal* (New Brunswick, N.J.: Rutgers University Press, 2001). See also Samantha Barbas, *Movie Crazy: Fans, Stars, and the Cult of Celebrity* (New York: Palgrave, 2001), esp. 85–108.

25. "Hollywood's First War Triangle," *Movieland,* August 1943, 16–18.

26. James M. Flagg, "Rita Hayworth Is Sketched by Flagg," *Los Angeles Herald Express,* c. 1941–42, in Rita Hayworth scrapbooks, vol. 1, Constance McCormick Collection, Cinema-Television Library, University of Southern California (hereafter cited as RHS).

27. Diane Waldman, "From Midnight Shows to Marriage Vows: Women, Exploitation, and Exhibition," *Wide Angle* 6 (1984): 40–48; see also Gaines, "War, Women, and Lipstick"; and Gaylyn Studlar, "The Perils of Pleasure? Fan Magazine Discourse as Women's Commodified Culture in the 1920s," *Wide Angle* 13 (January 1991): 6–33.

28. Gaines, "War, Women, and Lipstick," 43.

29. All quotations here from Louella O. Parsons, "Intermission for Romance," *Photoplay,* May 1946, 30–31, 109–112.

30. Pamela Pierce, "Happiness Doesn't Make Headlines," *Screen Guide,* January 1950, 54–55, 77. Irene Dunne was married to "one of the best dentists in the country," Claudette Colbert to a "recognized nose and throat specialist," Loretta Young to a "successful advertising executive." Marriages can work only when the "man can be respected and admired in his own right." And this respect and admiration must be professional; it apparently means nothing if it comes from wife and family alone.

31. See McLean and Cook, *Headline Hollywood.*

32. Danae Clark, *Negotiating Hollywood: The Cultural Politics of Actors' Labor* (Minneapolis: University of Minnesota Press, 1995), xiii.

33. "Hollywood's First War Triangle." See also Richard Addison, "Breakup—the Truth about Rita Hayworth and Victor Mature," *Photoplay,* August 1943, 84–85.

34. All quotations here from "Hubbub over Hayworth," *Movie Stars Parade,* November 1943, 22, 64–65.

35. Here and following from Hedda Hopper, "Hayworth's Child Has Rich Heritage," *Los Angeles Times,* c. 1944, RHS, vol. 2.

36. All quotations from Charles Vidor, "Exciting Woman," *Photoplay,* August 1946, 41–42, 86–87.

37. Leaming, *If This Was Happiness,* 18.

38. All quotations here from Dorothy Deere, "Feet That Danced," *Photoplay,* November 1946, 47, 110–114.

39. Parsons, "Intermission for Romance," 30–31, 109–112.

40. Clark, *Negotiating Hollywood,* 25.

41. Dyer, *Stars,* 45, contra Edgar Morin's assertions in *Les Stars* (Paris: Éditions du Seuil, 1957) that "the myth of stardom is love."

42. Leaming, *If This Was Happiness,* chap. 8.

43. All Parsons quotations from Louella O. Parsons, "It's Like This, Louella," *Photoplay,* July 1947, 36–39, 81, 82.

44. Leaming, *If This Was Happiness,* 124.

45. All quotations from Gardner Maxwell, "Psycho-Analyzing Rita," *Screen Guide,* 1948, RHS, vol. 3.

46. Gaines, "War, Women, and Lipstick," 45.

47. As Rochelle Gatlin points out, postwar women with "high occupational aspirations and steady commitment to a career" may have been marked as "deviant," but mothers themselves also became "the prime targets of popular misogyny" in the 1950s. See Rochelle Gatlin, *American Women since 1945* (Jackson: University Press of Mississippi, 1987), 17–19.

48. Sargeant, "Cult of the Love Goddess." For further discussion of this article see chap. 1.

49. Leaming, *If This Was Happiness.*

50. All quotations from Joan Curtis, "Hayworth Shocks Hollywood," *Film Album* (winter 1948): 4–5.

51. Sheilah Graham, "Hollywood's Dangerous Women," *Photoplay,* November 1948, 40, 110–113.

52. Jack Lait, "Sho' Is All Woman (Rita Hayworth)," *Photoplay,* November 1948, 46–47, 114–115.

53. For more on the scandal and a comparison of Hayworth's situation to that of Bergman see Adrienne L. McLean, "The Cinderella Princess and the Instrument of Evil: Revisiting Two Postwar Hollywood Star Scandals," in McLean and Cook, *Headline Hollywood,* 163–189.

54. For more on "Hayworth Ban Asked" see "This Affair Is an Insult to All Decent Women," *The People* (U.K.), January 9, 1949; and the clippings (all dated January 14, 1949) from the *Hollywood Reporter, Los Angeles Herald Express, Los Angeles Times,* and *Daily Variety* in the Rita Hayworth clipping file, AMPAS. See also Hedda Hopper, "Is Rita Hayworth Washed Up in Hollywood?" ("Her studio should ban her forever, says noted columnist, BUT . . . "), *Look,* March 16, 1949, 27–33, in which a bitter Hopper (she was not invited to the Hayworth/Khan wedding) lambasts Hayworth's abdication of her throne as Queen of Hollywood for a "globe-circling joy ride with a married Indian prince" (27). For more on Hayworth as the "Cinderella Princess" see Louella Parsons, "Cinderella Princess:

Colorful Career of Cinderella Girl Told by Film Writer," chaps. 1–6, *Los Angeles Examiner* (May-June 1949), RHS, vol. 4; Arno Johansen, "The Most Fabulous Love Story Ever Told," *Movieland,* May 1949, 42–43, 79–80; McLean, "Cinderella Princess."

55. All quotations here from Elsa Maxwell, "The Fabulous Life," *Photoplay,* October 1949, RHS, vol. 4.
56. Elsa Maxwell, "Title to Happiness," *Photoplay,* July 1950, 40–43, 77.
57. "Rita and Aly: The Most Dangerous Marriage of the Year," *Hollywood Yearbook* 1 (1950): 8–9.
58. Leaming, *If This Was Happiness,* chaps. 18–19.
59. In Ronald Rattigan, "Mr. and Mrs. Dick Haymes of Connecticut," unlabeled photocopy, 51, 70, from Caren Roberts-Frenzel.
60. "Why Rita Hayworth's Comeback May Fail," *Screen Guide,* c. 1952–1953, RHS, vol. 5.
61. Igor Cassini, "It *Had* to Happen," *Motion Picture,* August 1951, 38–39, 61–62. See also Igor Cassini, "Rita's Greatest Challenge," *Motion Picture,* c. 1950, 42–43, 54; and "Rita Hayworth: Fed Up with Aly?" *Quick,* May 8, 1950, 39–41, which discusses rumors about Aly's dalliances with "Negro dancer Katherine Dunham," then on a year-long tour of Europe, and how "a woman of Rita Hayworth's temperament would not take such treatment for very long."
62. In "Why Rita Hayworth's Comeback May Fail."
63. Arthur L. Charles, "What Now, Princess?" *Modern Screen,* November 1951, 37–38, 99–100.
64. Fredda Dudley Balling, "Marry the Boy Next Door," *Movieland,* May 1952, 6–8.
65. Louella Parsons, "Rita Tells All!" *Modern Screen,* c. 1952, RHS, vol. 5.
66. Charles, "What Now, Princess?"
67. All quotations here and below from Sheilah Graham, "Cinderella's Tired," *Modern Screen,* February 1953, 29, 65–66.
68. See Maxine L. Margolis, *Mothers and Such: Views of American Women and Why They Changed* (Berkeley: University of California Press, 1984), 218; Glenna Matthews, *"Just a Housewife": The Rise and Fall of Domesticity in America* (New York: Oxford University Press, 1987), appendix, 263–268; and May, *Homeward Bound,* 48–50, 55, 58–59, 75–76, 223.
69. All quotations here and below from Jane Corwin, "The Not-So-Private Life of Rita Hayworth," *Photoplay,* October 1952, 50–51, 105–107.
70. Liza Wilson, "Should Rita Change?" *Photoplay,* December 1951, 46–47, 93–94.
71. Peter Sherwood, "The Shadow in Rita Hayworth's Life," *Screenland,* September 1952, 26–27, 58–60.
72. All quotations here from Jane Morris, "Is Rita Hayworth Just a Lonesome Gal?" *Movieland,* May 1953, 36–37, 70–71.
73. Gretta Palmer, "Boom in Broken Homes," *Coronet,* May 1944, 23–26.
74. Gaines, "War, Women, and Lipstick," 43.
75. Quotations from May, *Homeward Bound,* 183, 193.
76. Ibid., 193.
77. Ibid.
78. James Wandworth, "Romantic Fireworks," *Motion Picture,* November 1953, 16, 72.
79. Florabel Muir, "She's the Marrying Kind," *Photoplay,* October 1953, 48–49, 84–85.

80. All quotations here and below from Thelma McGill, "Rita's Forgotten Child," *Modern Screen*, November 1953, 56–57, 92–93.
81. Rattigan, "Mr. and Mrs. Dick Haymes."
82. Earl Wilson, "This We Swear," *Motion Picture*, undated photocopy, from Caren Roberts-Frenzel.
83. "Rita, Goddess of Love," *Movieland*, April 1955, 34–35, 66–67.
84. May, *Homeward Bound*, 65 and chap. 8.
85. Ibid., esp. chaps. 3 and 8.
86. Interview with Jack Cole, in *People Will Talk*, ed. John Kobal (New York: Knopf, 1985), 593.
87. Alfred Garvey, "Why Rita Hayworth Walked Out on Dick," *Confidential*, January 1956, 14–15, 48, 50, 52.
88. *Togetherness* was a term and editorial policy introduced by *McCall's* magazine in 1954 (the Easter issue) to define the attribute of the ideal marriage and, in Steven Cohan's words, describes the "married couple who spent time together and shared equally in what had hitherto been familial duties determined by gender. . . . It implied a husband who was home oriented, who took seriously his responsibility for child rearing, and who viewed his wife as his primary companion" (Steven Cohan, *Masked Men: Masculinity and Movies in the Fifties* [Bloomington: Indiana University Press, 1997], 9–10). However, according to Helen-Damon Moore, *Magazines for the Millions: Gender and Commerce in the* Ladies' Home Journal *and the* Saturday Evening Post, *1880–1910* (Albany: State University of New York Press, 1994), the emphasis *McCall's* placed on togetherness "*failed* as a device to attract [new] readers" (190) [italics mine].
89. Ruth Seymour, "Love's Lonely Fugitive," *Movie Secrets*, August 1956, 26–29, 68–72.
90. What Hill did not recognize, too, is that Hayworth had probably begun to show signs of the onset of Alzheimer's disease—loss of memory, disorientation, bouts of strange behavior—during these years. See Hill, *Rita Hayworth*.
91. For more on Dyer's notions of authenticity in relation to Hollywood stardom see his "*A Star Is Born* and the Construction of Authenticity," in *Stardom: Industry of Desire*, ed. Christine Gledhill (New York: Routledge, 1991), 132–140.
92. Clark, *Negotiating Hollywood*, 82.

Chapter 3. I'm the Goddess of Song and Dance

1. *Weekly Variety*, review of *Tonight and Every Night*, dir. Victor Saville, in Production Code Administration file *(Tonight and Every Night)*, Margaret Herrick Library, Academy of Motion Picture Arts and Sciences (hereafter cited as AMPAS). Also in Gene Ringgold, *The Films of Rita Hayworth* (Secaucus, N.J.: Citadel Press, 1974), 155.
2. "Simulated singing" is from *Weekly Variety*'s review; the rest from Kate Cameron, *New York Daily News*, March 9, 1945.
3. Eileen Creelman, *New York Sun*, March 9, 1945.
4. In particular, extensive articles exploring *Down to Earth*'s numbers and dance sequences—in addition to straightforward reviews—appeared in virtually all of the

well-known organs of middle- or highbrow mass culture at the time: *Theatre Arts Monthly, Saturday Review of Literature, Dance Magazine, Life.*

5. Quite a bit of scholarly attention has been paid to *Yolanda and the Thief* and to *The Pirate* by anyone writing about Minnelli's work, of course, and also in virtually every treatment of the American film musical published from the 1980s on (e.g., Rick Altman, *The American Film Musical* [Bloomington: Indiana University Press, 1987]; Jane Feuer, *The Hollywood Musical*, 2d ed. [Bloomington: Indiana University Press, 1993]), particularly in work discussing the gay labor or camp dimensions of the Freed-unit musicals (e.g., Matthew Tinkcom, *Working like a Homosexual: Camp, Capital, Cinema* [Durham, N.C.: Duke University Press, 2002], chap. 1; Brett Farmer, *Spectacular Passions: Cinema, Fantasy, Gay Male Spectatorships* [Durham, N.C.: Duke University Press, 2000], chap. 2). The most peculiar canonization of the two films, however, is in Altman's book, in that he acknowledges gay labor and camp not at all but does base his analysis on the musical's importance in generating "community response." Because Altman's entire point about "symbolic spectatorship" and the significance of the film musical *in its own time* rests on detailing the musical's value to its community (with box-office success, presumably, being an important marker of this), it is unfortunate that he does not acknowledge that some of the films he chooses to canonize were not wholeheartedly accepted by the community to whom they were addressed. Although Altman claims, in other words, that the relatively unpopular (in its time) *Yolanda and the Thief* is one of the "true lost gems" of musical history (186) it has never been "lost" in the scholarly universe, whereas originally quite successful musicals like *Tonight and Every Night* and *Down to Earth* most assuredly have been.

6. Bruce Babington and Peter William Evans, *Blue Skies and Silver Linings: Aspects of the Hollywood Musical* (Manchester, U.K.: Manchester University Press, 1985), 13.

7. Eleanor Powell comes immediately to mind, but there are others whom we do not know about. Nita Bieber, who danced in many of Hayworth's musicals at Columbia, also performed as a soloist in several MGM musicals in the 1950s; when I asked her who did her choreography, she replied "I did!" (interview conducted by phone on June 9, 1992).

8. Jerome Delamater, *Dance in the Hollywood Musical* (Ann Arbor, Mich.: UMI Research Press, 1981), 100–101.

9. Here and below from Altman, *American Film Musical,* 54, 58.

10. Here and below from Michael Renov, *Hollywood's Wartime Woman: Representation and Ideology* (Ann Arbor, Mich.: UMI Research Press, 1988), 186–187.

11. Quotations from William Vincent, "Rita Hayworth at Columbia, 1941–1945: The Fabrication of a Star," in *Columbia Pictures: Portrait of a Studio,* ed. Bernard F. Dick (Lexington: University Press of Kentucky, 1992), 126.

12. In 1944 Columbia hired Jack Cole (1911–1974) to run the only permanent dance unit at a Hollywood studio and to choreograph Columbia musicals using this trained dance staff. See Dorothy Spence, "Hollywood Dance Group," *Dance Magazine,* July 1946, 16–19. Harry Cohn also gave Cole contractual control over the staging, shooting, and editing of the musical numbers Cole choreographed. The dance unit lasted through the late 1940s, but Cole's success enabled him to continue to insist on control over his numbers when he choreographed at other

studios for other directors in the 1950s (e.g., Howard Hawks and *Gentlemen Prefer Blondes* at Twentieth Century Fox in 1953). For more on Cole, who figures in my next chapter as well, see Glenn Loney, *Unsung Genius: The Passion of Dancer-Choreographer Jack Cole* (New York: Franklin Watts, 1984); John Kobal, ed., *People Will Talk* (New York: Knopf, 1985), 593–607; and Adrienne L. McLean, "The Thousand Ways There Are to Move: Camp and Oriental Dance in the Hollywood Musicals of Jack Cole," in *Visions of the East: Orientalism and Film,* ed. Matthew Bernstein and Gaylyn Studlar (New Brunswick, N.J.: Rutgers University Press, 1997), 130–157.

13. Virginia Wright Wexman, "The Love Goddess: Contradictions in the Myth of Glamour," in her *Creating the Couple: Love, Marriage, and Hollywood Performance* (Princeton, N.J.: Princeton University Press, 1993), 143–144. Despite the title of this chapter the only mention made of Rita Hayworth in the entire book is that Hayworth had her "hairline raised" in a listing of the "best-known examples of beauty regimens associated with the careers of Hollywood actresses" (136).

14. Ibid., 143–144.

15. See, e.g., Steven Cohan, "'Feminizing' the Song-and-Dance Man: Fred Astaire and the Spectacle of Masculinity in the Hollywood Musical," in *Screening the Male: Exploring Masculinities in Hollywood Cinema,* ed. Steven Cohan and Ina Rae Hark (New York: Routledge, 1993), 46–69; Richard Dyer, "'I Seem to Find the Happiness I Seek': Heterosexuality and Dance in the Musical," in *Dance, Gender, and Culture,* ed. Helen Thomas (New York: St. Martin's, 1993), 49–65; Tinkcom, *Working like a Homosexual;* and Farmer, *Spectacular Passions.*

16. Judith Mayne, *Framed: Lesbians, Feminists, and Media Culture* (Minneapolis: University of Minnesota Press, 2000), 20.

17. Cohan, "'Feminizing' the Song-and-Dance Man," 66–67. See also Alexander Doty, *Making Things Perfectly Queer: Interpreting Mass Culture* (Minneapolis: University of Minnesota Press, 1983). Doty, too, mentions the neglect in critical theory of "musical numbers performed by groups of women, with little or no participation by men" (13).

18. The version of Mulvey's "Visual Pleasure and Narrative Cinema" (1975) that I cite is in *Issues in Feminist Film Criticism,* ed. Patricia Erens (Bloomington: Indiana University Press, 1990), 28–39.

19. For a historical investigation of the meanings of one of the most famous of America's "showgirls," the Ziegfeld Girl, see Linda Mizejewski, *Ziegfeld Girl: Image and Icon in Culture and Cinema* (Durham, N.C.: Duke University Press, 1999).

20. Mayne, *Framed,* 17.

21. Maureen Turim, "Gentlemen Consume Blondes," in Erens, *Issues in Feminist Film Criticism,* 101–111.

22. Laura Mulvey, "Visual Pleasure and Narrative Cinema," esp. 33. Turim does not mention Jack Cole.

23. Lucie Arbuthnot and Gail Seneca, "Pre-Text and Text in *Gentlemen Prefer Blondes*" (1982), in Erens, *Issues in Feminist Film Criticism,* 112–125. They do not mention Cole's name either.

24. All quotations here from Turim, "Gentlemen Consume Blondes," 106.

25. I have always been puzzled by a simple logical inconsistency in Mulvey's definition of the "device of the showgirl." First, as mentioned, Mulvey defines musical

performance as erotic spectacle—"woman displayed as sexual object"—which tends "to work against the development of a story line, to freeze the flow of action in moments of erotic contemplation." At the same time, however, she notes how, in the musical, "song-and-dance numbers break the flow of the diegesis." The device of the showgirl eliminates such breaks, for when a film performer *plays* a performer, she can perform "within the narrative" and "the gaze of the spectator and that of the male characters in the film are neatly combined without breaking narrative verisimilitude." Yet Mulvey obviates the usefulness of this device by again insisting that the "sexual impact of the performing woman takes the film into a no-man's-land outside its own time and space." Since perhaps the most famous line from Mulvey's essay is "Sadism demands a story," it is unclear *why* removing a film to a no-man's-land outside of the narrative should sustain, rather than debilitate, voyeuristic pleasure. Can the showgirl simultaneously deploy an impact that can break the flow of narrative and also be the "reassuring rather than dangerous" fetishized icon/object of scopophilia? (33, 35).

Mulvey's 1986 essay "Changes: Thoughts on Myth, Narrative, and Historical Experience," in *Visual and Other Pleasures* (Bloomington: Indiana University Press, 1989), is also interesting considered both against "Visual Pleasure" and in relation to musical performance conceived as narrative rupture. First, Mulvey reproduces the no-man's-land formulation almost word for word in "Changes" in relation to Bakhtinian rites of carnival: these rites, Mulvey states, provided a "liminal moment outside the time and space of the dominant order" (172). Second, in terms of feminism, narrative, and spectacle, Mulvey argues that if narrative is conceived linearly, rather than in [binary] opposition to spectacle, a tripartite structure can be created in which narrative's return on the "other side" of the liminal space is *not,* or need not be, simply a return to the "order of everyday" (169). Even within the "stronger force" of narrative, the liminal space could "incorporate widened options" for behavior and demeanor. In this way, if women could not immediately change the world, they could "stake out *the right to imagine* another" (167, Mulvey's italics).

26. All quotations here from Richard Dyer, "Entertainment and Utopia" (1977), in *Genre: The Musical,* ed. Rick Altman (London: BFI, 1981), 177.
27. All quotations here from Robin Wood, "Art and Ideology: Notes on *Silk Stockings*" (1975), in Altman, *Genre: The Musical,* 57–69.
28. Rick Altman, in Wood, "Art and Ideology," 57, 58.
29. Angela McRobbie, "*Fame, Flashdance,* and Fantasies of Achievement," in *Fabrications: Costume and the Female Body,* ed. Jane Gaines and Charlotte Herzog (New York: Routledge, 1990), 39–58.
30. Jeanine Basinger, *A Woman's View: How Hollywood Spoke to Women, 1930–1960* (New York: Knopf, 1993), 147. Conversely, see the discussion of *Cover Girl* and *The Dolly Sisters* (Irving Cummings, 1945, with Betty Grable and Alice Faye) in Patricia Mellencamp, *A Fine Romance: Five Ages of Film Feminism* (Philadelphia, Pa.: Temple University Press, 1995), 25–35, in which Mellencamp claims that the "women are not responsible for their achievements" and "are literally made by men" (28).
31. Andrew Britton's claims about Katharine Hepburn resonate here as well: "The significance for feminist cultural studies of the great female stars of the Hollywood cinema lies in the contradictions they generate within narrative structures

which are committed overall to the reaffirmation of bourgeois-patriarchal norms" (Andrew Britton, *Katharine Hepburn: Star as Feminist* [New York: Continuum, 1995], 7).

32. See, e.g., the interview with Gene Kelly in the appendix of Delamater, *Dance in the Hollywood Musical.* Of course, were a woman to do a dance with herself or her own mirror image, she would likely be labeled and dismissed as a [typical] narcissist.

33. See Altman, *American Film Musical,* chaps. 2 and 3.

34. Susan Leigh Foster, "Choreographing History," in *Choreographing History,* ed. Susan Leigh Foster (Bloomington: Indiana University Press, 1995), 5.

35. All quotations here from Ann Cooper Albright, *Choreographing Difference: The Body and Identity in Contemporary Dance* (Hanover, N.H.: Wesleyan University Press, 1997), xiv.

36. Sondra Horton Fraleigh, *Dance and the Lived Body: A Descriptive Aesthetics* (Pittsburgh, Pa.: University of Pittsburgh Press, 1987), 32.

37. Judith Lynn Hanna, *Dance, Sex, and Gender: Signs of Identity, Dominance, Defiance, and Desire* (Chicago, Ill.: University of Chicago Press, 1988), 132.

38. Francis Sparshott, *Off the Ground: First Steps to a Philosophical Consideration of the Dance* (Princeton, N.J.: Princeton University Press, 1988), 399.

39. Joseph Margolis, "The Autographic Nature of the Dance," in *Illuminating Dance: Philosophical Explorations,* ed. Maxine Sheets-Johnstone (Lewisburg, Pa.: Bucknell University Press, 1984), 81.

40. Ramsey Burt, "Dissolving in Pleasure: The Threat of the Queer Male Dancing Body," in *Dancing Desires: Choreographing Sexualities on and off the Stage,* ed. Jane C. Desmond (Madison: University of Wisconsin Press, 2001), 219–220.

41. Margolis, "Autographic Nature of the Dance," 70–84.

42. Bieber, interview.

43. For more on the often contradictory relationships of real bodies, ideal bodies, and dance styles in the Hollywood musical see Adrienne L. McLean, "Feeling and the Filmed Body: Judy Garland and the Kinesics of Suffering," *Film Quarterly* 55 (spring 2002): 2–15.

44. For Jack Cole's description of performing with Rita Hayworth in *Tonight and Every Night* see Kobal, *People Will Talk:*

Well, baby, I didn't know what hit me when they turned the camera on, 'cause Rita was just like Monroe. When it was for *real,* look out! So for the first shot I just went up six ways from Sunday because suddenly this mass of red hair, and it looked like ninety-four more teeth than I'd ever seen in a woman's mouth before, and more eye-rolling, and more shoulder—I mean, the most animated object known to man. The minute *film* was rolling, it was for real, it was gonna be on a large screen, it was like, *Stand back, man, this is how it goes.* And I was not able to deal with it. I'd never seen so much animation and giving out. Rita always did it for real, whereas somebody like Betty Grable . . . could do it all in a haze, you know, while thinking about what horse was going to win that day. (597)

45. Jane C. Desmond, "Introduction: Making the Invisible Visible: Staging Sexualities through Dance," in Desmond, *Dancing Desires,* 24.

46. As I have mentioned, the notion that the ideal viewer posited by this governing paradigm is not only male but white and heterosexual has been challenged by many scholars who have worked to theorize how spectators of different racial, ethnic, class, or sexual identities might have "desired differently" or according to mechanisms other than voyeurism or fetishism. When I use terms such as *male* or *masculinity,* I mean them in the same way that Mulvey does—to signify white, middle-class, and heterosexual. Jane Feuer is one of the first film scholars to address explicitly the fact that, as she put it at the 1992 Society for Cinema Studies Conference in Pittsburgh, the musical is "gay as hell." Feuer added a section, "Gay Readings of Musicals," to the second edition of her book *The Hollywood Musical* (1993), in which she discusses gay production and reception practices in some Freed-unit musicals. See also Cohan, "'Feminizing' the Song-and-Dance Man"; Tinkcom, *Working like a Homosexual;* Farmer, *Spectacular Passions;* and anything by Alexander Doty.

47. Sound may be the medium of music, movement of dance, but neither attribute is necessary or sufficient to define them. In reference to dance particularly, as Sparshott puts it, although "[w]orkers in the humanities are regarded by all other academics as mushy" and all "philosophers despise aesthetics for its hopeless mushiness," the "aestheticians of dance are so mushy that even the other aestheticians notice. This is because . . . their topic systematically resists the establishing of a stable starting point, in a way that the aesthetics of the other arts does not" (*Off the Ground,* 398).

48. Altman, *American Film Musical.* Altman defines the features of the "musical corpus" in the first three chapters of the book.

49. Alan Williams, "The Musical Film and Recorded Popular Music," in Altman, *Genre: The Musical,* 156.

50. Altman, *American Film Musical,* 65.

51. Direct address represents self-reflexivity "that other genres of classic narrative work to suppress," according to Patricia Mellencamp ("Spectacle and Spectator: Looking through the American Musical Comedy," *Ciné-Tracts* 1 [summer 1977]: 33). See also Jim Collins, "Toward Defining a Matrix of the Musical Comedy: The Place of the Spectator within the Textual Mechanisms," in Altman, *Genre: The Musical,* 135–146; and Feuer, *The Hollywood Musical.*

52. Altman, *American Film Musical,* 230.

53. Seymour Chatman inadvertently makes somewhat the same point when he says that if we started actually *"listening"* to a movie's score, "it would probably mean that we had lost interest in the narration" (Seymour Chatman, *Coming to Terms: The Rhetoric of Narrative in Fiction and Film* [Ithaca, N.Y.: Cornell University Press, 1990], 9 [Chatman's italics]).

54. All quotations here from Susan McClary, *Feminine Endings: Music, Gender, and Sexuality* (Minneapolis: University of Minnesota Press, 1991), 23, 25.

55. David Burrows, *Sound, Speech, and Music* (Amherst: University of Massachusetts Press, 1990).

56. Ibid., 25.

57. Stephen Handel, *Listening: An Introduction to the Perception of Auditory Events* (Cambridge, Mass.: MIT Press, 1989), 547.

58. All quotations from Mark W. Booth, *The Experience of Songs* (New Haven, Conn.: Yale University Press, 1981), 17–18.

59. Burrows, *Sound, Speech, and Music,* 36–38.

60. Randy Martin, *Performance as Political Act: The Embodied Self* (New York: Bergin and Garvey, 1990), 167. Another reason for reconsidering dance in relation to the "one-dimensionality" of the female image is that, according to Christian Metz (*Film Language: A Semiotics of the Cinema,* trans. Michael Taylor [New York: Oxford University Press, 1974]), movement as a profilmic event is always "perceived as real" (8). As Metz puts it, "the spectator always sees movement as being present (even if it duplicates a past movement)"; movement entails "a higher degree of reality and the corporality of objects" (7).

61. Mulvey, "Visual Pleasure and Narrative Cinema," 33. For discussions of spectacle/narrative interaction see Mellencamp, "Spectacle and Spectator"; and Dana Polan, "'Above All Else to Make You See': Cinema and the Ideology of Spectacle," in *Postmodernism and Politics,* ed. Jonathan Arac (Minneapolis: University of Minnesota Press, 1986), 55–69.

62. Gene Kelly has always argued against there being *an* auteur for any Hollywood musical. See Donald Knox, *The Magic Factory: How M-G-M Made "An American in Paris"* (New York: Praeger, 1973).

63. See Richard deCordova, "Genre and Performance: An Overview," in *Star Texts: Image and Performance in Film and Television,* ed. Jeremy G. Butler (Detroit, Mich.: Wayne State University Press, 1991), 115–124; and Collins, "Matrix of the Musical Comedy."

64. That the film text is potentially a "site of struggle" is also the point of view taken by Tom Gunning in his "Film History and Film Analysis: The Individual Film in the Course of Time," *Wide Angle* 12 (July 1990): 4–19. See also Mayne, *Framed,* 3–22.

65. Altman, *American Film Musical,* 35.

66. It is with Hollywood musicals that the spuriousness of the practice of granting automatic authorship to a film's director is perhaps most clearly foregrounded.

67. See, e.g., Eleanor Powell and the Berry Brothers in *Lady Be Good* (Norman Z. McLeod, 1941); the dance direction is by Busby Berkeley, but Powell and the Berry Brothers choreographed their own routines. Powell receives top billing, but the "heterosexual couple" is [nondancing] Ann Sothern and Robert Young.

68. Albert A. Johnstone, "Languages and Non-Languages of Dance," in Sheets-Johnstone, *Illuminating Dance,* 175.

69. Annette Kuhn, "The Body and Cinema: Some Problems for Feminism," in *Grafts: Feminist Cultural Criticism,* ed. Susan Sheridan (London: Verso, 1988), 17.

70. See Wood, "Art and Ideology."

71. McRobbie, "Fantasies of Achievement." Other feminists, however, have tended in their discussions of dance to divide it into an exclusive and excluding triad: classical ballet, modern dance, postmodern dance. See, e.g., Elizabeth Dempster, "Women Writing the Body: Let's Watch a Little How She Dances," in Sheridan, *Grafts,* 35–54; and Janet Wolff, *Feminine Sentences: Essays on Women and Culture* (Berkeley: University of California Press, 1990), chap. 8. On Dempster's and Wolff's terms postmodern dance is the only truly subversive form because it does not reify or deify heterosexual romance or present the body as idealized, "seamless," or machinelike. Only postmodern dance represents movement as movement, effort as effort, the body as human—"real" and "individual"—body. But by leaving vernacular or popular dance forms out of such discussions, the argu-

ment that postmodern dance is better for women than ballet or modern dance becomes an argument that revolves essentially in an aerial aesthetic sphere. In the movies, on television, on the streets dance means in many different ways. The body is not, here, describable only according to this triad.

It is also significant that Gene Kelly felt compelled to proclaim at every opportunity that "dancing is a man's business." In fact, one of the historical situations that rarely receives nuanced attention in film studies is that dancing in America was largely a woman's business—a woman's business whose meanings and significance to feminism cannot be fully addressed if one limits the terms of the discussion to "gaze theory." Modern dance in America was substantially founded and developed as an art form by women (Isadora Duncan, Ruth St. Denis, Martha Graham) and is one of the few dance forms to remain a female-dominated aesthetic ground. Equally important, in America the history of professional and amateur dancing is closely aligned with female emancipation movements of all kinds. The liberation of many women from the confinement of the domestic sphere over the past hundred-plus years has always been powerfully symbolized by the physical liberation that dancing represents. The liberation of the body through fashion reform—or conversely the dismayed and angry responses in various public venues to that reform—came to signify the liberation of the mind, and vice versa. Indeed, the dominance of women in American dance by the end of World War II helps to explain its marginality, the marginality that made a Gene Kelly or a Fred Astaire so defensive about their pursuit of a career in it. See Elizabeth Kendall, *Where She Danced* (New York: Knopf, 1979), for a history of women and dance in America. See Jonas Barish, *The Antitheatrical Prejudice* (Berkeley: University of California Press, 1981), for a wider historical discussion of prejudice toward the performing artist. See the essays in Glenn D. Wilson, ed., *Psychology and Performing Arts* (Berwyn, Pa.: Swets and Zeitlinger, 1991), for discussions of how the performing artist *feels* about, and handles the effects of, that prejudice.

72. Hanna, *Dance, Sex, and Gender.*

73. Howard Hawks, e.g., who is usually credited as the auteur of *Gentlemen Prefer Blondes,* said in 1976 that he "had nothing to do with the filming of the musical sequences of *Gentlemen Prefer Blondes,* that he was not even on the set" (Delamater, *Dance in the Hollywood Musical,* 117). What we know about musical viewing patterns lends support to this: when asked, historical male viewers not only claimed to like movie musicals less than female viewers, but they actively disliked them more. See Leo A. Handel, *Hollywood Looks at Its Audience: A Report of Film Audience Research* (Urbana: University of Illinois Press, 1950), chap. 8, which contains charts of audience preference for both "serious" musicals and musical comedies. Since women were the primary viewers of musicals, the ideal spectator of musical spectacle may never have been a heterosexual male, at least from the industry's point of view.

74. See, e.g., Cohan, "'Feminizing' the Song-and-Dance Man"; Tinkcom, *Working like a Homosexual;* and Farmer, *Spectacular Passions.*

75. For a discussion of the representation of sexual difference in theatrical dance see Dempster, "Women Writing the Body"; and Hanna, *Dance, Sex, and Gender.*

76. Maxine Sheets-Johnstone, "Phenomenology as a Way of Illuminating Dance," in Sheets-Johnstone, *Illuminating Dance,* 132.

77. Examples might include beating pulses, twitching eyelids, engorged muscles, etc. See James Naremore, *Acting in the Cinema* (Berkeley: University of California Press, 1988), 65. See also McLean, "Feeling and the Filmed Body."
78. Edwin Denby, *Dance Writings* (New York: Knopf, 1986), 136.
79. Dempster, "Women Writing the Body," 51.
80. Theories that equate merely being a woman with performance (that femininity is a masquerade) have complicated the issue. As Lesley Stern points out, masquerade as a concept has become "slippery" because the term *masquerade* now functions mostly as a metaphor for or illustration of femininity itself. See Lesley Stern, "Acting Out of Character: The Performance of Femininity," in Sheridan, *Grafts,* 31. See also John Fletcher, "Versions of Masquerade," *Screen* 29 (summer 1988): 43–70. Fletcher, speaking of Joan Riviere's 1986 study "Womanliness as Masquerade," says that the "importance of Riviere's conception of the masquerade is that it constitutes a transgressive doubleness, an inscription of alternative wishes. The potential for a critical distance from the mythemes of femininity (passivity, responsiveness, deference, flattery, etc.) is lodged already within it and the narratives it might generate. This is in contrast to its current usage in film criticism to indicate the production of the fetishized image of the woman for the male spectator" (55).
81. A small sample of such films includes Hayworth's *Tonight and Every Night* and *Down to Earth;* the films of Eleanor Powell; Betty Grable and Carmen Miranda, *Moon over Miami* (Walter Lang, 1941; chor. Jack Cole); Betty Hutton, *Incendiary Blonde* (George Marshall, 1945; chor. Danny Dare); Ann Miller, *Eadie Was a Lady* (Arthur Dreifuss, 1945; chor. Jack Cole); Vera-Ellen, June Haver, Vivian Blaine, *Three Little Girls in Blue* (Bruce Humberstone, 1946; chor. Seymour Felix); Betty Hutton, *Annie Get Your Gun* (George Sidney, 1950; chor. Robert Alton); Leslie Caron, *Lili* (Charles Walters, 1953; chor. Walters and Dorothy Jarnac); Cyd Charisse, *Meet Me in Las Vegas* (Roy Rowland, 1956; chor. Hermes Pan, Eugene Loring).
82. On self-reflexivity and musicals see Jane Feuer, "The Self-Reflexive Musical and the Myth of Entertainment" (1977), in *Film Genre Reader,* ed. Barry Keith Grant (Austin: University of Texas Press, 1986), 329–343. See also Feuer, *The Hollywood Musical.*
83. It was well known at the time that Hayworth's singing voice was dubbed (here, by Anita Ellis). Hayworth sang quite often on radio, however, and when entertaining troops during the war. It was apparently Harry Cohn's preference for the "big band" sound that caused him to dub most of his stars (male stars as well; Larry Parks's voice is dubbed in all of his musicals, and some of Gene Kelly's high notes were dubbed in *Cover Girl*) with big-band voices. Hayworth actually had six film singing voices over the course of about fifteen years, and few reviewers, at least, ever remarked on the differences among them (see also chaps. 1, 4, and 5).
84. The war is not mentioned in the film, so the military uniforms remain mysterious throughout. The wartime context and the peculiarities of the film were noticed by some reviewers, however. *Photoplay* (July 1947) wrote, "Shots of white airplanes full of spirits heading upward into the unknown still make us a little nervous, especially when all this earthly merry-making and torch-singing are going on at the same time" (6).
85. All quotations here from Altman, *American Film Musical,* 45, 205, 336.

86. In terms of high/low, e.g., is heaven the same place as Mount Parnassus, or is heaven even "higher"? If there is a Terpsichore, is there also a different God, a Zeus (*yes,* according to the script)?

87. Eve Kosofsky Sedgwick, *Between Men: English Literature and Male Homosocial Desire* (New York: Columbia University Press, 1985), 89. See also Tinkcom, *Working like a Homosexual;* and Brett Farmer, *Spectacular Passions.*

88. Vincent, "Rita Hayworth at Columbia," 125.

89. Altman, *American Film Musical,* 336.

90. Feuer, "Self-Reflexive Musical," 336.

91. John Kobal, in *Rita Hayworth: The Time, the Place, and the Woman* (New York: Norton, 1977), writes that the "highbrow-versus-lowbrow theme" in *Down to Earth* "backfires" because the Greek Ballet is "by far the best musical number in it, not at all the constipated culture of previous, and even later, movie excursions into the ballet" (207).

92. For Cole's comment see Kobal, *People Will Talk,* 601.

93. Feuer, "Self-Reflexive Musical."

94. Altman, *American Film Musical,* 361.

95. All quotations here from Feuer, "Self-Reflexive Musical," 332–335, 361.

96. This foregrounding is, of course, interesting given the time in which the film was made. Straddling the end of World War II, *Down to Earth* embodies not only the tensions common to musicals mentioned earlier in this chapter but also the ideological tensions sustained in 1940s films in which female protagonists, however incompletely or briefly, are allowed to advance "from fetish to subject," in Michael Renov's terms *(Hollywood's Wartime Woman).*

97. Babington and Evans, *Blue Skies,* 168, 169.

98. Although it is possible that Danny has married someone else in the interim, Terpsichore's line "Will he wait for me?"—answered by Mr. Jordan with a wave of the hand toward the dead Danny—as well as the musical's generic focus on "ideal" couples obviate such an interpretation.

99. Steven Shaviro, *The Cinematic Body* (Minneapolis: University of Minnesota Press, 1993), 42.3. The "recent discussions" he names are Altman's and Feuer's books on the musical.

100. Arlene Croce, *Afterimages* (New York: Random House, 1977), 444.

101. Winthrop Sargeant, "The Cult of the Love Goddess in America," *Life,* November 10, 1947, 80–96 ("She is almost the perfect embodiment of that quality of passivity which poets, in more classically minded times, thought of as the essence of the female nature. . . . She causes or inspires action, but she does not act herself except in response to the desires of others" [89]). See also the discussions of Sargeant's article in chaps. 1 and 2.

Chapter 4. I Told You Not to Move—I Mean It!

1. See, e.g., Richard Dyer, "Resistance through Charisma: Rita Hayworth and *Gilda,*" in *Women and Film Noir,* ed. E. Ann Kaplan (London: BFI, 1978), 91–99; Mary Ann Doane, "*Gilda:* Epistemology as Striptease," *Camera Obscura* 11 (fall 1982): 6–27; Linda Dittmar, "From Fascism to the Cold War: *Gilda's* 'Fantastic' Politics," *Wide Angle* 10 (1988): 4–18; Kimberly Lenz, "Put the Blame on

Gilda: Dyke Noir vs. Film Noir," *Theatre Studies* 40 (1995): 17–26; and Angela Martin, "'Gilda Didn't Do Any of Those Things You've Been Losing Sleep Over!': The Central Women of 40s Films Noirs," in *Women in Film Noir,* ed. E. Ann Kaplan, 2d ed. (London: BFI, 1998), 202–228.

2. B. Ruby Rich, "In the Name of Feminist Film Criticism" (1978), in *Multiple Voices in Feminist Film Criticism,* ed. Diane Carson, Linda Dittmar, and Janice R. Welsh (Minneapolis: University of Minnesota Press, 1994), 35.

3. Laura Mulvey, "Visual Pleasure and Narrative Cinema" (1975), in *Issues in Feminist Film Criticism,* ed. Patricia Erens (Bloomington: Indiana University Press, 1990), 33, 35.

4. Patrice Petro, "Feminism and Film History," in Carson, Dittmar, and Welsh, *Multiple Voices,* 76.

5. Adrienne Rich quoted in B. Ruby Rich, "In the Name," 27.

6. J. P. Telotte, *Voices in the Dark: The Narrative Patterns of Film Noir* (Urbana: University of Illinois Press, 1989), 67.

7. I first learned that Van Upp had written *Gilda* when I acquired a photocopy of the screenplay in 1999 through interlibrary loan; I found it through the WorldCat database. On its first page is typed "Screenplay by Virginia Van Upp, FINAL DRAFT, August 29, 1945." That Van Upp wrote *Gilda* is also the conclusion of Lizzie Francke, *Script Girls: Women Screenwriters in Hollywood* (London: BFI, 1994), 59–66, although Francke does not explain *why* Van Upp is not given screen credit other than as producer. Van Upp was also remarkable in being one of the few women ever to achieve top executive status in the classical studio system (she was second in command to Harry Cohn at Columbia in the mid-1940s), but very little information has been published about her (she is mentioned exactly once, by name only, in Bernard F. Dick, ed., *Columbia Pictures: Portrait of a Studio* [Lexington: University Press of Kentucky, 1992]). A brief entry on her career can be found in Ally Acker, *Reel Women: Pioneers of the Cinema, 1896 to the Present* (New York: Continuum, 1991), and in the Francke book cited above. According to the Hayworth coworkers I interviewed, Van Upp exerted a lot of influence not only on *Gilda* but on Hayworth's film career during the star's years of greatest popularity in the mid-1940s.

8. All quotations here from Dyer, "Resistance through Charisma," 92–93, 96.

9. Orson Welles and Rita Hayworth were married from 1943 to 1947; Hayworth separated from Welles in 1945/46, and they were in the process of divorcing during the filming of *The Lady from Shanghai.*

10. Quoted in Lucy Fischer, *Shot/Countershot: Film Tradition and Women's Cinema* (Princeton, N.J.: Princeton University Press, 1989), 33.

11. It was interesting to learn, given Welles's frequent rendering of how he came to make *The Lady from Shanghai* (he was trying to borrow money from Harry Cohn by phone, noticed a secretary reading a book called *The Lady from Shanghai,* and spontaneously offered to make a film for Cohn of the same name in exchange for $50,000), that Welles was trying to buy the rights to *If I Die Before I Wake* by April 26, 1946: "Please try desperately to get 'If I Die Before I Wake' to Harry Cohn, Columbia, immediately. . . . Urgent as deal is pending" (Welles to Lolita Hebert, Mercury Productions, telegram, Orson Welles Collection, Lilly Library, Indiana University). *Gilda* had been released, very successfully, in March (and there was no book called *The Lady from Shanghai*).

12. See, e.g., E. Ann Kaplan, *Women and Film: Both Sides of the Camera* (London: Routledge, 1983), 60–72; Lucilla Albano, "The Accessibility of the Text: An Analysis of *The Lady from Shanghai*," in *Off Screen: Women and Film in Italy*, ed. Giuliana Bruno and Maria Nadotti (London: Routledge, 1988), 124–138; and Fischer, *Shot/Countershot*, 32–49.

13. Interestingly, Columbia's official pressbook does not mention that Welles and Hayworth were ever married (pressbook on microfiche at the British Film Institute).

14. For a characterization of the "erotic triangle" in which a woman is positioned as an object of exchange between two men see chap. 1, "Gender Asymmetry and Erotic Triangles," in Eve Kosofsky Sedgwick, *Between Men: English Literature and Male Homosocial Desire* (New York: Columbia University Press, 1985). See chap. 3 of this volume for how this triangle often functions in Hollywood musicals.

15. Another way that *Gilda*, like many Hollywood films, circulated publicly was as a fictional story version in movie story magazines. For analysis of three different story versions of *Gilda* from 1946—one very like a queer reading—see Adrienne L. McLean, "'New Films in Story Form': Movie Story Magazines and Spectatorship," *Cinema Journal* 42 (spring 2003): 3–26.

16. Elsa/Hayworth also never addresses the camera directly here.

17. Charles Higham, *The Films of Orson Welles* (Berkeley: University of California Press, 1970), 112.

18. James Naremore, *The Magic World of Orson Welles*, 2d ed. (Dallas, Tex.: Southern Methodist University Press, 1989), 133.

19. Higham, *Films of Orson Welles*, 116.

20. See Dyer, "Resistance through Charisma," 96.

21. Ibid., 112; see also Charles Higham, *Orson Welles: The Rise and Fall of an American Genius* (New York: St. Martin's, 1985), 242.

22. Hayworth's own singing voice can be heard in the first "Put the Blame on Mame" in *Gilda*, but Anita Ellis dubbed the film's other numbers. Ellis also dubbed *The Lady from Shanghai*.

23. Mulvey, "Visual Pleasure and Narrative Cinema." For further discussion of the "device of the showgirl" see chap. 3.

24. Claudia Gorbman, *Unheard Melodies: Narrative Film Music* (Bloomington: Indiana University Press, 1987), 20.

25. David Burrows, *Sound, Speech, and Music* (Amherst: University of Massachusetts Press, 1990), 24.

26. Lizabeth Scott's films may have been modeled on Hayworth's (*Dead Reckoning* [John Cromwell, 1947] was reportedly originally intended for Hayworth), and we need to consider the role Scott's singing plays in light of her wide characterization as a "good-bad girl." *Dark City* (William Dieterle, 1950) alone has five sung setpieces.

27. André Bazin, *Orson Welles: A Critical View*, trans. Jonathan Rosenbaum (New York: Harper and Row, 1978), 94.

28. As described in the previous chapter, one of the ways Rick Altman defines the musical formally is by its ability to reverse what he calls the "normal" image-over-sound hierarchy of classical Hollywood cinema, for "only in the musical does the sound actually generate the movement within the image" (Rick Altman,

The American Film Musical [Bloomington: Indiana University Press, 1987], 230). But it is unquestionably a feature of the song-and-dance numbers in *Gilda* as well, as is another characteristic feature of the musical number, direct address to the camera.

29. Alan Williams claims that films that "incorporate but do not privilege" musical performances do not use close miking of singing and musical accompaniment ("The Musical Film and Recorded Popular Music," in *Genre: The Musical,* ed. Rick Altman [London: BFI, 1981], 153). And although Williams does note the "important intermediary case" of close miking in film noir, he claims it is "visually justified" by the presence of microphones in nightclubs (153). But there are no microphones in *Gilda* or *The Lady from Shanghai* or *Affair in Trinidad* or in many other films noirs, such as *To Have and Have Not* (Howard Hawks, 1944), *The Big Sleep* (Howard Hawks, 1946), and *The Killers* (Robert Siodmak, 1946), all of which use close miking during most of their musical performances.

30. In "*Gilda:* Epistemology as Striptease" Mary Ann Doane characterizes "the image of woman" in *Gilda* as being "fixed and held—held for the pleasure and reassurance of the male spectator" (9), and she does not acknowledge Dyer or his countervailing argument at all (although she cites the anthology in which his essay appears).

31. All quotations here from Kaja Silverman, *The Subject of Semiotics* (New York: Oxford University Press, 1983), 230–232.

32. Kaja Silverman, *The Acoustic Mirror: The Female Voice in Psychoanalysis and Cinema* (Bloomington: Indiana University Press, 1988), 31.

33. Mark W. Booth, *The Experience of Songs* (New Haven, Conn.: Yale University Press, 1981), 17.

34. *Gilda* was choreographed by an uncredited Jack Cole.

35. Laura Mulvey, *Visual and Other Pleasures* (Bloomington: Indiana University Press, 1989), xi.

36. Marjorie Rosen, *Popcorn Venus: Women, Movies, and the American Dream* (New York: Coward, McCann, and Geoghegan, 1973), 211.

37. Doane, "Epistemology as Striptease," 9.

38. All quotations here from Svea Becker, "A Femme Fatale Communicates through Dance," *Proceedings of the Conference of the Society of Dance History Scholars* (1987), 45–56.

39. See, e.g., John Kobal's interview with Hayworth in the last chapter of his *Rita Hayworth: The Time, the Place, and the Woman* (New York: Norton, 1977).

40. Higham, *Orson Welles,* 242. See also Peter Cowie, *A Ribbon of Dreams: The Cinema of Orson Welles* (New York: Barnes, 1973), 104–105.

41. The "potential for evil" and "humane and liberal" are from the first version of James Naremore's essay on *The Lady from Shanghai* ("Style and Theme in *The Lady from Shanghai,*" in *Focus on Orson Welles,* ed. Ronald Gottesman [Englewood Cliffs, N.J.: Prentice-Hall, 1976], 135). In the 1989 version of the same essay (in *The Magic World of Orson Welles*), "potential for evil" has been replaced by "the full extent of his temptations" and "humane and liberal" has been reduced to "humane" (136). On Welles's "liberalism" my reading of the situation leads me to believe that what Raymond Williams once said of the Bloomsbury group can also be said of Orson Welles: "The social conscience, in the end, is to protect the private consciousness" (in John Higgins, "Raymond Williams and the Problem

of Ideology," in *Postmodernism and Politics,* ed. Jonathan Arac [Minneapolis: University of Minnesota Press, 1986], 112).

42. Theater patrons in 1948 probably guessed from the way *The Lady from Shanghai* was advertised (usually with a balefully glaring Elsa, sometimes holding a gun, captioned with the words "I told you—you know nothing about wickedness!") that Elsa was bad before the lights went down. And, as opposed to *Gilda,* they would have been right.

43. A comparison of Barbara Leaming's separate biographies of Welles and Hayworth reveals stunning differences in subject agency. Her *Orson Welles: A Biography* (New York: Viking, 1985) is based on extensive personal interviews of Welles by Leaming; but in *If This Was Happiness* (New York: Viking, 1989) she has to rely on third-person, usually retrospective, accounts. In fact, the Welles material in the Hayworth study is simply cut whole-cloth from the Welles book. Other biographies of Welles include Joseph McBride, *Orson Welles* (New York: Viking, 1972); Frank Brady, *Citizen Welles* (New York: Doubleday, 1989); Higham, *Orson Welles;* Simon Callow, *Orson Welles: The Road to Xanadu* (New York: Viking, 1995); and David Thomson, *Rosebud: The Story of Orson Welles* (New York: Knopf, 1996). As mentioned, archival material about Hayworth is hard to come by; in Matthew Bernstein's assessment Columbia is the "bane of the film historian" because it has never opened its archives (if they exist) to researchers (Matthew Bernstein, review of *Columbia Pictures: Portrait of a Studio,* ed. Bernard F. Dick, *Film Quarterly* 46 [spring 1993], 58).

44. Even in 1948, for example, Welles was referring in public to *The Lady from Shanghai* as "an experiment—in what not to do," announcing that he was "trapped" into making it because he owed Columbia $60,000. "But I'm not bitter," Welles was quoted as saying. "It taught me how to shoot a sexy dame singing a song and stuff like that" (*Time,* June 7, 1948, 100).

45. Quoted in Fischer, *Shot/Countershot,* 34.

46. Cowie, *Ribbon of Dreams,* 104–105, quoting Jacques Siclier, "Le Mythe de la femme dans le cinéma americain" (Paris, 1956).

47. McBride, *Orson Welles,* 104.

48. Joseph McBride, *Orson Welles: Actor and Director* (New York: Harcourt, 1977), 53.

49. McBride even claims that there is a "lot of love" in Orson Welles's screen vision of "Hayworth's personality" and produces as evidence that Welles's chauvinism is also "romantic" the following: "'Women are clearly the superior sex, you know,' [Welles] told David Frost. 'I really mean that. . . . If there hadn't been women we'd still be squatting in a cave eating raw meat, because *we made civilization in order to impress our girl friends*'" (McBride, *Orson Welles: Actor and Director,* 51, 52 [emphasis mine]).

50. Naremore, *Magic World of Orson Welles,* 128, 133–135.

51. Jon Tuska, *Dark Cinema: American Film Noir in Cultural Perspective* (Westport, Conn.: Greenwood Press, 1984), 172–173.

52. Telotte, *Voices in the Dark,* 67.

53. Fischer, *Shot/Countershot,* 47.

54. McBride, *Orson Welles,* 97; cited in Fischer, *Shot/Countershot,* 34. Frank Krutnik, in *In a Lonely Street: Film Noir, Genre, Masculinity* (London: Routledge, 1991), also claims (erroneously) that Hayworth's career was "devastated" by *The Lady from Shanghai* (230).

55. All quotations here from Kaplan, *Women and Film,* 62, 65, 58.
56. William Vincent, in "Rita Hayworth at Columbia, 1941–1945: The Fabrication of a Star," in Dick, *Columbia Pictures,* also notices Kaplan's misuse of Hayworth's name but excuses it, to my mind unconvincingly, as Kaplan's "conscious or unconscious" acknowledgment that it is "Hayworth's mystique that gives the role resonance" (129).
57. Hayworth's name in fact appears more often than variations on Elsa Bannister (some thirty-five times to thirty-three). My favorite example is "Michael is unaware that he is being consumed by monsters, dazzled as he is by Hayworth's image" (65).
58. See again Virginia Wright Wexman's caution that one "need not adopt a posture of naive credulity" to posit that audiences would grant more credence to the "facts" of a journalistic or fan article than to the "fictional forms of the films themselves" (Virginia Wright Wexman, *Creating the Couple: Love, Marriage, and Hollywood Performance* [Princeton, N.J.: Princeton University Press, 1993], 33).
59. Although, again, not publicly as screenwriter.
60. Quoted in John Kobal, *Rita Hayworth,* 222. See also Dyer, "Resistance through Charisma"; Michael Wood, *America in the Movies* (New York: Basic Books, 1975), 56; Leonard Michaels, *To Feel These Things: Essays* (San Francisco: Mercury House, 1993), 1–12.
61. Another document, a nine-page memo from Welles to Harry Cohn about the music for *The Lady from Shanghai* that begs Cohn to restore the music to Welles's specifications, implies that Welles very much cared about how *The Lady from Shanghai* turned out and that Harry Cohn ignored him. Excerpts from this memo appear in virtually every Welles book written since the early 1980s. But whether any of these memos were actually sent, or arrived at their intended destinations, is unknown.
62. Bob Schiffer, interview by author, May 14, 1992, Los Angeles, Calif.; Eddie Saeta, interview by author, May 16, 1992, Los Angeles, Calif.
63. FBI files available under the Freedom of Information Act ("Rita Hayworth [Margarita Cansino]"). I first learned about this particular notation in her and Welles's files from a clipping sent to me by a traveling friend from the *Calgary Herald,* Sunday, October 22, 2000, D2. See also note 76 below.
64. Orson Welles and Peter Bogdanovich, *This Is Orson Welles* (New York: Harper, 1992), 191.
65. Telotte, *Voices in the Dark,* 66.
66. Naremore, *Magic World of Orson Welles,* 115.
67. The article is "The Time, the Place, and the Girl: Rita Hayworth," *Focus on Film* 10 (summer 1972): 15–29.
68. Molly Haskell, *From Reverence to Rape: The Treatment of Women in the Movies* (New York: Holt, Rinehart, and Winston, 1974), 204. And, of course, there are numerous references in *The Lady from Shanghai* to Circe, sirens, etc.
69. In McBride, *Orson Welles: Actor and Director,* 50–51.
70. In Kobal, *The Time, the Place, and the Woman,* 218, 219.
71. Dana Polan, *Power and Paranoia: History, Narrative, and the American Cinema, 1940–1950* (New York: Columbia University Press, 1986), 14.
72. Bazin, *Orson Welles,* 94.
73. Polan, *Power and Paranoia,* 16–17.

74. All quotations here from Naremore, *Magic World of Orson Welles,* 262, 276.

75. Thomson, *Rosebud,* 275–276. Thomson continues: "For the first time in her life on-screen she had authority," but this is only true if you believe authority must be the ability to manipulate others instead of agency in the accomplishing of your own goals.

76. Barbara Leaming mentions that when *The Lady from Shanghai* began production, "Orson owed [Hayworth] approximately $30,000, which he had borrowed in the course of their marriage" (*If This Was Happiness,* 137). Actually, Welles seems to have owed Hayworth much more than $30,000; according to ledger sheets in the Welles Collection, Hayworth lent money on several occasions to Welles's Mercury Theatre, making her a virtual Mercury Theatre "angel." And, as far as the record goes, he appears neither to have noted to the Mercury Theatre's tax accountant that Hayworth had lent said sums nor to have paid her back. Frank Brady also claims that it was Hayworth who "had informally petitioned Cohn to let her star in a Columbia film directed by her estranged husband. She had asked Cohn to hire Orson because she believed it might save her marriage; it would also help Orson's career" (Brady, *Citizen Welles,* 385). By the time shooting began, Hayworth "had already set her mind on a divorce" but agreed to make the film "to help bolster Orson's income" (396). Hayworth's financial support of Welles was constant (and she raised their child, Rebecca [born 1944], with virtually no financial support from Welles).

77. Polan, *Power and Paranoia,* 19.

Chapter 5. This Is Hayworth as Hayworth Really Is

1. Richard Dyer, "Resistance through Charisma: Rita Hayworth and *Gilda,*" in *Women and Film Noir,* ed. E. Ann Kaplan (London: BFI, 1978), 91–99.

2. Laura Mulvey, "Visual Pleasure and Narrative Cinema" (1975), in *Issues in Feminist Film Criticism,* ed. Patricia Erens (Bloomington: Indiana University Press, 1990), 28–39; and Kaja Silverman, *The Subject of Semiotics* (New York: Oxford University Press, 1983).

3. Fortunately for us, Valerie Bettis (1919–1982) subscribed to a clipping service for most of her career and donated the resulting scrapbooks to the Dance Collection of the New York Public Library for the Performing Arts. These scrapbooks (hereafter referred to as VBS) were very useful in determining the nature of the critical reception of *Affair in Trinidad* by magazines and newspapers large and small and in considering how the relationship of the two women was constructed in popular discourse.

4. Danae Clark, *Negotiating Hollywood: The Cultural Politics of Actors' Labor* (Minneapolis: University of Minnesota Press, 1995), 82.

5. John L. Scott, "Valerie Bettis Tackles Dual Job in Film Fling," *Los Angeles Times,* March 9, 1952.

6. L. L. Stevenson, "Hayworth and Bettis vs. Movie Executives," *Detroit News,* September 4, 1952; review in *Los Angeles Herald Express,* March 6, 1952; Norton Mockridge, "Heat-Wave Dance May Scorch Creator," *New York Sun,* August 2, 1952 ["Bigwigs Nervous"]; all in VBS.

7. Stevenson, "Hayworth and Bettis." With reference to their subsequent collaboration on *Salome* (1953), Bettis called Hayworth "a natural dancer. Her arm and hand movements particularly are pure music. She has a rhythmic sense which is a joy to a dance director" ("The Credit Belongs to Valerie Bettis," *Erie [Pennsylvania] Dispatch Herald* [1952], VBS). See also Herbert M. Simpson, "Valerie Bettis: Looking Back," *Dance Magazine*, February 1977, 60.

8. Howard Thompson, "Valerie Bettis Doubles in Brass," *New York Times*, August 3, 1952.

9. It is intriguing that, according to a note on the last page of Gene Ringgold, *The Films of Rita Hayworth* (Secaucus, N.J.: Citadel Press, 1974), Hayworth is quoted as having once said that the only role she ever *sought* to play but that she never did was "Federico Garcia Lorca's *Yerma*" (256). One wonders whether the role was suggested to her by Bettis.

10. Valerie Bettis, interview by Wendy Laakso, April 3, May 10, 1979, transcript, Dance Collection, New York Public Library for the Performing Arts.

11. Valerie Bettis, radio interview by Walter Terry, 1952, Dance Collection, New York Public Library for the Performing Arts (transcribed by the author).

12. Marianne Goldberg, "Ballerinas and Ball Passing," *Women and Performance* 3 (1987–1988): 14.

13. Jane C. Desmond, "Introduction: Making the Invisible Visible: Staging Sexualities through Dance," in *Dancing Desires: Choreographing Sexualities on and off the Stage*, ed. Jane C. Desmond (Madison: University of Wisconsin Press, 2001), 7.

14. Mulvey, "Visual Pleasure and Narrative Cinema," 36.

15. Ramsey Burt, "Dissolving in Pleasure: The Threat of the Queer Male Dancing Body," in Desmond, *Dancing Desires*, 222.

16. I use Hayworth's name here, rather than that of her character, to indicate that this is not a narratively driven moment.

17. *Affair in Trinidad* was put together very quickly to capitalize on Hayworth's unexpected return to Hollywood in 1951, and the script, as Vincent Sherman put it to me (interview conducted in Los Angeles on May 13, 1992), was a "terrible rip-off" of several other movies. Whether intentionally so or not, the narrative structure of *Affair in Trinidad* is almost identical to that of *Notorious*. Bettis also plays the evil Veronica in *Affair in Trinidad* (who at one point drunkenly imitates "Trinidad Lady" before falling over the furniture).

18. A description of another film noir, *Dark City* (William Dieterle, 1950), also fits *Affair in Trinidad*: it is "a vision of the noir world without the emphasis of the noir ethos" (Alain Silver and Elizabeth Ward, eds., *Film Noir: An Encyclopedic Reference to the American Style* [Woodstock, N.Y.: Overlook Press, 1979], 82).

19. Steve later rescues Chris from Max, who also murdered his brother.

20. Bosley Crowther, review of *Affair in Trinidad*, dir. Vincent Sherman, *New York Times*, July 31, 1952, 14.

21. Otis L. Guernsey Jr., "Movie Stars Mark Time," *New York Herald Tribune*, August 17, 1952, VBS. For Bosley Crowther's scathing review see *New York Times*, July 31, 1952.

22. Patricia Parker, *Literary Fat Ladies: Rhetoric, Gender, Property* (New York: Methuen, 1987), 146.

23. Ibid., 65.

24. All quotations here are from Walter Terry, "Rita Hayworth, Barefoot Dancer, Emulates Valerie Bettis in Film," *New York Herald Tribune*, August 17, 1952, VBS.

25. Dyer, "Resistance through Charisma."

26. Svea Becker, "A Femme Fatale Communicates through Dance," *Proceedings of the Conference of the Society of Dance History Scholars* (1987), 45–56.

27. Bettis/Terry radio interview. For more on the history of the association of the bare foot with women's literal and figurative freedom—and therefore scandalous sexuality—see Janet Lyon, "The Modern Foot," in *Footnotes: On Shoes*, ed. Shari Benstock and Suzanne Ferriss (New Brunswick, N.J.: Rutgers University Press, 2001), 272–281.

28. Elizabeth Dempster, "Women Writing the Body: Let's Watch a Little How She Dances," in *Grafts: Feminist Cultural Criticism*, ed. Susan Sheridan (London: Verso, 1988), 52.

29. This and subsequent quotation from Mockridge, "Heat Wave Dance May Scorch Creator." It is important to remember here that this discussion was taking place almost a year before the release of Alfred Kinsey's report on female sexuality in August 1953 (see Alfred C. Kinsey, Wardell B. Pomeroy, Clyde E. Martin, and Paul H. Gebhard, *Sexual Behavior in the Human Female* [Philadelphia, Pa.: W. B. Saunders, 1953]).

30. In Marie Torre, "She Joined Show So She Could Sing," *New York World-Telegram and Sun*, December 23, 1950, VBS.

31. All comments in this and preceding paragraph from Bettis/Terry interview. I have speculated from time to time about Bettis's own sexuality, which on possibly spurious stereotypical terms—her deep voice, her forthrightness and independence, her wearing of trousers, and things of that ilk—seems unconventional, especially in the context of the 1950s. Bettis was married twice, first (1943–1955) to a Brazilian composer, Bernardo Segall (she said it was the easiest way to acquire good music), the second to Arthur Schmidt (1959–1969). The first marriage ended with divorce, the second with the death of Schmidt (see Simpson, "Valerie Bettis: Looking Back," 60).

32. Richard deCordova, *Picture Personalities: The Emergence of the Star System in America* (Urbana: University of Illinois Press, 1990), 145.

33. All quotations in this and subsequent paragraph are from Judith Butler, *Gender Trouble: Feminism and the Subversion of Identity* (New York: Routledge, 1990), ix, 145–147.

34. Sherman interview. See also his autobiography, *Studio Affairs: My Life as a Film Director* (Lexington: University Press of Kentucky, 1996), 228–239.

35. Sherman interview. Sherman also pointed out that, anyway, "Fred Astaire was no brain!" I mention this because, contra the case with female stars like Hayworth, Astaire's intelligence and knowledge are never called into question in scholarly discussions, although he had even less formal schooling than Hayworth did.

36. Gaines notes that *Flashdance* (Adrian Lyne, 1983) was "the first film in years" that many of her friends, lesbian and straight, "had gone back to see a second time. Does its 'fantasy of control,'" Gaines asks, "explain why women, after seeing the film, are dancing along with *Flashdance* videocassettes in their living rooms and signing up for classes in jazz dance?" (Jane Gaines, "Women and Representation: Can We Enjoy Alternative Pleasure?" in Erens, *Issues in Feminist Film Criticism*, 86). See also Brett Harvey, *The Fifties: A Woman's Oral History* (New

York: HarperCollins, 1993): "Did you ever think about the fact that all the fabrics we wore in the fifties were *stiff?*" (xi); Elaine Tyler May's use of "containment" as a metaphor for the fifties in *Homeward Bound: American Families in the Cold War Era* (New York: Basic Books, 1988); and the discussion of postwar domestic ideology in relation to Hayworth's image in chap. 2.

37. Francis Sparshott, *Off the Ground: First Steps to a Philosophical Consideration of the Dance* (Princeton, N.J.: Princeton University Press, 1988), 399.

38. Bettis appeared only in *Affair in Trinidad*. She choreographed *Salome*, with Hayworth, and *Let's Do It Again* (Alexander Hall, 1953), a musical remake of *The Awful Truth* (Leo McCarey, 1937).

39. Lucy Fischer, *Shot/Countershot: Film Tradition and Women's Cinema* (Princeton, N.J.: Princeton University Press, 1989), 132–171. All other references are from these pages.

40. According to Mary Ann Doane a woman with two different voices would threaten to reveal what Hollywood tries always to cover up, namely, that the material homogeneity of movie body and movie voice is an illusion ("The Voice in Cinema: The Articulation of Body and Space," *Yale French Studies* 60 [1980]: 33–50).

41. Janey Place, "Women in Film Noir," in Kaplan, *Women and Film Noir*, 35–54.

42. Judith Mayne, *Framed: Lesbians, Feminists, and Media Culture* (Minneapolis: University of Minnesota Press, 2000), 17.

43. All quotations here from Amy Lawrence, *Echo and Narcissus: Women's Voices in Classical Hollywood Cinema* (Berkeley: University of California Press, 1991), 147–154. *Miss Sadie Thompson* also starred José Ferrer and Aldo Ray and was shot in 3-D but widely released only in a "flat" version. Other film versions of the W. Somerset Maugham story ("Miss Thompson," 1921) include *Sadie Thompson*, with Gloria Swanson (1928), and *Rain*, with Joan Crawford (1932). Maugham himself thought Hayworth's version the best of the three, saying that he "was delighted that it was in a screen version of one of my stories that she proved just how superb an actress she really is" (in Ringgold, *Films of Rita Hayworth*, 47).

44. John McCarten, *New Yorker*, January 9, 1954, 75.

45. Both *Variety* and *Cue* reviews excerpted in Ringgold, *Films of Rita Hayworth*, 196–197.

46. Lawrence, *Echo and Narcissus*, 148.

47. Mary Ann Doane, *The Desire to Desire: The Woman's Film of the 1940s* (Bloomington: Indiana University Press, 1987), 39; quoted in Lawrence, 148.

48. As all of Hayworth's biographers note, one of the misfortunes of Hayworth's *Miss Sadie Thompson* is that Columbia advertised it as a steamy sex film rather than as the character study it really is. In *The American Movie Goddess* (New York: John Wiley and Sons, 1973), Marsha McCreadie makes an elision similar to Lawrence's between the advertising for *Miss Sadie Thompson* and the film itself—i.e., McCreadie "analyzes" the film but bases her analysis on the printed sheet music to its songs and several pinup photos of Hayworth from other contexts. But, as *Variety* noted, the numbers "don't come off with the s.a. [sex appeal] punch the advance ballyhoo would have you believe" (December 23, 1953).

49. Simpson, "Valerie Bettis: Looking Back," 60.

50. Burt, "Dissolving in Pleasure," 219, 222.

51. Robin Wood, "Art and Ideology: Notes on *Silk Stockings*" (1975), in *Genre: The Musical*, ed. Rick Altman (London: BFI, 1981), 67. As Katie Conboy, Nadia Me-

dina, and Sarah Stanbury write in their collection *Writing on the Body: Female Embodiment and Feminist Theory* (New York: Columbia University Press, 1977), "there is a tension between women's lived bodily experiences and the cultural meanings inscribed on the female body that always mediate those experiences" (1).

52. Horst Ruthrof, *Semantics and the Body: Meaning from Frege to the Postmodern* (Toronto: University of Toronto Press, 1987), introduction and 261. See also Susan Leigh Foster's discussion of "corporeal significance" in "Choreographics of Gender," *Signs* 24 (autumn 1998): 1–33.

Afterword

1. Even if a star has written an autobiography, his or her renderings of the past—given the many different motivations for writing about it in the first place—might differ substantially from the ones circulating at the time. An example that has been the subject of some anecdotal conversations with colleagues recently is Ginger Rogers, whose autobiography was an apparent attempt to revise her image as always having been free from baser appetites or meanings or experiences of any kind (see Ginger Rogers, *Ginger: My Story* [New York: HarperCollins, 1991]). Although I have not performed any sustained examination of Rogers's image in the 1930s and 1940s, what I have looked at makes this gloss on her career much too simplistic. Thus, what "really" happened in a star's words might be valuable in some senses but also needs to be considered against that star's previous textual incarnations.

2. The star scrapbooks of the Constance McCormick Collection at the University of Southern California would be a good place to start. This collection of articles and clippings, from 1934 on and covering more than a thousand stars, directors, and films, represents an enormous resource for work of this kind. Information about the collection and a list of the stars with scrapbooks devoted to their careers can be found at http://artscenter.usc.edu/cinematv/mccormick_collection.html.

3. See, e.g., Richard Lippe, "Kim Novak: A Resistance to Definition," *CineAction* 7 (winter 1986–1987): 51–74; Jackie Byars, "The Prime of Miss Kim Novak: Struggling over the Feminine in the Star Image," in *The Other Fifties: Interrogating Midcentury American Icons*, ed. Joel Foreman (Urbana: University of Illinois Press, 1997), 197–223. Byars's essay is primarily a close textual analysis of six of Novak's films.

4. All quotations here from "Replacement for Rita?" *Life*, May 2, 1949, 77–78.

5. For a summary of Novak's career by a Hollywood journalist see Ezra Goodman, *The Fifty-Year Decline and Fall of Hollywood* (New York: Simon and Schuster, 1961), 272–285. The ["unauthorized"] biography of Novak is Peter Harry Brown, *Kim Novak: Reluctant Goddess* (New York: St. Martin's, 1986).

6. See vols. 1 and 2 of the three Kim Novak scrapbooks in the Constance McCormick Collection, USC. See also Dick Pine, "Kim Novak: Glad to be Unhappy," *Photoplay*, August 1956, 32–37 ("'I don't like it—or want it!' Lovely Kim reveals the surprising reasons why she rejects the glitter of stardom"); Norma Kasell, "Is Kim Getting Married?" *Photoplay*, November 1957, 51–53, 110–113; Don Allen, "I Used to Be in Love," *Photoplay*, July 1958, 34–35, 88–89; Bill Davidson, "Kim Novak:

A Woman Who Can't Be Free," *Redbook,* March 1959, 38–41, 84–85 ("'Why don't they let me be *me?*' asks a young actress who has gained success by giving up the right to choose her clothes, her friends, even the kind of man to fall in love with").

7. In Goodman, *Fifty-Year Decline,* 276.

8. In a 1990 HBO documentary about Hayworth Novak said of working with Hayworth on *Pal Joey:* "She knew where it was coming from. She knew that it was Harry Cohn, and not me. She was always charming and gracious [to me]. . . . She was so beautiful and spectacular. Whatever she was feeling inside—because I knew what pressure she was under from Harry Cohn—she wasn't *about* to let anyone know something was getting to her."

9. George Sidney Collection, Doheny Library, University of Southern California.

10. All quotations here and in subsequent paragraph are in Goodman, *Fifty-Year Decline,* 272–273, 285.

11. Graham Fuller, "Legend: Kim Novak" ("The Rerelease of *Vertigo* Reminds Us of Kim Novak's Enduring Magnificence"), *Interview,* November 1996, 38–43, 116; and James Harvey, *Movie Love in the Fifties* (New York: Knopf, 2001), 84.

12. Brown, *Kim Novak;* and Kim Novak scrapbooks, vol. 3, Constance McCormick Collection, USC.

13. Danae Clark, *Negotiating Hollywood: The Cultural Politics of Actors' Labor* (Minneapolis: University of Minnesota Press, 1995), xii.

Cansino/Hayworth Filmography

A film designated (M) is a generic musical and features Rita Hayworth in a variety of singing and dancing numbers; (S) refers to a film in which she sings only; (D) indicates that she (or Rita Cansino) dances only.

As Rita Cansino

Under the Pampas Moon (Fox, 1935) *(D)*. Produced by Buddy G. De Sylva. Directed by James Tinling. Screenplay by Ernest Pascal and Bradley King, based on a story by Gordon Morris. Photographed by Chester Lyons. Edited by Alfred de Gaetano. Dance direction by Jack Donahue. Starring Warner Baxter, Ketti Gallian, J. Carrol Naish, John Miljan, Armida, Ann Codee, Jack La Rue.

Charlie Chan in Egypt (Fox, 1935). Produced by Edward T. Lowe. Directed by Louis King. Screenplay by Robert Ellis and Helen Logan, based on the Earl Derr Biggers character. Photographed by Daniel B. Clark. Edited by Alfred de Gaetano. Starring Warner Oland, Pat Paterson, Thomas Beck, Rita Cansino, Frank Conroy, Nigel de Brulier.

Dante's Inferno (Fox, 1935) *(D)*. Produced by Sol M. Wurtzel. Directed by Harry Lachman. Screenplay by Philip Klein and Robert Yost, suggested by a story by Cyrus Wood as adapted by Edmund Goulding. Photographed by Rudolph Maté. Edited by Alfred de Gaetano. Dance sequence choreographed by Eduardo Cansino. Starring Spencer Tracy, Claire Trevor, Henry B. Walthall, Scotty Beckett, Alan Dinehart.

Paddy O'Day (Fox, 1935) *(D)*. Produced by Sol M. Wurtzel. Directed by Lewis Seiler. Screenplay by Lou Breslow and Edward Eliscu. Photographed by Arthur Miller. Edited by Alfred de Gaetano. Dance direction by Fanchon. Starring Jane Withers, Pinky Tomlin, Rita Cansino, Jane Darwell, Michael Visaroff, Francis Ford.

Human Cargo (Twentieth Century Fox, 1936). Produced by Sol M. Wurtzel. Directed by Allan Dwan. Screenplay by Jefferson Parker and Doris Malloy, based on Kathleen Shepard's novel *I Will Be Faithful*. Photographed by Daniel B. Clark. Edited by Louis R. Loeffler. Starring Claire Trevor, Brian Donlevy, Alan Dinehart, Ralph Morgan, Helen Troy, Rita Cansino.

Meet Nero Wolfe (Columbia, 1936). Produced by B. P. Schulberg. Directed by Herbert Biberman. Screenplay by Howard J. Green, Bruce Manning, and Joseph Anthony, based on Rex Stout's novel *Fer de Lance*. Photographed by Henry Freulich. Edited by Otto Meyer. Starring Edward Arnold, Joan Perry, Lionel Stander, Victor Jory, Nana Bryant.

Rebellion (Crescent Pictures, 1936). Produced by E. B. Derr. Directed by Lynn Shores. Screenplay and story by John T. Neville. Photographed by Arthur Martinelli. Edited by Donald Barratt. Starring Tom Keene, Rita Cansino, Duncan Renaldo, William Royle, Gino Corrado, Allen Cavan.

Trouble in Texas (Grand National, 1937). Produced by Edward F. Finney. Directed by R. N. Bradbury. Screenplay by Robert Emmett, based on a story by Lindsley Parsons. Photographed by Gus Peterson. Edited by Frederick Bain. Starring Tex Ritter, Rita Cansino, Horace Murphy, Earl Dwire, Yakima Canutt, Dick Palmer.

Old Louisiana (Crescent Pictures, 1937). Produced by E. B. Derr. Directed by Irvin V. Willat. Screenplay by Mary Ireland, based on a story by John T. Neville. Photographed by Arthur Martinelli. Edited by Donald Barratt. Starring Tom Keene, Rita Cansino, Robert Fiske, Raphael Bennett, Allen Cavan, Will Morgan.

Hit the Saddle (Republic, 1937). Produced by Nat Levine. Directed by Mack V. Wright. Screenplay by Oliver Drake, based on a book by William Colt MacDonald. Photographed by Jack Marta. Edited by Lester Orleback. Starring Robert Livingston, Ray Corrigan, Max Terhune, Rita Cansino, Edward Cassidy, J. P. McGowan.

As Rita Hayworth

Criminals of the Air (Columbia, 1937) *(D)*. Produced by Wallace MacDonald. Directed by Charles C. Coleman Jr. Screenplay by Owen Francis, based on a story by Jack Cooper. Photographed by George Meehan. Edited by Dick Fantl. Starring Rosalind Keith, Charles Quigley, Rita Hayworth, John Gallaudet, Marc Lawrence, Patricia Farr.

Girls Can Play (Columbia, 1937). Produced by Ralph Cohn. Directed by Lambert Hillyer. Screenplay by Lambert Hillyer, based on a story by Albert DeMond. Photographed by Lucien Ballard. Edited by Byron Robinson. Starring Jacqueline Wells, Charles Quigley, Rita Hayworth, John Gallaudet, George McKay, Patricia Farr.

The Shadow (Columbia, 1937). Produced by Wallace MacDonald. Directed by Charles C. Coleman Jr. Screenplay by Arthur T. Horman, based on a story by Milton Raison. Photographed by Lucien Ballard. Edited by Byron Robinson. Starring Rita Hayworth, Charles Quigley, Marc Lawrence, Arthur Loft, Dick Curtis, Vernon Dent.

The Game That Kills (Columbia, 1937). Produced by Harry L. Decker. Directed by D. Ross Lederman. Screenplay by Grace Neville and Fred Niblo Jr., based on a story by J. Benton Cheney. Photographed by Benjamin Kline. Edited by James Sweeney. Starring Charles Quigley, Rita Hayworth, John Gallaudet, J. Farrell MacDonald, Arthur Loft, John Tyrrell.

Paid to Dance (Columbia, 1937). Produced by Ralph Cohn. Directed by Charles C. Coleman Jr. Screenplay by Robert E. Kent, based on a story by Leslie T. White. Photographed by George Meehan. Edited by Byron Robinson. Starring Don Terry, Jacqueline Wells, Rita Hayworth, Arthur Loft, Paul Stanton, Paul Fix.

Who Killed Gail Preston? (Columbia, 1938) *(S)*. Produced by Ralph Cohn. Directed by Leon Barsha. Screenplay by Robert E. Kent and Henry Taylor, based on a story by

Henry Taylor. Photographed by Henry Freulich. Edited by Byron Robinson. Starring Don Terry, Rita Hayworth, Robert Paige, Wyn Cahoon, Gene Morgan, Marc Lawrence. [Hayworth's singing dubbed by Gloria Franklin.]

There's Always a Woman (Columbia, 1938). Produced by William Perlberg. Directed by Alexander Hall. Screenplay by Gladys Lehman, based on a story by Wilson Collison. Photographed by Henry Freulich. Edited by Viola Lawrence. Starring Joan Blondell, Melvyn Douglas, Mary Astor, Frances Drake, Jerome Cowan.

Convicted (Central/Columbia, 1938). Produced by Kenneth J. Bishop. Directed by Leon Barsha. Screenplay by Edgar Edwards, based on a story by Cornell Woolrich. Photographed by George Meehan. Edited by William Austin. Starring Charles Quigley, Rita Hayworth, Marc Lawrence, George McKay, Doreen MacGregor.

Juvenile Court (Columbia, 1938). Produced by Ralph Cohn. Directed by D. Ross Lederman. Screenplay by Michael L. Simmons, Robert E. Kent, and Henry Taylor. Photographed by Benjamin Kline. Edited by Byron Robinson. Starring Paul Kelly, Rita Hayworth, Frankie Darro, Hally Chester, Don Latorre, David Gorcey.

The Renegade Ranger (RKO-Radio, 1938). Produced by Bert Gilroy. Directed by Davis Howard. Screenplay by Oliver Drake, based on a story by Bennett Cohen. Photographed by Harry Wild. Edited by Frederic Knudtson. Starring George O'Brien, Rita Hayworth, Tim Holt, Ray Whitley, Lucio Villegas, William Royle, Cecilia Callejo.

Homicide Bureau (Columbia, 1939). Produced by Jack Fier. Directed by Charles C. Coleman Jr. Screenplay by Earle Snell. Photographed by Benjamin Kline. Edited by James Sweeney. Starring Bruce Cabot, Rita Hayworth, Robert Paige, Marc Lawrence, Richard Fiske.

The Lone Wolf Spy Hunt (Columbia, 1939). Produced by Joseph Sistrom. Directed by Peter Godfrey. Screenplay by Jonathan Latimer, based on the novel *The Lone Wolf's Daughter,* by Louis Joseph Vance. Photographed by Allen G. Siegler. Edited by Otto Meyer. Starring Warren William, Ida Lupino, Rita Hayworth, Virginia Weidler, Ralph Morgan, Tom Dugan.

Special Inspector (Central/Columbia, 1939). Produced by Kenneth J. Bishop. Directed by Leon Barsha. Screenplay by Edgar Edwards. Photographed by George Meehan. Edited by William Austin. Starring Charles Quigley, Rita Hayworth, George McKay, Edgar Edwards, Eddie Laughton.

Only Angels Have Wings (Columbia, 1939). Produced and directed by Howard Hawks. Screenplay by Jules Furthman, based on a story by Howard Hawks. Photographed by Joseph Walker. Edited by Viola Lawrence. Starring Cary Grant, Jean Arthur, Richard Barthelmess, Rita Hayworth, Thomas Mitchell.

Music in My Heart (Columbia, 1940) *(M)*. Produced by Irving Starr. Directed by Joseph Santley. Screenplay by James Edward Grant, based on his story "Passport to Happiness." Photographed by John Stumar. Edited by Otto Meyer. Starring Tony

Martin, Rita Hayworth, Edith Fellows, Alan Mowbray, Eric Blore. [Hayworth performs one dance only.]

Blondie on a Budget (Columbia, 1940). Produced by Robert Sparks. Directed by Frank R. Strayer. Screenplay by Richard Flournoy, based on a story by Charles Molyneux Brown and comic-strip characters created by Chic Young. Photographed by Henry Freulich. Edited by Gene Havlick. Starring Penny Singleton, Arthur Lake, Rita Hayworth, Larry Simms.

Susan and God (MGM, 1940). Produced by Hunt Stromberg. Directed by George Cukor. Screenplay by Anita Loos, based on a play by Rachel Crothers. Photographed by Robert Planck. Edited by William H. Terhune. Starring Joan Crawford, Fredric March, Ruth Hussey, John Carroll, Rita Hayworth, Nigel Bruce.

The Lady in Question (Columbia, 1940). Produced by B. B. Kahane. Directed by Charles Vidor. Screenplay by Lewis Meltzer, based on a story by Marcel Achard. Photographed by Lucien Androit. Edited by Al Clark. Starring Brian Aherne, Rita Hayworth, Glenn Ford, Irene Rich.

Angels over Broadway (Columbia, 1940). Produced by Ben Hecht. Codirected by Ben Hecht and Lee Garmes. Screenplay and story by Ben Hecht. Photographed by Lee Garmes. Edited by Gene Havlick. Starring Douglas Fairbanks Jr., Rita Hayworth, Thomas Mitchell, John Qualen.

The Strawberry Blonde (Warner Bros., 1941). Produced by Hal B. Wallis. Directed by Raoul Walsh. Screenplay by Julius J. Epstein and Philip G. Epstein, based on James Hagan's play *One Sunday Afternoon*. Photographed by James Wong Howe. Edited by William Holmes. Starring James Cagney, Olivia de Havilland, Rita Hayworth, Alan Hale, George Tobias, Jack Carson.

Affectionately Yours (Warner Bros., 1941). Produced by Hal B. Wallis. Directed by Lloyd Bacon. Screenplay by Edward Kaufman, based on a story by Fanya Foss and Aleen Leslie. Photographed by Tony Gaudio. Edited by Owen Marks. Starring Merle Oberon, Dennis Morgan, Rita Hayworth, Ralph Bellamy, George Tobias, James Gleason.

Blood and Sand (Twentieth Century Fox, 1941) *(S)*. Produced by Darryl F. Zanuck. Directed by Rouben Mamoulian. Screenplay by Jo Swerling, based on Vicente Blasco Ibáñez's novel *Sangre Y Arena*. Photographed by Ernest Palmer and Ray Rennahan. Edited by Robert Bischoff. Starring Tyrone Power, Linda Darnell, Rita Hayworth, Nazimova, Anthony Quinn. [Hayworth's singing dubbed by Graciela Párranga.]

You'll Never Get Rich (Columbia, 1941) *(M)*. Produced by Samuel Bischoff. Directed by Sidney Lanfield. Screenplay by Michael Fessier and Ernest Pagano. Photographed by Philip Tannura. Edited by Otto Meyer. Dance direction by Robert Alton. Starring Fred Astaire, Rita Hayworth, John Hubbard, Robert Benchley, Osa Massen. [Hayworth's singing dubbed by Nan Wynn.]

My Gal Sal (Twentieth Century Fox, 1942) *(M)*. Produced by Robert Bassler. Directed by Irving Cummings. Screenplay by Seton I. Miller, Darrell Ware, and Karl Tunberg, based on Theodore Dreiser's story "My Brother Paul." Photographed by Ernest Palmer. Edited by Robert Simpson. Dance direction by Hermes Pan. Starring Rita Hayworth, Victor Mature, John Sutton, Carole Landis, James Gleason, Phil Silvers. [Hayworth's singing dubbed by Nan Wynn.]

Tales of Manhattan (Twentieth Century Fox, 1942). Produced by Boris Morros and S. P. Eagle. Directed by Julien Duvivier. Screenplay and stories by Ben Hecht, Ferenc Molnar, Donald Ogden Stewart, Samuel Hoffenstein, Alan Campbell, Ladislas Fedor, L. Gorog, L. Vadnai, Henry Blankfort, and Lamar Trotti. Photographed by Joseph Walker. Edited by Robert Bischoff. Starring Charles Boyer, Rita Hayworth, Ginger Rogers, Henry Fonda, Charles Laughton, Elsa Lanchester, Edward G. Robinson, George Sanders, Paul Robeson, Ethel Waters.

You Were Never Lovelier (Columbia, 1942) *(M)*. Produced by Louis F. Edelman. Directed by William A. Seiter. Screenplay by Michael Fessier, Ernest Pagano, and Delmer Daves, based on Carlos Olivari and Sixto Pondal Rios's "The Gay Señorita." Dance direction by Val Raset. Photographed by Ted Tetzlaff. Edited by William Lyon. Starring Fred Astaire, Rita Hayworth, Adolphe Menjou, Leslie Brooks, Adele Mara. [Hayworth's singing dubbed by Nan Wynn.]

Cover Girl (Columbia, 1944) *(M)*. Produced by Arthur Schwartz. Directed by Charles Vidor. Screenplay by Virginia Van Upp, adapted by Marion Parsonnet and Paul Gangelin, based on a story by Erwin Gelsey. Photographed by Rudolph Maté and Allen M. Davey. Edited by Viola Lawrence. Dance direction by Val Raset and Seymour Felix. Starring Rita Hayworth, Gene Kelly, Lee Bowman, Phil Silvers, Eve Arden, Otto Kruger. [Hayworth's singing dubbed by Martha Mears.]

Tonight and Every Night (Columbia, 1945) *(M)*. Produced and directed by Victor Saville. Screenplay by Lesser Samuels and Abem Finkel, based on Lesley Storm's play *Heart of a City*. Photographed by Rudolph Maté. Edited by Viola Lawrence. Dance direction by Jack Cole and Val Raset. Starring Rita Hayworth, Lee Bowman, Janet Blair, Marc Platt, Leslie Brooks, Florence Bates. [Hayworth's singing dubbed by Martha Mears.]

Gilda (Columbia, 1946) *(S, D)*. Produced by Virginia Van Upp. Directed by Charles Vidor. Screenplay by Virginia Van Upp [uncredited] and Marion Parsonnet, based on a story by E. A. Ellington adapted by Jo Eisinger. Photographed by Rudolph Maté. Edited by Charles Nelson. Dance direction and choreography [uncredited] by Jack Cole. Starring Rita Hayworth, Glenn Ford, George Macready, Joseph Calleia, Steven Geray. [Hayworth's singing dubbed by Anita Ellis.]

Down to Earth (Columbia, 1947) *(M)*. Produced by Don Hartman. Directed by Alexander Hall. Screenplay by Edward Blum and Don Hartman, based on characters from Harry Segall's play *Heaven Can Wait*. Photographed by Rudolph Maté. Edited by Viola Lawrence. Dance direction and choreography by Jack Cole. Starring Rita

Gilda
used men
the way
other women
use
makeup!

A COLUMBIA PICTURE

One of fourteen different "teaser" ads for *Gilda* from the *Gilda* pressbook. Copyright 1946 by Columbia Pictures Corp.

Hayworth, Larry Parks, Marc Platt, Roland Culver, James Gleason, Edward Everett Horton, George Macready. [Hayworth's singing dubbed by Anita Ellis.]

The Lady from Shanghai (Columbia, 1948) *(S)*. Produced, directed, and written for the screen by Orson Welles, based on Sherwood King's novel *If I Die Before I Wake*. Photographed by Charles Lawton. Edited by Viola Lawrence. Starring Rita Hayworth, Orson Welles, Everett Sloane, Glenn Anders, Evelyn Ellis. [Hayworth's singing dubbed by Anita Ellis.]

The Loves of Carmen (Beckworth/Columbia, 1948) *(S, D)*. Produced and directed by Charles Vidor. Screenplay by Helen Deutsch, based on Prosper Mérimée's *Carmen*. Photographed by William Snyder. Edited by Charles Nelson. Dance direction and choreography by Robert Sidney and Eduardo Cansino. Starring Rita Hayworth, Glenn Ford, Ron Randell, Victor Jory, Luther Adler. [Hayworth's singing dubbed by Jo Ann Greer.]

Affair in Trinidad (Beckworth/Columbia, 1952) *(S, D)*. Produced and directed by Vincent Sherman. Screenplay by Oscar Saul and James Gunn, based on a story by Virginia Van Upp and Bernie Giler. Photographed by Joseph Walker. Edited by Viola Lawrence. Dance direction and choreography by Valerie Bettis. Starring Rita Hayworth, Glenn Ford, Alexander Scourby, Valerie Bettis, Torin Thatcher, Steven Geray, Juanita Moore. [Hayworth's singing dubbed by Jo Ann Greer.]

Salome (Beckworth/Columbia, 1953) *(D)*. Produced by Buddy Adler. Directed by William Dieterle. Screenplay by Harry Kleiner, based on a story by Kleiner and Jesse L. Lasky Jr. Photographed by Charles Lang. Edited by Viola Lawrence. Dance direction and choreography by Valerie Bettis. Starring Rita Hayworth, Stewart Granger, Charles Laughton, Judith Anderson, Sir Cedric Hardwicke, Alan Badel.

Miss Sadie Thompson (Beckworth/Columbia, 1953) *(S, D)*. Produced by Jerry Wald. Directed by Curtis Bernhardt. Screenplay by Harry Kleiner, based on W. Somerset Maugham's story "Miss Thompson," and the dramatization *Rain* by John Colton and Clemence Randolph. Photographed by Charles Lawton Jr. Edited by Viola Lawrence. Dance direction and choreography by Lee Scott. Starring Rita Hayworth, Jose Ferrer, Aldo Ray. [Hayworth's singing dubbed by Jo Ann Greer; film initially released in 3-D.]

Fire Down Below (Warwick/Columbia, 1957) *(D)*. Produced by Irving Allen and Albert R. Broccoli. Directed by Robert Parrish. Screenplay by Irwin Shaw, based on the novel by Max Catto. Photographed by Desmond Dickinson. Edited by Jack Slade. Dance direction and choreography by Ken Jones. Starring Rita Hayworth, Robert Mitchum, Jack Lemmon, Herbert Lom.

Pal Joey (Columbia, 1957) *(M)*. Produced by Fred Kohlmar. Directed by George Sidney. Screenplay by Dorothy Kingsley, based on the musical play by John O'Hara, Richard Rodgers, and Lorenz Hart. Photographed by Harold Lipstein. Edited by Viola Lawrence. Dance direction and choreography by Hermes Pan. Starring Rita

Hayworth, Frank Sinatra, Kim Novak. [Hayworth's singing dubbed by Jo Ann Greer, Novak's by Trudi Erwin.]

Separate Tables (United Artists, 1958). Produced by Harold Hecht, James Hill, and Burt Lancaster. Directed by Delbert Mann. Screenplay by Terence Rattigan and John Gay, based on Rattigan's play. Photographed by Charles Lang Jr. Edited by Marjorie Fowler and Charles Ennis. Starring Rita Hayworth, Deborah Kerr, David Niven, Burt Lancaster, Wendy Hiller.

They Came to Cordura (Columbia, 1959). Produced by William Goetz. Directed by Robert Rossen. Screenplay by Ivan Moffat and Robert Rossen, based on Glendon Swarthout's novel. Photographed by Burnett Guffey. Edited by William A. Lyon. Starring Cary Cooper, Rita Hayworth, Van Heflin, Tab Hunter, Richard Conte.

The Story on Page One (Twentieth Century Fox, 1960). Produced by Jerry Wald. Directed by Clifford Odets. Screenplay by Clifford Odets. Photographed by James Wong Howe. Edited by Hugh S. Fowler. Starring Rita Hayworth, Anthony Franciosa, Gig Young, Mildred Dunnock, Hugh Griffith.

The Happy Thieves (United Artists, 1962). Produced by Rita Hayworth and James Hill. Directed by George Marshall. Screenplay by John Gay, based on Richard Condon's novel *The Oldest Confession*. Photographed by Paul Beeson. Edited by Oswald Hafenrichter. Starring Rita Hayworth, Rex Harrison, Joseph Wiseman, Gregoire Aslan, Alida Valli.

Circus World (Paramount, 1964). Produced by Samuel Bronston. Directed by Henry Hathaway. Screenplay by Ben Hecht, Julian Halevy, and James Edward Grant, based on a story by Philip Yordan and Nicholas Ray. Photographed by Jack Hildyard. Edited by Dorothy Spencer. Starring John Wayne, Claudia Cardinale, Rita Hayworth, Lloyd Nolan, Richard Conte.

The Money Trap (MGM, 1966). Produced by Max E. Youngstein and David Karr. Directed by Burt Kennedy. Screenplay by Walter Bernstein, based on the novel by Lionel White. Photographed by Paul C. Vogel. Edited by John McSweeney. Starring Glenn Ford, Elke Sommer, Rita Hayworth, Joseph Cotten, Ricardo Montalban.

The Poppy Is Also a Flower (a.k.a. *The Opium Connection*) (Comet Films, 1966). Produced by Euan Lloyd. Directed by Terence Young. Screenplay by Jo Eisinger, based on a story idea by Ian Fleming. Photographed by Henri Alekan. Edited by Monique Bonnot, Peter Thornton, and Henry Richardson. Starring Senta Berger, Stephen Boyd, Yul Brynner, Angie Dickinson, Rita Hayworth, Trevor Howard.

The Rover (L'Avventuriero) (Cinerama, 1967; U.S. release 1971). Produced by Alfredo Bini. Directed by Terence Young. Screenplay by Luciano Vincenzoni and Jo Eisinger, based on Joseph Conrad's novel. Photographed by Leonida Barboni. Edited by Peter Thornton. Starring Anthony Quinn, Rosanna Schiaffino, Rita Hayworth, Richard Johnson.

Sons of Satan (a.k.a. *I Bastardi*) (Warner Bros.–7 Arts, 1968). Produced by Turi Vasile. Directed by Duccio Tessari. Screenplay by Duccio Tessari, Ennio De Concini, Mario Di Nardo, based on a story by Di Nardo. Photographed by Carlo Carlini. Edited by Mario Morra. Starring Rita Hayworth, Giuliano Gemma, Klaus Kinski.

Road to Salina (Sur la route de Salina) (Avco Embassy, 1971). Produced by Robert Dorfmann and Yvon Guezel. Directed by George Lautner. Screenplay by George Lautner, Pascal Jardin, and Jack Miller, based on the novel by Maurice Cury. Photographed by Maurice Fellous. Edited by Michelle David. Starring Mimsy Farmer, Robert Walker, Rita Hayworth, Ed Begley.

The Naked Zoo (Film Artists International, 1970; U.S. release 1971). Produced and directed by William Grefe. Screenplay by Ray Preston from a story idea by William Grefe. Photographed by Gregory Sandor. Edited by Julio Chavez. Starring Rita Hayworth, Fay Spain, Stephen Oliver.

The Wrath of God (MGM, 1972). Produced by Peter Katz. Directed by Ralph Nelson. Screenplay by Ralph Nelson, based on the novel by James Graham. Photographed by Alex Phillips Jr. Edited by J. Terry Williams, Richard Bracken, and Albert Wilson. Starring Robert Mitchum, Frank Langella, Rita Hayworth, John Colicos, Victor Buono.

Bibliography

For fan and mass-market magazine articles see the notes to each chapter.

Acker, Ally. *Reel Women: Pioneers of the Cinema, 1896 to the Present*. New York: Continuum, 1991.

Adams, Patricia. "Dorothy Tutin and J. C. Trewin: An Essay on the Possibilities of Feminist Biography." *Theatre Studies* (1984–1985/1985–1986): 67–102.

Agan, Patrick. *The Decline and Fall of the Love Goddesses*. Los Angeles, Calif.: Pinnacle Books, 1979.

Albano, Lucilla. "The Accessibility of the Text: An Analysis of *The Lady from Shanghai*." In *Off Screen: Women and Film in Italy*, ed. Giuliana Bruno and Maria Nadotti, 124–138. London: Routledge, 1988.

Albright, Ann Cooper. *Choreographing Difference: The Body and Identity in Contemporary Dance*. Hanover, N.H.: Wesleyan University Press, 1997.

Altman, Rick. *The American Film Musical*. Bloomington: Indiana University Press, 1987.

———, ed. *Genre: The Musical*. London: BFI, 1981.

Arbuthnot, Lucie, and Gail Seneca. "Pre-Text and Text in *Gentlemen Prefer Blondes*" (1982). In *Issues in Feminist Film Criticism*, ed. Patricia Erens, 112–125. Bloomington: Indiana University Press, 1990.

Babington, Bruce, and Peter William Evans. *Blue Skies and Silver Linings: Aspects of the Hollywood Musical*. Manchester, U.K.: Manchester University Press, 1985.

Banner, Lois. *American Beauty*. New York: Knopf, 1983.

Barbas, Samantha. *Movie Crazy: Fans, Stars, and the Cult of Celebrity*. New York: Palgrave, 2001.

Barish, Jonas. *The Antitheatrical Prejudice*. Berkeley: University of California Press, 1981.

Barthes, Roland. *Image/Music/Text*. Trans. Stephen Heath. New York: Hill and Wang, 1977.

Basinger, Jeanine. *A Woman's View: How Hollywood Spoke to Women, 1930–1960*. New York: Knopf, 1993.

Bazin, André. *Orson Welles: A Critical View*. Trans. Jonathan Rosenbaum. New York: Harper and Row, 1978.

Becker, Svea. "A Femme Fatale Communicates through Dance." *Proceedings of the Conference of the Society of Dance History Scholars* (1987), 45–56.

Berlant, Lauren. "National Brands/National Body: *Imitation of Life*." In *Comparative American Identities: Race, Sex, and Nationality in the Modern Text*, ed. Hortense J. Spillers, 110–148. New York: Routledge, 1991.

Bernardi, Daniel, ed. *Classic Hollywood, Classic Whiteness*. Minneapolis: University of Minnesota Press, 2001.

Bernstein, Matthew. Review of Bernard F. Dick, *Columbia Pictures: Portrait of a Studio*. *Film Quarterly* 46 (spring 1993): 58–59.

Bhabha, Homi. "The Other Question—the Stereotype and Colonial Discourse." *Screen* 24 (November-December 1983): 18–36.

Bird, S. Elizabeth. *For Enquiring Minds: A Cultural Study of Supermarket Tabloids.* Knoxville: University of Tennessee Press, 1992.

Bobo, Jacqueline. "*The Color Purple:* Black Women as Cultural Readers." In *Female Spectators: Looking at Film and Television,* ed. E. Deidre Pribham, 90–109. London: Verso, 1988.

Booth, Mark W. *The Experience of Songs.* New Haven, Conn.: Yale University Press, 1981.

Bordwell, David, Janet Staiger, and Kristin Thompson. *The Classical Hollywood Cinema: Film Style and Mode of Production to 1960.* New York: Columbia University Press, 1985.

Brady, Frank. *Citizen Welles.* New York: Doubleday, 1989.

Brand, Peg Zeglin, ed. *Beauty Matters.* Bloomington: Indiana University Press, 2000.

Braudy, Leo. *The Frenzy of Renown: Fame and Its History.* New York: Oxford University Press, 1986.

Britton, Andrew. *Katharine Hepburn: Star as Feminist.* New York: Continuum, 1995.

Brown, Peter Harry. *Kim Novak: Reluctant Goddess.* New York: St. Martin's, 1986.

Burrows, David. *Sound, Speech, and Music.* Amherst: University of Massachusetts Press, 1990.

Burt, Ramsey. "Dissolving in Pleasure: The Threat of the Queer Male Dancing Body." In *Dancing Desires: Choreographing Sexualities on and off the Stage,* ed. Jane C. Desmond, 209–241. Madison: University of Wisconsin Press, 2001.

Butler, Judith. *Bodies That Matter: On the Discursive Limits of "Sex."* New York: Routledge, 1993.

———. *Gender Trouble: Feminism and the Subversion of Identity.* New York: Routledge, 1990.

Byars, Jackie. "The Prime of Miss Kim Novak: Struggling over the Feminine in the Star Image." In *The Other Fifties: Interrogating Midcentury American Icons,* ed. Joel Foreman, 197–223. Urbana: University of Illinois Press, 1997.

Callow, Simon. *Orson Welles: The Road to Xanadu.* New York: Viking, 1995.

Carroll, Noël. *Theorizing the Moving Image.* Cambridge, U.K.: Cambridge University Press, 1996.

Caughey, John L. *Imaginary Social Worlds.* Lincoln: University of Nebraska Press, 1984.

Chatman, Seymour. *Coming to Terms: The Rhetoric of Narrative in Fiction and Film.* Ithaca, N.Y.: Cornell University Press, 1990.

Clark, Danae. *Negotiating Hollywood: The Cultural Politics of Actors' Labor.* Minneapolis: University of Minnesota Press, 1995.

Cohan, Steven. "'Feminizing' the Song-and-Dance Man: Fred Astaire and the Spectacle of Masculinity in the Hollywood Musical." In *Screening the Male: Exploring Masculinities in Hollywood Cinema,* ed. Steven Cohan and Ina Rae Hark, 46–69. New York: Routledge, 1993.

———. *Masked Men: Masculinity and Movies in the Fifties.* Bloomington: Indiana University Press, 1997.

Collins, Jim. "Toward Defining a Matrix of the Musical Comedy: The Place of the Spectator within the Textual Mechanisms." In *Genre: The Musical,* ed. Rick Altman, 135–146. London: BFI, 1981.

Conboy, Katie, Nadia Medina, and Sarah Stanbury, eds. *Writing on the Body: Female Embodiment and Feminist Theory.* New York: Columbia University Press, 1977.

Cott, Nancy F. *The Bonds of Womanhood: "Woman's Sphere" in New England, 1780 – 1835.* New Haven, Conn.: Yale University Press, 1977.

Cowie, Peter. *A Ribbon of Dreams: The Cinema of Orson Welles.* New York: Barnes, 1973.

Croce, Arlene. *Afterimages.* New York: Random House, 1977.

Curry, Ramona. *Too Much of a Good Thing: Mae West as Cultural Icon.* Minneapolis: University of Minnesota Press, 1996.

Daly, Ann. "Dance History and Feminist Theory: Reconsidering Isadora Duncan and the Male Gaze." In *Gender in Performance: The Presentation of Difference in the Performing Arts,* ed. Laurence Senelick, 239–259. Hanover, N.H.: University Press of New England, 1992.

Davis, Ronald L. *Hollywood Beauty: Linda Darnell and the American Dream.* Norman: University of Oklahoma Press, 1991.

de Certeau, Michel. *The Practice of Everyday Life.* Trans. Steven F. Rendell. Berkeley: University of California Press, 1984.

deCordova, Richard. "Genre and Performance: An Overview." In *Star Texts: Image and Performance in Film and Television,* ed. Jeremy G. Butler, 115–124. Detroit, Mich.: Wayne State University Press, 1991.

———. *Picture Personalities: The Emergence of the Star System in America.* Urbana: University of Illinois Press, 1990.

Delamater, Jerome. *Dance in the Hollywood Musical.* Ann Arbor, Mich.: UMI Research Press, 1981.

De Marinis, Marco. *The Semiotics of Performance.* Trans. Aine O'Healy. Bloomington: Indiana University Press, 1993.

Dempster, Elizabeth. "Women Writing the Body: Let's Watch a Little How She Dances." In *Grafts: Feminist Cultural Criticism,* ed. Susan Sheridan, 35–54. London: Verso, 1988.

Denby, Edwin. *Dance Writings.* New York: Knopf, 1986.

Desmond, Jane C., ed. *Dancing Desires: Choreographing Sexualities on and off the Stage.* Madison: University of Wisconsin Press, 2001.

———, ed. *Meaning in Motion: New Cultural Studies of Dance.* Durham, N.C.: Duke University Press, 1997.

Dick, Bernard F., ed. *Columbia Pictures: Portrait of a Studio.* Lexington: University Press of Kentucky, 1992.

Dittmar, Linda. "From Fascism to the Cold War: *Gilda*'s 'Fantastic' Politics." *Wide Angle* 10 (1988): 4–18.

Doane, Mary Ann. *The Desire to Desire: The Woman's Film of the 1940s.* Bloomington: Indiana University Press, 1987.

———. "The Economy of Desire: The Commodity Form in/of the Cinema." *Quarterly Review of Film and Video* 11 (1989): 23–33.

———. "*Gilda:* Epistemology as Striptease." *Camera Obscura* 11 (fall 1982): 6–27.

———. "The Voice in Cinema: The Articulation of Body and Space." *Yale French Studies* 60 (1980): 33–50.

Doty, Alexander. *Flaming Classics: Queering the Film Canon.* New York: Routledge, 2000.

———. *Making Things Perfectly Queer: Interpreting Mass Culture.* Minneapolis: University of Minnesota Press, 1983.

Dyer, Richard. "Entertainment and Utopia" (1977). In *Genre: The Musical,* ed. Rick Altman, 175–189. London: BFI, 1981.

———. "Four Films of Lana Turner." In *Star Texts: Image and Performance in Film and Television,* ed. Jeremy G. Butler, 214–239. Detroit, Mich.: Wayne State University Press, 1991.

———. *Heavenly Bodies: Film Stars and Society.* New York: St. Martin's, 1986.

———. "'I Seem to Find the Happiness I Seek': Heterosexuality and Dance in the Musical." In *Dance, Gender, and Culture,* ed. Helen Thomas, 49–65. New York: St. Martin's, 1993.

———. "Resistance through Charisma: Rita Hayworth and *Gilda.*" In *Women and Film Noir,* ed. E. Ann Kaplan, 91–99. London: BFI, 1978.

———. "*A Star Is Born* and the Construction of Authenticity." In *Stardom: Industry of Desire,* ed. Christine Gledhill, 132–140. New York: Routledge, 1991.

———. *Stars.* London: BFI, 1979; new ed. London: BFI, 1998.

———. "White." *Screen* 29 (autumn 1988): 44–64.

———. *White.* London: Routledge, 1997.

Ellis, John. *Visible Fictions: Cinema, Television, Video.* London: Routledge, 1982.

Erens, Patricia, ed. *Issues in Feminist Film Criticism.* Bloomington: Indiana University Press, 1990.

Farmer, Brett. *Spectacular Passions: Cinema, Fantasy, Gay Male Spectatorships.* Durham, N.C.: Duke University Press, 2000.

Feuer, Jane. *The Hollywood Musical.* 2d ed. Bloomington: Indiana University Press, 1993.

———. "The Self-Reflexive Musical and the Myth of Entertainment" (1977). In *Film Genre Reader,* ed. Barry Keith Grant, 329–343. Austin: University of Texas Press, 1986.

Fischer, Lucy. *Shot/Countershot: Film Tradition and Women's Cinema.* Princeton, N.J.: Princeton University Press, 1989.

Fletcher, John. "Versions of Masquerade." *Screen* 29 (summer 1988): 43–70.

Foreman, Joel, ed. *The Other Fifties: Interrogating Midcentury American Icons.* Urbana: University of Illinois Press, 1997.

Foster, Susan Leigh. "Choreographics of Gender." *Signs* 24 (autumn 1998): 1–33.

———, ed. *Choreographing History.* Bloomington: Indiana University Press, 1995.

Fraleigh, Sondra Horton. *Dance and the Lived Body: A Descriptive Aesthetics.* Pittsburgh, Pa.: University of Pittsburgh Press, 1987.

Francke, Lizzie. *Script Girls: Women Screenwriters in Hollywood.* London: BFI, 1994.

Friedberg, Anne. *Window Shopping: Cinema and the Postmodern.* Berkeley: University of California Press, 1993.

Friedman, Lester D. "Celluloid Palimpsests: An Overview of Ethnicity and the American Film." In *Unspeakable Images: Ethnicity and the American Cinema,* ed. Lester D. Friedman, 11–35. Urbana: University of Illinois Press, 1991.

———, ed. *Unspeakable Images: Ethnicity and the American Cinema.* Urbana: University of Illinois Press, 1991.

Fussell, Paul. *Class: A Guide through the American Status System.* New York: Simon and Schuster, 1983.

Gaines, Jane. "War, Women, and Lipstick: Fan Mags in the Forties." *Heresies* 5 (1985): 42–47.

———. "Women and Representation: Can We Enjoy Alternative Pleasure?" *Issues in*

Feminist Film Criticism, ed. Patricia Erens, 75–92. Bloomington: Indiana University Press, 1990.

Gallup Looks at the Movies: Audience Research Reports, 1940–1950. Wilmington, Del.: American Institute of Public Opinion and Scholarly Resources, 1979.

Gatlin, Rochelle. *American Women since 1945.* Jackson: University Press of Mississippi, 1987.

Gaut, Berys. "Identification and Emotion in Narrative Film." In *Passionate Views: Film, Cognition, and Emotion,* ed. Carl Plantinga and Greg M. Smith, 200–216. Baltimore, Md.: Johns Hopkins University Press, 1999.

Goldberg, Marianne. "Ballerinas and Ball Passing." *Women and Performance* 3 (1987–1988): 7–31.

Goodman, Ezra. *The Fifty-Year Decline and Fall of Hollywood.* New York: Simon and Schuster, 1961.

Gorbman, Claudia. *Unheard Melodies: Narrative Film Music.* Bloomington: Indiana University Press, 1987.

Grant, Neil, ed. *Rita Hayworth in Her Own Words.* London: Hamlyn, 1992.

Gunning, Tom. "Film History and Film Analysis: The Individual Film in the Course of Time." *Wide Angle* 12 (July 1990): 4–19.

Hadley-Garcia, George. *Hispanic Hollywood: Latins in Motion Pictures.* New York: Citadel Press, 1990.

Handel, Leo A. *Hollywood Looks at Its Audience: A Report of Film Audience Research.* Urbana: University of Illinois Press, 1950.

Handel, Stephen. *Listening: An Introduction to the Perception of Auditory Events.* Cambridge, Mass.: MIT Press, 1989.

Hanna, Judith Lynn. *Dance, Sex, and Gender: Signs of Identity, Dominance, Defiance, and Desire.* Chicago, Ill.: University of Chicago Press, 1988.

Harvey, Brett. *The Fifties: A Woman's Oral History.* New York: HarperCollins, 1993.

Harvey, James. *Movie Love in the Fifties.* New York: Knopf, 2001.

Haskell, Molly. *From Reverence to Rape: The Treatment of Women in the Movies.* New York: Holt, Rinehart, and Winston, 1974.

Hershfield, Joanne. *The Invention of Dolores del Rio.* Minneapolis: University of Minnesota Press, 2000.

Heywood, Colin. *A History of Childhood: Children and Childhood in the West from Medieval to Modern Times.* London: Blackwell, 2001.

Higashi, Sumiko. "Ethnicity, Class, and Gender in Film: DeMille's *The Cheat.*" In *Unspeakable Images: Ethnicity and the American Cinema,* ed. Lester D. Friedman, 112–139. Urbana: University of Illinois Press, 1991.

Higgins, John. "Raymond Williams and the Problem of Ideology." In *Postmodernism and Politics,* ed. Jonathan Arac. Minneapolis: University of Minnesota Press, 1986.

Higham, Charles. *The Films of Orson Welles.* Berkeley: University of California Press, 1970.

———. *Orson Welles: The Rise and Fall of an American Genius.* New York: St. Martin's, 1985.

Hill, James. *Rita Hayworth: A Memoir.* New York: Simon and Schuster, 1983.

Johnstone, Albert A. "Languages and Non-Languages of Dance." In *Illuminating Dance: Philosophical Explorations,* ed. Maxine Sheets-Johnstone, 167–187. Lewisburg, Pa.: Bucknell University Press, 1984.

Kaplan, E. Ann. *Women and Film: Both Sides of the Camera.* London: Routledge, 1983.

Kendall, Elizabeth. *Where She Danced.* New York: Knopf, 1979.

King, Barry. "Stardom as an Occupation." In *The Hollywood Film Industry,* ed. Paul Kerr, 154–184. London: Routledge, 1986.

Kinsey, Alfred C., Wardell B. Pomeroy, Clyde E. Martin, and Paul H. Gebhard. *Sexual Behavior in the Human Female.* Philadelphia, Pa.: W. B. Saunders, 1953.

Klaprat, Cathy. "The Star as Market Strategy: Bette Davis in Another Light" (1976). In *The American Film Industry,* ed. Tino Balio, 351–376. Madison: University of Wisconsin Press, 1985.

Knox, Donald. *The Magic Factory: How M-G-M Made "An American in Paris."* New York: Praeger, 1973.

Kobal, John, ed. *People Will Talk.* New York: Knopf, 1985.

———. *Rita Hayworth: The Time, the Place, and the Woman.* New York: Norton, 1977.

———. "The Time, the Place, and the Girl: Rita Hayworth." *Focus on Film* 10 (summer 1972): 15–29.

Krutnik, Frank. *In a Lonely Street: Film Noir, Genre, Masculinity.* London: Routledge, 1991.

Kuhn, Annette. "The Body and Cinema: Some Problems for Feminism." In *Grafts: Feminist Cultural Criticism,* ed. Susan Sheridan, 11–23. London: Verso, 1988.

Landy, Marcia. "Mario Lanza and the 'Fourth World.'" In *Keyframes: Popular Cinema and Cultural Studies,* ed. Matthew Tinkcom and Amy Villarejo, 242–258. New York: Routledge, 2001.

Lawrence, Amy. *Echo and Narcissus: Women's Voices in Classical Hollywood Cinema.* Berkeley: University of California Press, 1991.

Leaming, Barbara. *If This Was Happiness.* New York: Viking, 1989.

———. *Orson Welles: A Biography.* New York: Viking, 1985.

Lenz, Kimberly. "Put the Blame on *Gilda:* Dyke Noir vs. Film Noir." *Theatre Studies* 40 (1995): 17–26.

Lippe, Richard. "Kim Novak: A Resistance to Definition." *CineAction* 7 (winter 1986–1987): 51–74.

Loney, Glenn. *Unsung Genius: The Passion of Dancer-Choreographer Jack Cole.* New York: Franklin Watts, 1984.

López, Ana. "Are All Latins from Manhattan? Hollywood, Ethnography, and Cultural Colonialism." In *Unspeakable Images: Ethnicity and the American Cinema,* ed. Lester D. Friedman, 404–421. Urbana: University of Illinois Press, 1991.

Lovell, Alan, and Peter Krämer, eds. *Screen Acting.* New York: Routledge, 1999.

Lyon, Janet. "The Modern Foot." In *Footnotes: On Shoes,* ed. Shari Benstock and Suzanne Ferriss, 272–281. New Brunswick, N.J.: Rutgers University Press, 2001.

Margolis, Joseph. "The Autographic Nature of the Dance." In *Illuminating Dance: Philosophical Explorations,* ed. Maxine Sheets-Johnstone, 70–84. Lewisburg, Pa.: Bucknell University Press, 1984.

Margolis, Maxine L. *Mothers and Such: Views of American Women and Why They Changed.* Berkeley: University of California Press, 1984.

Martin, Angela. "'Gilda Didn't Do Any of Those Things You've Been Losing Sleep Over!': The Central Women of 40s Films Noirs." In *Women in Film Noir,* ed. E. Ann Kaplan, 2d ed., 202–228. London: BFI, 1998.

Martin, Randy. *Performance as Political Act: The Embodied Self.* New York: Bergin and Garvey, 1990.

Matthews, Glenna. *"Just a Housewife": The Rise and Fall of Domesticity in America.* New York: Oxford University Press, 1987.

May, Elaine Tyler. *Homeward Bound: American Families in the Cold War Era.* New York: Basic Books, 1988.

Mayne, Judith. *Framed: Lesbians, Feminists, and Media Culture.* Minneapolis: University of Minnesota Press, 2000.

McBride, Joseph. *Orson Welles.* New York: Viking, 1972.

———. *Orson Welles: Actor and Director.* New York: Harcourt, 1977.

McClary, Susan. *Feminine Endings: Music, Gender, and Sexuality.* Minneapolis: University of Minnesota Press, 1991.

McCracken, Ellen. *Decoding Women's Magazines: From* Mademoiselle *to* Ms. New York: St. Martin's, 1993.

McCreadie, Marsha. *The American Movie Goddess.* New York: John Wiley and Sons, 1973.

McLean, Adrienne L. "The Cinderella Princess and the Instrument of Evil: Revisiting Two Postwar Hollywood Star Scandals." In *Headline Hollywood: A Century of Film Scandal,* ed. Adrienne L. McLean and David A. Cook, 163–189. New Brunswick, N.J.: Rutgers University Press, 2001.

———. "Feeling and the Filmed Body: Judy Garland and the Kinesics of Suffering." *Film Quarterly* 55 (spring 2002): 2–15.

———. " 'New Films in Story Form': Movie Story Magazines and Spectatorship." *Cinema Journal* 42 (spring 2003): 3–26.

———. "The Thousand Ways There Are to Move: Camp and Oriental Dance in the Hollywood Musicals of Jack Cole." In *Visions of the East: Orientalism and Film,* ed. Matthew Bernstein and Gaylyn Studlar, 130–157. New Brunswick, N.J.: Rutgers University Press, 1997.

McLean, Adrienne L., and David A. Cook, eds. *Headline Hollywood: A Century of Film Scandal.* New Brunswick, N.J.: Rutgers University Press, 2001.

McRobbie, Angela. *"Fame, Flashdance,* and Fantasies of Achievement." In *Fabrications: Costume and the Female Body,* ed. Jane Gaines and Charlotte Herzog, 39–58. New York: Routledge, 1990.

Mellencamp, Patricia. *A Fine Romance: Five Ages of Film Feminism.* Philadelphia, Pa.: Temple University Press, 1995.

———. "Spectacle and Spectator: Looking through the American Musical Comedy." *Ciné-Tracts* 1 (summer 1977): 27–35.

Metz, Christian. *Film Language: A Semiotics of the Cinema.* Trans. Michael Taylor. New York: Oxford University Press, 1974.

Meyerowitz, Joanne. "Beyond the Feminine Mystique: A Reassessment of Postwar Mass Culture, 1946–1958." In *Not June Cleaver: Women and Gender in Postwar America, 1945–1960,* ed. Joanne Meyerowitz, 229–262. Philadelphia, Pa.: Temple University Press, 1994.

———, ed. *Not June Cleaver: Women and Gender in Postwar America, 1945–1960.* Philadelphia, Pa.: Temple University Press, 1994.

Michaels, Leonard. *To Feel These Things: Essays.* San Francisco: Mercury House, 1993.

Miller, Randall M., ed. *The Kaleidoscopic Lens: How Hollywood Views Ethnic Groups.* New York: Jerome S. Ozer, 1980.

Mizejewski, Linda. *Ziegfeld Girl: Image and Icon in Culture and Cinema.* Durham, N.C.: Duke University Press, 1999.

Modleski, Tania. *Loving with a Vengeance: Mass-Produced Fantasies for Women.* Hamden, Conn.: Archon Books, 1982.

Morella, Joe, and Edward Z. Epstein. *Rita: The Life of Rita Hayworth.* New York: Delacorte Press, 1983.

Mulvey, Laura. *Visual and Other Pleasures.* Bloomington: Indiana University Press, 1989.

———. "Visual Pleasure and Narrative Cinema" (1975). In *Issues in Feminist Film Criticism,* ed. Patricia Erens, 28–39. Bloomington: Indiana University Press, 1990.

Naremore, James. *Acting in the Cinema.* Berkeley: University of California Press, 1988.

———. *The Magic World of Orson Welles.* 2d ed. Dallas, Tex.: Southern Methodist University Press, 1989.

———. "Style and Theme in *The Lady from Shanghai.*" In *Focus on Orson Welles,* ed. Ronald Gottesman, 129–135. Englewood Cliffs, N.J.: Prentice-Hall, 1976.

Negra, Diane. *Off-White Hollywood: American Culture and Ethnic Female Stardom.* New York: Routledge, 2001.

Packard, Vance. *The Status Seekers.* New York: David McKay, 1959.

Parker, Patricia. *Literary Fat Ladies: Rhetoric, Gender, Property.* New York: Methuen, 1987.

Peters, Anne K., and Muriel G. Cantor. "Screen Acting as Work." In *Individuals in Mass Media Organizations: Creativity and Constraint,* ed. James S. Ettema and D. Charles Whitney, 53–68. London: Sage, 1982.

Petro, Patrice. *Aftershocks of the New: Feminism and Film History.* New Brunswick, N.J.: Rutgers University Press, 2002.

———. "Feminism and Film History." In *Multiple Voices in Feminist Film Criticism,* ed. Diane Carson, Linda Dittmar, and Janice R. Welsh, 65–81. Minneapolis: University of Minnesota Press, 1994.

Place, Janey. "Women in Film Noir." In *Women and Film Noir,* ed. E. Ann Kaplan, 35–54. London: BFI, 1978.

Poitras, Guy. *The Ordeal of Hegemony: The United States and Latin America.* Boulder, Colo.: Westview Press, 1990.

Polan, Dana. "'Above All Else to Make You See': Cinema and the Ideology of Spectacle." In *Postmodernism and Politics,* ed. Jonathan Arac, 55–69. Minneapolis: University of Minnesota Press, 1986.

———. *Power and Paranoia: History, Narrative, and the American Cinema, 1940–1950.* New York: Columbia University Press, 1986.

Radway, Janice. *Reading the Romance: Women, Patriarchy, and Popular Literature.* Chapel Hill: University of North Carolina Press, 1984.

Ray, Robert B. *The Avant-Garde Finds Andy Hardy.* Cambridge, Mass.: Harvard University Press, 1995.

Reid, John T. *Spanish American Images of the United States, 1790–1960.* Gainesville: University Press of Florida, 1977.

Renov, Michael. "Advertising/Photojournalism/Cinema: The Shifting Rhetoric of Forties Female Representation." *Quarterly Review of Film and Video* 11 (1989): 1–21.

———. *Hollywood's Wartime Woman: Representation and Ideology.* Ann Arbor, Mich.: UMI Research Press, 1988.

———. "*Leave Her to Heaven:* The Double Bind of the Post-War Woman" (1983). In

Imitations of Life: A Reader on Film and Television Melodrama, ed. Marcia Landy, 227–235. Detroit, Mich.: Wayne State University Press, 1991.

Rich, B. Ruby. "In the Name of Feminist Film Criticism" (1978). In *Multiple Voices in Feminist Film Criticism,* ed. Diane Carson, Linda Dittmar, and Janice R. Welsh, 27–47. Minneapolis: University of Minnesota Press, 1994.

Ringgold, Gene. *The Films of Rita Hayworth.* Secaucus, N.J.: Citadel Press, 1974.

Roberts, Shari. "'The Lady in the Tutti-Frutti Hat': Carmen Miranda, a Spectacle of Ethnicity." *Cinema Journal* 32 (spring 1993): 3–23.

Roberts-Frenzel, Caren. *Rita Hayworth: A Photographic Retrospective.* New York: Abrams, 2001.

Rogers, Ginger. *Ginger: My Story.* New York: HarperCollins, 1991.

Rosen, Marjorie. *Popcorn Venus: Women, Movies, and the American Dream.* New York: Coward, McCann and Geoghegan, 1973.

Ruthrof, Horst. *Semantics and the Body: Meaning from Frege to the Postmodern.* Toronto: University of Toronto Press, 1987.

Scanlon, Jennifer. *Inarticulate Longings: The* Ladies' Home Journal, *Gender, and the Promises of Consumer Culture.* New York: Routledge, 1995.

Sedgwick, Eve Kosofsky. *Between Men: English Literature and Male Homosocial Desire.* New York: Columbia University Press, 1985.

Shaviro, Steven. *The Cinematic Body.* Minneapolis: University of Minnesota Press, 1993.

Sheets-Johnstone, Maxine. "Phenomenology as a Way of Illuminating Dance." In *Illuminating Dance: Philosophical Explorations,* ed. Maxine Sheets-Johnstone, 124–145. Lewisburg, Pa.: Bucknell University Press, 1984.

Sherman, Vincent. *Studio Affairs: My Life as a Film Director.* Lexington: University Press of Kentucky, 1996.

Silver, Alain, and Elizabeth Ward, eds. *Film Noir: An Encyclopedic Reference to the American Style.* Woodstock, N.Y.: Overlook Press, 1979.

Silverman, Kaja. *The Acoustic Mirror: The Female Voice in Psychoanalysis and Cinema.* Bloomington: Indiana University Press, 1988.

———. "Historical Trauma and Male Subjectivity." In *Psychoanalysis and Cinema,* ed. E. Ann Kaplan, 110–127. New York: Routledge, 1990.

———. *Male Subjectivity at the Margins.* New York: Routledge, 1992.

———. *The Subject of Semiotics.* New York: Oxford University Press, 1983.

Simpson, Herbert M. "Valerie Bettis: Looking Back." *Dance Magazine,* February 1977, 52–64.

Sollors, Werner. *Beyond Ethnicity: Consent and Descent in American Culture.* New York: Oxford University Press, 1986.

Sparshott, Francis. *Off the Ground: First Steps to a Philosophical Consideration of the Dance.* Princeton, N.J.: Princeton University Press, 1988.

Spigel, Lynn. *Make Room for TV: Television and the Family Ideal in Postwar America.* Chicago, Ill.: University of Chicago Press, 1992.

———. *Welcome to the Dreamhouse: Popular Media and Postwar Suburbs.* Durham, N.C.: Duke University Press, 2001.

Stacey, Jackie. *Star Gazing: Hollywood Cinema and Female Spectatorship.* London: Routledge, 1994.

Steinem, Gloria. "Women in the Dark: Of Sex Goddesses, Abuse, and Dreams." *Ms.,* January/February 1991, 35–37.

Stern, Lesley. "Acting Out of Character: The Performance of Femininity." In *Grafts: Feminist Cultural Criticism,* ed. Susan Sheridan, 25–34. London: Verso, 1988.

Stewart, Phyllis L., and Muriel G. Cantor. "Analysis: Occupational Control." In *Varieties of Work Experience: The Social Control of Occupational Groups and Roles,* ed. Phyllis L. Stewart and Muriel G. Cantor, 313–322. New York: John Wiley, 1974.

Studlar, Gaylyn. "Discourses of Gender and Ethnicity: The Construction and De(con)struction of Rudolph Valentino as Other." *Film Criticism* 13 (winter 1989): 18–35.

———. "The Perils of Pleasure? Fan Magazine Discourse as Women's Commodified Culture in the 1920s." *Wide Angle* 13 (January 1991): 6–33.

Telotte, J. P. *Voices in the Dark: The Narrative Patterns of Film Noir.* Urbana: University of Illinois Press, 1989.

Thomas, Bob. *King Cohn: The Life and Times of Harry Cohn.* New York: Bantam, 1967.

Thomson, David. *Rosebud: The Story of Orson Welles.* New York: Knopf, 1996.

Tinkcom, Matthew. *Working like a Homosexual: Camp, Capital, Cinema.* Durham, N.C.: Duke University Press, 2002.

Tinkcom, Matthew, and Amy Villarejo, eds. *Keyframes: Popular Cinema and Cultural Studies.* New York: Routledge, 2001.

Tuska, Jon. *Dark Cinema: American Film Noir in Cultural Perspective.* Westport, Conn.: Greenwood Press, 1984.

Vincent, William. "Rita Hayworth at Columbia, 1941–1945: The Fabrication of a Star." In *Columbia Pictures: Portrait of a Studio,* ed. Bernard F. Dick, 118–130. Lexington: University Press of Kentucky, 1992.

Waldman, Diane. "From Midnight Shows to Marriage Vows: Women, Exploitation, and Exhibition." *Wide Angle* 6 (1984): 40–48.

Weigert, Andrew J. *Mixed Emotions: Certain Steps toward Understanding Ambivalence.* Albany: State University of New York Press, 1991.

Welles, Orson, and Peter Bogdanovich. *This Is Orson Welles.* New York: Harper, 1992.

Wexman, Virginia Wright. *Creating the Couple: Love, Marriage, and Hollywood Performance.* Princeton, N.J.: Princeton University Press, 1993.

Williams, Alan. "The Musical Film and Recorded Popular Music." In *Genre: The Musical,* ed. Rick Altman, 147–158. London: BFI, 1981.

Wilson, Glenn D., ed. *Psychology and Performing Arts.* Berwyn, Pa.: Swets and Zeitlinger, 1991.

Wolff, Janet. *Feminine Sentences: Essays on Women and Culture.* Berkeley: University of California Press, 1990.

Woll, Allen L. *The Latin Image in American Film.* Los Angeles: UCLA Latin American Center Publications, 1977.

Wood, Bryce. *The Making of the Good Neighbor Policy.* New York: Columbia University Press, 1961.

Wood, Michael. *America in the Movies.* New York: Basic Books, 1975.

Wood, Robin. "Art and Ideology: Notes on *Silk Stockings*" (1975). In *Genre: The Musical,* ed. Rick Altman, 57–69. London: BFI, 1981.

———. *Hitchcock's Films Revisited.* New York: Columbia University Press, 1989.

Index

Page numbers in italics refer to illustrations.

About the Author

Adrienne L. McLean is an associate professor of film studies in the School of Arts and Humanities at the University of Texas at Dallas. She is the coeditor, with David A. Cook, of *Headline Hollywood: A Century of Film Scandal* (Rutgers University Press, 2001). She is currently at work on another book for Rutgers, *Dying Swans and Madmen: Ballet, the Body, and Narrative Cinema.*